D1348920

# HOW WE FOUND AMERICA

THE UNIVERSITY OF

NORTH CAROLINA PRESS

CHAPEL HILL & LONDON

# How We

# Found America

## MAGDALENA J. ZABOROWSKA

*Reading*

*Gender*

*through*

*East*

*European*

*Immigrant*

*Narratives*

The paper in this book meets
the guidelines for permanence
and durability of the Committee on Production Guidelines
for Book Longevity of the
Council on Library Resources.

Portions of the material in
Chapters 5 and 6 appeared in a
different format in the following articles:

"The 'Free-for-All Country':
Transcending the Boundaries
of Exile in the Works of Maria
Kuncewicz." *Pacific Coast Philology* 28, no. 1 (1993): 56–71.

"Eva Hoffman's Observing
Consciousness." *2b: Quarterly* 2,
nos. 3–4 (1994): 62–66.

99  98  97  96  95   5  4  3  2  1

Library of Congress Cataloging-in-Publication
Data

Zaborowska, Magdalena J.
  How we found America: reading gender
through East European immigrant narratives /
Magdalena J. Zaborowska.
    p.   cm.
  Includes bibliographical references and index.
  ISBN 0-8078-2203-5 (cloth : alk. paper).—
ISBN 0-8078-4509-4 (pbk. : alk. paper)
    1. American literature—East European
American authors—History and criticism.
2. American literature—Women authors—
History and criticism.   3. Women and literature
—United States—History.   4. Emigration and
immigration in literature.   5. East European
Americans in literature.   6. Authorship—
Sex differences.   7. Immigrants in literature.
8. Sex role in literature.   9. Narration
(Rhetoric).   I. Title.
PS153.E37Z33   1995                         94-33791
810.9'9287—dc20                                CIP

# Contents

# Preface: What We Find Here

My house in Kazimierz, where I've returned, is now standing in a world that's completely different from the one in which it was built. And I am different too. . . . Like in that short story, which I wrote in London during the attacks of V-2, I now see my house not so much as my regained living quarters, but as a historical monument. Yet, I loyally warn its future caretakers: apart from the living, they'll have to deal here with a phantom who is arranging flower bouquets for the guests long dead.—Maria Kuncewicz, *Natura*

**W**hen people ask me where I am from, instead of saying simply, "I'm from Poland," I sometimes give them my "narrative" answer. "It's a long story," I begin, and then, if my interlocutors are up to it, I go on to tell them that I was born in Kielce, Poland, where I also grew up; that I went to Warsaw University, where I got my master's degree in English, and, shortly after, embarked on my trip to the United States to pursue a doctorate in American literature; that I graduated from the University of Oregon in Eugene and that I now teach English in a college in South Carolina. The reason why I am summarizing my life story here is not to boast of my modest bicultural achievements, but to explain why, if it is to be completely honest, my answer to a simple question about my national identity has to be delivered in a narrative framework. As Julia Kristeva claims, "Beyond the *origins* that have assigned to us biological identity papers and a linguistic, religious, social, political, historical place, the freedom of contemporary individuals may be gauged according to their ability to *choose* their membership, while the democratic capability of a nation and social group is revealed by the right it affords individuals to exercise that choice."[1] Theoretically, with my Polish "identity papers," I could choose to live anywhere, as Kristeva implies, provided that the country I pick "affords" me the right to "exercise" this freedom. In practice it is not that simple, and the very act of explaining why it is not calls for a narrative framework defining one's national identity. Like millions of other people who were born in one place but ended up living in another, I know my own origins, yet also understand those of the culture that I have adopted.

Because of strict definitions of citizenship all over the world, emigrants and refugees do not have the freedom to "choose" the cosmopolitan status that Kristeva envisions for the future when there will be "nations without nationalism" and when everyone can choose territorial loyalties. The only "choice" we have today (provided of course that we are not forcibly expelled or forcibly confined) is to emigrate, thus renouncing any stable national identity. Once we leave our country of origin, we lose a clear sense of where we belong as we enter crosscultural narratives that always inscribe us all as either guests or aliens wherever we are: as emigrants, we lose touch with our homelands and can never truly return there; as newcomers, we are the "other" for the dominant culture, which alternately accepts and rejects us. Being characters who often feel lost amid various immigrant narratives written for us by law, literature, politics, and history, we resort to telling stories when asked where we are from because no simple answer is possible. As a reader of these stories and a character in an immigrant narrative myself, I therefore hesitate to call myself either Polish or American.

Because I have recently chosen to live in the United States, I have to accept that I will be forever suspended between Poland and America—a fact that nevertheless does not make me "Polish American." Currently, I am defined by that curious oxymoron "resident alien." As someone who "resides" in America but who is still considered an "alien" by it, I sometimes have to resort to my complicated "narrative" to define my national origins and my status according to the U.S. Immigration and Naturalization Service. This narrative approach to my national identity results also from the fact that, like the writers I study in these pages, I believe that once you have left your country and lived somewhere else for a while, there is no going back. For when I tell people that I am from Poland, I mean "my" Poland, the one I knew and belonged to in the past. In *Natura*, Maria Kuncewicz describes a reunion with her house in Kazimierz (Poland), where she returned after having lived in the United States for many years. Comparing herself to a phantom floating between the past and present, she emphasizes that it is not the house itself that has changed so much, but, rather, that she herself and the world in which the house is standing have become completely estranged.[2] Like Kuncewicz's house, "my" Poland is unchanged; it is embedded in memory and nostalgia; it is a "historical monument." However, no one knows this secret Polishness of mine because to everyone else I am defined in reference to the Poland of today, the country that my interlocutors envision when they hear that I am Polish, but in which I, a returned immigrant, am only a visitor who does not recognize herself and her homeland. From my "resident alien" vantage point in the United States, I see myself as suspended between Poland, where I was born but which I now know only through memories, and the United States, where I live but which I cannot fully enter as a foreigner.

Being neither here nor there is often painful, but it has its advantages, too—ones that I have especially appreciated while working on this book. For example, when I began reading Mary Antin's and Anzia Yezierska's immigrant stories, I could understand intercultural dilemmas and identity crises described in them quite easily. When I learned about Maria Kuncewicz's world of "phantoms," I recalled the experience of actually feeling like one myself last December when I went back home for the first time after nearly seven years. Once there, I felt as if I were walking in an old dream or a faded movie, where things and people seemed familiar yet strange. Having traced Eva Hoffman's linguistic journey of self-discovery, I understood better why my voice in English was sometimes such an "unreliable instrument." In short, through reading the stories of women who, like myself, had to produce narrative answers to explain their East European origins, I found the inspiration to construct a literary-critical explanation for our complex situation as female immigrants in the United States. As Anzia Yezierska would have put it, I have "found" my place—my "America"—in my study, my narrative about East European women writers who helped me understand my own story.

As this book shows, our particular versions of "America" as well as our backgrounds are very different, but, regardless of ethnicity, religion, and class, we all meet as aliens in the Promised Land, where our disappointments with its failed promises bring us together. Indeed, as a real place the Promised Land always fails, but as an embodiment of desire to pursue imaginary "Americas" it fulfills its promise on the frontiers of the mind. I wrote this book out of gratitude to the women writers who had crossed the cultural oceans separating East Europe and the United States before me and who showed me the way to my own frontiers, to my own "America." Their works redefine traditional notions about immigrant passages and provide inspiration to examine the ways in which we read American literature and culture. Speaking from the margin, they also redefine the insider's perspective by reflecting and challenging the dominant notions about gender, class, ethnicity, and sexuality. They teach us about ourselves, no matter where we are positioned and what stories we need to tell to explain our origins. As a scholar positioned between the Old and New Worlds, whose personal story is similar to the ones I am describing in these pages, I offer this work as another bridge thrown over the cultural ocean still separating East Europe and the United States.

This book would have not been written without the help and support of friends and family both in Poland and the United States. I express my sincere appreciation to Professor Joseph Hynes, who was a patient and resilient reader during the early and intermediate stages of this manuscript and who sustained my progress with intellectual generosity, friendship, and support. Professor Sam B. Girgus was a wonderful friend and teacher who inspired me to work on this particular topic; he and his wife Scottie "adopted" me as a member of their family and introduced me to their "America." Special thanks and recognition are due to Professors Mary E. Wood, Linda Kintz, and James L. Rice, whose advice, encouragement, editorial help, and friendship were invaluable in the research for and the first stages of writing this manuscript. Professors Beth Holmgren and Emory Elliott provided expert advice about how to revise my work, while Professor Nicholas Radel was an invaluable editor and friend during the most painful process of revision, offering insights and suggestions for improving my argument. I thank my colleagues at Furman University, Tracey Rizzo, Elizabeth Hodgson, Willard Pate, Ann Sharp, Linda Julian, and William Rogers, for reading my work and for offering encouragement, advice, and understanding during its final stages when the demands it made on me had to be reconciled with a full-time teaching load. Correspondence with Professors Halina Filipowicz and Hugh McLean and with Witold Kuncewicz—who also kindly consented to an interview about his mother—was a source of many important ideas for my work. My students at Furman University, especially Susan Greenwell, Kasia Hagemajer, Regenia Gatewood, Brenda Bruce, and Chong Lo, kept me on my toes as a teacher and scholar. They helped me articulate many of my ideas in the classroom and gave me even more of theirs before this book took its final shape.

In addition, I want to express my gratitude to my friends from the University of Oregon, Linda Strom, Pamelyn Dane, Carol Faulkner, and Barbara Żaczek, who offered many important suggestions for designing this study. I also would like to acknowledge the friendship and support of Richard and Carole Stein, Carol T. Silverman and Mark Levy, A. K. Weatherhead, Mary Hynes, Betty Johnson, Maria and Edward Frączek, Elżbieta and Andrzej Krzesiński, Juretta Nidever, Németh Zsuzsa, Elżbieta Sienkiewicz, Krzysztof Wojciechowski, Anna Szyndler, Shirley Bolles, and Joanna Kot.

My research received assistance from the University of Oregon Center for the Study of Women in Society, the Oregon Humanities Center, and Furman University. Special thanks are due to Robin M. Cochran, Ruthann L. Maguire, and Sherry Abernethy for their help in the production of this manuscript.

My greatest debt and appreciation go to my parents, Maria and Henryk, to my sister Gosia, and to my grandmother Stanisława and the rest of our family of Szymańscy and Zaborowscy in Kielce and Iłża, Poland, who have encouraged me and seen me through my first attempt at making Polish American literary connections.

# HOW WE FOUND AMERICA

# Introduction: Other "Americas"

The past was only my cradle, and now it cannot hold me, because I am grown too big; just as the little house in Polotzk, once my home, has now become a toy of memory, as I move about at will in the wide spaces of this splendid palace, whose shadow covers acres. No! it is not that I belong to the past, but the past that belongs to me. America is the youngest of the nations, and inherits all that went before in history. And I am the youngest of America's children, and into my hands is given all her priceless heritage, to the last white star espied through the telescope, to the last great thought of the philosopher. Mine is the whole majestic past, and mine is the shining future.—Mary Antin, *The Promised Land*

n 1912, Mary Antin, a Russian Jewish immigrant, published her autobiographical text, *The Promised Land*, which describes the story of her and her family's flight from the czarist oppression in the Russian Pale of Settlement to the freedom of American democracy. Since its first edition, Antin's book has become an "immigrant classic" and one of the better-known newcomer texts documenting the passage from the Old World into the New and praising the United States and its ideology. As an immigrant prodigy who rose from the poverty of the ghetto to a prominent position as spokesperson for the immigrant cause, the author of *The Promised Land* also wrote other paeans to celebrate her new country. In *They Who Knock at Our Gates* (1914), she envisions a worldwide utopia modeled on America: "This process of the removal of barriers, begun through conquests, commerce, and travels, is approaching completion in our own era. . . . 'The world is my country' is a word in many a mouth to-day. East and West hold hands; North and South salute each other. There remain a few ancient prejudices to overcome, a few stumps of ignorance to uproot, before all the nations of the earth shall forget their boundaries, and move about the surface of the earth as congenial guests at a public feast." Antin's vision of all the nations "forgetting their boundaries" and hastening to a cosmopolitan "public feast" seems to have come from one of the enthusiastic political speeches of our own time, with the economic powers proclaiming the "new world order" and boasting of their "victory over communism."

Nevertheless, these words were written as immigration propaganda designed to counter widespread American nativism and prejudice against the mounting numbers of homeless newcomers from East Europe and the Balkans. Already at that time slogans such as "America for Americans" were everyday reality, and Antin felt obliged to remind her new country about its ideological promise to be the "city on a hill": "The ghost of the Mayflower pilots every immigrant ship, and Ellis Island is another name for Plymouth Rock."[1]

Many descendants of those who came to America on the Mayflower preferred that Plymouth Rock remain where it was, in white, Protestant New England and not in the murky quagmire of New York Harbor. For instance, in her autobiography, Charlotte Perkins Gilman remembers how appalled she was by the multinational composition of New York, "that unnatural city where every one is an exile, none more so than the American" because of the "rapidly descending extinction of our nation, superseded by other nations who will soon completely outnumber us."[2] To Henry James, walking through the streets of "his" Boston, the Puritan legend of old seems irrevocably erased by "a huge . . . sponge saturated with the foreign mixture and passed over almost everything I remembered."[3] This "foreign mixture," the strangers flooding their cities, the crowd of aliens with their outlandish traditions, religions, customs, languages, and conduct were the undesirable other in the Promised Land.

In such a historical climate Mary Antin's enthusiastic writings also told another story, a story of an immigrant woman's oppression and fear hidden behind the optimistic visions that her texts projected for their American readers. *The Promised Land* begins with the author's introduction as she embarks on a puzzling journey of self-inquiry: "Is it not time to write *my life's story*? I am just as much out of the way as if I were dead, for I am *absolutely other than the person whose story I have to tell*."[4] Although she tells the reader that she is writing her autobiography, Antin concentrates on the tale about the person she no longer is. The careful reader realizes that Mary Antin was in fact two women. As a writer and a speaker for the immigrant cause, she was a public persona. As a private individual, however, she must have been acutely aware of the division in her identity caused by her transition into the new culture and ideology, which did not necessarily live up to the ideals subsumed under that seductive name, the "American Dream."

Seventy-seven years after the publication of Mary Antin's *The Promised Land*, Eva Hoffman wrote *Lost in Translation: A Life in a New Language* (1989). The subtitle of the book is a poignant summary of its author's story: "A Life in a New Language." For Hoffman, born and raised Jewish in postwar Poland, the new life began with her family's immigration to North America in the late 1950s. The transition across cultures—from Poland to Canada and the United States—changed their lives completely and made young Eva embark on a writing career. The most acute rites of passage she had to go through in her new country involved a linguistic rebirth and a recreation of herself as a person speaking, writing, thinking, and, finally, even dreaming in English. Although in her autobiographical novel she describes in detail how she mastered her new language and how she invented a new cultural identity for herself, Hoffman emphasizes that no "straight narrative" could tell her story, no orderly account of events could ever convey her complex experience.

Instead of presenting a traditional chronological account of the immigrant journey and rebirth in the New World, *Lost in Translation* mixes events in an unsolvable puzzle of the past, present, and future. It poses many questions impossible to answer and disavows any definite message or moral resulting from its fragmented narrative. We cannot even expect closure in this crosscultural story. The "multiple perspectives and their constant shifting"— America's kaleidoscopic culture in which the author-narrator recreates her new identity—are still in motion and transit when she ceases writing down her "life in a new language" on the last page of her text: "Be here now, I think to myself in the faintly ironic tones in which the phrase is uttered by the likes of me. Then the phrase dissolves. The brilliant colors are refracted by the sun. The small space of the garden expands into the dimensions of peace. Time pulses through my blood like a river. The language of this is sufficient. I am here now."[5] In the book's last sentences, the "phrase dissolves" and is translated into the moment in which the physical being of the narrator absorbs and reconciles with the language. Although the words of this message, its semantics, are "sufficient," Hoffman's story remains open, since it is impossible to stop telling one's life, impossible to cease remaking oneself in the new language. The "I am here now" is thus a witness to its author's living, but it can record only a fleeting moment, a sliver of time, by turning it into a text that escapes definitions and celebrates impermanence.

Although written in such different historical and political circumstances, Hoffman's text is a clear continuation of Antin's narrative of acculturation; it acknowledges this similarity and claims the heritage of the earlier story. Yet Hoffman's vision of America and of her immigrant predicament is almost a negation of Antin's. Instead of praising American ideology and drawing optimistic projects for the future, Hoffman is cautious and reserved. In her account she concentrates on the individual story of acculturation, on the pain, suffering, and fragmentation it involves rather than on its proverbial rewards. Hoffman's text writes straightforwardly what Antin did not dare disclose in hers—the intimate and personal, often unglamorous and embarrassing, side of the immigrant woman's story.

Despite their different messages, these two texts by immigrant women from East Europe engage in an interesting dialogue with each other. While reading

*The Promised Land*, we have the impression that Antin is consciously setting up a tradition and trying to create a space within American literary history for the writings of women who would come after her. Hoffman's book is tangible proof that Antin's endeavors flourished, since it acknowledges *The Promised Land* as its inspiration and as a story that could have been written by Hoffman had she lived then. In this way, two women representing two different historical moments are able to meet within the tradition they have created together. What are the consequences of this meeting to the readers of East European literature in the context of modern American culture?

This book examines the implications of this question and answers it through a discussion of literary and cultural exchanges between the United States and East Europe from the end of the nineteenth century until the present moment. It explores how this East-to-West dialogue is reflected in the works of lesser-known immigrant and expatriate writers, mostly women, from Poland and Russia. These writers have been left out of the so-called East European canon, which in American literature is dominated by the celebrated male dissident avant-garde (e.g., Czesław Miłosz, Joseph Brodsky, Milan Kundera). However, the writings of women, from Mary Antin to Eva Hoffman, comprise a distinct tradition without which it is impossible to talk about the East European literature not only in the United States but also in the whole cultural realm known as the "West." These female writers, too often left out of the politicized discussions of postwar émigré tradition, have contributed to American ethnic literature by presenting a woman's version of Americanization, which revises the traditional narrative models and opens up new readings of both male and female newcomer texts.

Basing my approach in Bakhtinian theories of dialogic reading and on select feminist, cultural, and historical criticism, I discuss immigrant and exiled women's novels as a part of an intercultural and open genre, one that invites fictional, autobiographical, and documentary expressions. Reading writers as diverse as Mary Antin and Eva Hoffman, writers who nevertheless meet within the larger tradition of literary exchanges between the United States and East Europe, calls for an approach that will reflect their differences and accommodate similarities. In emphasizing the interdisciplinary nature of my approach, I point out the complexity of this field of study and the need to create a unique narrative framework to relate its literary-historical development.

The opening chapter of this study presents a discussion of the relationships between the dominant culture and the newcomer. The play between the host country's interpretive powers and the marginalized newcomer's desire to belong places female immigrants in a doubly alienated position because of their gender and sexuality. For this reason, the particular dialogue between East Europe and America inscribed into the texts by immigrant and exiled women engages different types of narrative: one written for the newcomer by the host culture, one presented by the newcomer to her new country, and another one that often has to be hidden—a subtext in which the woman writer describes her frustration and disillusionment with the Promised Land.

Chapters 2 through 5 discuss the specific literary and ethnic otherness of such diverse Jewish and Catholic authors as Mary Antin (1881–1949), Elizabeth Stern (1890–1954), Anzia Yezierska (1885–1973), and Maria Kuncewicz (1899–1989) and concentrate on their ideological and authorial constructions of the transition between the Old World of East Europe and the Promised Land of America. In this context, the term "other" gains a multilayered meaning: it designates women as the other gender, as immigrant writers bringing their alien traditions and languages to the United States, and it refers to the "invention" of the newcomer female by the host culture, which expects her to fulfill the ready-made narrative of woman's acculturation. Traditionally, such a narrative of the feminine rites of passage into the Promised Land ends with a marriage to a native-born male. However, a close reading of the authors I consider suggests alternative readings focusing on the immigrant woman's oppression in the dominant culture, her awareness of being ideologically "written" as an alien female in a new country, and her realization that she has to follow the narrative prescribed for her in order to be published and speak out for the immigrant cause.

Mary Antin's *The Promised Land*, which I read closely in Chapter 2, contains a story about how the new language is simultaneously a key to freedom and social status as well as an inevitable instrument of repression through the ideological idiom that the newcomer has to acquire. This theme is explored further in Chapter 3, which discusses Elizabeth Stern's *My Mother and I* as a text that both elicits and rejects the cultural split imposed on the immigrant woman who insolently claims America as her birthright and resists acculturation on the host country's terms. The feminist texts of Anzia Yezierska—the subject of Chapter 4—seem to be defeated by the clichéd happy endings involving predictable intermarriages. I propose to reread their Hollywood-like conclusions as deliberate and provoking formal innovations that lead to alternative readings subverting the restrictive official narrative of female Americanization.

Chapter 5 reintroduces Maria Kuncewicz, an exiled Pole who became an American citizen and wrote and taught in the United States in the 1950s and 1960s. Kuncewicz's focus on the themes of female exile and textual oppression during the Cold War inspired novels and autobiographies that explore the implications of subjectivity and authorship in a world divided by the Iron Curtain. In my analysis I show that all the women I discuss are able to work out a polyphonous voice throughout history, despite their individual differences in class, religion, and education. Like earlier immigrant writers, Kuncewicz is acutely aware of being written by the dominant culture as an exile and a political refugee, but she is able to turn this condition into an inspiration for cosmopolitan novels and autobiographies. By defying the official construction of herself as a silenced foreign woman and displaced person, she joins the voices disrupting the traditional approaches to female East European newcomers, such as those of Antin and Yezierska.

In Chapter 6, I read closely Eva Hoffman's *Lost in Translation* and her recent journalistic account, *Exit into History: A Journey Through the New Eastern Europe* (1993), through Julia Kristeva's theories of the inner "foreigner" and international otherness from *Strangers to Ourselves* and *Nations without Nationalism*. Hoffman's texts provide an illustration for Kristeva's theory that we are all not only strangers to one another but also to ourselves as we go through different stages in our lives, as if through different countries. From Hoffman's focus on language and the alienation of individuals and American culture within the multicultural world, I move to Chapter 7, which contains a discussion of Vladimir Nabokov's *Pnin*, his "American" novel, as an immigrant narrative. I reread *Pnin* within the thematic context established by East European women's narratives and demonstrate that the larger cultural discourse in the novel between East Europe and the United States contains an interesting exchange between the male and female authors, both of whose stories often share the themes of gender-related oppression and ideological ambiguity. Looking at *Pnin* through the "feminine" themes of the oppression of sexuality and immigrant otherness shows its male protagonist in the feminized position that the dominant culture assigns to all newcomers regardless of gender.

The Conclusion examines my inquiry into the revised Other Europe as establishing a critical "America"—a theoretical framework—found and founded for reading the writers I study in relation to the larger discourse on multicultural literature. Like the authors we study, we cannot escape Kristevan strangeness as critics. Yet, like these authors, we too can reach across differences and learn about the traditions that provide the context of otherness for the subjects we examine. My project assumes that reaching out to embrace the East Europe narrated by women can be read as embracing a new approach to American literature, which is still coming to terms with its inherent conflicts over this country's ethnic origins, cultural freedom, and ideological message. In titling this study *How We Found America*, I am suggesting that what Maria Kuncewicz calls the "free-for-all country" of literature recreates in its diversity the strangeness of the dominant culture, the otherness of its margin, and their mutual dependence on each other. It is a dialogue of many writers and critics who ought to share more openly their "findings," their unique "Americas," across cultural, ethnic, religious, gender, and class differences.

# The "Other Europe" Revisited

## FROM IMMIGRANT NARRATIVE
## TO POSTTOTALITARIAN DISCOURSE

"There is no America!" Then came a light. . . . I saw
America—a big idea—a deathless hope—a world still in
the making. I saw that it was the glory of America that it
was not yet finished. And I, the last comer, had her share
to give, small or great, to the making of America, like
those Pilgrims who came in the *Mayflower*. . . . I began
to build *a bridge of understanding between the American-
born and myself*. Since their life was shut out from such as
me, I began to open up my life and the lives of my people
to them. And life draws life. In only writing about the
Ghetto I found America. . . . The Americans of tomorrow, the America that is every day nearer coming to be,
will be too wise, too open-hearted, too friendly-handed,
to let the least last-comer at their gates knock in vain with
his gifts unwanted.—Anzia Yezierska, "America and I"

**T**he enthusiastic narrator in this passage from Anzia Yezier-ska's short story delivers a eulogy to "America in the mak-ing," a paean to the ideological concept of the dominant culture, which she composes out of the despair and drudgery of her early twentieth-century, lower-class immigrant experience. However, her discovery that writing about her people—the East European Jewish ghetto—can build a bridge of understanding between them and the "native-borns" does not imply the unequivocal authorial success of being heard and understood. On the contrary, her insistence that it is only the "Americans of tomorrow" who will appreciate her contribution seems to suggest that a reward for her efforts cannot come in the present, that the "bridge of understanding between the American-born and myself" created by an immigrant writer is a utopian and futuristic construction, left best in the realm of "big ideas" and "deathless hopes."[1] This passage brings to mind a larger cultural analogy in a tradition of reading immigrant writers from Poland and Russia in the United States, a tradition that may also be seen in terms of a confrontation between the ideo-logical and political reality of the host culture and the idealistic longings and futuristic rhetoric of its newcomers.

I discuss this confrontation in this chapter, which sets up a theoretical framework for reading novels by East European immigrant women as com-plexly reflective of the interaction between the dominant culture and its newcomers. By approaching the novel through the paradigm of Bakhtinian dialogism, which defines this genre as always engaged in discourses with non-novelistic texts, I argue for its role as a meeting ground for intercultural nar-ratives and diverse authors. Because literary dialogues contained in the novel reflect also the diversity and relationships of power in the cultures supplying the texts, I emphasize that the one in America is especially rich in tensions and unique individual voices. My reading of the East European immigrant women writers' contribution to American literature focuses on their double "otherness"—as marginalized ethnics desiring inclusion and as the "other" gender—foreign women—which confronts patriarchal oppression both in the Old and the New Worlds.

As accounts of gendered Americanization, these women's texts register the conflict between the model narratives of feminine acculturation, which are constructed for them by the dominant culture, and their own accounts, which often challenge or revise the "master plots" they are expected to follow. Caught in this conflict, they often interrogate the ideological and gendered models of Americanization by offering alternative readings of both female and male rites of passage. I stress that, by pointing out the unfulfilled promises of the Promised Land, they subvert the traditional narratives of immigrant gratitude and success and revise the outdated, canonical approaches to the writings from the "Other Europe."[2]

### The Novel as Cultural Bridge

The cultural "bridge of understanding" connecting East Europe and the United States is a construction based on two seemingly mutually exclusive approaches in valuing the newcomer and the dominant culture to their respective others. Long before Anzia Yezierska wrote, work on this feat of cultural engineering started with the first Poles, Russians, Czechs, Slovaks, Bulgarians, and others, the newcomers from the "East" who were lumped into an ethnic minority group along with many other newcomers who had been inhabiting the territories of the "West," in the New World, practically from the time of the first colonies.[3] They were among the marginal groups taking part in the ambivalent American experiment—seen both as the making of an ideological concept and of a future United States—together with the Anglo-Saxons, who had built their new home often having almost wiped out the indigenous peoples' civilizations. Regardless of how much it is entangled in the murky history of the invasion and settlement of the New World, the contribution to bridge building between East European and North American cultures of the Poles, for instance, has not been widely recognized. Although we may have heard about the Revolutionary War battles in which Tadeusz Kościuszko and Kazimierz Pułaski led American troops (and we may probably recall a few towns named after them), we are generally unaware of the multitude of writings produced by immigrants and visitors from Poland alone.[4] We may recall the stereotypical "Polack," Stanley Kowalski, from Tennessee Williams's *A Streetcar Named Desire* and William Styron's ambivalent concentration camp survivor from *Sophie's Choice* and their appearance in the film versions of both. Or we may be aware of the recent Steven Spielberg movie, *Schindler's List*, which was shot on location in Poland. However, these historical, literary, and cinematic images of Poland and its people do not tell the whole story because they reflect only one aspect of a more complex cultural representation—"how we see them" instead of "how they see us and themselves." This aspect can best be studied in writings *by* rather than *about* immigrants from Poland and East Europe.

An especially interesting part of this little-known literary discourse involving East Europeans in America is that which has been taking place within the novel. I have structured my study of the writings of Polish and Russian immigrants and exiles in America around the novel, although I do not limit my discussion to the form as it has traditionally been classified. In my close readings of individual writers, I emphasize the openness of the novel as a genre, which invites boundary-crossing, and the mixing of extraliterary expressions with fiction. As an unbound medium—a "heteroglot" construction, in Mikhail Bakhtin's terms, in which many different voices find expression and engage in a dialogue with one another—it provides an ideal meeting ground for intercultural exchanges.

My approach is indebted not only to Bakhtin but also to his critics and interpreters, Michael Holquist, Katerina Clark, and Julia Kristeva, who emphasize his conception of the novel as a genre that constantly revises itself by engaging with extraliterary discourses. As Clark and Holquist note, Bakhtin saw the novel as a "fundamentally anticanonical" genre, one that insists on "a dialogue between texts that a given system admits as literature and those texts that are excluded from such a definition."[5] This dialogic nature of the novel, as Clark and Holquist describe it, indicates that texts produced on the margin of the traditional novel and "literature," and especially texts such as autobiographies, memoirs, and diaries, which are often deemed non-novelistic, are in fact indispensable voices in the Bakhtinian polyphonic genre. Kristeva expands this interpretation. For her, Bakhtinian dialogism strives toward harmony, but is "all the while implying the idea of rupture (of opposition and analogy) as a modality of transformation." In this context, the Bakhtinian novel can be also seen as produced through conflicts and contrasts between texts, which in turn may reflect the conflicts and contrasts among the individuals, groups, and cultures who wrote them. Like the novel, dialogues between literatures and cultures, as well as those contained within these literatures and cultures, produce larger polyphonic discourses, but they also allow individual voices to find expression within, even to disrupt, these discourses.[6]

Emphasis on the singular expressions of individual writers is crucial to Bakhtin's concept of the novel as dialogue. Gary Saul Morson reminds us that the Russian theorist "insists that it is always real and specific people, not texts or languages, that speak to one another." In the dialogic encounter of the act of reading, all participants must have "an irreducible voice," must be active and involved.[7] This meeting between the author and the reader over the printed page can be seen as a reflection of a larger cultural encounter in which specific peoples and individuals participate. The way America "reads" East Europe depends, then, on its desire to engage actively, to be an "irreducible voice," and to recognize such a voice in individual immigrants' texts. The decentered position of these texts is an advantage, as it allows them to be an alternative to the centralized version of the national literature, to challenge and revise, as well as show the national canon's dependence on its ethnic margin.

According to Stanisław Barańczak, literature is the best means of communication between cultures, as it carries deeper and more significant meanings than any political and scholarly commentary:

> Just as the differences between two ethnic languages create the need for translators, so all the incompatibilities between the Eastern European and American mentalities only make every form of semantic mediation all the more desirable. . . . I believe in culture as a possible go-between. A single novel by, say, Milan Kundera or Tadeusz Konwicki, when translated into English, tells the American audience more about Czechoslovakia or Poland than ten years of *Newsweek* coverage. . . . [It] is an incomparably better source of information about Eastern Europe than a thousand interviews with General Jaruzelski by Barbara Walters. A general can lie and be believed; in a work of art, we cannot fail to discover a false note because it simply hurts our ears. If you want to know why ten million unarmed people in an Eastern European country risked being crushed by Soviet tanks . . . don't ask party secretaries. Ask poets and artists.[8]

But if this type of intercultural communication is to work, America has to move beyond superficial media coverage and engage in the deeper dialogue embedded in the novel. By doing so, it will not only participate in the new world order it boasts of creating, but it will also perpetuate the dialogic nature of the genre that reflects so well the complexity of its own national character.

In my reading of American diversity through the lens of novels written by East European immigrants—mostly Polish and Russian women—I am not, however, concerned with defining general boundaries of the genre or the boundaries separating the particular subgenres within it. All the authors discussed in this study wrote fiction, novels, short stories, and autobiographies; they used prose and quoted poetry; they drew on the external discourses embracing and enriching literature. My focus is on individual writers and how they participate in the East-West dialogue through their literary expressions; it is on what they have to say about the experience of being a part—accepted or not—of a complex hybrid, the American novel. Therefore, although I discuss many texts, read passages closely, and ponder single words and phrases in these pages, my aim is to see—to make tangible—the individuals who wrote them and to bring out the ethnic, national, religious, gender, and class differences that define their unique voices.

My emphasis on individual men and women writing their stories is important, because every text, and every author, reaches beyond the boundaries of the immediate milieu within which a literary work has been created. As Milan Kundera argues, "Nothing is a local matter any more" in a world growing smaller and denser with every racing year.[9] No text pertains to just one nation, one ethnic or racial group, one author, or one isolated historical or personal event. Although in discussing novels we often talk about extreme individualism and alienation—the complex modern ailment of otherness—each person shares this predicament with the rest of the world.[10] Naturally, such an approach to reading authors and texts does not imply collapsing the boundaries of race, gender, class, ethnic origin, or religious denomination that still separate men and women, peoples, and cultures, but it does mean that, despite these boundaries, we have something in common to build bridges with. We can, in Jay Clayton's words, engage in the "pleasures of Babel."[11]

It is also true that we need to keep reaching over the boundaries of difference to protect our cultural sanity. As James Clifford claims, "pure products go crazy"; any isolated and homogeneous environment is prone to frustration because we naturally need an other to define ourselves.[12] In this context, we cannot talk about just the particular ethnic literature of the United States or any other nation without acknowledging foreign influences and presences that disrupt a superficial cultural "unity in diversity." Although from its beginning the American novel has been written as a mosaic of ethnic contributions and although it has orchestrated a choral discourse of numerous voices, many readings of this diversity tend to emphasize the unity of a nation and its ethnic or racial groups instead of individual contributions to this unity. Such an approach to the novel as a unified multilayered text, in which each group is granted a separate space, reveals tensions among individual voices and the relationships of power governing them that have often been neglected. That is why it is important to remember that even though the specific fictions written between East Europe and the United States stand for an individual voice in themselves, this voice nevertheless resonates with many different writers' often contradictory expressions. And because the East European contribution, in particular, belongs to that complex composition, the American novel, it is engaged in the tensions and relationships of power among many participants within a genre and a culture that escape traditional definitions of unity.

## America and Its Other

The particular relationship between the two interlocutors—East and West—who converse within the novel in America has been very much structured by the opposition of the powerful versus the powerless. Such a relationship exists between any host culture and any minority, and it utilizes the rhetoric of the center and the margin. Consequently, the encounter I am going to present does not seem altogether harmonious and reciprocal; the dialogue in this case does not necessarily preclude inequality of its participants. For example, in a desire to embrace minorities, to make them a part of the constantly evolving canon, some American critics turn to "authorizing" the immigrant texts, to validating them within the ideology they represent as insiders and agents speaking from the center, the host culture.[13] Such authorizations, or critical "colonizations," often obscure the original message of an ethnic text in their noble attempts to fit that text into the familiar American model, to insist that the dialogue is conducted in the common language of diversity. We often fashion elaborate arguments about how a given text *lives up* to the standards of the host culture instead of concentrating on how it sometimes does not agree with American ideology, or even fails to absorb the narrative models that this ideology expects it to embrace.[14]

Critical efforts of this type foreground the politics of making the literary trends and canons in this country. The virtual absence of women writers from the early anthologies and series depicting postwar East European writing in the 1960s, 1970s, and even 1980s can be easily traced to a patriarchal model of the curriculum and to outdated perceptions of so-called "literary greatness."[15] The well-known Penguin series edited by Philip Roth, Writers from the Other Europe, does not feature a single woman writer. By presenting the "Other Europe" as written exclusively by men, Roth establishes a one-gender cultural model for audiences in the United States and Western Europe. In this context, the title of the series is highly ironic—the use of the term "other" can be seen as signifying absent female authors within the canon of male novelists established by the series.[16] The literary merit of émigré authors promoted so far in the United States notwithstanding, the exclusion of women from the emerging canon seems to indicate that either there have been no good female writers coming to the United States from East Europe or that their stories have not coincided with what the mainstream editors, translators, and audiences in the West have wanted to promote, popularize, and hear.

Assuming that there are always interesting women writers to be found if we care to look for them—and my subsequent chapter on Maria Kuncewicz proves that—I would argue that the virtual absence, or marginalization, of women in recent discussions about East European literature in the United States results from a long history of reductive readings of immigrant writings by the host culture. In tracing these writings' appearance in scholarship and teaching, I notice a clear, politically motivated historical division into the pre–World War II and the Cold War eras that also reflects a gender split. Historically, we either read about the "huddled masses" crossing the Atlantic in search of better economic opportunities or political dissidents fleeing communist persecution, even as the stories of both groups play out the same immigrant scenario in different historical contexts. Nevertheless, both groups—the "huddled masses" and the dissidents, respectively—are perceived in terms of characteristic narrative patterns that are split still further along the lines of gender.

In the "huddled masses" tradition, we trace two superficial story lines, the male one of economic success or the female one of miscegenation. But in the predominantly male dissident tradition, we follow underground activities against the communist regimes and heroic defections to the free West.[17] In this tradition women hardly ever emerge as political activists and celebrated émigré dissidents. They are either sexual objects lost in the turbulent times around them—e.g., female characters in Milan Kundera's *The Unbearable Lightness of Being*—or they are figures too preoccupied with maintaining the domestic sphere to engage in the male-dominated public domain of ideological combat.[18] The distinctions between historical periods and gendered narratives make it difficult to study the East European contribution to American multicultural literature. Instead of divided, it should be read and taught as a heterogeneous, changing, and often controversial dialogue of diverse narratives and voices. The reason why such a divided perspective makes this reading difficult stems from the insistence of the dominant culture on receiving a reassuring portrait of itself from its ethnic margin—the "Other Europe."

Early twentieth-century American audiences were trained to admire the successful making of such an immigrant hero as Andrew Carnegie—"Scottish-born *American* industrialist and humanitarian," as the *American Heritage Dictionary* poignantly calls him (emphasis mine)—and to appropriate his story as a narrative model reflecting their national success. Subsequently, influenced by the Cold War politics and anti-Soviet propaganda, they expected post-war émigré stories to testify to the evils of communism and expected real-life plots in which the most talented East European intellectuals were seeking freedom of speech in the democratic West. The ideological emphasis on and popularity of the male story of success in both traditions have resulted in the emergence of a "canon" of sorts, a set of texts privileged by their propagation in scholarship, teaching, and publications. The dominant culture's preference for such male narrative models did not wholly preclude immigrant women writers, such as Polish-Jewish Anzia Yezierska or Mary Antin, from becoming popular during the 1920s, nor did it more recently prevent Eva Hoffman or Slavenka Drakulic from being published and read. However, the narrative models that have survived the passage of time had to be in tune with patriarchal American culture, which wanted to read in immigrant literature the reflection and continuation of its Founding Fathers' "defections" to the New World in search of economic and religious freedom.[19]

This desire to explain the East European other through the familiar model of American consensus informs even more recent, and more publicized, approaches to postcommunism, in which a male-dominated host culture reinforces patriarchal models of the Old World. For example, the program of the 1993 Annual Conference on Polish Affairs, "Poland between Two Worlds," did not feature a single session on women.[20] This is significant, given that it had been barely six months since the government's introduction of a national anti-abortion law in the wake of the church's campaign to restore "family values" in that increasingly capitalist ex-communist country. Perhaps this should not be a surprise, as studies on contemporary Poland's women have usually been rare, despite the fact that issues vital to their lives continue to be the battle-ground between the church and the state: contraception and abortion, divorce, women in politics, and so on. Immortalized in romantic poetry as mothers, lovers-muses, and upholders of national virtues, then praised by social-realistic propaganda as sturdy comrades unafraid of man's work, Polish women have often been objects of ideological descriptions, but they have hardly ever been listened to as independent voices speaking for themselves.[21] But no matter how their own culture presents them, a profound lack of interest in their version of "Poland between Two Worlds" displayed by the country in which the conference took place suggests that the West is perhaps still invested in continuing the dissident tradition beyond the Cold War era.[22]

Similar responses to historical and political changes have continued to fuel the debate on the canon in American literature, which, torn between the hegemony of traditional consensus and the need to include disruptive "other voices," has often resulted in half-hearted arguments for the inclusion of minority writings. It does not help in promoting a fairer picture of America's other literatures and ethnic groups that the available studies about them only self-consciously justify the validity of their projects. In the case of immigrant literature, it has for a long time served as illustrative material in sociological and historical studies of newcomer groups. When made a subject of a literary critical work, it had to be often mediated as not quite literary because of its closeness to these nonliterary disciplines. As a result, just as many other minority works, texts by immigrant writers have been often approached as helpful in providing background and in documenting historical changes important for understanding American culture, but not as interesting in themselves because of their literary qualities.

For example, in *America's Immigrant Women*, Cecyle S. Neidle explains her interest in the lesser literature of the newcomer: "While the experiences of immigrants in the American environment have made a considerable impact on American writing, the effect of immigrant writers themselves on the literary scene has been a modest one. . . . [W]ith the exception of Ole Edvart Rölvaag, Ludwig Lewisohn, and Abraham Cahan, *works of real literary stature are lacking*. Only in the field of autobiography can the claim be upheld that foreign-born autobiographers made a considerable impress in terms of numbers and effectiveness."[23] Neidle's value judgment concerning immigrant writing raises several important questions. What are the grounds for deciding which immigrant works possess "literary stature" and which do not? In evaluating the text's merits, do we take into consideration the author's gender (all writers Neidle praises are male) and its implications for the writing mode (female-autobiographical; male-intellectual)? Is it true that, in order to produce remarkable literature, one must not write autobiography? In her study on the relationship between gender and writing, Judith Kegan Gardiner suggests that "women's novels are often called autobiographical, women's autobiographies, novelistic." Must we conclude, then, that immigrant women's naturally and necessarily autobiographical writing did not have any impact on the history of the American novel?[24] (Or that male novels are never autobiographical?) Neidle claims that "as it was difficult to acquire the artistic distance needed to universalize an experience in which one's involvement was as total as that of an immigrant . . . the *fictive immigrant story* had to wait for the more detached observer" (256, emphasis mine). Because it is hard to imagine a "detached observer" recording his or her life in a new country, the immigrant woman's writing is condemned to a sphere of "explosive and emotional response," which cannot approximate fiction. For example, Anzia Yezierska's texts are seen as a "dozen different autobiographical guises," not as novels (262–264). The question whether there exists any novel, by a male or female, untainted by autobiography never arises in Neidle's discussion.

On the other hand, more recent scholarship often approaches immigrant women's texts as basically documents registering the ethnic history of America. For example, Maxine Schwartz Seller acknowledges "women as subjects rather than objects and ethnic life not as an aberration, but as an enduring and valuable . . . feature of the American social landscape." Seller's introduction and anthology succeed in presenting women from abroad as "problem solvers rather than problems," and her work proves to be a rich source of bibliographical information on diverse ethnic groups. Nevertheless, she still recognizes women's texts mostly for their "authenticity and effectiveness in conveying the thoughts, feelings, and experiences of immigrant women"— that is, for their autobiographical and documentary role rather than for artistic or literary value.[25] Thus Anzia Yezierska's "The Free Vacation House" is rendered as an example in the chapter "Community Life," even though it is a perfectly constructed and masterfully executed short story. I might ask more questions: Why should we decide that a piece of immigrant writing is either a document or "pure fiction"? How can we possibly know whether it relates a "real" first-hand experience or whether it only uses the mode of autobiographical fiction to present an invented story? Cannot all immigrant texts— male and female, novels, autobiographies, documents, narratives of historical facts—be simply treated as valuable contributions to American literary discourse?[26]

But even the act itself of restoring lesser-known immigrant texts, in particular these by women writers from Poland or Russia, to the position they deserve may involve validation through the powerful ideologies of the dominant culture, thus reinforcing the traditional canon. A revised East European canon would have to be mediated by publishers, editors, and critics representing a center that consented to hear and promote marginal voices according to its preferences. In this context, even a feminist approach waging war against the outdated canon can be seen as *taking in* powerless marginal texts and mediating them *into* a separate category of feminist fiction, which constitutes a powerful ideological center of its own. A female newcomer would have to be mediated into such a center in order to be recognized as a participant. Often in the course of such mediation, her particular otherness, her unique class, religious background, and ethnicity, will be subdued or muted because of the critical desire to concentrate on validating her gender.

Therefore, although it is necessary to look for common denominators if we want to bring many texts together and build a chronological tradition of female writings from the Other Europe, it is also important to note and emphasize differences and tensions within this very tradition, especially those that pertain to the diverse experiences of gender represented by women from different backgrounds. Even though all the women I study come from the same geographical location and have had similar experiences of passage into American culture, their individual accounts have to be read as unique experiences determined by specific class, religious, and ethnic conditions. A Jew and a Catholic—Anzia Yezierska and Maria Kuncewicz—may be brought together in the general immigrant women's literary tradition. Yet their individual concepts of nationhood, the dominant culture, the political and ideological implications of immigration, their social status, and authorial success are bound to be very different. Moreover, because of how the United States approached the political issue of immigration before and during the Cold War, they would be received on very different terms by the dominant culture. For Elizabeth Stern, writing against the sexism, xenophobia, and anti-Semitism of the early twentieth-century United States, gender and sexuality were inseparable from her Jewishness and lower-class origins and made her able to identify with the suffragists' cause and thus boldly claim Americanness as "a woman and a Jew."

However, even Stern's efforts to combine the immigrant cause with the American women's movement have to be read in the context of the ambivalent attitude of native-born women reformers to their foreign counterparts. In her case, individual difference of the newcomer intersects with the canonical mediations and classifications of her by the host culture. Females from East Europe and the Balkan countries were often seen as a threat to the late nineteenth-century cult of the New Woman and were consequently left out of it because they wanted emancipation on their own terms.[27] Immigrant women with backgrounds similar to Stern's were also excluded from the women's suffrage movement because some of its conservative members rejected the idea that any immigrant, female or male, should have a vote equal to theirs and thereby influence matters concerning their country. In lumping immigrants of both genders together as unwanted voters, the anti-immigrant suffragists contradicted the basic assumptions of their own ideology of essential difference between the sexes, suggesting that its political tenets held true only for American women.[28]

We can see more recent examples of such a confrontation between the ethnic woman's concept of gendered identity and that held by the dominant culture in Eva Hoffman's autobiographical novel *Lost in Translation: A Life in a New Language* (1988). Hoffman's complex postmodern journey into multicultural America shows the female newcomer coming of age in the New World, where her linguistic and emotional record of female acculturation mingles with the political discourse of the Cold War anti-Soviet rhetoric around her. However, despite her peers' desire to see communism—and, to a certain extent, the narrator who has lived under it—as stereotypically evil, Hoffman resists the temptation to use the enthusiastic, traditional immigrant discourse to defend herself, a discourse that is often as reductive as anticommunist propaganda. In her emphasis on the uniqueness of an individual immigrant experience, Hoffman targets the insecurities and imbalances in the dominant culture who needs its other—the ambivalent "resident alien"—to read through the ideological discourses defining the world divided as much by the Iron Curtain as by the "battle of the sexes."

### Inverting the Balance of Power

In this study of the outsiders in the traditional East European canon and of gendered narratives in the immigrant novel in the United States, I propose to read newcomer authors and their texts as active agents who desire participation in American culture. Rather than proving that an author fits some central model, I prefer exploring the particular textual yearnings of these authors for acceptance and their desire to be heard by the host country—as the narrator in another Anzia Yezierska short story exclaims: "I want America to want me!" I also want to follow failures of immigrant ideals and critiques of the American Dream in those who were supposed to perpetuate it, those who expected to be welcomed and accepted by the dominant culture in return for that. My readings of Slavic-Jewish women writers such as Mary Antin, Anzia Yezierska, and Elizabeth Stern stress the themes of alienation, oppression, and the fight for freedom in an environment that was often far from friendly. Perceiving these writers' texts as active voices depicting America from *outside* its powerful ideology of integration leads to a reevaluation of, for instance, the seemingly successful Americanization of Mary Antin and reveals Anzia Yezierska's disillusionment with the political and ideological implications of an immigrant female author's career in this country.

I realize that my efforts to concentrate on marginal texts while inevitably writing from a center of power, which I necessarily create as a critic and a scholar, may be seen as an improbable masquerade. Gayatri Chakravorty

Spivak claims that each explanation we give pertains to some center—some cultural code, political stance, opinion, subjectivity—that may conceal repression. We need the margin as a circumference of what is inside and what is defined in opposition to the outside, which often leads to the exploitation of the margin: "The putative center welcomes selective inhabitants of the margin in order to better exclude the margin."[29] A critic who wants to engage in an inquiry about "displaced" authors is bound to "shuffle" between the center—the academic and ideological position—and the margin—authors, texts, facts, politics—that he or she wants to validate and empower. On the other hand, as Jay Clayton suggests, seemingly limiting critical center-margin-center oscillations have "positive, creative uses." They make us realize our ability to resist power both from above—"by those with power over others"—and from within—"[in our] own cherished disciplines"—and to use this resistance to promote the "legitimating power of culture—its ability to legitimate the dominant ideology, of course, but also its ability to consolidate subterranean values, to preserve marginal traditions, and to confirm as subjects people who have long been denied that status" (23–4).

We can use this creative approach to power in connection with the Bakhtinian dialogic model mentioned earlier, in which each cultural encounter is unique and requires individual treatment. Thus, in my readings of immigrant women's writings, I analyze texts *from* their outsider's position and in terms of *their* marginal idiom directed *toward* the dominant culture that they want to revise. After all, each newcomer writer creates his or her unique "America," from his or her unique center of paradoxical power—marginality—which can challenge and rewrite the dominant culture, often without this culture's even realizing it.[30] In thus emphasizing the marginal power of newcomer writers to re-create the dominant culture, I do not intend to substitute one gendered narrative for another. In reading women's writings created between East Europe and the United States, I am aware that their experience can be understood fully only through cross-references to the male canon, for which their narrative models and authorship provide the margin. Moreover, since women's writings reflect a larger dialogue engaging diverse backgrounds, their version of America has to be read, again, through the magnifying glass of difference, through their individual Jewish, Catholic, lower-class, middle-class, proletarian, or intellectual approaches.

### Playing on the Borders

Immigrants' revisions of their host cultures are recorded in diverse texts, often isolated from one another and classified as belonging to social sciences, history, or cultural studies—disciplines that would not readily use the word "novel" in relation to Mary Antin's *The Promised Land*, for example. Because it deepens the otherness of immigrant women's writings, this diversity calls for an interdisciplinary approach, which can only enrich the reading of the outsider's message and can only read the novel as a dialogic and intercultural genre. Therefore, without collapsing the borders between various approaches, we can still use them to construct a complex reading of diverse authors within a dialogic American–East European novel.

Using such an interdisciplinary approach in this study, I found my critical "center" already on the outskirts of any definite ideology. Obviously, as a critical stance, my work necessarily claims some interpretive power. However, I mean to channel this power, my readings, toward voicing the "power of the outsider" that I see in the immigrant texts. My own background as a scholar positioned between two cultures, languages, and literary traditions— East European and American—is naturally decentralized and "alien," and, in a sense, similar to that of the immigrant women writers. Yet, as a critic, I see myself empowered by this similarity to venture into the otherness of the newcomers' messages about this country. My exploration of these messages in this study coincides with a desire to validate my own theoretical perspective as the critical other—the outsider-participant in American literary scholarship. While keeping in mind that all our literary and critical efforts are, to a lesser or greater degree, fictions, I am aware that mine is also telling a story. This story is not only about empowering the marginalized immigrant women's writings but also about claiming a voice for myself as a bicultural scholar.

My perception of a critical position in this context rests on the clear reversal of the cultural power structure that is seen from the in-between perspective of the outsider. As such, I offer intercultural translation and, for the time being, a definite dislocation of the core of power onto the outside of the host culture. Similar ideas have been already advocated by such critics as Jeffrey Goldfarb, Mary Dearborn, Stanisław Barańczak, Margaret O'Brien Steinfels, and many others. Yet while these critics concentrate on *America* learning from the foreigners, I emphasize what *the foreigners want to teach*. Obviously, I do not intend to praise arrogant intrusions of aliens who know better, but to stress what they see as the most truly American feature of this cultural discourse— its being constantly in the making by minorities and newcomers who claim it for their own, despite its frequent resistance to and rejection of them.[31]

Critical inversion of the power structure, decentering, is necessary if one wants to engage in the immigrant accounts of a search for freedom—a passage from the Old World into the New. Traditionally, the crucial part of the immigrant transition has been the shedding of the Old World skin and taking on the New World one. A backstage struggle to retain the ethnic origins and to balance a precarious identity while suspended between two incompatible worlds has not been as emphasized. In some criticism, the immigrant writer's perspective as an outsider has been appreciated as an invaluable contribution to the American national character.[32] The welcoming culture, which makes such a writer over and into "one of us" within an all-embracing democracy, however, still remains the main point of reference, thus placing the outsider in the subordinate position as an object rather than a subject. We can see the past and present version of this perspective already in a classic immigrant play by Israel Zangwill, *The Melting Pot* (1909), and in works by recent critics such as Werner Sollors, Sacvan Bercovitch, and Myra Jehlen.[33]

Nevertheless, newcomer authors can be read as subjects when we focus on the failures and disillusionments they relate rather than on standard Americanizations that they were expected to undertake. Having come here, the immigrants find themselves caught in the juxtaposition of the Old World and the New—and both are unavailable to them. The two alien cultures facing each other over their respective differences produce an immigrant conflict of in-between identity. An individual case of this conflict in an immigrant text can be read as a mirror reflection of the East-West discourse in the novel. Just as an East European and an American might, two novels can—and do—find themselves positioned on the extremes of ideological, economic, and social spectrums. Nevertheless, despite the ocean of difference between them, or precisely because of it, these novels are engaged in a dialogue that started with the individual immigrants at the end of the nineteenth century and that is still going on, despite the demise of an ideology stigmatizing the Eastern part of Europe as America's and the West's political other.

Being the other in America, the country which in itself is a stranger to any newcomer, the immigrant is entangled in an identity conflict with no way out. Remaining an alien enclosed within a hermetic ethnic shell—that is, holding on to the Old World identity within the minority group—the newcomer is marginalized and excluded from the longed-for dream of mythical America. Yet entering the strange Promised Land as a naturalized citizen, one who abandons ethnic roots, indicates an affirmation of otherness as a permanent condition. The new identity is born suspended between the remainders of the old alien self and the invitation to American otherness, and thus is rendered permanently split and alienated. Such dangling identity, or identities, may be the only kind capable of engaging in intercultural dialogue and of remaking the host culture. Immigrant texts, even those that reach this country in translation, attest to the creative quality of such a balancing identity act.

In the works of early Jewish women from Poland and Russia, this conflict becomes a catalyst for writing. For the Catholic Maria Kuncewicz, a refugee and immigrant-visitor from Poland who went back to her motherland as an American citizen, exile within international otherness became a main theme of fiction and autobiography. Eva Hoffman's recent memoir, *Lost in Translation*, celebrates an awareness of being different, of being simultaneously lost and found in the precarious new linguistic existence in America, while cherishing the lost paradise of her Polish childhood.

### Female—A Special Case of Otherness

The otherness conflict is especially acute in women writers, as their identity is doubly oppressed because of gender. They are trapped between the mythical construction of an America they cannot attain as immigrants and the quotidian realities they have to cope with in the New World as females. The early newcomers, especially those originating in lower-class Orthodox Jewish backgrounds, such as Yezierska and Antin, find, instead of the "land of milk and honey," the ethnic ghetto, where they are segregated and where they discover that "we the people" refers to the cool Anglo-Saxons who look down on Hester Street and on its inhabitants' emancipatory aspirations. Paradoxically, the female immigrant, like the female slave, can be seen as an especially oppressed alien in a land that has been always mythologized in terms of a woman's body.[34]

Henry Nash Smith's works present America as a myth and a metaphor—a feminine landscape and a fertile womb that is possessed and fertilized by the settlers. Annette Kolodny's more recent studies of this myth through gender concentrate on sexual and reproductive connotations of its metaphors—the woman-land is penetrated, "laid," and gives birth to a new race of people.[35] The whole genre of Adamic literature and criticism addresses themes such as "the virgin wilderness," "the New Eden," and "the New World Garden." Although the assaults and "regenerations through violence" are acknowledged in the paradise, the overall vision stresses the warmth and comfort of the Promised Land, which gathers all children to "her" breast like a forgiving mother-lover.[36] Even Kolodny's feminist approach, which offers alternatives to the masculine-biased readings of the land as a woman's body, still emphasizes the same myth's importance for women by calling for a "feminized" attitude toward the landscape.[37]

The sexual connotations of the myth of the Promised Land coincide with the female newcomer novel, which seems to be preoccupied with the theme of sexual unfulfillment in the new country and which often rejects the feminized vision of America for one centering on an idealized WASP male. In these texts the host culture prefers the idealized vision of itself to crude reality on the one hand, and is both fascinated with and scared of the exotic otherness of the immigrant woman on the other. As an alien body, a carrier of foreign sexuality, the female newcomer represents a threat to the centralized ethos of American womanhood and can provide a temptation for native-born males.[38] But she is often rejected by both genders for being an outsider to the American courting customs and for her desire to be accepted as the "other gender"—a woman—on terms that are alien to the dominant culture.

For instance, because the dominant rhetoric of the nativist years 1890–1920 did not accept and acknowledge her alien identity and sexuality, the immigrant woman of that time can be read as oppressed within the dominant culture she desires to enter. Not only is she already made inferior by the patriarchal traditions of the Old World and by the immigrant communities in the New World that continue these traditions, but she is also the "other" in relation to the native-borns of both genders. She is caught up in a struggle to acquire the language, to fight poverty, and to work out her precarious existence in the new country, but she must also come to terms with being alienated due to her foreign sexuality (e.g., unaccompanied single women or those not claimed by men were not admitted into the country; neither were single mothers). Therefore, her individual perception of herself as a female is constantly threatened, as she cannot fit into the existing models of femininity and cannot work out alternative ones without risking self-denial. As we can see in many stories by Anzia Yezierska, who fights her way toward becoming an American woman, Jewish females in her texts suppress their sexuality in order to be accepted. In their new home their bodies are carriers of the brain that acquires the language, earn money as laborers ("hands"), but are expected to be desexualized to avoid the stigma of foreign female carnality. In the context of the Promised Land, which is identified as feminine and sexual, such a situation produces paradoxes. Unable to identify with their new "motherland," female immigrants are still expected to be model American mothers and wives; forced to suppress their sexuality in order to prove themselves as workers and students, they are nevertheless constantly under surveillance because the dominant culture wants to see them as its sexual other.[39]

This split between gendered identity and sexuality is necessary in order to deliver the newcomer into the host culture. As a desexualized woman, she is safe and acceptable and can play her immigrant roles without disturbing the image that her new environment expects her to fit. In Yezierska's novels the woman who wants to rise out of the ghetto has to virtually renounce sexual gratification for the sake of becoming somebody, for "making from [her]self a person." Even if her intellect carries her out of the tenements and lets her pass for an American, her body still remains in the metaphorical ghetto-prison of repressed sexuality. When she falls in love, she loves platonically and flees from sex; a figure of a mature mentor who appreciates her intellect replaces a lover who desires her body.[40] We can see this pivotal theme in *Salome of the Tenements, All I Could Never Be,* and *Bread Givers* as well as in Mary Antin's immigrant classic, *The Promised Land.* An iconographical representation of this theme can be seen at the Ellis Island Museum of Immigration, which displays a "before and after" advertisement of an agency making over the exotically but extremely uncomfortably and outmodishly dressed immigrant women and girls into inconspicuously fashionable Americans. This insistence that newcomer women's appearance fit into the accepted norm suggests that the host culture is invested in ensuring successful assimilation of both genders through controlling females, who in turn could influence their families as mothers as wives.[41]

Nevertheless, control or rejection by the dominant culture is not the only reason for the oppression of the immigrant woman's gendered and sexual identities. She suffers in the confrontation not only with the male-dominated Anglo-Saxon mentality, but also with that of her male fellow immigrants, fathers, lovers, husbands, and sons, who condemn the emancipatory efforts of their women as a sin against or a betrayal of the Old World traditions. This is especially true of the early immigrant Jewish families described by Anzia Yezierska and Elizabeth Stern. In their particular cases, the trauma of repressed sexuality—which exacts a price for the rebellion against the old and the new narratives writing a woman's life—produce very interesting literary accounts of female liberation. In these texts we follow the female authors' and their characters' struggles for identity, which are triggered precisely by the gender-related lack of freedom that a female immigrant, regardless of her race or religious persuasion, experiences between the two worlds as a marginal other.[42] That is why a struggle with a father and a denial of ethnic lovers for the sake of utopian relationships with Americans become almost a clichéd story in the novels I discuss. On the other hand, these repetitious narratives, reappearing in different versions throughout most of the immigrant women's writings, converge into an interesting subtext that allows for an alternative reading in which all these individual women participate and can be read.

But even this collective text is delivered into the new culture by mediators, people who substitute for the immigrant women authors as intercultural go-betweens. As Mary V. Dearborn stresses, an ethnic female author needs "midwives" to bring her text into the host country and to validate it. Authors of prefaces and glossaries, the mentors who boast of their immigrant prodigies, are the necessary "translators" of the newcomer woman's foreignness.[43] As Sandra Gilbert, Susan Gubar, and other feminist critics claim, the writing woman *is* her text, which she produces in order to liberate herself from the safety and closure of a patriarchal tradition that relegates her to the domestic sphere. And although we can see a similar development in male immigrants and their texts (they are usually autobiographical and often sentimental in a curiously feminine way), they, too, sometimes get mediated. Nevertheless, the woman writer presents a special case because she is the other gender. In depriving the immigrant woman of a direct contact with the readers, the mediators and "midwives" abort her efforts to be accepted on her own terms as an author and a female.[44] Thus, even "bodily" writing, writing rendered as a metaphor of "giving birth" to her children-books, is denied to the newcomer. (In the case of Anzia Yezierska, we may speculate that such mothering of texts was a substitute for her unfulfilled American sexuality, as she gave up marriage and her daughter to be able to write.) This fact symbolizes the erasure of the woman's gendered identity by her mediators, her sacrifice for the texts she produces for the audiences in her new home.

Hence, the ethnic female's freedom to create is often available only after she pays for it by renouncing a successful sexual identity and the gender roles her freedom implies in the new culture: her ability to intermarry, to take an upper-class lover, to adopt an American family model. In my discussion of how the immigrant women's texts elicit this dilemma, I argue with Dearborn's conviction that miscegenation is a possible "re-embodiment" of a female subject in Yezierska, Antin, and Stern. Dearborn claims that the immigrant woman enters the culture through marriage or a union with a native-born male. Thus successful Americanization entails a sexual merging with the new country. I argue that it is precisely this model—another scenario of imposed assimilation—that the immigrant women's texts are challenging and revising.

In summary, the gender-related oppression of the immigrant women raises the following implications for my argument about the novelistic dialogue between America and East Europe.

First, a close reading of the "powerless" discourse, into which ethnic women from East Europe have been inscribed so far, uncovers their empowerment as outsiders-participants in American culture. I inquire into their version of the dialogue between East and West because it constitutes the margin necessary for grasping an overall picture of the intercultural encounter between the two alien literatures, both participants in the American novel.

Second, the texts describing this paradoxical female empowerment by their lack of freedom tell a story of frustrated female sexuality. The newcomer woman's body has to be repressed as a result of a clash between the dominant culture's and the newcomer woman's different ideologies of sexual conduct and their incompatible concepts of femininity. As a result of this repression, the immigrant rejects the feminized vision of America as a woman-mother-lover and replaces it with a myth of an idealized WASP male; a mentor-lover replaces the virgin-land myth, since his image embodies the male-dominated host culture that the immigrant desires to enter.

Moreover, in the rites of passage into America, every newcomer is bound by the official scenarios prescribed for her by the dominant culture, since this culture wants to see a confirmation of its ideology in the narratives produced by its margin. Nevertheless, despite being bound by the official story line, with which she has to comply in order to get published, the immigrant woman writer is able to smuggle an alternative story—a subtext or an alternative reading—under the seemingly complacent surface. Yet as an author, she has to be mediated into the American culture by translators and mentors of her alien otherness. The momentary freedom she enjoys as a maker of texts is thwarted because of the host country's inability to grasp and accept her foreign nature without a translation.

Although such accounts of unsuccessful female Americanization attest to these women's failures to be entirely accepted by the host culture and to achieve individual gendered identity, they still remake and develop the dialogic, intercultural novel. This genre is often perpetuated by otherness and denial, and the immigrant women's accounts of ambivalent acculturation open up opportunities for rereading the history of the American novel and of its cultural work. In this way, their texts form a specific tradition of their own, which is still continued by such contemporary writers as Eva Hoffman or Izabela Filipiak.[45]

These factors involving women from East Europe lead to more general questions concerning the larger theater of East-West dialogue: Is the experience of frustrated gendered identity limited to immigrant women writers? How do the results of this inquiry change our reading of the East European canon in the United States? What do they tell us about the politics of engaging in the dialogues with ethnic literatures and gendered narratives?

## Rereading Male Story through Female

An answer to the first question may seem obvious, since, as readers trained in reading for two incompatible spheres—male and female—we would expect that a man's account of Americanization should be the opposite of the woman's. After all, it is the "fathers" who have made the rules in America or who deny the woman's right to the public sphere in the name of the Old World domestic and conduct traditions.[46] Thus, as participants in the powerful patriarchal discourse, both immigrant and native-born males should constitute the indispensable other to women—the oppressive center. However, having positioned the immigrant women's texts in the space of the outsider-participant who is in fact remaking the host culture, I will use the results of this critical operation for an inquiry into Vladimir Nabokov's "American" novel, *Pnin*, which we can read as an immigrant narrative. Displacing the female perspective into the position of power, which, too often, is automatically prescribed for men, enables us to revise the suspiciously stable and definite place occupied by the male immigrant subject.

I agree with Mary Dearborn's argument that "no feature of ethnic female tradition is exclusively female" (189). There is no question about the unique character of the woman's experience; yet there is still the possibility of dialogue between male and female stories within the shared immigrant rites of passage. Each gendered narrative needs the other in the constant play between their otherness and between their respective concepts of alien sexuality constructed for them by the dominant culture. For this reason, even in disagreement the male and female immigrant texts constantly engage in textual discourses that are contained within the larger dialogue involving America and East Europe. There is no clearly and completely female novel versus a definitely male novel; even if a text talks about one gender only, the other is implied anyway, precisely because of its absence (as some French feminist critics would agree).

But where does the female sphere end and the male one begin in the dialogic terrain of East-West encounter? The crowd streaming into America through the gates of Ellis Island in the black and white documentary pictures and films is genderless and faceless; people from different countries blend into one tentacular body that is deprived of a specific sexual identity or preference. Thus all immigrants are seen as other and, in this sense, occupy a somewhat feminized position in the dominant culture. Mary Antin calls this genderless organism—the immigrant body—the "sinew and bone of all the nations."[47] In what has been generally considered the classic embodiment of immigrant propaganda, *They Who Knock at Our Gates*, Antin talks about newcomers as icons and ideological symbols rather than as individuals or sexual beings. The frontispiece in her book features a sturdy-looking man, and this is the image, not incidentally, that we have of immigrants—workers, peasants, peddlers— a crowd of gray humans rather than of individuals who look curiously very much alike.

An image of an immigrant may depict a man or a woman, but it does not necessarily imply a male or a female, since "the sinew and bone" are the ideological synecdoches rather than symbols for specifically gendered bodies. If we read the traditional rags-to-riches male narratives in the light of such "feminine" themes as oppression of gender and frustrated sexual identity, we will see that even the male story has been constructed and thwarted by the dominant center. Since we are culturally and ideologically conditioned to read male writers as always placed in the position of power, we often ignore the instances where they occupy the feminine space of the other. For example, reading Vladimir Nabokov's *Pnin* within the thematic context established by the analysis of immigrant and exiled women writers opens up the possibility for exploring this text's latent romantic and sentimental aspects.[48]

Therefore, the accounts by immigrant women describing female sexual suppression in the dominant culture can make us question the masculine vitality and unequivocal sexual power that we usually take for granted in men's stories. The explanations for the female, and, consequently, for both gendered narratives about alien sexuality can be found in the dichotomy between the sexuality of the Old World and the New. The foreign woman is caught in this double bind of otherness in two patriarchal cultures and thus marginalized twice. In contrast to that, the male rites of passage usually involve a narrative of struggle against social or natural forces, economic success, and rise to political power.[49] However, reading beyond this alluring façade of success, we can see that the male story, too, often addresses the theme of repression of sexuality, since, as a newcomer, the male is placed on the margin of otherness usually assigned for the female. Abraham Cahan's protagonist in *The Rise of David Levinsky* is a good example of a character who demonstrates such a conflict between the superficial story of economic success and the "feminized" subtext exploring sexual frustration and unfulfillment in the already sexually ambivalent Promised Land.

As can be expected, the most obvious depictions of this frustration are present in immigrant women's texts, where males figure as an additional oppressive factor. However, the angry portrayals of Orthodox Jewish patriarchs and lovers by Yezierska or Stern also curiously indicate sexual frustration in Old World men, who feel threatened by their women's American ideas and ambitions of emancipation. These new desires usually arise as a result of the immigrant woman's encounters with American males, whom she sees as superior and more desirable in their native-born otherness than the Old World men. Yet such encounters often construct the WASP male as the temperamental inferior of an exotic ethnic heroine—e.g., in Yezierska's *Salome*—a repressed Puritan afraid of the passionate immigrant. That is why, having rejected the males of her ethnic group and disillusioned by native-borns, the newcomer female does not fail to criticize them in her writings.[50] In this way, the seemingly powerless female discourse implies a gender-related dilemma both in the traditionally stronger male immigrant and in the idolized American male. According to the accounts by women, the trauma of acculturation affects both genders, whether they are Old World patriarchs or "real" Americans representing the dominant culture.

The theme of threatened gendered identity in men is present also in male émigré careers and writings. In particular, it is striking in the novels that originate within and seemingly support the center of ideological power. For example, the careers of Jerzy Kosiński and Vladimir Nabokov, two prominent émigrés from Poland and Russia, fit the success story of postwar America perfectly. The position of recognized authors from the Other Europe makes them parts and products of the dominant culture; they are chosen to represent East European literature not only because of their unequivocal literary merit but perhaps also because their images fit the political and cultural agenda of the Cold War era (Sirin in Nabokov's *Pnin* is an ironic example of such a commercialized ethnicity). In its hospitality to male dissidents heroically defecting from the countries suffering under communist regimes, American culture constructs a model desirable alien, whose presence within it attests to its political and cultural superiority over the Evil Empire. Therefore, both their cosmopolitanism and their ability to retain ethnic identities—and thus to require translators and ideological mediators much in the way women writers would—have often been male dissident writers' ticket to fame.[51]

However, if we use the approach derived from the discussion of immigrant women writers, we will discover that, for example, some of Jerzy Kosiński's characters suffer from a paradoxically "feminine" suppression of their sexuality. For example, as ethnic others, they often pay for success in the New World with impotence (*Being There*) or sexual repression and frustration (*Steps, Cockpit*). On the other hand, Nabokov's charming Timofey Pnin is presented as a sexless, possibly sterile, and sick body running away from the virile Sirin—a symbol of commercialized ethnicity—while Humbert Humbert from *Lolita* can embrace America only as a pedophiliac. Therefore, the seemingly dissonant dialogue between female and male within the immigrant writings produces a surprisingly harmonious duet: the body and sexuality—the most conspicuous differences—bring the two interlocutors together on the margin from which they present the dominant culture with their respective embodiments of otherness.

### Female-Male Dialogue and the East-West Cultural Discourse

The dialogic encounter between female and male immigrant texts brings us back to the juxtaposition of center-margin, other-other, East-West. Within the novel, where autobiography and fiction are never clearly separated and where the feminine space is not necessarily gender-specific, the reading of woman's experience enables us to detect oppression and frustration in the deceptively powerful structures and concepts.[52] The propagandistic accounts of female assimilation, such as Antin's *The Promised Land*, disclose alternative stories recording the newcomer woman's oppression. On the other hand, in these stories written from the vantage point of the marginal author, the dominant culture—which is trying to absorb and "melt" the newcomers—appears as an ambivalent other and confronts its own insecurities. Finally, the dominant sex of both worlds—the males representing the Old Country and those embodying the WASP "law of the fathers"—are rewritten in the women's texts. As a result of this rewriting, they can then be reread as the other occupying the feminized position—a feminine narrative space—which can be found even in the seemingly powerful male story of immigrant economic success.

Once again, going back full circle to the beginning of this chapter's argument, we can read the East European writings in the United States as a dialogue of individual voices and genders without collapsing the boundaries that delineate sexual differences and the relationships of power. With these boundaries intact—to honor and appreciate the individual participants, as well as their often dramatically different backgrounds—we can conceive of a literary chorus voicing difference together, through texts attesting to a multitude of religious, ideological, and ethnic origins. As a result, instead of a posterlike, happy "melting pot," we face a frustrated and disembodied discourse of otherness, from which America has been always trying to escape into the safety of the "one in many" ideology.

The reluctance to embrace uncertainty and fragmentation in place of the utopian melting pot is the reason why writing of the East European other has not been fully recognized as an indispensable contribution to the American novel. It has been usually as remote and intangible as the late communist states—the demonized threat to freedom and democracy. Since East Europe has ceased to exist as a political adversary, we have a tendency to forget that it refuses to disappear, that it still looms as the cultural other, despite the by now almost mythical fall of the Iron Curtain. We can trace this otherness within the numerous texts, the historical and individual narratives, even within the "oral tradition" that live immigrants can share with us when asked about their stories. It is time we included their versions of "America" within the scattered and demystified interplay between the center and margin, a playing in which two forces revise each other, talk and argue with each other, within and without that fascinating puzzle that is the American novel.

# The Perils of Woman's Americanization

MARY ANTIN'S *THE PROMISED LAND*

I was born, I have lived, and I have been made over. Is it not time to write my life's story? I am just as much out of the way as if I were dead, for *I am absolutely other than the person whose story I have to tell*. Physical continuity with my earlier self is no disadvantage. I could speak in the third person and not feel that I was masquerading. *I can analyze my subject*, I can reveal everything; for *she*, and not *I*, is my real heroine. My life I have still to live; her life ended when mine began.—Mary Antin, *The Promised Land*

## Inventing America's Ethnic "Other"

Since the end of the nineteenth century, before any discussion of their art could begin, the immigrant writers in America have had to be carefully labeled with their ethnicity, their distinctive otherness. They have been designated as German Americans, Russian Americans, Mexican Americans, Jewish Americans, and so on. Such an approach may seem odd in a country consisting solely of strangers and minorities, a country whose ideology is inherently based on consensus to difference—"unity in diversity"—or, more fashionably, multiplicity and multiculturalism. According to Oscar Handlin's famous and much-quoted introduction to *The Uprooted*, "Immigrants [are] American history." More recent scholarship takes Handlin's assumption even further. In their emphasis on an America created by minorities, contemporary critics include also Native Americans and African Americans. In the scholarly discourse, then, difference has been generally accepted as an underlying factor of multidimensional Americanness. What was un-American in the popular discourse of the beginning of the century, in the era of nativism and xenophobia, has now become the epitome of national character.[1]

Despite this rhetorical change of perspective, however, the average reader usually expects Old World linguistic, ethnic, and gender traits to surface in even the most eloquent expressions that immigrant authors might produce in the New World. Although diversity is the norm, ethnic otherness is still a requirement and places authors in often stereotyped positions. Being truly multicultural requires ethnic "proofs" validating authors' authentic foreignness. Thus, in classifying immigrant writers as aliens who desire communication with their new country's audience in its own language and cultural idiom, an American tradition constructs them as such ethnic others, outsiders who long to be admitted among insiders. According to Werner Sollors, emphasizing the national or racial origins of a writer—the so-called ethnic perspective—creates a conflict within literary history: "The total emphasis on a writer's descent—all but annihilates art movements."[2] Sollors develops this theme further in an introduction to *The Invention of Ethnicity*, where he claims that audiences and critics have a tendency to "invent" ethnicity as an artificial construct, which enables them to approach neatly categorized groups of writers rather than to pursue diverse themes and problems across and beyond ethnic boundaries.[3] He adds, in a foreword to William Boelhower's *Through a Glass Darkly: Ethnic Semiosis in American Literature*, that what really matters in our readings of ethnic literature is "the context of the reader's own 'gaze'" because, according to Boelhower, "the ethnic sign is everywhere, and ethnic writing *is* American writing."[4] Therefore, it is the beholder of the ethnic other who assigns ethnic identity to him or her; it is the dominant ideological consensus that makes distinctions between "American" and "ethnic," even though, as Sollors and Boelhower see it, there is no nonethnic writing in this culture.

Sollors's focus on ethnicity as an "invention" stresses politics and power as the forces instigating the inventive act: "It is always the specificity of power relations at a given historical moment and in a particular place that triggers off a strategy of pseudo-historical explanations that camouflage the inventive act itself."[5] The famous concept of "unity in diversity" underlying a multinational America can thus be seen as a self-conscious ideological construct rather than a completely spontaneous historical development. Because the late nineteenth and early twentieth centuries brought a lot of otherness into America, the concept of the ethnic other became incorporated into the ideological model that the host country wished to perpetuate in theory, even if it often rejected that other in practice.

The margin of otherness, from which outsiders such as the immigrant writers reach toward the dominant culture, can therefore be seen as invented to guarantee the security and stability of the central ethos of Americanness. Since this culture is composed of minorities and immigrants, the only way to create a superior core is through marking the newcomer as the other who is not *yet* American. Seen in this way, the concept of ethnicity separates instead of joining, because the line between the insider and the outsider is drawn arbitrarily across nationalities and races existing on both sides. Besides making it hard to study what Sollors terms "the cultural interplays and contacts among writers of different backgrounds, the cultural mergers and secessions that took place in America," such a separatist notion of ethnicity also obstructs a full understanding of the newcomer's perspective by "true" Americans (*BE* 14).

From the immigrants' vantage point, the interior often seems a mysterious other; in the eyes of an outsider the host country is as foreign as he or she is to that country. This newcomer's perspective implies an inversion of the center-margin juxtaposition and an invitation to a discourse on equal terms—between the two "others." Since, however, no center is usually willing to flip the perspective and find itself as the other approached by an empowered outsider, it often resists taking into account the alternative vantage point proposed by the immigrant.

In the case of newcomers who are also writers, this resistance creates a subtle form of textual oppression. If an outsider wanted to be heard by the center when ethnic texts were fashionable in America at the beginning of this century and later, during the nativist years of 1880–1920, he or she had to acquire not only American English but also the dominant ideology. Succeeding in both respects, Mary Antin's *The Promised Land* (1912) gained a reputation as the classic documentary of Americanization. Nevertheless, this very reputation often stands in the way of reading her text beyond the well-established clichés of acculturation. Her book remains all that an immigrant classic is expected to be—a sociological documentary, an autobiography, an archetype of immigrant passage and glorious Americanization.[6] Yet it is hardly ever read as the imaginative and intricate novel that it is.

## Cases of Otherness: Immigrant Woman, Writer, and Textual Oppression

As previously stated, the subject positions of newcomers are suspended between the remainders of their "old," supposedly fading identities and their invitation to an American otherness. Such a condition suggests permanent cultural frustration, for it entails a double otherness: the newcomers are perceived as the other by the center, but this center is in itself strange and alien to all immigrants, despite their desire to enter it. For a female this concept has an additional dimension because she is the other in both the patriarchal Old World and in the male-dominated Promised Land. In her case, adopting the dominant idiom is often accompanied by mediation or "translation" performed by mentors, sponsors, and native friends, who ease her text into the new culture so that it can be understood and accepted by insiders.[7] Although mediation makes possible a relative success in America—for example, Elizabeth Stern (1890–1954) wrote as "one of us," an educator and a social worker—it frequently obscures the immigrant woman's original message of oppression and identity conflict in confrontation with America. Moreover, it obliterates the opportunity for the center to see itself as the newcomer's other—a source of oppression and anxiety—in that message.

Reading immigrant women's texts beyond the traditional narratives of acculturation is a chance to show how the American novel engages in the intercultural discourse, how it can have a look at itself in the mirror held to it by its margin. The complex otherness of the immigrant woman writer enables her to engage in the intercultural dialogue and to propose a remaking of the host culture beyond the traditional male-made models. Besides disclosing the perils of female Americanization, texts by immigrant women also present an America that often does not live up to the outsider's expectations, an America that, as the center of power, is not always aimed toward the best ends and that, as an ideological construct, has often little to do with everyday reality.[8]

### The Woman behind Her Text

For authors such as Anzia Yezierska, Elizabeth Stern, and Mary Antin, being female in addition to being alien and Jewish implies the necessity not only of working out an American "socialized" identity in their transition to the United States but also of discovering a new dimension of their gender within the dominant culture and their ethnic traditions. They have to reconcile the tenets of Judaism and its view of women with the ways in which their new country sees its female citizens and also with the ways in which it sees those who are not citizens *yet*. In other words, they have to reconcile themselves with their new constructions as the ethnic other defined by sex, religion, class, language, nationality, and ethnicity. To trace their struggles to describe the ethnic woman's social roles as well as her individual sexual identity requires a reading beyond the typical stories of passage, rebirth, and success. Within the critical tradition, their stories are usually constructed according to male models, and they are expected to omit the woman's carnality as a topic not worthy to be included in serious tales about Americanization.[9]

The characters in many immigrant female texts are trapped between the mythical and idealistic construction of an America as the Promised Land that they cannot attain and the quotidian "realities" they have to cope with as newcomers in the New World's ghetto. Instead of the "land of milk and honey," many early female immigrants find themselves in the ghetto, where they discover that "we the people" refers to the uptown Anglo-Saxons who look down on Hester Street and its aspirations for emancipation. Among many discoveries about their new country, they find that class and social origin matter as much as they did in the Old World. There are divisions and animosities, a miniature class society among the immigrants, too, as Stern's hero, Steve, learns from his experiences of climbing the social ladder from the ghetto to the millionaire's home in *This Ecstasy* (1927).

The immigrant women's Old World dreams and expectations are cruelly shattered within the poverty and drudgery of lower-class tenement existence. Their new country treats them as inferiors of their fathers, sons, and husbands and thus reinforces the dogmas of Old World Judaism, which claim that women were created solely to serve and please men and to provide them with offspring. But this second-class status clashes with the responsibilities immigrant women have to shoulder in the New World, where they often work both within and outside the household and heroically struggle to keep their families above the starvation level. As Maxine Seller notes, "Women came to the United States to escape the economic, political, and religious oppression" of the Old World, but "in the workforce as in the family, [they] usually fared differently from men." They were limited to "traditional women's occupations"—domestic service, needlework, clothing manufacture—and still burdened by "housework, pregnancy, childbirth, and childcare [which] gave their lives dimensions of pleasure and pain not shared even by the men closest to them." In a lot of cases, a woman had to terminate her pregnancy, as the family could not afford another mouth to feed; often she would miscarry or give birth to a sickly infant who would soon die of malnutrition or disease, as happens to many siblings of Stern's heroine in *My Mother and I* (1917). In addition, women's access to education—and the chance it offered for a better life—was often limited. When courses for women were organized by charitable organizations, they focused mainly on "American-style domestic skills" rather than on instruction in more attractive, practical, and better-paying jobs, which were usually reserved for men (foreman, supervisor, bookkeeper, etc.).[10] Such gendered division of labor also indicated that women were not considered fit for occupations requiring typically male intellectual pursuits. When Anzia Yezierska's narrator in the short story "How I Found America" comes to the Immigrant School and wants to share her ideas about "how to make America better," she is told: " 'It's nice of you to want to help America, but . . . the best way would be for you to learn a trade. That's what this school is for, to help girls find themselves, and the best way to do is to learn something useful.' " [11] The answer of Yezierska's enraged heroine echoes in one of the displays at the Ellis Island Museum of Immigration, where a young girl, when asked about how she would wash stairs, from the top or from the bottom, responds: " 'I don't go to America to wash stairs.' "

In addition to being seen as a body fit for manual labor only, the immigrant woman in America of the late nineteenth and early twentieth centuries was also often perceived as "loose" and vulgar because she brought in a different morality and alien sexual conduct. For example, in Doris Weatherford's *Foreign and Female: Immigrant Women in America, 1840–1930* we read about the reluctance to admit single mothers or unwed pregnant girls to this country, whereas a father of an out-of-wedlock child would be granted entry without any problem. The immigrant woman's carnality evokes fear in her new home—she is not welcome unless she is made acceptable and safe by a male accompanying her or receiving her from the immigration officials. Weatherford mentions an interesting anecdote concerning a publication by "more sexually liberated Poles" for "girls and married women." The book was condemned fiercely by the Vice Commission of Chicago, which shunned such attempts at female education. No matter what, an immigrant woman was a loser in matters concerning her sexuality—being ignorant about it brought her shame as a promiscuous and "oversexed" female; attempting to educate herself about contraception in order to avoid an "accident" and curb the breeding of the oversexed was seen as immoral.[12]

Seller stresses that all immigrants, regardless of gender, were vulnerable to nativist prejudice in America but that women received a greater share in connection with their gender roles. They were considered bad mothers and poor housekeepers; East European women, especially, were blamed for the rise of juvenile delinquency and the decline in family life during the years of early twentieth-century urbanization (8). In the movement against prostitution, a lot of blame was laid on newcomer women, although statistics show that they were not very likely to "fall" in the first generation. But if immigrant females were commonly considered more "corruptible" than puritanical American women, it would actually be the second or the third generation—native-borns, who had no memory of the Old World—who would be more prone to trade in their bodies. What the host culture took for signs of promiscuity and lack of restraint in ethnic women were usually traditional ways of sexual conduct. Many peasant women, for example, who became factory workers in America were very open about their sexuality because they had grown up in close quarters and in big families where a girl was witness to nudity, sex, and birth from her earliest years. To many American women, such awareness and acceptance of the body and its functions was considered proof of being a loose woman. As Weatherford rightly points out, "It was unusual for society to forgive and for women to think themselves worthy of forgiveness" in the vicious circle of societal pressure and guilt and in the women's own often-held belief in the inferiority of their sex, which was ingrained in them in the Old World and perpetuated by their economic conditions in the New (64, 123).[13]

### The Woman behind the Myth

Because of the emphasis that the host culture placed on her sexuality and gender roles, the lower-class female immigrant, like the female slave, can be seen as the most oppressed alien in the land that has been always mythologized in terms of a woman's body. The multitude of texts that constitute "Adamic" literature and criticism addresses themes such as the "virgin wilderness," the "new Eden," and the "New World Garden." In these depictions of America the landscape is seen as female, and the allegorical Promised Land gathers her children to her breast like a mother-lover. Such a masculine perspective, discussed, for example, in Henry Nash Smith's *The Virgin Land* (1950), does not leave space to account for the newcomer woman's vision of her adopted country, since it is entirely focused on the man-made heterosexual myth of exploiting the female body. This traditional vision attests to the contribution of the first male immigrants, the "fathers" of the country, who came from the Old World and claimed America—both as a land and a myth—as their bride. It does not acknowledge the female version, which would not fit the rugged imagery and masculine notions concerning the conquest and appropriation of the Promised Land—the mute and willing virgin wilderness.[14]

The rhetoric of the Garden of Eden was nevertheless adopted readily by some male immigrant writers. Israel Zangwill's acclaimed drama, *The Melting Pot* (1909), operates within clearly masculine imagery evoking the visions of the first settlers. According to Zangwill's protagonist, David, the "melting" of the nations—the production of multicultural Americans—takes place within the Crucible, or God's vessel. This highly symbolic vessel-womb pertains to nature and is perceived as clearly female: "There *she* lies, the great Melting Pot . . . Can't you hear the roaring and the bubbling? There gapes *her* mouth" (emphasis mine). By envisioning America as the Crucible giving birth to a new race of people, Zangwill remakes the Garden of Eden myth, adjusting it to fit the immigrant rhetoric of the 1920s. Interestingly, he also hints at miscegenation as a possible way for the newcomer male to enter the dominant culture.[15] For his East European Jewish hero, the ultimate embodiment of Americanization is his love for Vera-America, who "gathered [him] to her breast" just like the virgin land that received the pioneers into its fertile womb.[16]

In contrast to Zangwill's sensual visions of Edenic America, which perpetuate a patriarchal perspective, imagery created by the immigrant woman challenges the myth. Her writing remakes the bodily image of America by stripping it of the feminine qualities she cannot identify with.[17] In many texts by newcomer women, America is symbolized by the cool Anglo-Saxon males whom the heroines worship and native women, who are often seen as hostile and condescending. Her rejection by native-born women and her confrontation with the predominantly male WASP culture make the newcomer confused about her gender and sexuality.[18] On the way to establishing a precarious identity in the new country, the immigrant woman's gendered self is constantly threatened, because in order to succeed in her ambitions, she has to defy the traditional roles prescribed for females by her own ethnic group and dare to modify the ones defined by the host culture she longs to enter. Taking a stand against both traditions, then, entails a confrontation with two aspects of her identity: with her sexuality, because it is her body and its carnality that predominantly define her existence, and with the social roles as rules governing the new world in which she tries to find herself. She often rejects female carnality in herself as well as in the mythical representation of her new environment, because they are male constructs that oppress her and often prevent her emancipation as the independent individual she aspires to be.

As a result of this resistance to her sexuality, the immigrant heroine sometimes has to renounce traditional gender roles—marriage and motherhood—to attain an education in America. She rejects becoming like the ghetto mother from Elizabeth Stern's *My Mother and I*, who is pregnant every year and who is chronically imprisoned within the Old World language and customs that have been transplanted into New World poverty. The newcomer must strike out on her own and give up the security of marriage and family if she wants to join the ranks of New Women. As a result, her body ceases to be anything more than a means to her goal—a carrier of the brain acquiring the language, a skilled worker earning the necessary income. A woman who wants to rise out of the ghetto has to virtually renounce sexual gratification for the sake of becoming "somebody"—an ironic pun for describing her disembodied status in the new milieu.

As much as this problem can be argued in terms of every liberated woman's experience with renouncing the domestic body for the sake of intellect and career in the public sphere, it is particularly vivid in the immigrant, who is perceived and constructed as overtly carnal even by native females. Although her intellect may carry her out of the tenements and allow her to "pass" as an American, her body remains in the metaphorical ghetto-prison of repressed sexual identity, as she does not even fit the image prescribed for liberated women by some upper-class feminists. Charlotte Perkins Gilman's enlightened notions, for instance, totally excluded "immigrant whores," for she strove to keep America's blood pure and unmixed with too much foreign element. In her autobiography, *The Living of Charlotte Perkins Gilman*, Gilman cannot hide her xenophobic feelings toward her foreign maid, "this unpromising Irish woman." "Her density," Gilman writes, "was such that any direction had to be given with a slow explicitness suitable to [the] under-witted. . . . [T]hat moron . . . stayed on, in the face of clearest suggestions of departure" (108–9). It is ironic that Gilman could fight for the women's cause and be at the same time so insensitive toward other females. Clearly, she did not think her ideology inclusive of servants and immigrants.[19]

Gilman, however, was reacting in accordance with the predominant mood of her times, when the belief in "one hundred percent Americanism" emerged as an attractive ideology and when newcomers were made the subject of pseudoscientific research that was to determine their desirability as prospective citizens. In the face of such xenophobia in the 1890s and then during the period 1914–24, when a "new racism" emerged, the immigrant woman had either to accept the model life prescribed for her by the host culture or try defying it.[20] On the one hand, her options ranged from being a hand in a sweatshop to spending the rest of her days as a house servant hoping to marry rich, as in the life narratives offered by charity organizations and "houses for working girls." On the other hand, her longing for what the American upper-class feminists of that time were beginning to claim—education, influence in politics and culture, freedom to live as one chooses—were seen as "out of this world."

### The "Other" Woman: An Antistory

The world from which some immigrant women came prepared them, in most cases, for the reaction of the dominant culture to their foreignness. The particular geographical location where the Russian Jew Mary Antin grew up and the historical frame within which her family embarked on their exodus to the United States marked her background with profound imprints of otherness. As a Jew in Diaspora and a repressed minority in Russia, Antin felt acutely aware of the tightness of the ethnic and gendered boundaries that confined her. Jews had to live in the *shtetl*—a nineteenth-century Russian version of a reservation—and could not pursue education or even religious worship publicly because both were against the czar's edicts. Even in her childish games, described so vividly in the first part of *The Promised Land*, Antin recreates the world divided into the sphere of the Christians—the powerful Gentile majority she liked to mock in playing church rituals with other children—and that of the Jews—the despised ethnic minority who had no choice but to take abuse from their Gentile neighbors and from the anti-Semitic Russian government. From a young age, a girl in the Pale of Settlement—the restricted area where Jews were forced to live under the czar's edict and where Antin grew up—knew also that she was not made for education and intellectual pursuits. A Jewish "girl was born for no other purpose" than instruction in the "laws regulating a pious Jewish household and in the conduct proper for a Jewish wife; for, of course, every girl hoped to be a wife."[21] Marriage was the only way out of her father's house and meant a transition from serving one man to serving another. This transition entailed serving her race as a mother, a procreating body stripped of any other qualities, firmly planted within the domestic sphere separate from the more intellectually stimulating world of men: "But while men, in addition to begetting, might busy themselves with the study of the Law, woman's only work was motherhood" (PL 35). Having brought such a split ethnic and gendered perspective to their idolized haven, America, immigrant women often accepted their newcomer otherness without much difficulty. Their ease in adapting to ethnic and gender marginality, on the one hand, and in acquiring the dominant insider's idiom that they felt entitled to, on the other, usually surprised native-borns.

As Mary Dearborn and Werner Sollors note, the successful Americanization of Mary Antin and Elizabeth Stern was met with contempt by those who considered themselves "true" Americans, those descended from the first settlers of "three hundred years ago" (PD 41; BE 88–89).[22] The paeans to America that these two women composed in their "immigrant classics," The Promised Land (1912) and My Mother and I (1917), were rejected by some because of their authors' bold claims on the host culture. Stern, especially, having constructed a heroine who pronounced: "I knew that America had always been mine," drew hostile comments from the critics.[23] However, underneath the paeans that caused some critical frowns, these two texts actually attest to a failure of female Americanization, for they debunk the predictable surface story and point to the darker sides of the immigrant woman's experience. As such they witness the textual oppression that their authors had to endure while writing, their being torn between the necessity of gratitude and the desire to find a literary outlet for their frustrations.

At first glance, Antin's and Stern's novels call for alternative readings because their deceptively conventional structures imply openness and incompleteness. For example, in her introduction to The Promised Land, Antin emphasizes that her authorial voice is completely different from that of the autobiographical narrator. This confession, about the story of her life being really about somebody else, discloses the whole narrative as highly ambivalent because Antin disassociates herself so clearly from her work and from its subject matter. To a careful reader this fact signals that *The Promised Land* should not be read as a simple document of immigrant experience, but as a work of fiction in which the politics of female authorship in general and of autobiography in particular are interrogated. Although preceded by President Roosevelt's foreword classifying it as an "Americanization story," Stern's *My Mother and I* rejects the narrative of the immigrant rites of passage because its heroine views herself as an insider, despite the dominant culture's classifying her as a newcomer other.[24] The dissonance between the authorial voices and the narrative models they employ and a conspicuous lack of successful conclusions to Antin's and Stern's novels invite open-ended interpretive possibilities. Their seemingly smooth and brilliant stories of young women's Americanization point to the dubiousness of the ideological messages in both texts. Such unfinished immigrant narratives suggest alternative readings, or "antistories," that challenge the traditional tale of female acculturation as a repressive "official version" enforced upon the newcomer writer by the host culture lost in its narcissistic gaze.

### Mary Antin's Untold Story

In the concluding pages of her autobiographical novel *The Promised Land*, Mary Antin (1881–1949) justifies certain omissions from the story of her life.[25] She explains to the reader why she did not include such chapters as her romance with an American man and her entrance into Boston's high society in what was supposed to be her autobiography: "These are matters to which I long to testify, but I must wait till they recede into the past" (*PL* 362). She admits, then, that some parts of her experience have to be hidden, and her "premature biography" cannot be completed or ever written: "A proper autobiography is a death-bed confession" (359, xx). Nevertheless, she follows her desire to reveal as much of her life to the reader as she can, because her story "is illustrative of scores of unwritten lives" as well as "a matter of my private salvation" (xxi).

Mary Antin's desire to confess her life story in *The Promised Land* arises from a belief that authorship can exorcise the past:

> I can never forget, for I bear the scars. But I want to forget—sometimes I long to forget. I think I have thoroughly assimilated my past—I have done its bidding—I want now to be of to-day. It is painful to be consciously of

two worlds. The Wandering Jew in me seeks forgetfulness. I am not afraid to live on and on, if only I do not have to remember too much. A long past vividly remembered is like a heavy garment that clings to your limbs when you would run. And I have thought of a charm that should release me from the folds of my clinging past. I take the hint from the Ancient Mariner, who told his tale in order to be rid of it. I, too, will tell my tale, for once, and never hark back any more. I will write a bold "Finis" at the end, and shut the book with a bang! (xxii)

However, *The Promised Land* did not provide its author with the "private salvation" from the past. She was not a great Romantic poet, but an immigrant woman, a Russian Jew, and a spokesperson for her people. As an author, Antin could not follow the example of Coleridge's phantom story-teller, but had to reconcile her individual authorial desires with the urgency of the "immigrant cause" and with the expectations of her native-born and newcomer readerships.

On the pages of her book, which seems at once a memoir, an autobiography, and an imaginative novel, she travels between the conflicting desires to write and to remain silent. Voicing her story means empowering the masses of immigrants she represents and wants to testify for in her work, subtitled "The Autobiography of a Russian Immigrant." On the other hand, her simultaneous need to remain opaque and withdrawn about certain aspects of her private tale implies that she is unable to write without inhibitions. And although such reticence may be true of most autobiographies, Antin's omissions and self-censoring seem consciously and purposely foregrounded.

The sense of her obligation to her people, on the one hand, and her reticence about such aspects of her life as class- and gender-related issues, on the other, are two major currents pervading *The Promised Land*. We can read this book as a biography of an immigrant woman, since, despite the first-person narrative, the writer clearly treats her narrator-I as somebody separate from herself: "I am absolutely *other* than the person *whose story I have to tell*" (ix, emphasis mine). She has to unburden herself of the tales of her passage from the Old World into the New and thus repay the debt of gratitude she owes to her people and to her new country. But aside from this, the text is her intimate "fictional autobiography" because, even in denials and omissions, she inadvertently presents a persona behind the narrator, a presence that would like to remain obscure in some instances but who cannot be passed by undiscerned. The "other" author of *The Promised Land* is writing a deep-structure subtext, which questions and debunks the superficial tale of an immigrant girl's successful Americanization.[26]

## The Official Version

It is worthwhile to look at the facts—the well-known scenarios describing both Mary Antin and her books—before we analyze the subtext in which she subverts and challenges the official version of her story. Biographical notes about this writer stress her love for education, which she expressed already as a little girl, in her home town of Polotzk, within the Pale of Settlement in Russia. She crossed the Atlantic in 1894 to join her father, who had gone ahead to prepare for the coming of his family to settle in Boston.[27] From the very beginning of her life in America, Mary was an ardent student of the new language and culture. Her teachers, friends, and family supported her efforts at public schools in Chelsea and Boston and later at the Girls' Latin School. However, in 1901, while Mary was attending Teachers College at Columbia and Barnard, she married and never took her degree. In his introduction to *The Promised Land*, Oscar Handlin calls Mary's marriage "a personal crisis" that "disrupted her career" (*PL* viii). She married Amadeus William Grabau, a geologist of Lutheran background whom she had met in the Natural History Club of the Hale House and with whom she had a daughter, Josephine Esther.

In 1899, at the age of sixteen, Mary Antin published her first book. *From Polotzk to Boston* is based on a diary letter to her uncle describing her voyage from Russia to Boston. She composed it in Yiddish when she was eleven and translated it into English, in America, at the age of thirteen. When she was fifteen, her first piece, "Snow," was printed in the *Boston Herald* with her teacher's introduction. *The Promised Land* came out in 1912, having been serialized by the *Atlantic Monthly*, and was later revised for schoolchildren as *At School in the Promised Land or the Story of a Little Immigrant* (1912). The book gained immediate success and popularity, despite the growing number of restrictive immigration laws and the general anti-immigrant sentiment sweeping through the United States. It was followed by *They Who Knock at Our Gates* (1914), which praised American democracy while urging it to abandon xenophobic tendencies. Her other contributions were short stories printed chiefly in the *Atlantic Monthly*; lectures on immigrant, Jewish, and feminist issues; and speeches for the National Americanization Committee, the National Security League, and the U.S. government's committee on public information. Antin was a liberal and a member of the National Academy of Arts and Sciences until 1918, when she retired from public life due to her suffering from neurasthenia.

"Except for brief flashes, the power of expression which shone in *The Promised Land* now left her," writes Handlin about the rest of Antin's life (xiv). She cultivated her interest in transcendentalism and anthroposophy—legacies of her friendship with sisters Emma and Josephine Lazarus—and contributed occasional stories to the *Atlantic*. She retained her sentiments for Judaism, though she never went back to it actively, having become a Quaker, a true convert to things American. However, on the eve of the Second World War, she expressed her solidarity with her people in the essay "House of One Father," published in *Common Ground* in the spring of 1941, which called upon the world to stop the catastrophe. Helen J. Schwartz sums up the writer's achievement: "Antin's work, though not presenting incisive social criticism, provides a sensitive and idealistic chronicle of immigrant experience in the early twentieth century."[28]

Early reviews and criticism usually term Mary Antin a chronicler, a sociological and autobiographical author. In the words of Israel Zangwill, who wrote an introduction to *From Polotzk to Boston* (1899), she "enables us to see almost with our own eyes how the invasion of America appears to the impecunious invader"; her writing is "'a human document' of considerable value, as well as a promissory note of future performance."[29] The author of *The Melting Pot* recognizes Antin as a bright pupil of his own philosophy by suggesting that she sees the immigrants taking over America and not vice versa. To Zangwill's praise of the young author, Josephine Lazarus adds hers, emphasizing that Antin's first text "record[s] not only . . . her own personal experience, but also that of the vast mass of Russian immigrants who crowd our shores, and of whom we know so little."[30] A review of *The Promised Land* (1912), published in the *New York Times*, also praises the successful collective document. The reviewer is pleased that Antin's book allows the reader "for the first time . . . [to] see with the eyes of a Russian Jewish immigrant woman," whose narrative "finds its greatest value" in the "ordinariness" of people's lives. Antin is praised for successfully combining a personal memoir with the "record of the experience of a typical immigrant," which makes her text "a unique contribution to our modern literature and to our modern history."[31]

While most of the sources stress Antin's contribution to the history of American immigration and praise her for taking on a collective voice, there are some that find the personal part of her narrative more interesting, and even a little disturbing. A review printed in *The Independent* in 1912 sees the "charm" of *The Promised Land* in its "frank egotism." The critic also emphasizes Antin's "genius for self-study, and a felicity of expression in the *richer terms of the New World*," where "George Washington is now in her background, and 'Old Glory' swings over her as one of the fellow-citizens in the land he won for all exiles."[32] Elisabeth Woodbridge, in the pages of the *Yale Review*, perceives the book as an "experiment in self-portrayal" as well as a text full of "rare bits of reading" for the student of social change and for the "lover of the curious and the picturesque" (in its portrayal of Jewish life). She praises the first part, its descriptions of the Pale of Settlement and of czarist oppression, as the most satisfying of the whole book. On the other hand, she claims that Antin lacks authenticity in her portrayal of America and that is why the first part is more valuable and authentic: "We are, in very truth, through her eyes, looking back into the middle ages."[33]

This approach is an interesting misreading of the text, which the author herself divides between the distant—less "true" and belonging to the "dead" past—memories of her Russian childhood and the more recent and tangible—more "accurate" and pertaining to her new reborn persona—account of her Americanization. Oddly enough, Woodbridge credits Antin with more accuracy in her tale's depiction of the distant Old World, even though Antin admits to having composed this first part—chapters I through VIII—in fits and starts of fragmented nostalgic recollections: "One day I found myself thinking of the time I went to school in Polotzk, and I wrote about that. Another day, I kept seeing the little girls I used to play with, and I put them in. Then it was the market-place that *haunted me*, or the Dvina gurgled in my ears all night, or there came into my mind the tales the women used to tell while picking feathers on a winter evening. I put these things down just *as they came, and so grew the book*."[34] Antin stresses that she did not follow any definite narrative, that the first part of her text "grew on her" as a nearly fictitious expression of the glimpses of the past and fragments of stories, which she retained about her homeland. Thus, the critic's emphasis on how well the "middle ages" are presented in *The Promised Land* seems definitely far-fetched.

Woodbridge's claims about this part's authenticity are not as much grounded in the actual text as in the typical and predictable reading of an immigrant story. As Gerald Graff claims, we usually know so much about texts before we start reading them that "often we do not need to read them at all in order to talk fluently about them and even to write about them."[35] For reviewers of Antin's autobiography the main attraction was her exotic Old World Jewishness—the accounts of ritual ablutions, Yiddish and Hebrew words explained in the glossary at the end, prayers, holiday meals, and the reports about persecution by the Gentiles. Because she was an alien, Antin was supposed to know better and to write about the world she came from rather than plunge into detailed descriptions of the host culture. Reluctant "real" Americans were not ready to admit that her version of America could be trusted. Such an approach to *The Promised Land* arises, then, from the reviewer's conviction that Antin is too "egoistic" in her writing. Thus, Woodbridge writes: "Self-expression is undoubtedly the goal towards which all humanity is striving, but if it is accepted as the goal of the individual, without the check of social service, it is apt to swing off into a hard and ruthless egoism, the penalty of which is ultimate blunting of one's sense of finer, indeed, of the ultimate values. The pitfall of the artistic temperament is egoism." [36]

Woodbridge would rather see Antin limited to her collective Old World voice than become a trespasser into an exclusive American individualism. The accusation of artistic egoism seems a little out of proportion in the case of the writer who naturally wanted to be published but who called herself an "unwilling celebrity." [37] Nonetheless, Woodbridge's misinterpretation is an interesting reaction to Antin's book because it works along the lines of conventional readings of the immigrant narrative: the Old World is supposed to be presented as more vivid and exotic than new and stunning America, and the newcomer is to remain in the marginal position of an ethnic other who does not dare trespass onto the insider-restricted terrain of Americanness.

As an ethnic text written by a Jewish woman from Russia, *The Promised Land* was expected to acquiesce in predictable modes of expression—that is, it was to be a documentary. This expectation about its form, then, logically implies a particular reception, for the reader of immigrant texts desires "realistic" facts and "true" stories. Therefore, even an act of reading in this context can be seen as "invented," because it expects to follow the ready-made narrative pattern that the dominant culture has presented to the newcomer. To Cecyle S. Neidle, Antin's text is a perfect example of "immigrant autobiography." The critic dwells on the "usual pattern of sketching in the European background, followed by the experiences of the family in Boston" and emphasizes that the book is "worshipful throughout" about the New World. [38] She does not push her analysis beyond well-established and predictable limits of anticipated and ideologically predetermined readings of immigrant narrative. Even Betty Bergland's more recent study claims that, "attached" to the ideologies of her age, Antin as narrator "lacked a language for articulating the contradictory positions of the Historical Antin." [39] Although Antin the narrator makes it very clear in the introduction that there is another story behind the "immigrant classic," Bergland insists that *The Promised Land* remains a paradigm of superficial Americanization. It is not surprising, then, that Antin never made it into the *Twentieth-Century American-Jewish Fiction Writers* volume of the *Dictionary of Literary Biography*. Although she would fit the ethnic part, she would not fit the genre one, as her writing was not seen to be fiction full of subtext and ambiguity. Paradoxically, even her short stories were either forgotten or mistaken for transcripts of social cases. They were never considered literature.[40]

The example of Mary Antin's "official story" clearly shows that an immigrant writer's persona is as much invented as her texts. The dominant culture constructs such writers according to its expectations of the newcomer and the version of the passage from the Old World into the New that it would like to hear.[41] Therefore, even though immigrant writers were certainly grateful to be published, they were also expected to internalize their gratitude, to flaunt and emphasize it in their texts. Although this implies textual oppression, advertising the dominant ideology in this way is seen as a small price to pay for an opportunity to be heard. In Dearborn's opinion, Mary Antin's book "staggers under the weight of gratitude" (*PD* 34). On the other hand, Cecyle Neidle sees *The Promised Land* as "a *persuasive advertisement* for the wonders of the public school and what it could achieve in educating aliens."[42] The two critics agree that she has completely internalized the dominant idiom and the ready-made image of the immigrant writer. They read her as constructed by America rather than as her own independent person. Although critically stimulating on some level, such approaches engender a certain oppression of the writer by assuming her one-dimensional identity within the new culture—Antin's gender and ethnicity actually limit her readings instead of opening up new ones. As a result, the writer is perceived only within the limits of clichéd experiences involving the space between the Old and the New Worlds and often prevented from delivering a message alternative to this predictable scenario, from expressing the other immigrant story, and, thus, thwarting the neat categorization of gendered immigrant writing.

Critical approaches such as these show clearly how much Antin was already a construct of the reading public and how much the image of her was "sold" simultaneously with her books. Already in her time she was made into an epitome of the immigrant chronicler, a recorder of the American myth of freedom and individualism, or into an egoistic foreign artist who dared to claim the new country without asking. Werner Sollors quotes a reaction against Antin voiced by Barrett Wendell, who complained in a letter that the "Russian Jewish immigrant prodigy Mary Antin 'has developed an irritating habit of describing herself and her people as Americans, in distinction from such folks as Edith [Wendell's wife] and me, who have been here for three hundred years.'" While expected to proceed with her acculturation and to provide a good example for others, the writer ought not acquire too much of an insider's voice, perhaps because she was a Jew and one of the lower-class "unwashed" so despised by the elite. According to Wendell's "genetics of salvation," only third-generation newcomers could aspire to becoming American. Rather indignant about her undeserved claims to his exclusive concept of Americanness—assuming that his is the only one—he never specifies where a woman like Antin, who would eventually be a grandmother to the "third generation," is supposed to fit (*BE* 88).[43]

Despite some of her audience's hostility and its conservative reluctance to share the insider's position with Zangwill's "impecunious invader," Mary Antin was rather successful in her adopted country. Even in recent criticism she is very much perceived in line with this contemporaneous image. She is still regarded as a "model of successful assimilation," "a New Woman," but one who is "still her parents' child" in her shuttling between the Old and the New Worlds.[44] As a Jewish writer she is often discussed as a successful transition-maker between her Old World Judaism and her New World "religion," Americanism. But such approaches often omit what an emphasis on her successful assimilation in such a transition entails: the pain of separation from the faith and the dream of being among the chosen people, what Antin beautifully compares to "the dream to which I was heir, in common with every sad-eyed child of the Pale. . . . This . . . living seed which I found among my heirlooms, when I learned how to strip from them the prickly husk in which they were passed down to me" (41).

Surprisingly, most recent feminist scholarship reflects contemporary criticism of *The Promised Land*. Mary Dearborn approaches Antin as an almost forgotten author, whose obscurity is due to the fact that she "thoroughly internalized the dominant culture's vision of the ethnic and the foreign" and who "lack[s] any alternative, protesting voice." She classifies *The Promised Land* as a text of American patriotism and a document attesting to American "values and typologies." It is not of much interest to the contemporary reader because it does not voice a rebellion against the schematic immigrant expression of gratitude for the new country. According to this reading, Antin's is too successful and too integrated a text to be considered an important ethnic contribution, at least according to contemporary feminist standards. Dearborn stresses the way all Antin's writings appeared with explanations and prefaces—mediating introductions by an important sponsor who validated her texts for the American reader. Antin's success depended largely on such mediations, which elevated her works to the status of officially approved immigrant propaganda. As Dearborn sums it up, "Her stories only attain that status by virtue of the story of her life"—the author of *The Promised Land* was lucky to have had a biography that lent itself to such uses (*PD* 34).[45] As does Bergland, Dearborn sees Mary Antin aligning herself with the dominant culture and thus abandoning a position of a gendered and ethnic marginal subject that the contemporary reader would like her to explore boldly and openly.

Helen J. Schwartz expresses a similar opinion in her biographical sketch on Antin: "Successful as a chronicler, she often fails to *acknowledge or analyze adequately* the problems of marginality evidenced in her autobiography. . . . She deals with the disintegration of family life, threats to moral education and religious integrity in slum conditions, and assimilation; but such problems are drowned in her paean to American opportunities."[46] These critics see Antin as a feminist failure who yielded willingly to the "colonization" of the immigrant woman by the host culture (*PD* 83–90). But Antin might be seen to respond to their readings with an anecdote from her childhood that contains a meaningful authorial comment: "What proof has he [the reader] . . . that I am not lying on every page of this chronicle?" (135).

Although not embraced by the feminist critics, Antin inspired some innovative approaches that go beyond reading her as little less than a grateful prodigy. Allen Guttman, for example, stresses Antin's heroine's drive to question authority in religion; a spiritual departure from her faith coincides with her leaving Russia for America.[47] To Eric Homberger, the story line in *The Promised Land* is a "classic example of the liberation-from-slavery narrative" because its structure contrasts the constraint of the Pale with the freedom of America.[48] Sam B. Girgus attributes to Antin's autobiographical writings "one of the strongest expressions of the myth of America as an ideal and vision," but also a power to evoke an antimyth, unmaking this vision.[49] This approach, stressing the way an alternative message arises from the seemingly conformist one, opens up Antin's work to interpretation beyond the clichés of successful immigrant Americanization and points to the existence of a critical voice within paeans to the Promised Land.

### Behind the Official Version

Mary Antin's *The Promised Land*, then, contains an alternative, protesting voice, but not the one that Dearborn or Schwartz would have. Although these feminist critics stress the writer's schematism and responsiveness to the dominant ideology, they do not take into account that Antin was, and still *is*, made into this image of a successful immigrant girl by her audience and critics. They do not seem to realize that, at the time when she was writing, Antin did not have any other choice but to participate in some of the "paeans" if she wanted a chance to speak for the immigrant cause, if she wanted to see her text in print at all. However, even in her very use of the dominant narrative, Antin is aware of how she is being manipulated and she tries to communicate this awareness to her reader: "I did not even discover my own talent. It was discovered first by my father in Russia, and next by my friend in America. What did I ever do but write when they told me to write? . . . *I never heard of any one who was so watched and coaxed, so passed along from hand to helping hand, as was I.* . . . But so it was always with me: somebody did something for me all the time" (*PL* 214–15, emphasis mine).

Mary's success is often deliberately underlined with a degree of helplessness, as she is pushed along her path to Americanism by all around her. Her father expects his unrealized dreams of education to come true in his daughter. Her sister needs Mary's progress to certify her, Frieda's, sacrifices for the younger girl's schooling. As for her mother, she wants to see Mary become the New American Woman that the older immigrant females will never be. To her teachers Mary is a prize pupil to be shown off as living proof that public education does miracles for the ghetto; to the Jewish community she is a proud reminder of their intellectual abilities.

As a little girl, Mary is so coached and conditioned to fulfill these roles that some of her paeans to America sound a little unconvincing, as if she were reciting a lesson learned by heart: "What more could America give a child? Ah, much more! As I read about how the patriots planned the Revolution, and the women gave their sons to die in battle, and the heroes led to victory, and the rejoicing people set up the Republic, it dawned on me gradually what was meant by *my country*. . . . For the Country was for all the Citizens, and *I was a Citizen*" (225). Although in this passage the narrator seems to claim America in the conformist way of an integrated alien, her "adoption of America by the immigrant" refers to the drama of a people without a country, who are in permanent exile. As an immigrant, Mary was indeed a "citizen" but not an American—a term she does not use in reference to herself. In fact, her emphasis on America *and* herself, on an immigrant *and* her new country, sets up a juxtaposition and suggests a separation rather than a fusion.

We can see her awareness of her difference on an occasion when she is chastised by her classmates for claiming that there is no God. "Nature made me," says rebellious Mary to her pious Christian friends. Later on, she is listening to her teacher's admonitions with a comprehension of her ambiguous position in America: "She made me understand . . . that it was *proper American conduct* to avoid religious arguments on school territory." And although she "felt honored by this private initiation into the doctrine of the separation of Church and State," there is clear self-directed irony in this lesson on Americanness that meant to teach her—always an immigrant Jewish girl—not to challenge the opinions held by the Christian majority (242–44). The lesson on the separation between church and state becomes a metaphor for Mary's experience as an eloquent user of the dominant idiom, for her realization that what she wants to say is not always what her audience would like to hear from her.

When she recites her poem about George Washington in class, she stresses that, although Washington, she, and her classmates are all "Fellow Citizens" in American democracy, a "special note" in her poem can be understood only by her fellow Jewish immigrants: "For I made myself the spokesman of the 'luckless sons of Abraham,' saying—'Then we weary Hebrew children at last found rest / In the land where reigned Freedom, and like a nest / To homeless birds your land proved to us.'" Mary as narrator emphasizes that *"only* Israel Rubinstein or Beckie Aronovitch could have *fully* understood, besides myself" (231, emphasis mine). This sense of kinship with other Jewish students serves to elicit the contrast between them and the rest of the class and the teacher: "The boys and girls who had never been turned away from any door because of their father's religion" and Miss Dwight can appreciate Mary's praise of America embodied by George Washington, but they cannot fully understand what it means spoken by a poor Russian-Jewish immigrant. America as the "nest to homeless birds" sounds oddly ironic in the context of being rejected because of one's "father's religion." The mature narrator also half-jokingly recalls how her audience did not really hear her plea for equality: "If they got any inkling of what the hail of big words was about, it must have been through occult suggestion" (230). She also comments, a bit ironically, on the enthusiastic reception of her performance. The Gentile students, who "sat as if fascinated in their places . . . woke up and applauded heartily . . . following the example of Miss Dwight, who wore the happy face which meant that one of her pupils had done well." The well-behaved American kids follow the example of their teacher in reacting to the words which, according to the narrator who knows well her new country's holidays, were "only to be expected on that occasion" (231).

The reception of Mary's poem is a metaphor for her situation as an immigrant prodigy. She is rewarded for her command of her new religion—Americanism—but continues to feel acutely different as a newcomer who has to use the dominant idiom to be accepted. The authorial voice recalls how her childish pathos later turned to embarrassment: "I can laugh now at the impossible metres, the grandiose phrases, the verbose repetitions of my poem. Years ago *I must have laughed at it, when I threw my only copy into the wastebasket*" (230, emphasis mine). Did she indeed laugh while destroying her poem? Why would she get rid of the only copy of her first published work? The determination young Mary feels while reciting her poem suggests an answer: "I was face to face with twoscore Fellow Citizens, in clean blouses and extra frills. I must tell them what George Washington had done for their country—for *our* country—for me" (230). The change from the past to the present tense between her description of the event—"I *was* face to face"—and of her actual performance—"I *must* tell them," as well as the gradual movement from "for their country," through "for *our* country," to "for me" show the narrator's awareness of her mission as a model "spokesman" for the immigrant cause. She remembers her stage fright and otherness in the past, and she realizes the incongruity between ideals and reality that made her discard her poem, yet she reminds herself that she still must perform, tell them—America—that George Washington meant democracy for the "huddled masses"—"for me"—too.

What Mary learns from the experience with her poem is that she can use the words of her new language and ideology to remind the dominant culture about the promise of equality that she took to heart as a young girl. Thus the exterior immigrant and pro-American propaganda that Mary as narrator delivers in the pages of *The Promised Land* can be seen as a self-conscious tool used in the fight against increasing nativist prejudice in Antin's time. Antin's versatile use of the dominant ideology has been often read as proof of the one-dimensional nature of her novel. However, by juxtaposing the idealized story with Mary's sense of alienation and difference, the writer points to the historical context in which the immigrants were viewed as inferior and subhuman, as undesirable in America and incompatible with its "true" citizens.

The racist beliefs that were quite openly expressed in the 1890s, and later during World War I, held that the peoples of the Mediterranean and East European regions were biologically different from the ones inhabiting the northern and the western parts of Europe.[50] This conviction led to a division of immigration history into the "old" and the "new," where the former referred to the "superior" stocks of newcomers coming to America from countries such as Ireland, England, or Germany before 1890 and the latter to the "large and increasing number of the weak, the broken, and the mentally crippled," fleeing the Balkans and East and Central Europe. The pseudoscientific findings and the publications of the Dillingham Commission, the clearly racist *Dictionary of Races*, and the predominant prejudice against foreigners strengthened by the world war and rapid urbanization were contributing to a very hostile climate.[51]

Therefore, it is not surprising that Antin's rhetoric was openly used for political reasons—as an already famous author she campaigned for President Roosevelt and the Progressive party. Nevertheless, this fact should not be read as a proof of her complete assimilation into the dominant culture and ideology.[52] She explains her hunger for a patriotic mission in *The Promised Land*: "A little Jewish girl in Polotzk was apt to grow up hungry-minded and empty-hearted; and if . . . she was set down in a land of outspoken patriotism, she was likely to love her new country with a great love, and to embrace its heroes in a great worship. Naturalization, *with us Russian Jews*, may mean more than the adoption of the immigrant by America. It may mean the *adoption of America by the immigrant*" (228, emphasis mine). Antin praised the Puritan America of the Founding Fathers in *They Who Knock at Our Gates* (1914), but she used their ideals as a weapon against the anti-immigrant sentiments she saw emerging all over the country. She utilized the long-established clichés of patriotism, but with an intent to criticize its ill use by those who called on it to oppose the coming of the "new Pilgrims" from Russia or Poland. Her references to American ideals were perhaps echoes of her youthful fascination with democracy and George Washington, but later they became conscious chastisements of the dominant culture for its failure to live up to these ideals.[53]

Behind its deceptively correct ideological surface structure, *The Promised Land* challenges the traditional rags-to-riches immigrant narrative. As James Craig Holte stresses, *The Promised Land* offered an alternative to the clichéd tale of success in its celebration of intellectual rather than materialistic values. In contrast to the typical male stories of Americanization—the autobiographies of Andrew Carnegie and Edward Bok—Antin's America "is a land of opportunity not because it offered a way to wealth, but because it offered a chance to acquire an education." Holte sees Antin's text as an interesting example of a conversion narrative, in which the conversion process is secular and takes the heroine from being foreign to being American: "Antin has ceased to be a stranger in the new land and has become an evangelist for it." Despite his astute reading, however, Holte does not define what being an American means for a young newcomer woman; being such a one and being an "evangelist" for the new country are not the same thing.[54]

Indeed, as an "evangelist" for America, Mary from Antin's text cuts a somewhat unconventional figure. The introduction and final eulogy to her new home speak about an ambivalent approach to the narrator's past, her writing, and her new identity. She does finish her tale with a predictable "happily ever after"—we learn that Mary will marry an "American"—but sternly refuses to conclude her personal transformation; we never learn what became of her educational ambitions and plans for the future. In this respect, she gives the conversion narrative Holte speaks about an ironic twist, because her final "triumph" can be also read as an acknowledgment of failure—she disassociates herself from her earlier incarnation not because she is completely "made over" but because she resists this process and is unhappy about the ending she is expected to write to her life story. As a mediated narrative of immigrant success, *The Promised Land* is supposed to end happily, yet Antin deliberately leaves her readers' curiosity unsatisfied. Before she launches into her final, much-quoted paean—"Mine is the whole majestic past, and mine is the shining future"—she tells the reader: "My favorite abode is a tent in the wilderness, where I shall be happy to serve you a cup of tea out of a tin kettle, and answer further questions" (360–62). Apparently, the "wandering Jew" in her has not found a home and the "lying" author expects her audience to inquire about what she is hiding from it between the lines.

In this respect, Antin's book depicts a deeply personal drama about a girl growing up in America, going through an identity crisis, being torn between Jewish and Gentile values, and experiencing gender-related oppression in the midst of the Promised Land. According to June Sochen, some Jewish women writers often describe "identities within identity," since "the Jewishness is a pale adjective describing American women's lives in the twentieth century." Sochen stresses that the characters' identities in such writers' books are largely defined by their femaleness.[55] Although avoiding explicit references to sexuality, Antin's story is mostly concerned with the life of a female whose "egoistic" dreams overshadow her ancestry and religion without erasing them. Mary's is an identity within identity—a woman and a body within the model immigrant constructed by others. In addition to being a newcomer, a condition that marginalizes both males and females, her gender determines how she perceives the world around her and how she narrates it in her story; it also makes her vulnerable to textual oppression as a writer and the immigrant other.

### No Paradise for a Woman

Even though most feminist critics fail to appreciate it (another lesson in how easily we all get used to stereotypical readings), *The Promised Land* offers a definitely feminist perspective on the American education of a Jewish immigrant female. Antin challenges the ideology of women's domesticity shared by both the old and the new patriarchal cultures. She presents the American reader with a book that subverts the traditional narrative of a woman's life in its forsaking of the domestic sphere for the male world of success, narcissism, and heroic self-making. The book also clearly cuts itself off from such typical "girl" themes as marriage and romance. Antin is conscious of making her character a heroine who violates the conventional story about a "nice girl" with her experience of growing up amid the harshness and lack of privacy in the ghetto, and this may be another reason why there is no chapter about Mary's romance and sexuality. The book ends with the girl being in charge of her life and conscious of her individual achievement, which would not have been possible if she had been securely and traditionally married.

Antin also shows the sacrifices of other women who contributed to Mary's schooling and in this way counterbalances the "egoism" in her depiction of Mary's sequence of successes. For example, the realization that her elder sister had to work in a sweatshop to provide money for Mary's American Dream is just one among many bitter discoveries concerning the workings of her new country's "equal opportunity" system:

> But whatever were her longings, she said nothing of them; she bent over the sewing-machine humming an Old-World melody. In every straight, smooth seam, perhaps, she tucked away some lingering impulse of childhood. . . . If a sudden shock of rebellion made her straighten up for an instant, the next instant she was bending to adjust a ruffle. . . . If, in America, [my father] had been able to support his family unaided, it would have been the culmination of his best hopes to see all his children at school, with equal advantages at home. But when he had done his best, and was still unable to provide . . . [t]here was no choosing possible; Frieda was the oldest, the strongest, the best prepared, and the only one who was of legal age to be put to work. My father has nothing to answer for. He divided the world between his children in accordance with the laws of the country and the compulsion of his circumstances. (200–201)

In the contrasting stories of the two sisters, two versions of female Americanization come into confrontation: Mary's—the idealized and exalted one, and Frieda's—the quotidian and repressed. Antin interweaves them craftily to show us how the official narratives are often underlined by those attesting to the unattractive "compulsion of circumstances." (These two story lines are analogous to the father's two incarnations—the Old World one, who can do nothing to help his children, and the New World one, who can help only some of them and has to face responsibility for the mixed blessings of being in the land that makes such choices possible.) [56]

Throughout her story, Mary repeatedly stresses her gratitude to Frieda, yet does not hesitate to take advantage of her elder sister's devotion. Werner Sollors names Mary's tendency a "cult of gratitude," which he sees as characteristic of Antin's (and Phyllis Wheatley's) "excessive assimilation and submissiveness . . . [in] equating themselves with George Washington" (*BE* 45). However, in light of what immigrants' lives were like, Mary's "equation" seems a little ironic. After all, she learns from her sister and mother, and from the whole world of the ghetto, that both in Russia and America economic conditions, religion, and class determine social status and gender roles.[57]

In neither country is an ethnic woman free to do as she pleases; she is expected to succumb to the prevalent ideology, be it religious or political. A Jewish woman of the Pale hopes to escape her lot in America, where "a long girlhood, a free choice in marriage, and a brimful womanhood are the precious rights of an American woman" (*PL* 277). Yet for a lower-class Jewish female in the Promised Land the dream hardly ever comes true, since she is often confronted with the necessity to work at an early age, as does Fetchke/ Frieda, who then gets married off by a marriage broker to take on the burden of housekeeping for her husband instead of for her father. "The precious rights of an American woman" hardly work in the cases of first-generation immigrant women. Although Mary succeeds in the end and concludes her story with the much publicized, exalted cliché "Mine is the shining future," there is no indication of what her life is going to be like beyond this dazzling, vague conclusion.

The refusal to write a closure to her heroine's story points again to Antin's counternarrative, which, for instance, uses a "biographical" lie about the honors taken by Mary at Barnard College. As we know, the author never took a degree herself. Nonetheless, her heroine-narrator, who is supposed to be telling a "true" story, "lies" to the reader to make at least the educational part of her Americanization successful (360). The "matters to which I long to testify," she says, have to remain untold, but she gives us hints about what she so conspicuously pretends to leave out of her "picture of that double life": "the romance of Dover Street," "afternoon tea with gentle ladies whose hands were as delicate as their porcelain cups," "Mr. Casey lying asleep in the corridor; and the shock of the contrast . . . like a searchlight turned suddenly on my life," "poems, in which I figured as a heroine of two worlds" (*PL* 360– 61). This indication that there is another story of her Americanization that nevertheless remains hidden recalls the introduction, where Mary Antin tells us herself: "I have been made over . . . I . . . chose my own books, and built me a world of my own. . . . And so I can say that there has been more than one birth of myself, and I can regard my earlier self as a separate being, and make it a subject of study" (xix, xx). This sense of fragmentation and alienation from herself clearly binding the beginning and the end of her narrative should not be read as a happy affirmation of rebirth in America. It indicates instead the inevitable loss of the immigrant woman's identity amid the Americanization narrative prescribed for her by the dominant culture—the Promised Land, which is not interested in listening to her other story—in which she nevertheless remains Jewish and female, "a princess, in memory of my forefathers who had ruled a nation," in which she goes "in the disguise of an outcast" although she feels "a halo resting on [her] brow" (40).[58]

### Told in Absences: The Other Story to Which "I Long to Testify"

At the end of *The Promised Land* the narrator invites the reader to participate in "imagining" a conclusion to Mary's story: "The rest of the course may be left to the imagination. Let us say that from the Latin School on I lived very much as my American schoolmates lived, having overcome my foreign idiosyncrasies, and the rest of my outward adventures you may read in any volume of American feminine statistics" (360).

Antin's ironic innuendoes about how "typical" her life became after graduation from the Latin school incite the reader's curiosity instead of appeasing it at the end of *The Promised Land*. After all, in a version clearly different from the ones usually presented by "feminine statistics," the writer points to the immigrant woman's difficulties in accepting the construction of her gender and sexuality in both the Old World and the New. Despite Mary's desire to do so, it is not possible to overcome her "foreign idiosyncrasies," even when she can escape her ethnic milieu temporarily. An immigrant woman has to be ruthless and egoistic (very much in the sense that Elisabeth Woodbridge condemned) if she wants to break away from the prison of the ghetto and step up on the American social ladder; the sacrifices by parents and siblings have to be accepted and taken advantage of.[59]

And although she can eventually make it into high society, as Mary does as a guest of the Boston élite, she will always be seen as an immigrant Jewish female, a prodigy of the tenements whom it may be fashionable to ask to tea. As such, though, she is a disembodied icon, a symbol of the charitable causes her wealthy benefactors are involved in, but definitely not one of the Americans. She remembers the contrast between her poverty, that of a scholarship recipient from the ghetto, and the wealth of her aristocratic classmates at the Latin School: "To make myself at home in an alien world was also within my talents; I had been practicing it day and night for the past four years. To remain unconscious of my shabby and ill-fitting clothes when the rustle of silk petticoats in the schoolroom protested against them was a matter still within my moral reach. Half a dress a year had been my allowance for many seasons; even less, for as I did not grow much I could wear my dresses as long as they lasted" (294). The obvious bitterness of this passage contrasts with the ones in which the narrator praises the "cordiality" of the "girls who came to school in carriages" and who "rated" her by "my scholarship, and not by my father's occupation" (295). Although seemingly accepted by her "democratic" classmates, Mary also learns about the "incongruity of Commonwealth Avenue entwining arms with Dover Street" in the Latin School. Her relation with aristocracy there may have been "graciously American," but it has taught her the rules of "friendly distance" that pervade social conduct in the land of the free.

As Mary learns later, being a specimen of the Old World, she may be an exotic curiosity to upper-class society, but she is not perceived by it as a person and a sexual body on her own terms. The narrator comments on the physical otherness of the immigrant woman as written on her body by her economic condition: "The haunting consciousness of rooted poverty is an improper bedfellow for a woman who still bears. It has been known to induce physical and spiritual malformations in the babies she nurses. . . . Care, to the man, is a hound to be kept in leash and mastered. To the woman, care is a secret parasite that infects the blood" (310–11). Not only is the ghetto woman stigmatized with the "sickness" of poverty as a body, but she is also affected by it in her sexuality. And, as Mary has learned in the Latin School, she has to be acceptable sexually—nonsexual, that is, safely stripped of her carnality—to be fit company for the Daughters of the American Revolution, for example. In tracing Mary's bodily transition from the Old World to the New, Antin's text shows us how her heroine is desexualized in the course of her Americanization, how she is expected to forsake her Old World, "Middle Ages" sensuality for the repressed mind-set of the Puritan New World.

### "Nature Made Me": Absent Body in the Promised Land

The division of Antin's book into two parts—the first describing the Pale of Settlement and Russia and the second dealing with America—serves to elicit two incarnations of the heroine. The narrator-I who self-consciously tells the story, with occasional invocations to the reader and from her vantage point as an adult in America, is, as previously mentioned, spinning the "official" version. In this narrative, Maryashe, Mashke, Marya comes to America and is reborn as Mary Antin, the prodigy of public schools and living proof that immigrants are good for America and vice versa. However, when we follow the events that lead to Mary's success and find ourselves at the end of the story, we realize that the immigrant Bildungsroman we have just witnessed conspicuously lacks one of the most important elements in any girl's story—a depiction of her sexual identity. In chapter XV, "Tarnished Laurels," the narrator tells the reader: "Wheeler Street recognizes five great events in a girl's life: namely, christening, confirmation, graduation, marriage, and burial" (276). Of all the "great events," which sound New World "generic," having been stripped of their Jewishness, we are introduced to only one—the story of Mary's graduation; a new dress, her speech, and the praises she received from school officials are discussed in detail. Although her elder sister, Frieda, marries somewhere in the same chapter, the "egoistic" account of the public event of American graduation is presented as more important.

In the context of an emancipated, antidomestic story of a young girl's acculturation, this emphasis on education and success in the outside world can be easily understood. However, the description of her transition into the New World as a gendered and sexual being should enter her discussion as well. But that is instead significantly repressed, even beyond the sexual openness allowed at her time.[60] Antin's antistory, the subtext narrated by the other persona aware of the official narrative's hold, points to a deep recess separating Mary's Old and New World sexual incarnations. The retrospections into her childhood in Russia reveal a world that is perceived in a much more sensual way than Mary's beloved America. There are lessons in domesticity and preparations for the "pious burden of wifehood," as that is every girl's ultimate vocation. Although, from the vantage point of America, Mary rebels against the superiority and freedom granted to Jewish males, she nevertheless expresses sentiment for the old ways (34, 35). In contrast, "a long chapter of the romance of Dover Street is left untold" and we never find out about the heroine's American marriage and courtship (360).

Therefore, although Antin mentions Mary's marriage at the end, she still suggests that the Pocahontas myth of acculturation through miscegenation is just another superficial scenario. Her heroine finds a husband, but their union is carefully stripped of any sexual qualities because they cannot exist as male and female bodies within the official version. As we have seen, however, sexuality is at the core of an ethnic woman's passage into the new culture; it defines her as other and sets her against the native-born of both sexes. Thus by conspicuously removing it from the second part of her text, Mary Antin is proving its importance. By setting up exotic Old World sensuality against New World repressive sophistication, she shows how an ethnic woman is always oppressed, how she is trapped between two incarnations that either construct her as primarily sexual or deprive her of this part of her identity.

We can see this dichotomy in Mary's perceptions of the Pale and of her new environment. Compared with the memories of tastes and smells of the Old World, America appears strangely sanitized and sterile. Whereas the past reveals a group of unabashed female bathers who "were accustomed to see each other naked in the public hot baths," the American present mentions the body only in the educational context of social work. The detailed insights into Russian-Jewish women's cleanliness, the traditional purifying ablutions and the rites of faith associated with the body, have no counterparts in the portrayal of the New World. For the narrator of the second part, who talks about fostering physical education among the poor, "the boy's own body" is the "fittest *instrument for his uplifting*" through exercise and application of scientific principles to his development and growth. Needless to say, there is no mention of what charity organizations could do about a "girl's body" (89, 287–8, emphasis mine).

Not only is the narrator-I reticent about issues of sexuality in the New World, but she rarely refers to herself as a carnal presence. For example, in the description of her first school dress, tailored for her by her devoted elder sister, Frieda, Mary is looking up at her new garment hanging upon the wall— "my consecration robe awaiting the beatific day" (199). The "girl theme" of fashion and dressing up is sacrificed in this scene to elicit the almost religious rites of education—Mary's metaphorical New World baptism—which will deliver her into "civilized" society. Later on, at the usual age of teenage vanities, Mary appears underdeveloped, fragile, and sickly. At the age of seventeen, she looks twelve and, after a visit to a friend's house, hates her look in the mirror: "I studied myself long in my blotched looking-glass. *I saw just what I expected.* My face was too thin, my nose too large, my complexion too dull. My hair, which was curly enough, was too short to be described as luxurious tresses; and the color was neither brown nor black. My hands were neither white nor velvety; the fingers ended decidedly, instead of tapering off like rosy dreams. I was disgusted with my wrists; they showed too far below the tight sleeves of my dress of the year before last, and they looked consumptive" (347, emphasis mine).[61]

Mary's self-examination is prompted by a sponsor's desire to paint her portrait. The girl cannot understand why anybody would look for beauty in her fragile ethnic appearance. Her comparison of herself with females one usually sees in the paintings (those with velvety hands and "rosy dreams" of fingers) comes out very unfavorably. She assumes that people want to paint others because of their beauty, and it disturbs her that her own body is the antithesis of a stereotypical portrait of an upper-class female. In this confrontation of sorts with *her* upper-class "other"—a sexually attractive female of "luxurious tresses," "velvety" skin, and "rosy" fingers—Mary discovers disgust toward and a fear of her own body. (On the other hand, we can also discern in this scene a subtle ironic reference to the clichéd and unrealistic, portraitlike, static and artificial standards of American women's beauty.) It is her external appearance that her wealthy friends want to capture and buy from her, her being as an antithesis to the Anglo-Saxon female beauty, her "type" as an immigrant elevating her to the position of a subject worthy of a portrait.

This disturbing confrontation with her commodified carnality in the dominant culture is counterbalanced by a logical explanation, in which Mary decides resolutely, "It was because I was a girl, a person, a piece of creation. . . . [W]hy should not an artist be able to make an interesting picture of me?" It never crosses her mind that she could be fascinating precisely because of her ugliness and shabby, "ethnic" appearance. This fragment is characteristic of the whole New World part of *The Promised Land*, where there is a rational explanation attached, sometimes too forcibly, to any instance where the narrator should engage in gender- or class-related issues. Clearly influenced by Darwinism, Emersonian thought, and a transcendentalist approach to nature, Mary indulges in descriptions of her affiliations with the universe, but she has trouble dealing with her own body, whose growth into womanhood she cannot help but notice. Nevertheless, when she ventures into the world of living creatures as a member of the Natural History Club, she learns to experience nature sensually, as if to make up for the loss of contact with her own carnality.

At first, any reference to the body in America requires a "scientific," nature-bound explanation. Following her private evolution theory, the heroine draws a parallel between one's physical appearance and social standing—upper-class people look nice, and that is why they pay for their portraits; she is poor and ugly, and that is probably why she is getting paid for her sittings. Mary is now much more conscious of social status and class, although she does not engage in a discussion of people's different economic standing as openly as she did in the first part, which laid out clearly the social strata of Polotzk. We can see her self-consciousness in the careful selection of images in the mirror passage, in which she replaces the picture of her emaciated body—what she *expected* a poor starved child to look like—with a plea to regard her for only her humanity. It bothers her that she gets paid for the sittings, but she dismisses such "hair-splitting analyses" because she also needs money for rent, which her father is no longer able to earn because "America, after all, was not going to provide for my father's family" (349, 291). In this way Mary unwillingly sells herself to make her Americanization possible. Such an approach to her bodily image arises from her social status, of which she learns by observing and comparing herself with others and which teaches her that her appearance is a commodity one can use or disregard but never enjoy.[62]

Therefore, the sensuous bodily incarnation of the heroine sketched in her descriptions of the Old World—where she saw herself as a daughter of the fertile Old Testament women Rebecca, Rachel, and Leah—seems to fade with her progress and initiation into the New World (40). In place of the superstitious, lively recollections of Old World tastes and smells, she introduces her American "jar of specimen." The narrator remembers, with a bit of irony, how she has developed a whole collection of "phantom dishes" in America:

> Do you think all your imported spices, all your scientific blending and manipulation, could produce so fragrant a morsel as that which I have on my tongue as I write? Glad I am that my mother, in her assiduous imitation of everything American, has forgotten the secrets of Polotzk cookery. . . . and I am the richer in memories for her omissions. Polotzk cheese cake, as I now know it, has in it the flavor of daisies and clover picked on the Vall; the sweetness of Dvina water; the richness of newly turned earth which I moulded with bare feet and hands; the ripeness of red cherries bought by the dipperful in the market place; the fragrance of all my childhood summers.
>
> Abstinence . . . is one of the essential ingredients in the phantom dish. (91)

There are no real meals and tastes in the second part of *The Promised Land*. In the New World, which should be so rich in tastes to the newcomer, so "flowing with milk and honey," Mary joins the Hale House Natural History Club, where she learns about spiders and sea creatures and where she discovers her "promised land of the evolution." Now she sees the world as "much nobler than it had ever been before" (335). Gone are the Old World flavors and particular sensory sensations as Mary ventures into the world of philosophical and scientific thought. Interestingly, the prominent scholars at the club are named Mr. Emerson and Mr. Winthrop, as if to certify even further that the reborn heroine took the right course ideologically with her belief in nature and her desire to contribute to the city on a hill.[63]

However, despite her superficial faith in American philosophy and natural sciences, Mary feels profound nostalgia for a past so full of joy and sensuality that it often colors her perceptions of the new culture. When she falls in love, there is a mysterious friend who comes to her, carrying "the golden key that unlocked the last secret chamber of life" for her, although he is never named and we never find out what impact this particular revelation, perhaps about sex and marriage, had on her life (356). Apparently, such topics were not a part of the puritanically scientific discourse within the Natural History Club, with Messrs. Emerson and Winthrop presiding. However, despite this conspicuous absence of the body, despite its exchange for the world of natural sciences, Antin's subtext suggests that Mary does learn about responding to the world around her by using her senses. The description of the "phantom dishes" is developed in a sensual language, as if by reaching into the past from her present in America Mary were stretching a hand toward her old, familiar self. In the Old World part she writes: "I imbibe wisdom through every pore of my body. . . . The earth was my mother, the earth is my teacher. I am a dutiful pupil: I listen ever with my ear close to her lips. It seems to me I do not know a single thing that I did not learn, more or less directly, through the corporeal senses. *As long as I have my body*, I need not despair of salvation" (136, emphasis mine). While recollecting her growing up in the Pale from the present of her American milieu, Mary is able to connect with her old self. In the context of the Old World, she can admit that she learns "by the prick of life on my own skin" rather than through "borrowed experience." And although these theories may superficially sound like Emerson (or even Jonathan Edwards), the other story embodies Mary as a sensual and vibrant girl and woman. Her split and fragmented identity in America is a result of the abyss separating the two worlds, the two narratives, and the two "embodiments" of the same woman.

### Reaching across the Abyss: Dialogue with the Other

As she has proven by constructing her story from seemingly incompatible narratives, Antin believes in a possibility of communication between Mary's fragmented incarnations. At the end of the novel, when she is getting ready to deliver her final speech about the "shining future," Mary has just come back from a Natural History Club trip, with her hair "damp with sea spray; the roar of the tide . . . still in [her] ears," and she feels that "my jar of specimens in my hand . . . I was hardly conscious of the place where I stood . . . the familiar world around me was transfigured" (363). Thus her rejected, repressed body is lurking behind the paeans to her new country, even though Mary is never allowed to emerge fully as a flesh-and-blood female. Antin's insistence on the separation of Mary's two incarnations, on the one hand, and her desire for a dialogue between them, on the other, suggests that the opposites can meet, that the alternative story can transform, or just chip at the foundation of, the dominant one.

At the end of the book, Mary does not emerge as an unequivocal body; she may be seen as a mere phantom who "soars above" the mire of the slum because her sexuality cannot fully emerge in the repressed America, because the textual oppression Antin had to deal with did not make such a heroine entirely possible then.[64] In the passages that can be read as the writer's ironic authorial comments, Mary regrets that she never learned to write poetry, but she is happy that she at least learned to "think in English without an accent," to imitate the native-born others in some of her ways. She realizes that the passions and desires she could have expressed openly in verse were not allowed to surface, as she had to follow the "scientific" course of Americanization and became caught in the narrative prescribed for her by the dominant culture. In her desire to deliver the vision of the immigrant expected from her, she realizes nevertheless her authorial limitations, as she implies when she writes: "The fault was partly mine, because I always would reduce everything to a picture" (220).

In Antin's Promised Land there may be no Adam and Eve, no "eating of the apple," yet there are "bold-faced girls who passed the evening on the corner, in promiscuous flirtation with the cock-eyed youths of the neighborhood, [who] unconsciously revealed . . . the eternal secrets of adolescence" (339). There are also Mary's "moments of depression," when she wishes to run away from the slum life because she feels "defiled by the indecencies [she] was compelled to witness"—subtle, yet poignant hints that her life did not consist solely of educational success and tea parties (297). These downplayed parts of *The Promised Land* question the easy idealism of its official narrative and, once again, lead us into the alternative reading underlying it. Just as Mary's conspicuously absent body, relegated from the official version to the subtext, can engage in a dialogue with the disembodied character of the surface story, so does the alternative reading of Antin's text emerge as a contrast and necessary other to the tale of seemingly successful female Americanization. In another self-conscious moment of authorial sincerity she refers us to another "picture," this time from her past, which gives us further clues to reading her complex narrative. While describing her Old World house, she recalls a garden "where lived the Gentile girl who was kind to me" and the flowers that grew there: "Concerning my dahlias I have been told that they were not dahlias at all, but poppies. As a conscientious historian I am bound to record every rumor, but I retain the right to cling to my own impression. Indeed, I must insist on my dahlias, if I am to preserve the garden at all. . . . It is only that my illusion is more real to me than reality. And so do we often build our world on an error, and cry out that the universe is falling to pieces, if any one but lift a finger to replace the error by truth" (81). This picture is not reductive. In its glimpse of another world—the forbidden garden of Gentiles—it reveals to a careful reader-beholder the depth of the vision of its creator. As a metaphor eliciting the technique of writing her life story, Antin's "dahlias" represent her subtext for those of her readers who want to look beyond the "historical" poppies.

In this sense, we can see Antin making the best of her entrapment and consciously utilizing the textual oppression of an immigrant woman writer to construct a dialogue between the stories she wrote into *The Promised Land*. Only by putting together fragments of her heroine's shattered self is she able to present us with a collage portrait of a newcomer woman. Conversely, by providing us with a seemingly intact and conventional text, she makes us see how it is nevertheless engaged in self-unmaking, how its antistory is undermining the official one. The peculiar dialogue between diverse narratives, concepts of sexuality, ideologies, and perceptions of freedom that perpetuates her novel challenges the conventional, one-dimensional portrayal of the writer and her text. It makes us see her as a one of the most important forerunners in the tradition of female newcomer writing as well as in the larger cultural and literary discourse involving East European writers in America.

Mary Antin writes: "My life has been unusual, but by no means unique. . . . It is because I understand my history, in its larger outlines, to be typical of many, that I consider it worth recording. My life is a concrete illustration of a multitude of statistical facts" (xxi). Although she repeatedly stresses the "statistical facts" as a larger frame for her story, Antin proves that the narrative into which she turned it in *The Promised Land* is a rich and unique text of its own, and herself an intriguing and engaging voice, without whom it is not possible to talk about the novel in America.

# Pride over Tears

ELIZABETH STERN'S
INSOLENT AMERICANIZATION

The mere writing of this account is a chain,
slight but never to be broken; one that will
always bind me to that from which I had
thought myself forever cut off.

—Elizabeth Stern, *My Mother and I*

n her autobiographical novel *My Mother and I* (1917), Elizabeth Gertrude Levin Stern (1889–1954), a Polish-Jewish writer, seems to be writing a second-generation sequel to Mary Antin's account of female acculturation in *The Promised Land*. Stern's seemingly fully assimilated narrator is looking back into her Polish-Jewish ethnic past from the comfortable interior of her model middle-class American home, just as Antin's narrator might have done had she decided to tell us a story of her marriage and family life. However, instead of emphasizing the separation from the immigrant's Old World incarnation as Antin does in her introduction, Stern's novel begins with a claim that it is impossible to break away from the past one is "chained" to by birth. *My Mother and I*, thus, responds to Antin's text in two ways: first, as a continuation in which Stern describes a young woman's rite of passage into the dominant culture where she embraces enthusiastically, as Mary did, "American womanhood" and her adopted country's ideology; second, as a revision in which her story advances the rewriting of the immigrant narrative in its focus on the price female immigrants have to pay for acculturation by both refusing and having to embrace the narrative models expected from newcomer authors.

In the few available reviews and critical studies of Stern's work, *My Mother and I* is largely perceived as completing and complementing Antin's novel. This emphasis on continuation—and the classification of a genre—is positive, for it points to critical affirmation of the rapidly developing tradition of East European immigrant women's writings in American literature. Yet such readings that welcome a relatively new tradition often miss the fact that Stern's text represents both its continuation and a separate voice revising and questioning it. As the close inquiry into Antin's seemingly unproblematic narrative has already revealed, reading such writings requires a dialogic approach—

not simply looking for similarities but inquiring into the alternative subtexts, interpretations, and dialogues taking place within and without a given text.[1]

In this chapter I show that a close reading of Stern's *My Mother and I* suggests that one ought to read women's immigrant narratives as a tradition, but one needs to see that this tradition's primary characteristic is a desire to revise and rewrite itself rather than to complacently imitate earlier models. I argue that Elizabeth Stern's novel reveals many ways in which her heroine's ambivalent Americanization subverts the typical newcomer narrative. *My Mother and I* illustrates the immigrant woman's necessary fragmentation in the process of becoming American, or of claiming Americanness as her "birthright." This fragmentation also disrupts the usual happy ending with an emphasis on the narrator's mother's antistory—the alternative narrative leading to metaphorical death and obliteration of the mother who represents the heroine's ethnicity. Interestingly, with its oscillation between the mother's and the daughter's story, its lack of names, and its emphasis on both the general and the individual aspects of the narrator's life, Stern's text challenges both the stereotypical tale of female Americanization and the archetypal female Bildungsroman. As a tale about acculturation, *My Mother and I* points to the loss of self and to the heroine's subsequent fragmentation as the price to be paid for claiming her "birthright," for writing her own "America." As a story about separation from the maternal sphere and about the necessity to erase the father's, Stern's text shows too that any immigrant woman's narrative had to be read through the dominant culture's stereotypes of the female Bildungsroman, which had to end in marriage.

I also argue that the poignant use of the dominant idiom to express these themes presents another example of how *My Mother and I* both elicits and rejects the necessary cultural split imposed on the newcomer woman who insolently claims America. Stern shows that her heroine's sign of Americanness, her educated English, can express both her dominant American ethnicity and her fragmented self to her audience. Michelle Cliff talks about the phenomenon of "split consciousness" in the woman writer who succumbs to the use of dominant language. The realization of the woman's ethnicity and ethnic loyalty causes this split, because she cannot express her conflict otherwise than in the "colonial" idiom of the dominant culture that molded her into its own image. A struggle to find herself in such a situation—to construct a self that could deal with this crisis—means attempts to build wholeness from fragmentation. The split self that a woman writer becomes between incompatible cultures and languages is the only "material" she has to thus re-create herself.[2]

I see this process of self-recreation emerging from the fragmented narrative of Stern's novel. Like Cliff, the narrator of *My Mother and I* begins with an illusion of the complete American self constructed by the "colonizer"— the dominant culture—and from there reaches into her past, working out a liberating ethnic "rage" that reveals the fragmentation and frustration underneath the official façade of the model immigrant (who is, let us not forget, made "model" by the dominant culture). Superficially, Stern's story is told by a holistic and self-assured narrator who knows exactly who she is: one who has already embraced the inevitable fragmentation, the constructions of herself as an ethnic immigrant insider.

Despite her seemingly perfect assimilation, Stern's texts—a variety of fiction, autobiography, memoir, and historical, biographical, and didactic pieces —reflect a difficult story of intercultural transformation *within America* and engage a complex discussion of women's gendered and social roles in American and Jewish cultures. Although there is no passage from the Old World into the New, no crossing of the actual ocean in *My Mother and I* and *I Am a Woman—and a Jew*, for example, there are many crosscultural transitions and conflicts that Stern's heroines have to go through while growing up in an America that insists on seeing them as outsiders and others. These transitions can be likened to the immigrant-passage scenario in the sense that they involve a move from an ethnic background into an American one. Stern can be thus read as an immigrant author. In fact, she has been read as such regardless of the context in which her audience wanted to place her—one highlighting her newcomer otherness or another her model assimilation of the dominant culture's values—because of this culture's desire to see the other in both the outsider and the ethnic insider. Her texts have been usually perceived through the writings of other newcomer women, and her stories have been defined by the familiar and inherently enigmatic label "tales of acculturation."

But such superficial labels arise from superficial readings of the tradition to which Stern belongs. This chapter shows that contemporary critical analyses of writers such as Stern and Antin ought to challenge their own reliance on earlier responses to these immigrant narratives in order to appreciate and welcome their complex messages.

## A Problematic Immigrant

At first sight, the life and career of Elizabeth Stern, a daughter of Polish-Jewish immigrants, follow the traditional trajectory of the newcomer narrative. A poor ghetto girl fights her way into the American Dream through education, self-reliance, and perseverance. Her achievement materializes in marriage with a native-born man and in her career as a successful social worker, journalist, and fiction writer.[3] This exemplary story of another immigrant prodigy in the New World involves also the predictable transition from the oppressive Old World. Stern immigrated to the United States from Poland at the age of two and a half in 1890 and settled with her parents in Pittsburgh, where she received a degree from the University of Pittsburgh in 1910. Her education at the New York School of Philanthropy brought her in contact with her husband, Leon Stern. Their union—a successful partnership between two strong professionals—eased her into an almost utopian life of work and companionate married love, which she would repetitively describe and idealize in her writings.[4]

In the predictable course of her immigrant story of success—seeming almost too good to be true—Stern has been often compared to Mary Antin. In fact, the publication of *My Mother and I* in 1917, just five years after the appearance of Antin's *The Promised Land*, was considered a response to the new tradition of the immigrant Bildungsroman by newcomer women. However, Stern was more aggressive than Antin in her open rebellion against the treatment of women in Jewish families. Her heroines' defiance of patriarchal Judaism, which was personified by unbending Orthodox rabbi-fathers in *My Mother and I* and *I Am a Woman—and a Jew* (1926), brings to mind similar conflicts between fathers and daughters in Anzia Yezierska's texts, especially in *Bread Givers* (1925). In exploring this conflict between the first and the second immigrant generations, between men and women of both worlds, Stern, like Yezierska, also writes her own unique story into some of her novels.

On the other hand, Stern's active involvement in the fight for women's suffrage and the right to work side by side with her American feminist counterparts, whose language and beliefs she easily adopted, sets her apart from Yezierska, who insists on the privacy and individuality of the ethnic woman's story, as well as from Antin, who took a collective perspective on the immigrant predicament. In her model life of a married working woman who proves to the patriarchal culture and its institutions that it is possible to have a career and a family at the same time, Stern seems much more American than ethnic. She was, after all, brought to the United States as a baby and, although born in the Old World, truly knew it only through the immigrant ghetto where she grew up, her mother's stories, and her conservative father's insistence upon preserving traditional Jewish ways.

Due to these somewhat contradictory factors that describe her both as an outsider and an insider, Stern has been often categorized as an embodiment of a perfectly pliable immigrant, one who blossomed into a modern American "new woman." Her extensive journalism, especially a collection of essays entitled *Not All Laughter: A Mirror to Our Times* (1937) and her novels, *This Ecstasy* (1927), *A Marriage Was Made* (1928), and *When Love Comes to Woman* (1929), project an image of an author who, among other issues, is deeply involved in and concerned about the changing mores of female conduct within American society. Stern's social work and feminist contributions to the case of working mothers, her understanding of women involved in unconventional love affairs, even her engagement in many Quaker initiatives and her sympathy for the temperance movement, all seem to single her out as an "immigrant" who let herself be "melted" into the more progressive part of the dominant culture.[5]

## Readings and Misreadings

As previously mentioned, Elizabeth Stern's public image after the publication of *My Mother and I* was largely constructed on comparisons with Mary Antin. One early reaction to her book sums up Stern's approach to the theme of female acculturation: "The note struck in Mrs. Stern's book appears to be a more sincere one than that sounded by Miss Antin, because, though the narrative is a personal one, the reader is not oppressed by the ego of the writer."[6] Although Antin's autobiographical text clearly expresses the collective struggle of the immigrants, in this case it was perceived as an overdrawn, egotistical account of Mary's success. The reviewer finds Antin's personal narrative "insincere," although the author claims to have written a "true" story. On the other hand, Stern's text, a purely individualized account of a Jewish girl's transition from the ghetto into an American marriage and middle-class happiness, seems modest and acceptable. Apparently, Stern's individualism appeared less overwhelming than Antin's, possibly because she uses the dominant idiom with more ease as an insider and does not introduce the unfamiliar Old World, with its exotic glossary and alien topography, into her story.

However, in the opinion of another critic, who was more concerned that the immigrant narrative be a documentary, Stern's book is inferior to Antin's: "It is much shorter than the work which presumably inspired it, and as a sociological document it is less valuable because less explicit."[7] To this critic, writing in *The Nation*, Stern's *My Mother and I* is an exaggerated outpouring of unmitigated immigrant enthusiasm: "Since we are likely to have many more of these *piquant narratives from our new Americans*, it is perhaps worth suggesting to them that their contributions to the *literature of the happy immigrant* will probably gain in thoughtfulness and mellowness if they postpone the announcement of their accomplishment till their first natural elation wears off, and they perceive that there are attainments more remarkable than marrying an American husband—splendid as that 'of course'—as Mr. Roosevelt would say—is."[8] The anonymous reviewer in the liberal *The Nation* is visibly ironic and condescending toward Stern's emotional account. The sentiments conveyed in the review are, as we have seen, not an isolated example of a hostile reaction to the immigrant rhetoric and especially to that expressed by a woman who had "made it" as successfully as Stern. In the era of nativism and anti-immigration legislation, resentment toward the newcomer was common enough, as those who felt themselves the only "true" Americans feared the encroachment of the alien masses. New books by immigrants also created competition for native writers and their ideology on the literary market. Conservative society, including critics and scholars, were against admitting that there was any connection between their Puritan ancestors immigrating to the Promised Land in the seventeenth century and the "huddled masses" of their own time, those who dared to use the rhetoric of the Old Testament exodus and renewal appropriated by the Founding Fathers.[9]

Mary Dearborn sums up such resistance in the dominant culture by focusing on the reception of women's texts: "The ethnic woman who mediates too successfully, who writes from the perspective of the dominant culture (which has insisted on her Americanization and conversion to its values) . . . is roundly scolded" (*PD* 41). The critic stresses a paradox that arises from the fact that the new country—and the review in question suggests this clearly—wants the immigrant to stick to "details" of her background, to be "foreign" and "ethnic" instead of American, while simultaneously expecting her to speak the "central" idiom so that she can be understood (and her book sold and bought) by insiders. In such an approach, the fact that Stern is not identical with other immigrants, that her background is ambivalent and complex, becomes completely lost.

As an atypical immigrant and an unacceptable American, Stern is a versatile user of the dominant ideology and language. She cannot identify with the "exotic" ethnic part as much as the reviewer from *The Nation* would like her to. Her books are written from the position of an insider who completely identifies with her country and who is already too much removed from her ethnicity to be able to supply a plethora of desired "details." In fact, while reading *My Mother and I*, the reader often has the impression that it is more about America than about the narrator's ethnic origins. In thus stressing her perspective as an insider, Stern cuts herself off from the usual writings that an immigrant writer was expected to produce at her time, ones that provided a measured comparison between the Old and the New Worlds. Since she claims

Americanness without undergoing the traditional rites of passage, without earning her position by a hard transitory struggle contrasting the oppressive childhood in the old country and the difficult freedom in the new, she meets with critical resistance.[10]

The comparison of Antin's and Stern's critical receptions reveals that both writers are chastised in either case—whether they are too ethnic (egotism) or too American (trespassing). Their "double fault" results from the fact that the host culture resists any overtly successful mediation, as Dearborn eloquently argues. However, what should be emphasized more in reference to both Antin's or Stern's reception is the open hostility of the dominant culture toward the alien woman who dares to transgress the sacred terrain of the insider's privilege to decide who is American and who is not—to assign and construct ethnic identities from its position of power as the majority. As Stern's narrator in *I Am a Woman—and a Jew* finds out the hard way, her employer's discovery of her Jewishness completely changes his attitude to her—a fact that makes her quit a lucrative managerial position in an upper-class department store. When confronted with her superiors' blatant anti-Semitism, she sees clearly that its source lies not only in the racist stereotypes prevalent then, but also in the prejudice that influences the capitalist market. Wealthy WASP clients cannot be served by Jews in a store with upper-class pretenses if it is to make money in a racist society. As soon as her ethnicity is discovered—and it takes naming and "commodifying" it, as, obviously, no one is able to see it—Stern's heroine becomes a different person to her superiors: her trade value changes. This is a painful lesson for an enthusiastic ethnic who considers herself American and is unknowingly passing for a WASP, one whose own ethnicity, in a sense, does not even exist for her until it is made real by the dominant culture's prejudice. Thus the narrator's Jewishness becomes tangible to her, even makes her realize its inherent meaning for her identity, only after it has been classified as such by those who despise it.

In light of the anti-immigrant feelings presented in *I Am a Woman—and a Jew*, even the condescending review from *The Nation* sounds sympathetic. It looks self-critically at the middle-class aspirations that the immigrants want to emulate, suggesting that "our new Americans," should take the American Dream and its guarantees of success with a grain of salt, because "not every daughter of the ghetto marries an American in an honorable profession" or "becomes the social companion of Daughters of American Revolution and descendants of the Mayflower pilgrims." Besides presenting a rather ironic approach to the idealistic accounts of Americanization, these comments suggest the existence of a superior group of immigrants—Mayflower Pilgrims.

Ironically, such a class-conscious construction of Americanness is based on the appropriation of the newcomer's experience, remaking that cultural idiom into the dominant ideological jargon. The immigrant propaganda of the era 1890–1920 was based on the same Old Testament rhetoric that had been used by the first settlers, who termed their journey to America a passage to the "New Canaan." In both cases the rhetoric points back to the history of the Jewish Exodus from Egypt and the search for the Promised Land, which was made into a metaphor for the mythical American experience. And yet, despite her employment of the dominant ideological idiom, Stern, a Jew, is rejected as a trespasser. Once again, both the ethnic woman and the user of American idioms are defined, accepted, or rejected by the powerful center for whom they provide the necessary minority margin and an official ideological discourse.

Because Stern's narrator in *My Mother and I* boldly encroaches upon territory forbidden to the outsider, she becomes suspect as being one who may not have reached success exclusively by virtue of her individual merits. As *The Nation* reviewer suggests: "What impecunious Jews in Poland will require is an analysis of success in America: what part was played by private benefactors, scholarships, prizes, hard work in odd hours?—what part was due to talent and personal charm?—how does one get a 'pull' with Mr. Roosevelt?" The justified realistic and class-conscious liberal attitude notwithstanding, the reference to Roosevelt's introduction to *My Mother and I* as a "pull" diminishes Stern's accomplishment as an author and suggests that the book won its recognition as a political statement rather than as a worthwhile literary work. Moreover, reading today, we can see that the ironic references to marriage as an "accomplishment," to "personal charm," and to "private benefactors" all point to the author's gender as inferior and perhaps reveal latent hostility toward her ethnicity.

As a woman, Stern should have been humble, grateful, and modest instead of being bold and proud. In place of the boastful celebration of her new life in America, she should have confined herself to being like other girls "of such origins," who are content with living and recording the "details" of domestic existence, who never dream about making it into the intellectual elite of the insiders. As an "impecunious Jew" (and here gender does not make much difference), the writer is perceived according to the anti-Semitic stereotypes that define Jewish immigrants as manipulative, cunning, and greedy for reward and recognition—getting the "'pull' with Mr. Roosevelt" would probably not be commented upon if she were a WASP. Thus Stern's fault is her inability to speak as an outsider who is aware of and does not question her marginal position, who, moreover, supplies a plethora of humble justifications for her marginality. Although her mixed voice is natural in one who immigrated at such a young age and never really knew another country, some of her audience would like her to remain, or even pretend to be, an alien ethnic heroine, one who never completely crosses into the privileged center of Americanism.[11]

In contrast, some recent critical responses, which acknowledge her integrated perspective, approach Stern as a writer whose work tries to reconcile her outsider's and insider's perspectives a little too overtly. As Mary Dearborn puts it, "Like the best ethnic texts, her work sets forth the ethnic American's double allegiance to ancestry and to the American community" (*PD* 42). Although she admits that some of Stern's work is interesting and worthwhile, Dearborn nevertheless refers to her as an unsuccessful writer who let herself be mediated too much and who eventually turned to ghostwriting (*PD* 41).[12] On the other hand, Helen M. Bannan defends Stern, whom she admires for her emphasis on the "sacrifices involved in family relationships complicated by cultural change" and for her faithful recording of the lives of the "first generation." Yet, although she admits that Stern "accurately accounts the costs and benefits of both the Americanization process and the application of feminist principles to life," Bannan also sees her books as "dated by their romanticism and frequent concentration upon battles considered long won."[13] The "battles" Bannan refers to—such as the right of married women to work—are indeed a thing of the past to us. To a contemporary reader who is looking for strong feminist stands that question and advance the white middle-class paradigms, Stern may lose her attractiveness as the contesting alien other; she is too "mild" in her otherness, too American for today's audience, who sometimes values a writer's exotic ethnic background more than her actual work. Thus, while blamed by these critics for being too much of an insider, Stern is in fact criticized for being the other who renounced the position of an outsider, which she should have embraced more readily as an ethnic writer.

However, Stern's Jewishness is at the core of her work, although this aspect of her ethnic otherness has not been emphasized enough in the scholarship about her. In her introduction to *I Am a Woman—and a Jew* (republished in 1986 after many years of oblivion), Ellen M. Umansky calls Stern's text "a rare and valuable record of a woman's struggle to come to terms with Jewish self-identity." Her reading offers interesting insights into the differences between Stern's own life and that of her first-person narrator, ones that are important in light of early twentieth-century readings that tend to approach immigrant literature as documentary and autobiography. For example, she stresses that Stern consciously wrote books that could be read as autobiographies but that were often far removed from the actual events of her life. Umansky sees *I Am a*

*Woman—and a Jew* as a fictional "spiritual odyssey" that remains "completely contemporary" rather than as a classic immigrant autobiography. But while praising Stern's concern for her Jewish background, Umansky chastises her for using the novel "as a springboard for expressing her social and religious beliefs."[14] Much like Dearborn and Bannan, Umansky blames Stern for her identification with the dominant culture that obscures her ethnic otherness.

In thus approaching Stern as a writer who was too much concerned with fictionalizing her social and political views as a perfectly integrated other, the critics avoid dealing with the conflicts that are present underneath her model scenarios of acculturation. By classifying her either as an immigrant or as an insider, they define her texts' complex characters, but they avoid dealing with narrative tensions resulting from this complexity. At the closure of the first chapter of *My Mother and I* we read: "It is six years since I left home; it is six years since *my life has been made over* again. With my mother's coming then fell open the door closed upon the past. It *does not lie in my power to tell how strange it seemed to me to look back*" (14). In this passage, highly reminiscent of Antin's introduction to *The Promised Land*, we read about the now familiar immigrant woman's dread of looking back into her past, of reconstructing her rites of passage for the American audience. In her novel Antin tells us that she is "completely other than the story she has to tell," whereas Stern in *My Mother and I* stresses her inability to communicate about this other, herself in the past, whom she has to confront after six years of what she thought was a completely new and separate life.

Although, in their respective stories, we can see both women trying to establish bridges between their ethnic and American backgrounds, we can also see how their texts reflect separations and ruptures inherent in such processes of cultural bridge building. Their accounts document ways of coming to terms with the splits they realize in themselves; their ethnic and American embodiments are separate and incompatible but necessary for each other, just like the Old and the New Worlds between which they are caught in the movement of the traditional immigrant narrative. Even though it entails facing their fragmented selves—the ethnic, the sexual, the gendered, the integrated parts of themselves—Antin and Stern engage in their narratives in order to communicate this fragmentation and intercultural conflict to their readers. In this way they prove that it is possible to work out their unique stories from bits and pieces of how immigrant females are written by the dominant culture and how they write themselves beyond the official scenario that this culture expects them to embrace.

Coming to terms with her ambivalent identity is especially interesting in Stern, whose textual shuttling between the positions of the insider and the outsider suggests a separation *and* a connection between the two. Stern's seemingly unproblematic and "assimilated" writings point to a definite split and conflict in the ethnic woman she creates in her writings. Early on in *My Mother and I*, she refuses to identify with other immigrants: "It may be because everything is so normal in my life that I cannot think of myself as a 'problem'; I cannot think of my mother as a 'problem.' Part of our work during the past six years has been in the settlement house, in the playground, in the night school. The young people I have met there have come to me with their problem, the problem of 'how to be American.' I have never thought in all those last six years that there was a relationship between them and me." [15] The protagonist-narrator of *My Mother and I* is startled to see how she and they will always have something in common both as strangers trying to be "Americans" and as "new" insiders in the Promised Land. She realizes that she has been repressing the awareness of this shared strangeness during the long years of her seemingly unproblematic life as a successful American woman. In this way she faces a dichotomy: she sees herself as cut off from other newcomers yet cannot deny the intercultural alienation she shares with them in the country that sees them all as foreigners.

When looking back into her past, she is also shocked by realizing the inevitable cruelty of her separation from her ghetto mother, a woman who could never become as American as her daughter. Stern is torn between the sense of an incurable loss necessary for her New World success, on the one hand, and the discovery of an invisible "chain" binding her to her parents and to her ethnic roots, on the other, no matter how well she does in her acculturation: "Perhaps I should never have seen into mother's heart, into her life as related to my own, if she had not come last winter to visit us. That brief visit of mother's brought back old pictures" (13). In juxtaposing the mother and the daughter and the spheres they inhabit in America, the novel contains a parallel story of the mother's "anti-Americanization" that can be read as an alternative commentary on the daughter's triumphant progress into New World womanhood. The narrator's earlier insistence on this separation, her hatred for her own ethnicity, and her refusal to be considered an immigrant at all resulted from her initial uncritical acceptance of the acculturation model she was supposed to fit. The visit of her mother brings together the two stages of her life she has believed incompatible. She realizes that, instead of spelling rebirth and renewal, the acculturation scenario she embraced earlier has actually resulted in the metaphorical death of her parents and of her own ethnicity. While reconstructing her life story, Stern's narrator is thus unmaking the model tale of female acculturation in which such a "death" is a desired result; she is illustrating a larger ideological paradox, which implies the inevitability of such loss and the necessity of otherness both in America's ethnic insiders and outsiders.[16]

In light of her separation from her parents and the past they represent, the narrator's insistent claiming of an American identity can be seen as a conscious, or even desperate, filling of the void left by her "dead" ethnic one. This insistence on replacing one identity with another proves that the narrator is somehow attached to "that from which I had thought myself forever cut off"; it suggests conflict rather than harmony at the core of her assimilated identity. She proclaims that she is American, has always been American, and she does so especially forcefully when she spends an evening with a group of Russian immigrants and finds herself an outsider among them: "I sat there as one outside. I was alone in all that ardent group singing the songs of another land. . . . I knew that evening that America had always been mine. Among these young men and women with dreams and desires . . . I was a stranger" (147). This statement separates her completely from the ethnic group to which she belongs by birth and from the heterogeneous group of international immigrants, while it affirms her deep conviction of being an American insider. She emphasizes: "I had not one moment, not one inkling of the feeling, which stirred them, except as one feels for that which is noble and fine—outside one" (146–47). At the same time, however, her discovery of being a stranger to other immigrants implies a renewed conflict with the dominant culture that would like to see her as one of the newcomers instead of as one of the insiders. In this way, her entrance into Americanness can happen only on her own terms, only within the story of acculturation that she writes for herself about the dominant idiom and ideology, her ethnic past, and her vivid imagination of an ambivalent insider.

When Stern's heroine insists boldly that she is an American, she engages in a literal interpretation of her adopted country's ideology. She declares, "I had always felt that America was my birthright. . . . My mother country has always been—America" (147). Although she was brought over from the Old World and raised in the ghetto, she claims America already in her childhood: "The American flag has always seemed to me a personal possession as if I had been its Betsy Ross" (51). These affirmative and propagandistic statements show her ability to see herself as an insider, despite the fact that the dominant culture may refuse to do the same. However, her bold usurpation of Americanness also becomes proof of her inevitable metaphorical death to her ethnic parents, from whom she is pulled away by force of generational necessity. Although she pursues her dream of insiderism, she also acknowledges, "I had been caught in some eddy that had pulled me away for many years from that which was mine" (147). As a combination of individualistic choice and generational necessity, the narrator's bold Americanization entails fragmentation. Although she thinks she has left her ethnic past behind, she cannot erase it; it comes back to her embodied by her mother and her mother's pain when the two of them can no longer speak the same cultural language.

Although written in the bold tone of an insider, *My Mother and I* resounds with the frustrations of its confused heroine. On the one hand, it claims the new country, "colonizes" it for the immigrant girl-narrator, who stands alone, as if a conqueror of her newly discovered land. On the other hand, it expresses the alienation of Stern's heroine from any ties with other newcomers as she enters America. This fact makes her doubly other to the dominant culture concerned with defining its minorities as groups, not individuals. As a Jew, she is also an outsider among strangers because she does not have a "real" country of her ancestors beyond the ocean and because her only "mother tongue" is Yiddish—the dialect of exile, of Diaspora, and of homelessness unsuitable for expressing American patriotism. Therefore, in her desire to be American, to immerse herself in English—her "step-mother tongue"—she in fact makes the only available choice, escaping from alienation within the immigrant margin into alienation within the dominant culture. Whatever she does turns against her; she has to learn how to live among her conflicting identities, torn between the Old and the New Worlds.

While studying in New York, she realizes that she belongs neither to a Jewish circle nor to the "other circle," that of her American friends: "At the school in New York there was an entire group which had come from the Soho of New York—from the East Side. In the lecture hours they sat together. Walking they were companions. They had lunches at the same table. With me they were shy and embarrassed. Had I not understood I would have been bewildered and offended, but I realized that they were keeping me out of their life because they were afraid of the other circle of which I was a member" (143–44). To her Jewish peers the narrator is already too integrated to be an unproblematic companion. However, seeing that, she wants the impossible from her American life: "I did not wish to lose the one group at the school, nor the other. I wanted the American environment in which I felt at ease and happy, but I hoped also not to lose my old life" (144). As she realizes in the course of her story, she can be a member of both groups only in her own narrative, in which she writes her own "America."

## The Invader Claims Her America

At the beginning of her story, the narrator of *My Mother and I* identifies her position between the perspectives of the outsider and the insider: "I am writing this for *myself* and for those who, like me, are *America's foster-children, to remind us of them*, through whose pioneer courage the bright gates of this beautiful land of freedom were opened to us, and upon whose tumuli of grey and weary years of struggle *we, their children*, rose to our opportunities. I am writing to those . . . who will come after this devastating war to America, and to those who will receive them" (12, emphasis mine). By defining herself as one of "America's foster-children," Stern stresses her otherness as a newcomer and emphasizes the power of the dominant culture to adopt the immigrants. At the same time, by using the first-person plural—"we, their children"— she aligns herself with the dominant culture, which claims it was made by immigrants-colonists who adopted this land and gave it its ideological and economic power—its "bright gates of freedom" and "opportunities." This binary opposition informs the narrative of acculturation that Stern's heroine goes through; it becomes a catalyst for her subtext, unmaking the oppressive narrative model which, as she finds out through her authorship, has the power to both subdue and liberate her. The journey to this realization is written into the surface narrative of the immigrant rites of passage and reflects the main character's discovery and appropriation of American English—the idiom of assimilation—which separates her from her parents.[17]

### Rewriting the Immigrant Narrative

Looking closely at Stern's illustrations of the mixed blessings of woman's Americanization, the careful reader notices that *My Mother and I* is full of subtle stabs at the traditional immigrant story, as if the author wanted to show us her own authorial separation from the mode in which she was expected to write. For example, when the heroine sees the Atlantic Ocean for the first time, she resists any connection between this event and her crossing of it as a newcomer baby. Having heard about the passage from her parents, she can only fantasize about what other immigrants might feel, what she herself should have felt perhaps, having perceived "Lady Liberty": "I always *imagined* the entrance to America as a gleaming, vast expanse of water where tall ships came sailing in, to stop directly before Bartholdi's great statue of Liberty, that welcomes strangers at the gate to America" (18). Since she cannot remember it, she feels obliged to imagine her reaction, but in doing so she reveals the rather detached perspective of the insider talking about foreigners. A ship full of immigrants is for her "a ship bearing *strangers to us* in America" (150, emphasis mine). However, as an American she has to embrace otherness of the insiders who are alien to her parents and to her past. When she marries, she leaves her traditional Jewish mother for a WASP, "a *stranger* whose language she [her mother] did not understand [and whose] life she did not know" (160, emphasis mine). There is a finality to her act that is the logical outcome of her lifelong aspiration to Americanism, but that does not imply an unproblematic fulfillment of the miscegenation scenario. Interestingly, once she thinks she has separated herself from her roots, everybody is a stranger, even herself. The heroine's Americanization is an exercise in alienation and fragmentation, qualities not welcomed in the so-called "literature of the happy immigrant."

Nevertheless, the narrator's marriage can be read as another possible metaphor for an "immigrant crossing," but this time one within her adopted country. She thinks of her mother: "I left her, as she had left her mother when she went on the far voyage to America." The crossing and the Old World are seen as fairy tales and anecdotes that one is told by one's parents (160). Although unable to remember her coming to these shores, the narrator relives her passage not in the memories of immigrant ships, but in joining her life with an American male's. But she does not make a typical ethnic bride. She marries as an "American college woman" to have a typical American home. Therefore, her crossing does not entail two worlds—Old and New—but, rather, it takes place within the America that she has divided into her mother's sphere—the ghetto—and her own—the idealized "American home"—that she yearns to establish away from her parents' space (147–48). More generally then, Stern's story can be read as an account of any woman's, "everywoman's," separation from the maternal sphere and from the realm of the father.

This tendency to make her story open and, possibly, all-inclusive is stressed by the narrator's namelessness, which emphasizes not only her remoteness from her ethnic family and from their religious faith but also her anonymity as an "American woman." Consequently, an important component of the immigrant narrative, the rites of renaming in America, the ritual of shedding the Old World and taking on the New World name, are conspicuously absent. In fact, if we look around the heroine, no one has firmly attached names. Her mother is only "Mother"; just once a peddler calls her "Miss Sarah" (24). There are "Father" and numerous nameless siblings who die, sisters Fanny and Mary; there are many anonymous friends and relatives. The book's characters, one might argue, could thus be anybody, and the story Stern presents to the reader may be seen as open—to be peopled by any ethnic group, to relate any woman's story.

The inevitable element in the traditional narrative, the American lover, is nameless, too, and thus unspecified as a descendant of any earlier immigrants. "I did not describe my lover except to tell my parents that he was an American," says the narrator, who, after all, is an American, too. However, there are hints of a class and ethnic difference that overshadow the young couple's superficially unproblematic sense of all-inclusive nationality. The bride-to-be admits: "I would not permit my lover to tell *his people* about us until he had seen my home, my folks, *my environment.* With all the new and beautiful and intimate meaning that an American home held to me I went to my mother's home in Soho to wait for him there" (154, emphasis mine). She goes back to the home she rejected before because to her future husband she is still an immigrant woman defined by her roots in the ghetto and she has to accept that. Interestingly, she calls her home in Soho "my mother's," as if her return were limited to the return into the mother's sphere only. (In fact, after the argument when the father tried to prevent her from going to school in New York, he disappears from the story completely.) After her marriage, the mother's house is the only space that used to be hers to which the young woman can refer from within what is clearly her husband's home and life: "My home is that kind of home in which *he has always lived.* With my marriage I entered into a new avenue" (161, emphasis mine). Her new life as an American wife and mother, as a working woman, happens in the shadow of another man-husband-"father," one whom the emancipated heroine of *I Am a Woman—and a Jew,* for instance, will have to fight for his New World paternalism almost as hard as she has fought her Old World rabbi-father. As if to emphasize the ambivalence of miscegenation, its inadequacy as an ending, Stern does not close her novel with the wedding but with a reunion of the mother and the daughter.

They meet, after years of separation, in the narrator's "unpretentious but pretty" house, "situated in a charming old suburb of an American city where attractive modern residences stand by the side of stately old Colonial houses, as if typifying young America in the shadow of old America" (12). Their reunion in this generic American middle-class "anywhere" is sadly unsuccessful. They no longer have a language in common because the narrator cannot explain her new world and her new identity to her mother, nor can the mother expect her grown-up daughter to share the ghetto life's pain and everyday struggle any more. This last meeting echoes the mother's questions before the wedding about her future son-in-law, questions that remained unanswered ("And are his people very different from us?"), because the daughter could not translate her lover's difference to her parents. That first encounter between the narrator's mother (the father is conspicuously absent) and her daughter's lover is not much of a meeting, though: "They tried to speak to one another. And my lover knew only English, and my mother only Yiddish. They had no common plane on which to meet. . . . Even in me each saw a different person" (160). The narrator's marriage is thus another illustration of her fragmentation—another intercultural passage, another removal further away from her mother's sphere: "So we were married. And mother said good-bye to me" (160–61).

When the mother comes to see her daughter's baby boy, who supposedly represents the Old America and the New, instead of a hopeful message about the growth of a new generation, we read about the daughter's and mother's sorrow upon the realization that they are even further apart because of this child of two worlds. The narrator hopes for a happy ending before the mother's visit and then sees it dissolve in her inevitable disillusionment: "Mother called to little son a quaint love name, and he turned to her with his bright smile. . . . Then he quietly turned away from her to his toys again. . . . And mother stood there in that strange white baby world which was her grandson's. . . . She was afraid to touch the crib, to soil the spotless rugs. Here was her grandchild, they were together, it is true. And her grandchild had no need of her. She felt alien, unnecessary. . . . I felt tears in my eyes" (164–65). Instead of a positive closure to the daughter's story, we witness the mother's drama when she sees a symbolic end of her traditional family line in this little boy with whom she cannot communicate: "You say he speaks, daughter. I do not understand the words he means to say now. And—he will never learn— learn my language." At this point the mother's and the daughter's stories are juxtaposed as separate and isolated with more insistence than anywhere else in the novel. It is as if, at the end of her narrative, Stern were showing us how the metaphorical death of the mother's world has to follow that of the heroine who has abandoned it for her America.[18]

"She did not understand," says the narrator about her mother's wonder and surprise at her daughter's American home, friends, lifestyle: "In this short visit of hers, for the first time mother saw me as that which I had always wished to be, an American woman at the head of an American home. But our home is a home which, try as I may, we can not make home to mother. She has seen come to realization those things which she helped me to attain, and she cannot share, not even understand, them" (168). Instead of a happy ending, Stern's text offers the mother's metaphorical erasure. And in causing and witnessing this erasure the daughter obliterates a part of herself. In her little grandson's nursery, the ghetto mother finally realizes that she has "died" for her child many years ago and that she does not and will not truly exist for her daughter's little boy. Although within the same country, they are separated by an insurmountable barrier of cultural and generational difference. The mother's story can be thus read as an antinarrative running parallel to her daughter's ambivalent Americanization. It surfaces in the end and destroys any possibility for a happy resolution. In fact, Stern's title, *My Mother and I*, suggests the simultaneity of the two narratives and implies the mother's story as the one that sets up and gives momentum to the daughter's.

Therefore, the price for the narrator's new life is largely paid by the mother —the inspirer of and the conspirator in her daughter's Americanization. The heroine's realization of the mother's pain and of the necessity to continue to inflict and endure it is the cost of making it on her own, of maintaining her ambivalent identity amid her America. One of the reviews notes that Stern's book can be read as an account of the mother's "pain and separation."[19] Despite the first-person narrative, we can read the story of the mother's suffering and sacrifice between the lines of the daughter's. She appears as a lone and heroic figure who gives her child willingly to the culture and life she does not know and cannot understand. When they attend the baccalaureate sermon at a college, the daughter asks, "Do you want me to be like them?" (meaning the beautiful crowd of happy graduates). The mother's affirmative answer means a declaration "to give me to that strange new womanhood of America" (115–16).

While she watches her daughter grow more and more alien to her, the mother is cruelly and inevitably left behind. But so are the past and the legendary girl with a name we never learn, who once crossed the Atlantic to come to America with other immigrants and who was to be her mother's joy and support. The young American woman whom her mother visits after years of separation seems to be hardly her flesh and blood. The two women confronting each other at the end of Stern's novel are strangers, although they both collaborated to make "this woman that I am, this woman mother helped me to become" (168). The heroine's fragmented American self is a product of both the mother's and the daughter's stories, even though these stories are written in different languages and run along tracks that cannot converge.

The unsuccessful meeting between the mother and the daughter at the end of Stern's novel symbolizes not only the narrator's confrontation with her ethnic past but also with her "mother tongue," in which she used to communicate with her parents but which she had to forego to embrace the language of the dominant culture. The fact that she cannot "translate" her new world for her mother during their reunion prompts the actual writing of her story, as if the narrator were trying to explain on paper what she has failed to convey in their conversations. Because the mother's visit binds the opening and closure of *My Mother and I*, its focus on language suggests that the movement from the mother tongue into the dominant idiom is central for Stern's narrative of immigrant fragmentation. By retracing her passage from the ghetto to her model American middle-class home, the narrator also retraces her linguistic transformation that ends with a symbolic death of her mother tongue—the erasure of her ethnicity.

The first part of the book, all of which is written in the eloquent and educated language of the insider who is versatile in the central idiom, describes the narrator's family life in the ghetto tenements, their economic struggles, and her parents' occasional memories of the Old World. The ethnic otherness of the heroine-narrator is remembered in vivid pictures from the past: the one-room apartment in which the whole family began their American Dream, the father's face grown tired over his Hebrew books, the mother's patient cooking by the stove to feed numerous babies, the streets of the ghetto teeming with crowds and peddlers' carts, the faces of illiterate immigrant women waiting for the narrator to read and translate letters for them. "Those old pictures!"—exclaims the heroine at the beginning of her tale, as if looking through an album of faded photographs. "Somehow they had all been wiped out from my mind by the beautiful new things in my life." "I am so happy, so blessed," she adds, as if to emphasize once more the double perspective of an insider and outsider who seems not to remember ancient history at one moment, but who reconstructs it rather vividly immediately thereafter (13). Significantly, she switches to first-person plural right after this statement, once she begins remembering "our" past, the collective meaning of which perhaps could not be described in the happy singular voice of an assimilated "American."

In both *My Mother and I* and *I Am a Woman—and a Jew* the writer-narrator sees the language of her parents' new country—which they themselves never learn—as a means to educational success and as a vital tool to construct and express her new American identity. English is not so much the language she grows up with, as she is raised speaking Yiddish, but the language that grows *on* her while she is going to school, talking to other ghetto children who substitute it more and more for their parents' dialect while playing forbidden games in the streets and tenement courts. English—a symbol of the dominant culture's pervading influence on the second generation of immigrants—erects a wall between the narrator and her parents; it marks and verbalizes both the new life of the child and the metaphorical death of her parents, who came too late to learn to translate their Old World foreignness into the idiom of the dominant culture.

As a child, Stern's heroine can still run away from school, back to the enclave that her ghetto-dwelling, Yiddish- and Polish-speaking family provides, to the familiar world of her mother and father. In her parents' home she can even indirectly communicate with the Old World by means of writing letters for her mother's illiterate women friends (31–43). The letter writing puts her in touch with the "far corners of the world" and makes her first realize the intercultural dramas that are taking place in her most immediate environment, the dramas in which she is also a heroine: "Those who replied to letters I wrote had, it appeared, the same troubles (no matter in which city or on what continent they lived) as had our neighbours next door to us, or on the floor above us" (43). But the "wide, wide world" that opens to the narrator within the ghetto brings about both a global and an individual perspective which, although multilingual at the beginning, can later be described only in the educated American English that estranges her from her family. In the course of her ambivalent Americanization, the narrator finds out that these two perspectives—the global (multilingual) and the individual (American English) further fragment her already split identity.

Stern's heroine, then, develops a sense of two separate spheres within her one country: America in the wider world and the ghetto in America. On the individual level her growing up is a constant shuffling between these spheres—the ethnic home that she can identify with less and less and the world of her educated American friends that she enters more and more confidently as she distances herself from her parents' influence. Consequently, the only idiom she has available to express this split is her very proper, educated English, which projects a comfortable insider, on the one hand, and a suppressed ethnic increasingly less able to speak in her mother tongue, on the other. Thus her text projects a conflict between the content of her story, the ethnic part, and the language used to describe it, the insider's idiom that brings about and embodies the ethnic outsider's metaphorical death.

We can see this conflict in the narrator's reluctance to identify basic details of her background. At the beginning of her story, the narrator confesses to having invented a fictitious name, Soho, for the actual "sorry district" in the "ghetto of a city in the middle west" where her family lived (15). Not only does she abstain from reproducing the language of her characters, but she also substitutes fictional names for actual ones and does not even name herself, her parents, and the place where they live, as if to make them and their environment as generic as possible. For example, while looking back at her early childhood, Stern describes typical ghetto scenes: "I can never remember my mother in my childhood in any other than one of two positions, standing at the stove cooking, or sitting in the corner; her foot rocking the cradle, and her hands stitching, stitching. . . . On rare occasions when mother was obliged to leave the house she would tie Fanny to one leg of the table, and me to the other. It was most uncomfortable all around, and especially to the neighbours, for we two children protested with the full power of our lungs until mother would return" (21). Although presented with sincerity and warm sentiment, the images of the poor, hard-working mother and the two screaming girls are subdued and softened by the balanced and composed language. The "pictures" she presents are static and seem remote and almost indifferent to the narrator, who recalls that the situation she describes was "most uncomfortable." Her emphasis on the neighbors' discomfort indicates her concern with how their environment perceived them rather than with how she and her sister really felt when they were left alone. In writing her account, the narrator speaks like an educated American woman, one of those who might pick up her book out of interest in "exotic" immigrant lore. Just as she has learned at school that Americanization "had nothing at all to do with the little kitchen in Soho," the narrator now uses language that has little to do with her subject matter (45). Unlike Yezierska, Stern does not attempt any American Yiddish vernacular; her language is cool and measured, without the passionate outbursts that so characteristically mark the ethnic intensity of Yezierska's texts. And yet, although Yezierska's "barbaric yawp" was often too much for the critics, Stern's "Gentile" way of writing did not win approval either, since it was not "authentic" enough.

It is possible, as Dearborn suggests, to express ethnicity even by means of the dominant idiom (*PD* 43). In some respects, that is precisely what Mary Antin accomplished in *The Promised Land* with her passionate account of Jewish life in Russia written in, possibly, an English even more impeccable than Stern's. But *My Mother and I* shows how the only "ethnicity" that the dominant idiom can adequately express is an Americanized one; the fragmented and frustrated one that marks the "death" of the original ethnic narrator. Thus, to a certain extent, Stern's heroine seems imprisoned within her immaculate English, which makes her less and less able to communicate with her parents and older relatives while she is growing up and which also makes the Old World characters metaphorically mute in her story.[20] Written without clearly punctuated emotional outbursts, the whole book speaks about the tragic severance of ties with Judaism and with traditional East European Jewish family ways in the acquisition of English and the culture that follows. In her descriptions of the ghetto children playing, Stern shows how the slow erasure of their background begins as English sifts into the playground lingo: "Though my intercourse with my elders was in Yiddish, in the street we little folk spoke a curious jargon Yiddish and English. It was almost a dialect, and later as a big girl in the sixth grade I once sorely puzzled the teacher by spelling bananas 'pennennies,' that being the Soho version of the name of the fruit. . . . I learned also at school of strange things altogether different from those father and mother knew. Indeed, much that was taught us by our teacher had nothing at all to do with the little kitchen in Soho" (44–45). The isolated Soho version of the word "banana" is the only trace of the dialect Stern recalls but cannot reproduce because it is a part of her foregone past. Her American education proves that the public school system could indeed spell miracles for the second-generation immigrants in helping them integrate, but it also reveals the insistence of the dominant culture on remaking the newcomers, on erasing their alien ethnicity in the efforts to produce uniform and compatible Americans. This idea of the melting pot might seem attractive as a theory, but, as Stern shows us, it meant virtual death to the immigrant's ethnicity in the process of his or her Americanization.

The most powerful metaphor describing such ethnic erasure can be found on the first page of *I Am a Woman—and a Jew*, where the narrator describes her father's funeral: "I remember looking down at the face of my father, beautiful and still in death, and for a brief, terrible moment feeling my heart rise up—surely it was in a strange, suffocating relief?—as the realization came to me: 'Now I am free!'" (1). The ambivalent relief expressed in the narrator's well-punctuated English arises from a conviction that her rabbi-father, who has always loomed like "an image of fine-carved stone, immovable, unbending, demanding that I submit my will and my thought," wanted to sacrifice everything, even her happiness, to uphold the creeds of Old World Judaism. It is only now that he is "at peace at least," and so is she, the daughter who has forsaken the "language of the Jews" for her passionate pursuit of English and Americanization (1).

As a symbol of her Jewishness and Old World roots, the narrator's father in *I Am a Woman—and a Jew* also represents her ethnic language, and his death can thus be seen as its metaphorical obliteration. As Sander Gilman stresses, language has been historically a "marker of Jewish difference," and it is this linguistic difference that has to be removed if a rabbi's daughter wants to be accepted in a culture created by Christian Founding Fathers. The young woman's Yiddish and Hebrew have to be replaced with English, her Jewishness has to be removed in order for her to become American. Thus the feeling of relief at her father's death marks the symbolic death of the narrator's ethnicity, while her ability to use only sophisticated English to describe this scene is proof of that death. The dominant idiom that the narrator embraces so readily erases her while accepting because, by using it, she participates in its cultural "violence" against her ethnic group. Gilman stresses that the language of the Western culture "provides all the vocabularies of difference in Western Europe and North America" and, through its "Christianized" rhetoric, makes the "negative image of difference of the Jew found in the Gospel into the central referent for all definitions of difference in the West."[21] Therefore, by using English to narrate their acculturation—the erasure of their difference—Stern's narrators in both novels describe their own ethnic deaths with the idiom that embodies this death. Nevertheless, as we have seen in the case of Mary Antin, this "death" does not have to mean obliteration of the ethnic's memory; the past cannot be erased as easily as a dialect or a way or life and, for a careful reader, can light up even the most repressive idiom used to narrate it.

### Paying the Price

Although she reaches back into her past and recreates warm familial scenes in appealing English, the narrator of *My Mother and I* feels acutely alone as the first truly assimilated member of her family. In a sense, she seems to be not the chronological second-generation immigrant—her parents' child—but a more remote and estranged third-generation insider. We can see, then, a generational dynamic in Stern's narrator's fervent assimilation, the rhetoric of which suggests that she has made a leap into a "redemptive third generation." In his analysis of this type of generational dynamics in American culture, Werner Sollors states that a "generation is first and foremost a mental concept which has been experienced as well as used to interpret experience throughout American history." According to Sollors's approach, the traditional immigrant movement from the first, to the second, to the third generation is ideological rather than historical because it is based more on a theory of consent rather than descent. In Marcus Lee Hansen's "Law," this third generation represents the ideal; it has the power to redeem the first one, reconcile it with the usually rebellious second, and pragmatically choose for itself whatever best qualities of the two preceding generations it desires (*BE* 214–21). In this context, America can be seen as *born* out of the rebellion of the second generation against its British "fathers," but as *formed* by the truly American third generation's conscious choice of ideology and ancestry.

A newcomer may skip generational gaps *within* the dominant culture for ideological reasons, because, although one may be "numerically second generation," one may nevertheless choose to be the third "in spirit" (*BE* 210, 219). Stern defies her Old World parents as a historical second generation, but chooses to feel completely assimilated and to return to some selective aspects of her past as the ideologically motivated third who narrates her ethnic death. In doing so she also illustrates the effects such choices have on the immigrant woman's identity.

Her mother's visit triggers the narrator's storytelling; it brings back confusing pictures and feelings from her seemingly "dead" past that are channeled through the power of writing. The narrator realizes that their worlds are different, that she has grown apart from her parent; and yet she realizes, too, that the silenced mother is one of the major "problems" in her story, perhaps even a catalyst for writing it or its coauthor.

### In the Name of the Mother

Stern's awareness that her story interconnects with her mother's becomes visible in a scene in which the narrator recalls her introduction to the "real American home" and to the "strange" American mother of her native-born friend:

> There was no mother whom I had ever seen in Soho who could approach my mother. I was very proud of the little curls blowing about her rosy cheeks, of her trim, plump, little figure in its close fitting waist and apron. . . . All my standards fell before the vision of the strange mother I saw at a party given by my classmate. . . . A woman in *white*! Why, mothers dressed in brown and in black, I always knew. And this mother sang to us. She romped through the two-steps with us. . . . I had always thought mothers never "enjoyed," just worked. *This strange mother opened a new window to me in the possibilities of women's lives.* To my eyes my mother's life appeared all at once as something to be pitied—to be questioned. (110, emphasis mine)

Superficially, the two images of the ethnic and the American mother are another in a series of binary oppositions pertaining to the heroine-narrator's fragmented identity. However, as a close reading of the quote reveals, the two mothers are inseparable, even becoming one, as the narrator moves from the description of the ethnic to the American. The "plump, little figure" of the ghetto mother provides the necessary contrast for the attractive American— "this strange mother" who "sang to *us*" and "romped through the two-steps with *us*" (emphasis mine). The use of the first-person plural projects the narrator's identification with the "us"—the American mother's children. This identification foreshadows her abandonment of the ethnic mother who symbolizes the Old World. The narrator's choice of seductive America—an attractive "stepmother"—is easier because of her ethnic mother's unattractive life, which should be "pitied" and "questioned." It is this combination of the two contrasting yet inseparable images of the ghetto and the American mother that truly defines what she wants to be as a woman, that has really "opened a new window" to the narrator in "the possibilities of women's lives."

The attraction she feels for American ways and people causes the narrator to hurt her flesh-and-blood mother with the overawed description of the American woman's superior qualities. The hurt is intended, as the narrator is aware of a strange need to make her mother realize how inferior she now seems to her daughter. Although she says, "Somehow I was afraid that mother would be hurt at the picture of that white-gowned, laughing, young mother," she goes on to describe it to her: "I dropped my own [eyes] until I had finished; I could not endure to see that strange look which for the first time in my life, mother turned to me" (111). Thus, while consciously wounding her mother's feelings, she chooses a stepmother America over her parent and consents to pay the price for it. Paying the price obviously entails not so much the suffering of the narrator herself, but rather her enduring the necessity to inflict the pain on her mother. This cruelty results from the fact that neither Stern's heroine nor her parents have any other choice in the Promised Land. For the narrator, that is what *her* country is about; the separation between generations is at the roots of Americanness with its migrations over the territories that are both geographical and linguistic. The parents have to be left behind while their child explores the frontiers unattainable to them.

However, despite this necessity to be left behind, the female parent becomes a fellow conspirator in the young woman's Americanization because she is connected to her not only as the "transitional" Old World–America mother, but also as the woman of the first generation who lives her impossible assimilation vicariously through her daughter's success, who can thus "enjoy" the fruits of her unglamorous "work." Therefore, although they may not have a language in common, the mother and the daughter write the child's American story together: "I could think of no words which I could say to [Father]. . . . It was mother who, due to her natural quickness and her deep sympathy with all her children, *understood*. She did not question whither my desires would lead me, nor what part she would have in their consummation. Mother and I were always chums. Though she could not read one word of English *there was not one book I read of which she did not know the narrative*. She knew my 'marks' at school. She knew my friends. She hated and loved my teachers as I did. It was as if she lived my life with me" (85–86, emphasis mine). The mother works as a "buffer" for her ambitious daughter and always takes her side against her stubborn and tyrannical rabbi-father. Despite the fact that the passage describing this mother-daughter alliance anticipates another, in which the heroine bemoans the inevitable loss of her mother in the course of her cultural crossing ("I thought it was Soho I was leaving behind me. But mother—not mother"), her narrative continues to hinge on the presences and absences of her female parent, who provides the necessary generational context for and perpetuates the young woman's independent story. But, as it becomes clear later in the narrator's life, the "diverging point of her life and mine" does not mark the separation of the mother's and the daughter's narratives but anticipates the moment when the two become one in Stern's text (131–33).

The inseparability of the mother's story and the daughter's narrative of acculturation is projected through the language describing their deathlike separation as the price one must pay for Americanization—the pain that both parent and child endure within the generational movement into the New World. The narrator's recollections of the past bring back the pain she felt she had to inflict on her parents and on herself in order to prove that, as her high school teacher told her, she could "make [her]self an American woman, no matter whether my parents or environment were American or not" (112).

Interestingly, she is henceforth repeating the actions of her mother who, many years ago, had to abandon her own parents to get married and to go to America: "She had lived near her mother . . . but on that wedding day she did not foresee that four years later she was to leave her mother as one leaves the dead, for she came to America, and her mother died without ever seeing her again" (155). These two women's stories—so distant and yet so similar in sharing the narrative of separation from the mother (and the motherland)— are two versions of the same tale describing female Americanization. No matter in what way she enters America, whether she lets herself be assimilated or not, an immigrant woman has to go through the metaphorical death of her parents—generational separation—and, since she dies to them because of her geographical removal or ideological estrangement, the death of herself to them as well. Yet even in separation she remains connected to her parents. This is especially true of the immigrant daughter, for the same narrative pattern writes her life and her mother's. Obviously, this model must be, to some degree, true of all newcomers, but it is perhaps more poignant in females whose gender roles imply giving life, nurturing, and caring—familial continuity rather than severance of ties. Consequently, once Stern's narrator has to leave her mother, when her education and new friendships take her further and further away from the sphere of her loving parent, she also breaks away from the traditional gendered narrative of her culture. She chooses independence and emancipation over the pious duties of a Jewish wife and mother who serves others instead of pursuing her own ambitions.

In contrasting the mother's and the daughter's narratives, Stern's novel emphasizes further the first-generation parents' necessary "death" to their third-generation child. Yet *My Mother and I* also describes a metaphorical death of the seemingly unproblematic and assimilated narrator. When she wants to tell her mother about a surprise birthday party her college friends gave her, she realizes that "the words lay dead upon my tongue" (133). It is her mother tongue that thus figuratively dies in this utterance, but also herself as a "new woman" who cannot ever become "alive" to the mother left behind in the ghetto. For now she does not exist in any other idiom than English. The narrator's desire to leave Soho and go to college opens another chasm between her and her parents. She tells them she feels no longer at home: "It's like living in a foreign land here" (139). To the family council, which deliberates over whether she is setting a bad example for her siblings and cousins, she wishes to say a lot, but she cannot speak at all and lets her mother do the talking for her: "When I would enter a room to find a group heatedly discussing me, mother would begin to speak in the sudden dead silence, nervously, without stopping, amidst all the unspoken disapproval, until I left" (142). In the absence of adequate language in which the narrator can explain herself to her "dead" ethnic past, her mother becomes a translator of her daughter's and, to some extent, her own story.

The narrator's fierce determination to follow through with her separation from the ghetto manifests itself in her desire to be American in every way. Realizing the price for her Americanization that her mother has to pay, the daughter decides to hide some parts of her story from her loving parent. While in school, the girl throws away the "ethnic" lunches wrapped in indecorous newspaper that her devoted mother prepares for her every day. Having come back home, she refuses to speak anything but English. In spite of this, just as her mother does for her in the family council, the daughter is able to translate her new experience for her mother. Her past chatty conversations with her mother are now replaced with her translating the English stories and newspapers to her awed parent: "My books were doors that gave me entrance into another world. Often I think that I did not grow up in the ghetto but in the books I read as a child in the ghetto. The life in Soho passed me by and did not touch me, once I began to read. . . . Books built a world, fanciful and strange, for mother and me, when I sat, translating to her word for word from the story before me. . . . However, she told me that such a little girl as I must not desire such wonderful things" (71–72).

The desire to become like people in her English books is so strong that the narrator admits her willingness to exchange the fantasy world for the reality of the ghetto. Unconsciously she has already started to invent her new life and identity, as if she were writing herself as a heroine in an American storybook. In this sense, these occasions when she reads to her mother become their first exercises in separation; the girl can translate the stories "word for word," but she can never make her mother inhabit them the way she is able to as an "American." The mother's warning about the "wonderful things" attests to her realization of this fact; it also points to the paradoxical intertwining of their seemingly incompatible and yet same stories of female immigration.

Despite their generational separation, both mother and daughter coauthor Stern's heroine's new life. By providing the space for her dreams and cheering the girl on in her desire for strange, "wonderful things" that her parents cannot understand, the mother makes her daughter's narrative possible. She also provides her literally with "a room of her own" by designating the special "Sabbath" parlor for the exclusive use of the avid scholar, into which the girl "migrates" already within her parents' home, building her own world apart without even realizing the foreshadowing that this implies (100). In the girl's first writing exercises, the mother is a necessary mediator and translator between her daughter and the Polish and Jewish women for whom the girl writes and translates letters. This maternal assistance makes it possible for the girl to indulge in her first creative texts—writing passionate love letters, heartwrenching condolences, and persuasive pleas, which the writer endows with more than their due share of rich rhetoric and flowery metaphors (32–43). Throughout the narrative letters are also exchanged between the mother and the daughter that weave threads connecting their stories back to the moments when they seem to break away from each other for good. Therefore, although she proclaims and mourns their inevitable separation, Stern's narrator actually proves that it is through writing—perhaps fictionalizing and withholding parts of the truth—that the mother and the daughter remain together in a subtext to the official narrative of their separation inscribed within the larger text of a woman's story.

## Beyond the Fathers

The narrator's realization that becoming an American woman involves the inevitable pain of separation from her mother and her nurturing ethnic roots also informs the way she sees her relationship with her father. In contrast to her textual connection with the mother, there is a definite writing out, or crossing out, of the father from the narrative of the third-generation insider. For example, her initiation into "girlhood" is via Alcott's *Little Women*, for which she boldly abandons the Yiddish novelettes her father wants her to read. She knows he desperately wants her to preserve her Jewishness, and thus, she rejects her father's word—both the readings he would like her to peruse and the ideology of female conduct he professes (69–70). The narrator-I renounces her male parent and the Jewish heritage he stands for as a patriarch and a rabbi.[22]

Her successful education and scholarly achievements make the narrator into a vehement enthusiast of democracy founded by American "fathers." We can see her desire to enter the world of the books she reads, to live within the realm of the English language and the native-borns, as a rejection of her own parents:

> There was nothing that seemed to me more wonderful than to have been born of parents that were Americans. Some of my classmates had names which had been the names of children when first Plymouth Rock was touched by the first immigrants of America. On Decoration Day girls and boys who sat by my side in school went with their parents to place flowers on the graves of members of their *families*. The sorrows, the dead of their land, her pride were their sorrows and their pride. Sometimes at home it seemed to me impossible that I could be in the same city with those children who were of, and part of, America. (107)

Although she cannot change her parents' Jewish names into Anglo-Saxon ones, the heroine makes sure that her "ancestral envy" is made up for with her American education. When she goes to college, it seems "as if I had in truth been born anew. . . . I learned that *I was an American college woman*. . . . I grew into American womanhood" (117, emphasis mine). Yet in her stubborn pursuit of education against all odds, the daughter actually resembles her scholar-father and, as she admits, follows masculine vocations and ambitions that upset her traditional family and their world, which is split neatly into two gendered spheres. She calls herself a "spoiled tomboy" and dreams about joining that "line [which] held only boys," who "strode up to a certain corner, turned, and disappeared from sight" on their way to school (29, 47). Her ambitions to embrace America are also curiously fed in the classroom of her Hebrew school, where she is "the only girl" and where she learns about American patriotism amid the "Oriental atmosphere" of Judaism (51–52). Prompted by the attractiveness of a seemingly less repressive American patriarchy—girls can go to school there—she chooses between the Old and the New World "fathers." However, in her choice she does not follow the dominant culture's paradigm of assimilation uncritically, but having completed her metaphorical, ambivalent "immigrant" journey, she invents her own version of Americanness. In this way, she becomes like the descendants of Plymouth Rock, no matter if the actual descendants object to her. By thus usurping the dominant ideology and fictionalizing it for herself, however, Stern's heroine is in conflict with the patriarchal dominant culture, which, as we have seen, objected to immigrants' taking too much for granted.[23] Her high school mentor's fatherly suggestion that "you must be the interpreter of the old to the new world, and of the new to the old" is disregarded, as the girl declines to interpret the Old World patriarchy to the New.

She vehemently refuses to follow her father's orders to leave school and to prepare for a Jewish marriage; in fact, she has to defy her whole family in order to prevail and continue her schooling away from home (112–15). The narrator's desire to leave home—and what it represents of her ethnic and religious roots—is incomprehensible to her father. Her refusal to "interpret" the father to her America, or her America to him, results from a conviction that they would never understand each other. As he admits himself, he belongs to the fifteenth century and his daughter to the twentieth. "Mother and I could not make him understand," the girl says after another argument when he chastises her for rejecting the ways of her people. His is the "proper" ethnic way of preserving the Old World customs as an enclave within the melting pot that graciously makes him a citizen. He would like his daughter to marry a Jew and be a good wife and mother, but in order to claim her America, the narrator has to cut herself off from this father who blocks her way into the future on her own terms: "Father could not even see that what I hated, nor why I loathed it. He liked the 'happy crowds' of dirty, pitifully underfed children 'playing' in the filthy gutters; he did not even perceive the unspeakable plumbing in the yards about us. . . . For him the ghetto, so real to me and to other young people like me, does not exist. For father lives in a world altogether cut off from the world about him; his is a world of the past, built by the ancient rabbis in whose footsteps he walks" (139–40).

This denial of her male parent is openly cruel and defiant; the father seems to be a scapegoat embodying all that the narrator despises about the ghetto—both the material poverty and sentiment for the "happy crowds" in their little Old World enclave. However, the changing tenses in the passage quoted above suggest a split in the narrator. She uses the past tense to describe her loathing of the environment where she grew up, the place where her father has decided to spend the rest of his life. Then she switches to the present to describe the world in which her father "lives," the world of a nostalgic past created by rabbis and scholars, the world she comes from and has left. In this way, she writes her story as an adult, looking back into her past, both rejecting parts of and trying to embrace some of the ethnicity embodied by her father and the unbending patriarchal tradition he represents. At the same time, she looks up to her new country as a foster father of sorts and embraces its ideology. This ambivalence is the price she pays for becoming and being an "American woman," a state that can be understood only through direct experience of the contradictions it contains.

The American womanhood the narrator desires to embrace is not only the cause of her conflict with her father. It is also the condition that, paradoxically, brings her closer to her mother while foreshadowing their inevitable separation. Caught between their need to erase the father and their desire to hold on to some of the values he represents, both mother and daughter find themselves collaborating once again to make the young woman's narrative of Americanization possible. They win against the unbending patriarchy despite the father's refusal to let the girl go to college. Their joint victory indicates that he is pushed out not only from his daughter's sphere but also, to some extent, from his wife's. This rejection of the father's values follows in the wake of the heroine's own symbolic cultural death—her ethnic uprooting and her feminist defiance of patriarchal power—which she has to experience in order to become part of the New World. This implies both her own metaphorical erasure and her father's, while simultaneously suggesting a paradoxical dependence on the past and the male parent whose scholarly zeal and stubbornness the daughter inherits and uses to push him away. As was the case with her impossible separation from her mother, the narrator learns that the "death" of one's cultural identity does not preclude a certain resurrection of the past, that it is possible to be of two worlds, even though this means living a conflict.

Stern's conflicting approaches to her textual oppression as an immigrant woman writer are very much like Antin's and Yezierska's; her texts seem to carry forth the tradition opened up by Antin and to anticipate Yezierska's ambivalent treatment of female acculturation; they even foresee Eva Hoffman's preoccupation with language and the past seen as generational heritage in *Lost in Translation*. Different from these others, however, Stern is able to convey the immigrant conflict—the fragmentation in the ethnic-and-insider woman's identity—more fully by showing how the dominant culture always marginalizes such a woman because of her gender and ethnicity. She emphasizes that the woman's own ethnic group—Jewish and Polish—often rejects her as too Americanized and pushes her to make an impossible choice between the two inseparable identities that comprise her. Stern's heroine's ability to come to terms with the marginality and fragmentation induced by both the dominant culture she feels a part of and the ethnic group she cannot completely abandon leads to a wholeness, a paradoxical identity based on her cultural split and perpetuated by the conflicts within which she has to live. This precarious wholeness is projected through her text, which in itself is a collection of conflicting readings and fragmented narratives unmaking one another. The narrator discovers the oppressive "chains" binding her to her past as well as the ones linking her to America, but she can still make the best of her ambivalent predicament; she can turn it into powerful texts that convey her struggle and make it worth the fight for the women writers who come after her.

*My Mother and I* is perpetuated by the heroine's resistance to the traditional immigrant narrative, which she has to both follow and rewrite if she wants to work out an identity that is uniquely her own. The heroine-narrator does not want to be an immigrant—a fragmented alien self—and that is why she constructs herself as complete, her own complex and American self; she chooses living in conflict and being aware of it instead of pretending that it could be resolved. Although this action calls for adopting the dominant idiom, she chooses the "stepmother tongue" consciously, to be able to tell her story herself rather than agree to being "melted" in the typical narrative, which would require a make-believe marginal idiom. She does not follow the classic rites of passage and resists mediation into the culture she knows she can take on her own. Stern's text is proof that such insolent usurpation of America is the only way an alien woman can avoid the humiliating process of acculturation on the dominant culture's terms.

Such a reading of Stern makes us realize how much the critical discourse about immigrant writers has been an artificial construct, how it has followed certain narrative patterns that suppress textual conflicts and tensions in its expectations concerning such texts as *My Mother and I*. As the recipient culture and the powerful center able to grant or withhold entry, America, with its literary canons, its people's expectations, its laws, has dictated the rules for the newcomer. We have been looking at the "strangers" from within the confident center and have expected the immigrants without to translate everything into our familiar language. Stern, and earlier Mary Antin, appeared to do just that and were accused of lacking the "protesting voice" (*PD* 42). However, it is not that the voice was absent but that the reading has not gone far enough beyond the clichés we have constructed ourselves and expect to find in every immigrant text. Instead of requiring instant intercultural translation, we could have tried learning the language of the newcomer's complex experience.

# Beyond the Happy Endings

ANZIA YEZIERSKA REWRITES

THE NEW WORLD WOMAN

This is a story with an unhappy ending. And I too
have become Americanized enough to be terrified
of unhappy endings. Yet I have to drop all my work to
write it.—Anzia Yezierska, "Wild Winter Love"

## Critical Ends and Happy Endings

**W**riting after Mary Antin's *The Promised Land* and Elizabeth Stern's *My Mother and I*, another Polish-Jewish immigrant author, Anzia Yezierska (c. 1885–1970), emerges in the 1920s as a new voice in the tradition of East European women's writing with her best-selling short story collection *Hungry Hearts* (1920). In her employment of what can be called a typical female newcomer's narrative, she continues and develops the story-writing techniques that, as I have demonstrated, both compartmentalize and liberate Antin's and Stern's autobiographical texts. Yezierska's skillful use of these well-established narrative models to construct popular "immigrant realism"—vivid pictures of the Lower East Side and its Jewish inhabitants presented in a stylized English-Yiddish dialect—produced a variety of texts, from short stories, to novels, to autobiographies, all of which also lend themselves to close readings and inquiries into narrative subtexts. In contrast to Antin and Stern, however, Yezierska makes the issues of gender and authorship not only central but pivotal for her books depicting female Americanization, and she shows how these issues intertwine with the literal and figurative immigrant journeys that an ethnic woman writer has to pursue in American culture.

Anzia Yezierska's heroines are usually self-made ethnic women who escape the constraints of patriarchal Judaism represented by Orthodox rabbi-fathers and, like Sara Smolinsky in the semiautobiographical *Bread Givers*, leave the ghetto for education, American life, and an inevitable Americanized marriage. Despite her renewed popularity in the last two decades, when her books have been republished and reintroduced onto reading lists, the academic debate about Yezierska has produced as much praise as criticism. For instance, while Carol B. Schoen, Mary V. Dearborn, and Alice Kessler-Harris praise her for constructing liberated and independent females in the novels *Salome of the Tenements* (1923), *Bread Givers* (1925), and *Arrogant Beggar* (1927), they still criticize the conclusions, in which the heroines are married off anticlimactically.[1]

Apart from finding ideological faults with her texts, critics of Yezierska seem also to engage in rewriting her story within their own scholarly discourses. Although there is no doubt that every interpretive act implies some recreating of a writer or a work of art, the fact that Yezierska's books and career lend themselves to such rewritings with visible ease may be proof of her complexity and ambivalence.[2] The degree to which the critics desire to alter and to "improve" her story is particularly interesting, since it seems that even now she is expected to fit some model of the immigrant woman writer.

For example, in the biography-memoir about her mother, Yezierska's estranged daughter, Louise Levitas Henriksen, talks about her yearning to change the ending to Yezierska's career. At the end of her introduction to *Anzia Yezierska: A Writer's Life* (1988), Henriksen evokes the image of her mother on the train going westward, toward Hollywood of the 1920s, fame, and money, but also, inevitably, toward her destiny as the forgotten and underestimated writer. This picture of Yezierska is also projected by most critics and literary historians—the once-famous immigrant author who fell into oblivion after a short time in the limelight, a celebrity from the Lower East Side ghetto, a "sweatshop Cinderella" in Hollywood, who ended up poor and obscure on a WPA project. No wonder that, many years after her mother's death, while working on a book about her and going through the writer's letters and unpublished manuscripts, Henriksen pleads guilty to the "incurable hope for a happy ending," in spite of irreversible history: "Knowing only too well what would happen next made me apprehensive as I went on reading. I had to resist the overwhelming urge to change some words in the letters, smooth out the growing disparities *between what she said and what I felt she should have said*. As if by editing I could have changed Anzia's destiny—and thereby my own."[3] This desire to change the language documenting her mother's story only proves that, although Henriksen pretends to be writing Yezierska's objective biography, she is doing what she seemingly forbids herself to do—she is fictionalizing the writer's life. Her work is of an apparently documentary character—a memoir and a collection of quotes from letters and reviews, arranged in a particular order, and following a more or less chronological narrative pattern. Yet the author of *Anzia Yezierska* is rewriting the woman Anzia Yezierska by means of gathering these "facts," pictures, and fragments of her mother's "autobiographical" fiction into her own book, by making her mother a heroine of a biographical narrative.

This may be the only approach available to the critic who is also rewriting her own life story along with that of her subject. Henriksen admits in the afterword: "Only now, in her absence, can I come this close to her again" (301). Chronological distance from the persona of the mother-writer empowers the daughter-critic to construct her own version of Yezierska's life. Once the mother has become a text written and read by others, the daughter is able to work with it; she can now embrace her mother's life and work within her own critical narrative. In this way, Henriksen can establish a "happy ending" of sorts to Yezierska's life by suggesting a particular reading of her story to the readers.

The desire to revise Yezierska's life and works is also shared by other critics, not necessarily as privileged in their biographical proximity to the writer as Louise Levitas Henriksen. In the case of scholars who became interested in reviving this writer's works after her death in 1970, David Bromwich's statement that biographies "define the range of plausible interpretations of an author" sounds especially convincing.[4] Most criticism of Yezierska seems to reflect the trajectory of her career. She started with the breathtaking success of *Hungry Hearts* (1920), her first collection on the ghetto life of Jewish immigrants that was later bought by Hollywood and turned into a film under the same title by Samuel Goldwyn. But she ended obscure and forgotten in a nursing home. As if to mirror this progression from fame to oblivion, Yezierska's critics acknowledge her initial originality and freshness of topic but dismiss her insistence upon writing about the same themes even after they held no interest for readers and publishers.

Another factor prompting critical efforts to "revise" or adjust Yezierska's story results from the dearth of solid evidence concerning her coming to America. For example, in her introduction to *Bread Givers*, Alice Kessler-Harris, who brought back into print many of Yezierska's texts, suggests that the place of the writer's birth in Poland (Plinsk) was different from that stated by Henriksen in her biography (Plotsk). Kessler-Harris claims as well that Yezierska's family came to America from Poland via Ellis Island in the 1890s, whereas the daughter cites the earlier immigrant processing station, Castle Garden, in her version of the writer's story.[5] According to Diane Levenberg, the facts of Yezierska's life are "murky." Nevertheless, the critic is sure of the arrival date (1901) and of the writer's age on her coming to America. Levenberg's "facts" are still different from those of Kessler-Harris and Henriksen; so are they also from those given by Mary V. Dearborn and Thomas J. Ferraro. How can we decide who is right?[6]

Apart from biographical revisions, Yezierska invites rewritings of her literary texts. In her study of the writer's life and work, Carol B. Schoen slightly changes the ending of one of the short stories to make it suit her own interpretive narrative. The ambivalent conclusion of "A Bed for the Night" prompts Schoen to write her own meaning onto Yezierska's; in Schoen's version a homeless girl is taken in by "one old woman . . . [who shoves] her out in the morning." However, the text actually concludes with the homeless girl's realization that the woman who helped her is a prostitute (and not a very old one)—the only person capable of charity in the whole of indifferent New York. The girl is discouraged from coming back the next night because the woman fears that her reputation may hurt the innocent youth.[7] Why did not Schoen want this important fact in her study? Was she embarrassed by the heroine's final tribute to the "holiness" of the charitable and Christlike prostitute? Did she want a happier ending—a less sentimental one—for the sake of her study?[8]

The critics' imaginative, or simply careless, renderings of her biography and fiction may stem from the fact that Yezierska has not been taken very seriously as a writer. She may be one of the so-called forgotten voices of "immigrant realism" that should be restored in the general effort to revise the canon, but, instead of being recognized for her own merits, she is often approached as a marginal author whose rediscovery needs to be justified, as if some of the critics feel guilty for engaging in such a minor and imperfect subject.[9] On the other hand, it is true that Yezierska's life and writings—because they are so colorful and exciting—often prompt the modern reader's desire to revise and change some of the passages or resolutions, which even to the writer's daughter seemed "exaggerated and sentimental" (*AY* 6). What she "should have said" or written may easily haunt a critic who plunges into the plenitude of interesting and innovative texts and who may become dismayed at too many melodramatic conclusions, too many scenes depicting a young immigrant woman's pathetic encounters with America, and too much of an emotional and overdramatic a style full of "Oi weh!" and "God from the world!"

For example, at the close of *Arrogant Beggar* (1927) and *All I Could Never Be* (1932) Adele and Fanya sit lonely and forlorn in their maiden rooms dreaming of love. All of a sudden, there is a knock at the door and, as in a fairy tale, a "prince" appears to save the conclusions from having to feature single, critically minded women. Such disappointing endings happen in many of Yezierska's texts, much to the regret of feminist readers who would prefer a defense of a single woman's independence to a conventional romantic resolution. After all, freedom from the traditional narrative binding a female to her family and domestic chores was Yezierska's proudly defended choice of life.

Why, then, did she need clichéd conclusions in her fiction? Why did she not express her liberated views consistently in both her life and writings?

These are the questions I am going to answer and explore through close readings of Yezierska's short stories and novels in my own critical "rewriting" of her. I do not think that we have to prove that Yezierska is a "great author" (what is a great author anyway?) if we want to read and study her. Nor do I believe that we need a happy ending to her literary career to perceive her as equally good as, or even better than, the recognized male authors of a similar background, such as Henry Roth and Abraham Cahan, with whom she is always compared unfavorably. My goal is to challenge the "happy endings" offered by some critics and to look closer at those which Yezierska pasted onto her texts so conspicuously. Yezierska, like many other immigrant authors, was expected to produce "happy" portrayals of acculturation that arose from preconceived narrative structures and implied predictable conclusions. As previously stated, all stories of acculturation, male and female, follow a more or less set pattern—an Old World character goes through a transition from the oppressive native country to the Promised Land and is reborn there as a New World citizen. The conclusion of such a narrative in America—the immigrant dream come true—is its crucial element. Marking the fulfillment of the rites of passage into a new culture, this closure to the newcomer narrative constitutes a happy ending to the sequence of ordeals involved in the transfer from one world to another.[10] For the reader, the anticipated happy conclusion to the immigrant journey is a comforting goal at the end of a sequence of events that may tell of persecution and suffering but that is still pervaded with the promise of a final reward. The ending of the immigrant narrative can thus be seen as a fixed, expected, and even somewhat anticlimactic resolution both to stories in which real or fictional men and women go through hardships and trials in order to achieve fulfillment in the New World as well as the readers' efforts to follow and vicariously participate in these stories.

Moreover, in their concern for the reader's comfort, the endings of the newcomer narratives accommodate gender difference. The texts describing male passages usually conclude with closures influenced by Horatio Alger's, Edward Bok's, and Andrew Carnegie's rags-to-riches scenarios, where the newcomer's success is measured in economic terms—material gain and business stature. In the female story, which is the underlying scenario behind such novels as Antin's *The Promised Land* and Yezierska's *Bread Givers*, a happy ending usually entails an ethnic heroine's metamorphosis into the New World woman through education and marriage with a native-born or Americanized Jewish man. This clear distinction in the conclusions to male and female acculturation tales lends itself to generalizations—the reader is relieved when a poor immigrant man finally "makes it" in the capitalistic New World and usually rejoices when a marriage concludes a woman's rites of passage into the new culture-home.[11]

In the context of our present feminist expectations, which dismiss the happy endings as clichéd and unrealistic, we often miss the fact that these endings may serve other purposes than simply closing the predictable narrative movement. When read closely and with an awareness of the larger historical and cultural contexts to which she was responding, Yezierska's texts disclose a richness that goes far beyond the predictable immigrant scenario. She challenges this model in her autobiographical piece "Mostly about Myself," which opens her second collection of stories, *Children of Loneliness* (1923). She talks about her sense of isolation in the new country: "When I first came to America [in the 1890s], the coldness of the Americans used to rouse in me the fury of a savage. Their impersonal, non-committal air was like a personal insult to me. I longed to shake them out of their aloofness, their frozen stolidity."[12] This feeling of being rejected and ignored by the self-absorbed host culture is the lot of all Yezierska's heroines. They are hungry for personal response, love, and sympathy from the native-borns, but often find these Anglo-Saxons indifferent, or even hostile, toward the immigrant woman's emotional outpourings. It is very difficult for them to convince their new compatriots that they are individuals and complex human beings, not specimens representing particular ethnic groups. In the story "To the Stars," Sophie Sapinsky's plea to be given an opportunity to study writing, to find expression for her feelings, is met with an ironic comment from the dean: "There are too many writers and too few cooks. . . . The trouble with you is that you are a Russian Jewess. You want the impossible" (*ChL* 71). Yezierska shows that the immigrant woman of the early twentieth century who desires a career beyond the sweatshop and the chores of a domestic is treated like a person out of her mind, since she longs for the impossible—a fairy tale ending to the story which from the start presupposes a "realistic" narrative of manual labor and lower-class existence for the alien female.

Yezierska, then, insists on unrealistic happy resolutions in which her characters achieve implausible success and acceptance. The "love affair" between the immigrant woman and America always ends happily in her texts, as if to mock the writer's own. Yezierska's decision to abandon a traditional family life, to be a writer rather than a wife and a mother, may be read as her defiance of a scenario prescribed for a woman's life.[13] Compared with Mary Antin, who conspicuously avoided them, Yezierska exploits the themes of love, sex, and marriage with ironic insistence. They come into her texts as familiar mo-tifs that never fail to change the heroine's most difficult circumstances for the better, as if with the touch of a fairy godmother's magical wand. In fact, in "Mostly about Myself" Yezierska compares her writing to composing a fairy tale: "I, buried alive in the killing blackness of poverty, could wrest the beauty of reality out of my experiences no less than the princess who had the chance to live and love, and whose only worry was which of her adorers she should choose for a husband" (16). Juxtaposing the "killing blackness of poverty" with the "princess" and her "adorers"—the realistic dark side of the immi-grant story and the American fairy tale—Yezierska shows us how she is going to use the dominant narrative to translate a newcomer woman's experience. Her female characters are usually married off at the end, but such a conclusion to the immigrant story should make us read *beyond* the clichéd ending, as it only makes the alternative reading of the woman's loneliness and alienation all the more acute and poignant.[14]

This study does not intend to prove that there is one definite classifica-tion and perception of Anzia Yezierska's works and life. In my analysis of her novels and stories, I argue that she did not fall prey to her clichéd romantic endings, as most of the critics suggest, but, rather, used them for an ironic and self-conscious contrast highlighting the unglamorous side of female Ameri-canization. In this context, I concentrate on the conflict that arises between the host culture and the woman newcomer, on the clash between the Old World and the New as prompting textual oppression in the writer and identity crises in her heroines.

Much like the characters in Antin's and Stern's novels, Yezierska's female characters are frustrated about their Old and New World gender roles and the discovery of the oppression of their sex. But Yezierska's emphasis on these themes results in an interesting contrast that elicits the failure of the American Dream—the immigrant happy ending—and the disillusionment with their new home that many immigrant women experience in her novels and short stories. Yezierska's insistence on the themes concerning her own ethnic background, biography, and political views—her Jewishness, her re-lationship with John Dewey, or her persistent criticism of the inadequacies of American democracy—is valuable and intriguing, even though it contrib-uted to her later obscurity as an author who "writes the same story" over and over again.

In reading beyond the happy endings to her texts, I examine Yezierska's vision of America and present her unmaking of the myth of the virgin land as woman's body. All Yezierska's heroines experience frustration in their gendered identity as newcomer women in the host culture, which they perceive as decisively male, and they identify with WASP mentor figures.[15] Their gendered identity crisis affects the way in which the newcomer women see themselves as sexual beings as well as how they perceive the males of the same ethnic group and those of the dominant culture. The repression of their carnality leads to fear of the male body and of sexuality in general in most of Yezierska's female characters. Still, they display a pervasive desire for fulfillment with an American male—a yearning for a happy, Cinderella ending through miscegenation. The irreconcilable conflict between sexual repression and desire for gratification, between female and male, ethnic and native-born, Jewish and Protestant, is the price an immigrant woman has to pay for acculturation according to Yezierska. This conflict reflects her inability to completely embrace America and to shed her stigmatizing garb of the alien other.

In this context, the autobiographical and repetitious—according to some critics, "obsessive"—themes in Yezierska's texts can be used to illustrate her approach to the woman writer's position in America. I trace her career's "unhappy ending" to her philosophy of constant rebellion and to the uncompromising critique of American ideals that she pursued faithfully throughout her whole life, in all the texts that compose her unconventional and intriguing "story." I argue that in their very unreality her literary conclusions provide us an opportunity for making paradoxical contrasts with the life stories of actual lower-class women at Yezierska's time. In the present, an inquiry into the reasons *why* such happy endings were used so widely, rather than a brusque dismissal of them, can teach us again that the immigrant narrative models, and our readings of them, do not always correspond very closely to the contents and meanings of the stories they carry.

## "There Is No America!": No Happy Endings in the Promised Land

### Ambivalent Dream

The "virgin land"—mythical America—to which millions of immigrants have been fleeing for centuries is never a lush garden or an Edenic landscape in Yezierska's writings. The pastoral visions of, for instance, John Smith's *The Description of New England* (1616), idealistic depictions of the fertile land and of its happy inhabitants in Michel-Guillaume Jean de Crèvecoeur's *Letters from an American Farmer* (1784), or even Willa Cather's emphasis on the nurturing richness of American soil in *My Antonia* (1918) belong to the tradition of writing about America as a Garden of Eden, a paradisiacal haven for the world's refugees. In these texts, written by and about newcomers from different cultures, the host country is modeled on an image of a motherly and beautiful woman whose body-landscape welcomes the immigrants and offers them home. The belief that the United States is a life-giving "divine creation" is emphasized in Carl Wittke's *We Who Built America* (1946): "Here was a 'melting pot' for all the world, and for centuries one of the most compelling convictions of the American people was the thought that their country was destined to become the mother of a mighty race."[16]

In contrast to this tradition, Anzia Yezierska's texts often present the Promised Land as a desert where the American Dream is a thirst that can never be quenched or a dark night filled with nightmares in which dreary economic and social factors overshadow any chance for betterment and renewal for lower-class Jewish newcomers. The narrator of "America and I" confesses: "I began to read the American history. . . . But the great difference between the first Pilgrims and me was that they expected to make America, build America, create their own world of liberty. I wanted to find it ready made. . . . I, when I encountered a few savage Indian scalpers, like the old witch of the sweatshop, like my 'Americanized' countryman, who cheated me out of my wages—I, when I found myself on the lonely untrodden path through which all seekers of the new world must pass, I lost heart and said: 'There is no America!'"[17] Instead of the green meadows they envisioned while still in Russia or Poland, immigrants from East Europe usually find themselves in the dark jungle of New York's "dumbbell" tenements, living amid poverty and engaging in a tough Darwinian struggle for everyday survival. Thus their hope for an instant happy ending in the land of plenty is shattered; there is no other America beyond the imperfect one they have found here; the dream ends in the very place that gave birth to it. A "hand" in a sweatshop complains about her disillusionment on the pages of Yezierska's "America and I": "Day after day, week after week, all the contact I got with America was handling dead buttons. The money I earned was hardly enough to pay for bread and rent. I didn't have a room to myself. I didn't even have a bed. I slept on a mattress on the floor in a rat-hole of a room occupied by a dozen other immigrants. I was always hungry—oh, so hungry!" (*HF* 148).

The metaphor of hunger is often a key to Yezierska's characters, who are starved for human kindness, respect, and appreciation. The uncritical vision of a Promised Land that offers nourishment, a land flowing with milk and honey, one that made them cross the Atlantic with the "huddled masses," is replaced with a conviction of the permanence of unfulfillment: "America of my dreams never was and never could be" (*HF* 152). In Yezierska's writings, the cherished rhetoric of the American Dream available to all struggles with the disillusioning language describing an America-Arcadia that can never be attained; the dominant narrative of passage and renewal is juxtaposed to a subtext depicting a failure of the American Dream in the newcomer, whose "journey of discovery" leads to the realization that there is a disparity between immigrant rhetoric and everyday life. For instance, the idealistic heroine of the story "America and I" identifies herself with the Pilgrims: "They had left their native country as I had left mine. They had crossed an unknown ocean and landed in an unknown country, as I." She finds her dream in the conviction that America is still in the making and that she, "the last comer," can contribute by "build[ing] the bridge of understanding between the American-born and [her]self," by writing about the ghetto (*HF* 152–53).[18]

However, despite the fact that she finds consolation in the ideology of her new country, the first-person narrator finishes her tale about Americanization with a surprising confession of guilt. She realizes that, even though she may succeed, others will fail in the competitive world where everybody desires "America to want" him or her and where only those who are capable of making themselves heard can surface (*HF* 151–53). That is why her final manifesto of belief in universal democracy sounds more like a question than a firm statement: "The America of tomorrow, the America that is every day nearer coming to be, will be too wise, too open-hearted, too friendly-handed, to let the least last-comer at their gates knock in vain with his gifts unwanted" (*HF* 153). Will it truly be so? The "great revelation" with which Yezierska closes her story is much less convincing than the passionate acknowledgments of difference and alienation that her heroine expresses having learned English and having tried in vain to become a person similar to and accepted by the native-borns. She has arrived "pregnant with the unlived lives of generations clamoring for expression," but finds out later on that "between my soul and the American soul were worlds of difference that no words could bridge" (*HF* 144, 152). The birth of a new race is not possible in American Dystopia. Her decision to devote her life to exploring this difference—to write about the immigrants for their host country—does not imply the eradication of her otherness but seems to emphasize its permanence as an ambivalent source of lifelong authorial inspiration.

In this context, the story's end can be read as an ironic comment on the rhetoric of immigrant success that was expected from a writer such as Yezierska in the 1920s. She had to produce an enthusiastic text that would sing the praises of the New World, despite the fact that the actual experience of female Americanization was far removed from this depiction. The "bridge of understanding" could be built only with the imperfect material available to the newcomer woman writer, with the familiar narrative of immigrant success that could not really bridge any differences.

And yet, although the words she uses cannot close the gulf between the two worlds, a careful reader knows that Yezierska recognizes the influence of her writing on the public. She gives her readers a seemingly optimistic conclusion, one that can either make a fairy tale ending or inspire them to search for some hidden subtext. Such ambivalent closure reveals the impossibility of direct understanding not only between the newcomer and America but also between the writer and the reader, both of whom cannot approach mutual comprehension even within the same idiom. In this situation, the newcomer writer has to use codes and subtexts to communicate meanings that have outgrown available narrative models.

Yezierska's self-conscious and ironic use of the ending in "America and I" indicates how remote her story is from any immigrant woman's reality. Pasting a clichéd happy conclusion onto an otherwise pessimistic story about the drudgery of a working-class woman's manual labor allows the text to pass politically as immigrant propaganda while it discloses the oppressive structure of the ideological message it is expected to carry. The alternative reading of the official Cinderella narrative suggests, then, ambiguities and darker sides to the immigrant woman's Americanization that no success can ever obliterate; in the narrator's words, "The drudgery that I had lived through, and the endless drudgery still ahead of me rose over me like a withering wilderness of sand" (*HF* 152). Moreover, even Yezierska's acknowledgment of the possibility of success suggests that a person's unexpected luck or well-earned achievement entails somebody else's inevitable failure in the competitive Promised Land. She seems to see that one often has to renounce solidarity with one's ethnic group and class to rise to being American. After that "great revelation"—"I saw America"—the narrator admits: "Great chances have come to me. But in my heart is always a deep sadness. I feel like a man who is sitting down to a secret table of plenty, while his near ones and dear ones are perishing before his eyes. My very joy in doing the work I love hurts me like a secret guilt" (*HF* 153). Although she herself may have succeeded, hers is an isolated happy ending—an exception rather than an example illustrating everybody's predicament. The final call to an America "of to-morrow . . . that is every day nearer coming to be" sounds very hollow in this context; indeed, the vision of the host country as the "vast sea of sand" in which the narrator "lost [her]self deeper and deeper" makes her voice like that of "one crying in the desert" and, perhaps, suggests the disillusioned newcomer's "drowning" in the sea of difference that would not part to provide the passage into the land of freedom.

In an interview with Richard Duffy, "You Can't Be an Immigrant Twice," the transcription of which concludes *Children of Loneliness*, the author uses her own story to illustrate the results of American success in a female immigrant writer. In what reads more like a first-person narrative than a dialogue, Yezierska, a celebrity then, reminisces about her vacation in Europe and presents her attempt to relive her immigrant journey through a return to America in steerage, with the crowd of immigrants to whom she had once belonged. However, she cannot repeat the childhood experience of her passage into the Promised Land that she has idealized so much in her writings. Although she compares the look on the poor people's faces with the one that the Pilgrims of the *Mayflower* must have had, she fails to survive more than a day in their crude company. Everything offends her now-refined tastes, and she requests removal to second class, where overnight she finds all the comforts she has become used to as a successful and well-paid American author.[19]

As a consequence of this "betrayal" of her past, she feels guilty. She tries to expiate for her success with a praise of the spirit and character she observes in the multilingual crowd of immigrants and with a eulogy for the American democracy that has allowed her "a chance to become articulate" (*ChL* 270). Nevertheless, this optimistic ending may serve as an ironic response to the episode immediately preceding it, where she introduces a young immigrant Ukrainian painter to the luxuries of first class. Having compared the steerage and the world of the rich, the boy declares that he would give up his painting for money, if it could make so much difference in one's life. Yezierska responds with more guilt for showing him the things he should not have known about. "I only made him unhappy," she concludes (269). She feels uneasy for being already on the other side—that of the insiders who enjoy their American success—the side unattainable by the poor young artist. From this scene she moves to a discussion of the possible improvements for "esthetic diversion" in third class so that the passengers would not "feel their condition so keenly," proving that she realizes that she has indeed crossed over to the other world, from which there is no return to her sentimentalized past (269).

The emotional maneuvering visible in this piece again shows us Yezierska's awareness of her writing. Superficially, the interview is simply another version of the Cinderella rags-to-riches story. But if we try to look beyond its rather propagandistic ending, it becomes clear that the author has intended the ambivalence of her message. You cannot be an immigrant twice, because once you gain a little bit of your American Dream—success—you pay for this happy ending with being estranged from your own people. Although she is a celebrity in this story, the writer also demonstrates how lonely and alienated it is to exist between the two incompatible worlds—a very shaky resolution to the fairy tale of immigrant passage.

In a story included in Yezierska's much-heralded first collection, *Hungry Hearts*, we read about a young girl's experience of such a mythical passage to America:

> "In America is a home for everybody. The land is your land." . . . "Everybody is with everybody alike, in America. Christians and Jews are brothers to-gether. An end to the worry for bread." . . . "Plenty for all. Learning flows free like milk and honey." . . . "Land! Land!" came the joyous shout. . . . Men fell on their knees to pray. Women hugged their babies and wept. Children danced. . . . Age-old visions sang themselves in me—songs of freedom of an oppressed people. America! America![20]

The religious fervor with which the immigrants in "How I Found America" share mythical stories about America and express their joy about their new country is seen through the eyes of a little girl, the narrator. The nameless heroine, so vulnerable because of her age, gender, and ethnicity, is also an excellent vehicle for conveying the emotionally charged retrospective reality of the shtetl from which her family is fleeing: "Every breath I drew was a breath of fear, every shadow a stifling shock, every footfall struck on my heart like the heavy boot of the Cossack" (250). The cruel picture of oppression in the shtetl serves as a contrast to the dream of the happy ending in America and calls for the fairy tale vision of a paradise of freedom and democracy.

The very title of the story, "How I Found America," seems to declare the feasibility and attainability of an ideal conclusion, with its emphasis on the past indicative of the verb. It is what we would expect after the trauma of the passage: "Steerage—dirty bundles—foul odors—seasick humanity—but I saw and heard nothing of the foulness and ugliness around me. I floated in showers of sunshine; visions upon visions of the new world opened before me" (260). Having experienced the constant danger of pogroms, the narrator faces the inhuman conditions on the immigrant ship with unfaltering faith in their quick erasure by the paradisiacal reality of America-Arcadia. However, the dream never comes true, as she and her family struggle through economic adversity and the drudgery of the worst-paying jobs in the ghetto. The girl, now stripped of her dreams, rebels constantly against her fate, but she has to "ben[d] to the inevitable" and accept her "defeat"—work in the sweatshop to help her family survive.

Although she finally feels that she "rose triumphant even in [her] surrender" because an understanding teacher, a woman descended from the Pilgrims, quotes Waldo Frank to her, it is not this happy ending and moral victory that really appeal to the reader, but the bitterness of the struggle and her disappointment. The use of Frank's *Our America* seems almost ironic in the context of the narrator's wasted years and youth: "'We go forth all to seek America. And in the seeking we create her. In the *quality of our search shall be the true nature of the America* that we create'" (297–98, emphasis mine). The young woman's desire to become "articulate," to contribute to the making of America with her thoughts and ideas, can never be fulfilled. Her search for the Promised Land has to be confined to manual labor in a sweatshop and her ambitions appeased within the low social position prescribed for her by the dominant culture. That is what Yezierska's heroine "found" in her new country. The ending, featuring her illumination about "creating in the seeking," is a fine piece of immigrant propaganda, but it provides an ironic coda to the narrator's endless everyday struggle and the intellectual ambitions unheard of in one from her social class.

In "The Miracle," a tale about a penniless young woman looking for her ideal man, Sara Reisel leaves her home in Poland with high hopes for a happy ending in the American paradise. Like the narrator of "How I Found America," she comes to the New World to chase her dreams of a better life— in this case to find a husband—since another girl from her village has married a rich man there. Sara makes her family pawn their Sabbath candlesticks and the Saifer Torah to provide money for her ticket, for it is their duty to help a girl find a man. Her father has his doubts and is reluctant to let her go: "*Are there miracles in America?* Can she yet get there a man at her age and without a dowry?" (*HH* 121). But Sara succeeds in her efforts to leave home and soon, on board the ship, envisions her happy ending as a love story. "I didn't see the day. I didn't see the night. I didn't see the ocean. I didn't see the sky. I only saw my lover in America, coming nearer and nearer to me, till I could feel his eyes bending on me so near that I got frightened and began to tremble. My heart ached so with the joy of his nearness that I quick drew back and turned away" (127). The passage across the ocean is a metaphor for a young woman's passage into womanhood and suggests her future initiation into sexuality. The

Cinderella dream scenario she envisions interestingly combines the myth of America as a land of miracles (thus the title) and a nurturing land of physical love; as the title of another story in *Hungry Hearts* proclaims, America is the place "Where Lovers Dream."[21]

However, the text of "The Miracle" begins with a clear reference to making up stories and fantasies: "Like all people who have nothing, I lived on dreams. . . . And what happened to me when I became an American is more than I can picture before my eyes, even in a dream" (114). In the context of this setup, her initial fear of being physically close with a strange male in a strange land passes by hardly noticed. When Sara's handsome teacher falls in love with her and proposes marriage, the happy ending surpasses the narrator's wildest dreams, as then she "could only weep and tremble with joy at his touch . . . the miracle of America come true!" (141). Sara seems to finally get her reward; after hard work and struggle in the sweatshop and in the school for immigrants, after waiting and suffering, she can be finally content that she has earned her piece of the American Dream. And yet the sexual tension that Yezierska builds up between her heroine and her "repressed" WASP teacher remains conspicuously suspended; because it suggests inequality rather than partnership, the tension raises questions about the validity of the story's romantic resolution.

Despite the happy endings in both stories, the voice of the author emerges clearly in the narration, with its controlling distance and mature knowledge. Beyond the superficially unproblematic resolutions of these texts, there are again ironic and self-conscious subtexts that Yezierska offers us as alternative readings. The endings seem very superficial and hardly credible when compared to the "realistic" descriptions of the hardships and disillusionments that the two heroines have to go through in the Promised Land. The young woman in "How I Found America" simply walks away from her new teacher-friend's office into an unclear future; we do not know for how long her enthusiasm will suffice, when she will have another moment of doubt in her new home (and they happen consistently throughout the whole story), whether the "quality of the search" alone will be able to sustain her. In the conversation she has with a fellow shop worker, the reader detects the clear and bitter voice of the author: "Why don't you learn yourself to take life like it is? What's got to be, got to be. In Russia you could hope to run away from your troubles to America. But from America where can you go?" (*HH* 277). There is no escape from this Promised Land to another, better one. There is no other place to dream of or to flee to from present misery and disillusionment; no one can envision anything beyond America. In this context the title, "How I Found

America," refers also to the reevaluation of the dream by a disenchanted immigrant who says good-bye to her visions of finding "America" as she hoped it would be.[22]

In "The Miracle" Sara's fear of an American lover is only superficially eradicated at the end. After a hopeless encounter with a ghetto matchmaker, she does not have any other choice but to take what comes to her—a cold-blooded WASP male who wants her to be his teacher-savior: "You can save me. You can free me from the bondage of age-long repressions. You can lift me out of the dead grooves of sterile intellectuality" (141). It is she who has to be the stronger character in this union and to help her Anglo-Saxon spouse connect his mind to his earthly desires. But she is praised exactly for her unintellectual "ethnic" qualities, for being a stereotypical East European Jewish female— an ironic complement, considering her desperate craving for knowledge and education. In a sense she ends up marrying because she has no other way to resolve her life in America, to become "like the native-born."

Although her teacher-lover marvels at her alien abilities and temperament, it is clear earlier in the story that she feels definitely inferior to him and acutely aware of the gap of otherness separating them: "'I'll help you,' he said. But you must first learn to get hold of yourself'" (134). The story's end is like a romantic letter from her friend whose marriage prompted the heroine to come to America—completely divorced from reality: "In America is a law called 'ladies first.' . . . In the cars the men must get up to give their seats to the women. The men hold the babies on their hands and carry the bundles for the women and even help with the dishes. There are not enough women to go around in America. And the men run after the women, and not like in Poland, the women running after the men" (117). No one is "running after" Sara when she leaves the shirt factory exhausted at the end of the day; no American working-class woman could see (or can do so today) any part of her experience in this utopian description. Thus the "miracle" in the title, as well as the one closing the story, may be read as ironic comments on the dreams about miscegenation—a successful union between the newcomer and the native-born is more possible in fiction than in reality. What Yezierska was avoiding in the "miraculous" closure of her tale could be, perhaps, an unwritten tale about her own choice of a lonely and loveless life over the miscegenation model; in her story an American male never dared to commit himself to "such a love as youth could never know."[23]

Yezierska's artificial and unconvincing endings in these stories might also result from a desire to satisfy a public greedy for Hollywood conclusions. The endings could reflect a need to be accepted and recognized as a spokesperson for her people, which, as Carol B. Schoen stresses, was one of Yezierska's main goals. Similarly, Mary Dearborn points out that Yezierska was always trying to meet the market's needs and expectations and wrote immigrant propaganda to help build a favorable image of the newcomer at a time of growing xenophobia and nativism. Creating a friendly, sympathetic picture of the immigrant who never fails to "find" his or her America was essential in the times when "communists," such as Emma Goldman, were being deported in a wave of fear of the "reds," when anybody from the East was considered a potential carrier of ideas that could hurt American democracy. According to Dearborn, Yezierska was thus consciously "inventing" an ethnic heroine in her desire to promote the immigrant cause. She sold her stories as vehicles for her own Cinderella image.[24]

Although we can see Dearborn's point, it is important to keep in mind that Yezierska did two things simultaneously: she worked both for economic success and intellectual recognition in the market of her times. She was a publicity-made heroine in Dearborn's terms, but she could control only a part of this process, for she had to "write" herself into the sort of "text" composed by the dominant culture. Nevertheless, she consciously "smuggled" alternative subtexts into her tales beneath their commercial happy endings; in doing so, she challenged the dominant narrative and its reductionist depiction of an immigrant woman's experience. Her ironic and self-conscious alternative readings thus serve as authorial commentaries on her own art and play to the politics of the cultural market in America with which she had to comply and of which, to a certain extent, she was inevitably a product. In the stories from *Children of Loneliness* and *Hungry Hearts*, Yezierska makes us see the immigrant woman's pain, struggle, and inability to settle down to the fact that America did not live up to her expectations. In this context, the rather Whitmanesque beginning of "America and I" ("As one of the dumb, voiceless ones I speak. One of the millions of immigrants beating, beating out their hearts at your gates for a breath of understanding") is both a propagandistic political appeal and an acknowledgment of the impossibility of conveying the truth about her experience.

### "The Statue in the Bay" Is a Man

The female characters' inability to fulfill their immigrant dreams in Yezierska's earlier texts shatters the image of mythical America that they brought with them from the oppressive Old World. What had been a happy vision often becomes a nightmare of poverty and disillusionment, of loveless and forlorn life amid the unattainable riches and happiness of others—the native-borns.

However, no women ever give up in Yezierska's writings. They press on, despite their disillusionment. After the initial shock, when they come face to face with the everyday struggle of their new lives, the women begin to create an alternative vision. They relentlessly pursue a new dream, and they hope for still another happy ending. Since the "creating in seeking" would never be finished in time to give them satisfaction, they construct another America for themselves, another dream to strive for amid the drudgery of day-to-day acculturation.

This new America replaces the myth based on the rhetoric of the virgin land, which constructs the New World as a metaphor—a female, a mother's body, flowing with the proverbial milk and honey and welcoming her exiled children to a comforting embrace. Emma Lazarus's famous poem "The New Colossus," engraved in bronze and now adorning the wall in the museum inside the base of the Statue of Liberty, is a clear example of this Promised Land rhetoric:

> Not like the brazen giant of Greek fame,
> With conquering limbs astride from land to land,
> Here at our sea-washed, sunset gates shall stand
> A mighty woman with a torch . . .

The "mighty woman" carries a torch that is the "imprisoned lightning," her name is "Mother of Exiles," and she cries "with silent lips": "'Give me your tired, your poor, / Your huddled masses yearning to breathe free, / The wretched refuse of your teeming shore. / Send these, the homeless, tempest-tossed to me.'"[25] This image of America—a mighty woman welcoming the refugees into the New World—replaces the ancient male heroes and gods who symbolize the Old World. The mighty woman combines their masculine power with feminine traits of nurturing and compassion; her torch is both "imprisoned lightning" (Zeus) and a lamp-new dawn that she "lift[s] beside the golden door" (Eos) of her inviting home. Yet the woman with a lamp, as well as Lazarus's poem, may still be seen as projecting an image of a land-bride waiting for her betrothed—the newcomer–New Man—and thus reaffirming rather than debunking the masculine mythologization of America.

In contrast to the myth, however, Yezierska's heroines find out that no one is going to lead them into the well-lit chambers of happy New World lives. The America they enter is a place where Darwinian notions of survival characterize everydayness more aptly than does Lazarus's poem. Lower-class people are the "wretched refuse" coming to the United States, and they are unable to read the lofty symbolism of Lazarus's poem. "But from my high visions, my golden hopes, I had to put my feet down on earth" admits the narrator of "America and I," even though in their efforts not to succumb to this reality, Yezierska's characters replace the old myth with a new one—a male mentor who serves as the alternative to the traditional representation of this country as a nurturing female. This new image, of a man-father-lover, is more connected with the reality of their lives, for it suggests a yearning for a relationship with a person who can mediate the heroine into the patriarchal Americanness that she so much desires.

On the biographical level, this new dream and desire in Yezierska's characters can be traced to the author's much publicized relationship with the educator John Dewey.[26] They met in 1917, and Yezierska attended his seminar at Columbia, having become captivated by his *Democracy and Education* (1916). Henriksen dramatizes their meeting in her biography of Yezierska: "It seemed only logical to try to enlist this eminent crusader in her own fight for democracy. Fired with the aptness of her cause, she walked into Dewey's office the next morning to make an appeal. The fact that she did not have an appointment made her visit more dramatic from her point of view. She brushed past the secretary and, once she started speaking, not giving him time to learn who she was, she found it easy to capture Dewey's attention" (*AY* 85). From the start, it was clear that Yezierska intended their relationship to assist her in pushing the immigrant cause against the increasing xenophobia of wartime America. To a struggling and lonely writer, the father-figure and the supportive authority that Dewey became in the course of the ensuing years of their friendship and work together was a reembodiment of the dream. Yezierska felt that she had finally found a true American friend.

Although Yezierska describes their friendship as based mostly on intellectual bond, her fictional depictions of it, in virtually all her major texts, add an interesting sexual twist to it. As Henriksen interprets it, on the basis of talking with her mother and studying their letters, Yezierska was perceived by Dewey primarily as an exciting and attractive woman: "Her intensity, the aggressive and impassioned speech, even her blouse pulled partly free of her skirt, her red hair slipping out of its pompadour in wisps around her flushed face—all these unconventional traits, which had so offended school principals and deans, were persuasive to Dewey" (88). The famous educator enlisted his support for the aspiring writer and advised her to quit teaching cooking classes and devote herself to writing. His faith in her talent and in the validity of her message fired Yezierska in her work and helped her find enough trust in herself to become a full-time author. However, as Henriksen suggests, based on Dewey's letters and poems to her as well as Yezierska's reaction to the resulting trauma, he expected to become involved in a sexual liaison. This misunderstanding ruined their friendship and left Yezierska torn between disgust and regret. She gives outlet to these feelings in novels depicting the clash of the Old and New World temperaments.

For example, in *Salome of the Tenements* and *All I Could Never Be*, she presents a stately WASP male falling in love with an exotic and unconventional immigrant female. The clash between the two worlds they represent surfaces in their different approaches to sexuality: he is looking forward to be freed from repressive Puritan conventions of conduct, while she tries to disassociate herself from carnality in her pursuit of knowledge and intellectual advancement. Thus their union is doomed from the very beginning because, as it happens in *Salome*, even if they get married, the differences separating such a mixed couple ethnically, socially, and sexually are going to destroy it.[27]

The image of a male teacher-friend who opens up the worlds of American education and intellectual growth to the immigrant woman can be found even in Yezierska's first collection, *Hungry Hearts*. "Wings" tells the story of an orphan girl who was rescued from Russian pogroms by an uncle in America and who wastes away her youth tending to her aging benefactor. Shenah Pessah's dreams of love, caused by a lonely ray of sunshine that has found its way into her dingy tenement apartment, are answered with magical immediacy—a young WASP sociology student stands at her door inquiring about a room to rent: "It was as though the god of her innermost longings had suddenly taken shape in human form and lifted her in mid-air" (*HH* 3). The man is now the symbol of America; his polished manners and handsome appearance encode the new dream for an immigrant girl starved for kindness. Although to him she is a "perfect type" to study and not a flesh-and-blood woman, the girl vividly imagines the young American male as a symbol of the culture and tradition that she is desperately trying to enter. Therefore, she falls in love not so much with the person as with the dominant center he represents, the center that has the power to accept and validate her as a human being. When, after a kiss he "didn't mean," the young student leaves his tenement "research apartment" (so as not to be a "cad" toward the "poor lonely little immigrant"), the story ends with a heart-broken Shenah, who nevertheless realizes that her fairy tale prince "opened the wings of [her] soul" (29–34).

After her love has been rejected, Shenah realizes that the ideals of freedom and individualism she saw in the American student are possible only in an America that she creates for herself. In "Hunger," a sequel to "Wings," she mythologizes her sociology student into a demigod—"'He was not a man! He was God Himself! On whatever I look shines his face!'" (*HH* 36). Once again, her desire is not for John Barnes, with his beautiful clothes and polished manners, but for what he represents—the "higher" life of an American who has made himself into a person, who is free to "pursue his happiness." Instead of a flesh-and-blood person, Shenah worships an idea she creates for herself out of disillusionment with the culture that perceives her only as a "poor little immigrant." Paradoxically, both the student and the immigrant girl are guilty of the same stereotypical attitude toward their respective other.

However, while the young man retreats from the ghetto, whose inhabitants have scared him off with their effusive emotionalism and nagging need for love, Shenah's infatuation becomes a productive hunger, propelling her ambitions and pulling her away from tenement drudgery to pursue her independence. She finds work and leaves her old uncle. She is determined to persist in the existential task of turning suffering into a fulfilling life: "'I have suffered, and must yet go on suffering. I see no end. But only—there is a something—a hope—a help out—it lifts me on top of my hungry body— the hunger to make from myself a person that cannot be crushed by nothing or nobody—the life higher!'" (64). Shenah's beautiful dream, delivered in passionately ungrammatical Yiddish-English, may sound pathetic and melodramatic. Yet it expresses the feelings of the character as well as of her author, who fought all her life to "make from myself a person."[28] In this sense, Yezierska enters into her text herself, with a message about deriving satisfaction from disappointment. As she proved with her life and career, it is possible to become a person without being attached to a man, without living a traditional domestic scenario. In this way Yezierska was living and writing a new narrative of a woman's life for which, in Carolyn Heilbrun's words, "there were no models . . . no exemplars, no stories."[29]

Yezierska's entrance into her text can be seen in another story, "To the Stars," which portrays Sophie Sapinsky's constant craving for a better life. Sophie's dream is to become a writer, despite the mockery she inspires in everybody who learns about her aspirations. The unsympathetic dean tells her that, as a Russian Jewess, she wants the impossible. He laughs at her and suggests she become a cook. In another instance her English professor ridicules her for comparing herself with Emerson in her ungrammatical idiom. In contrast to these unsympathetic men, the college president is the only kind person, the only "true" American who, she assumes, can understand her. But before she actually meets this embodiment of wisdom, and tells him about her plans, the young woman quits her job, finds a little dirty room of her own in a tenement cellar, and begins her struggle to write a story that would "show them" what she is capable of.

The picture of the president, hung on the cracked wall, is her source of strength and inspiration: "'Then what is it in me that's tearing and gnawing and won't let me rest?' she pleaded. The calm faith of the eyes leveled steadily at her seemed to rebuke her despair. The sure faith of that lofty face lifted her out of herself. She was humble before such unwavering power. 'Ach!' she prayed, 'How can I be so sure like you? Help me!'" (ChL 79). She actually worships the icon of the man and endows it with magical powers, even though she has never spoken to him. After all, he is a symbol of power and authority and, like the president of the country, he should represent an almost divine ability to change one's life. In this sense, as much as she is writing her story, she is also writing, constructing an ideal president of an ideal America who would listen to her and would understand her desire for expression and spiritual life—qualities unnecessary in the sweatshop. Under the icon of her new American deity, whom she worships with all the zeal her Jewish faith has taught her, Sophie struggles to prove that her "hand" can write as the extension of her passionate and feeling heart.[30]

As soon as she has completed her story, an account of raw ghetto life written in her raw ghetto idiom, Sophie is ready to show it to her idol, whom she has by now met. Her meetings with the celebrated teacher-father-figure are the projections of her picture worship, for the college president takes on all the qualities with which she has endowed his portrait—she has completed writing him as well as her story. Not surprisingly, Yezierska's story ends with a fairy tale moral: the girl wins a contest—five hundred dollars for the best short story—and becomes a celebrity of the ghetto. Hard and persistent work is always rewarded with success in American tales of self-making. Obviously, as Cinderella now transformed, Sophie is also recognized by those who rejected her before, but her joy is not complete until she shares it with the president. They spend a Victorian evening together at his office—a temple of wisdom and understanding—where he shares with her his ideas about the future of American democracy. The president's mission is to build better schools and thus educate American society and its people in enlightenment and tolerance. He invites her to teach him all that the immigrants can give to this vision of a better world. Thus a young woman writer from the ghetto finds her America in the friendship with the president who, at the end of the story, symbolizes not only a mythological person—an icon—but also embodies the archetypal

(Founding) father figure. He becomes another impossible dream, rewriting the myth of the Promised Land and gender relations in it.

### Writing the Disembodied God, Writing Herself

In all three stories, "Wings," "Hunger," and "To the Stars," the male figures are disembodied icons and images rather than human bodies, and the America they symbolize consists mainly of intellect, virtues, and ideas. This America is not a body in the sense that it was in the myth of the virgin land, with its female landscape imagery and its rhetoric of motherly love and nurturing. For Sophie, in "To the Stars," the president is "the living light of the late afternoon glow"—we do not know what he looks like because all the references to him are fictitious projections of the heroine's worship (*ChL* 93). Similarly, for Shenah in "Wings" and "Hunger," the young man becomes the "Other One," the epitome of the desire for betterment "that will make from you a person who'll yet ring in America" (64). Both women build their alternative versions of the American Dream around a happy ending involving an idealistic relationship with disembodied American men who help them enter the new culture.

However, in the process of thus remaking their visions, the women in Yezierska's texts threaten to endanger their own identities in the dominant culture. In the hero worship of their mentors and mediators, they not only disembody their idols by envisioning them as asexual demigods but also deprive themselves of a clear sense of sexual identity. The subtext in these stories suggests that the price one pays for constructing such male father figures, or platonic American lovers, to initiate the immigrant woman into the new culture is the loss of sexual identity. In "Wings," Shenah takes John's rejection not only as his statement that he would never treat a "little immigrant" seriously as a woman, but also as a hint suggesting that sex would hinder her ambitious resolutions. He is afraid of her ethnic sexuality, which might spoil his research, whereas she, in her worship of his sophisticated aloofness, rejects what she is—Jewish, sexually desiring and desirous—to be like him. In practice, she challenges the gender roles prescribed for her by both the Old and the New World and thus rejects her body in her struggle for intellectual growth. If she wants to become an American, she has to counter the stereotype of the Jewish woman's inadvertently sexual nature; she has to renounce her ethnic identity—which is linked to "Oriental" carnal longings—for the sake of embracing the spiritual values of the work ethic and the ideology of self-reliance. These values would make her acceptable to the host culture.

Therefore, in "Hunger" Shenah's feminine dreams about a fairy tale prince ripen into an ambition for things beyond simple marriage to an American, and John Barnes turns into a bigger-than-life demigod. That is why she rejects a wealthy Jewish coworker, Sam Arkin, who falls in love with her sexy vitality and enthusiasm. Having refused his proposal—his checkbook and promises that he would "give [her] dove's milk to drink . . . silks and diamonds to wear"—she tells him to use the experience of unrequited love the way she did. She advises him to "make a person of himself" through suffering rejection, which should inspire his ambition for "higher things" (60–64). Hence, repression of sexual identity and the gender roles it implies—Shenah has to be tough not to fall for men who offer the temptations of marriage and family— is the price to pay for becoming a self-made woman in America. Thus, by rejecting sexual dependence and the economic reliance it involves, Yezierska's heroine simultaneously rejects the institution of marriage as an obstacle preventing a woman from becoming her own person.[31]

In "To the Stars," Sophie writes her story depicting the ways in which she and her people contribute to the American ideal by sacrificing her bodily presence to language. While wasting away in the cellar, Sophie creates a text that will change her life. Yet to write it, she has to literally cut down her body's nourishment and needs for comfort. She tells the president later: "I feel I can learn you to put flesh and blood into your words so that everybody can feel your thoughts close to the heart." For a newcomer female, writing means a transformation of bodily sensuality into rhetoric, and that is why she expects such a text "written with the body" from others as well. After meeting with her idol, Sophie goes back home, to her work, with "a new light in her eyes, new strength in her arms and fingers" to guide her "hand" in writing (97–98).

Sophie's flight "to the stars" leads away from her body, which is seen as a mere vessel for the mind of a writer. The almost religious evocations in the ending ("tears of a soul filled to the brim," "new dawn, of hope and of faith fulfilled") suggest that Sophie has been transformed from being a "hand" in a shop, from being just a laborer's body, to being a "hand of God" in fulfilling her spiritual mission as a writer.[32] Inspired by her mentor, she becomes a disembodied presence that creates texts; but in gaining her voice she has to renounce her body and her sexuality. Such a "happy ending" implies that she can succeed, but she has to pay for it with the denial of her femininity.[33]

## "All They Ever Wanted to Be": Immigrant Women and Oppression of Sexuality in Yezierska's Novels

### Why Is God Male?

Yezierska's heroines' desire for education and intellectual fulfillment entails their denial of their bodies and their challenge to traditional gender roles in both cultures, but it does not so much alter the roles that are constructed for them by the dominant culture. Paradoxically, because they exist in America as primarily ethnic females—the other mothers, daughters, wives—they cannot escape being perceived within these gender roles. For example, Yezierska's own two unsuccessful marriages and the fact that she surrendered the custody of her daughter to her husband to be able to write classified her as a rebel by emphasizing her acts as incongruous with acceptable feminine behavior—she was an "unnatural mother" and a "selfish wife."[34] Thus both Yezierska and her heroines remain defined in terms of their gender roles, although they often challenge them and renounce, or are forced to renounce, the sexuality from which these roles arise.

In replacing the myth of the virgin land with the worship of disembodied male mentors, Yezierska's female characters separate the body and the mind and thus repress any flesh-and-blood desires in themselves. They also deny the existence of such desires in their idols. These denials are necessary if they want to subvert the feminine aspect of the myth of America and to emphasize their own intellectual capabilities instead. Yet even their alternative America—a happy ending through an intellectual friendship with a man—fails when the ideals they have cherished become live people, when the icons turn into male bodies that crave physical response and reciprocation of desire from their disciple-devotees. While most of Yezierska's stories explore platonic relationships with ideal Americans, it is in her novels, which are called by some critics "autobiographies," that she deals more extensively with the ambivalences of sexuality that her heroines experience on their way into the new culture.[35]

The crisis of sexual identity and its effects on the immigrant woman and her position within the dominant culture are presented vividly in Yezierska's first novel, *Salome of the Tenements* (1922). The story concerns a poor ghetto girl who has her mind set on marrying a millionaire and attaining the "higher life" reserved for privileged WASPs. The novel was inspired by the much-publicized marriage of a Jewish ghetto reporter, Yezierska's good friend Rose Pastor, to an uptown scion and philanthropist, Graham Phelps Stokes.[36] The text is particularly interesting because it shows Yezierska's craft in exploiting a typical "happy ending" to convey a subtext that describes the oppression and exploitation of the ethnic woman's femininity.

Although *Salome* seems deceptively clear about its heroine's sexuality—superficially, she is a stereotypical, passionate Jewish female—it explores her sexual frustration under the seeming cover of Hollywood melodrama.[37] The discovery that she has been deceived and used comes to Sonya Vrunsky after what should have been a "happy ending" in any tale of miscegenation—a marriage to a WASP who is an embodiment of her American Dream man. Because she is an alien who has trespassed into the forbidden territory of the upper class, she finds that it is not possible to "mix fire and water." Her beauty is proof to her husband's scandalized family and friends that she must have attracted him primarily as a sexual object, and her wit evidence that she entrapped her "catch" with ruthless and cunning sexual manipulation. Her lower-class social standing and Jewishness leave no doubt that, at a time when many immigrant and working-class women were forced into prostitution by low wages, she is a loose female who can skillfully capitalize on her charms.[38] After all, why else would a rich and intelligent man marry her? Sonya learns all this in the course of her story and discovers that intermarriage does not work in the Promised Land. Yezierska's deceptively simple romance is thus a study of the immigrant woman's realization that her insistence on constructing her American Dream around a male friend-mediator-husband is unrealistic because it frustrates her sexuality. Thus, it definitely revises the traditional ending of melodrama.

On the very first pages of *Salome of the Tenements*, in the chapter entitled "Salome Meets Her Saint," Sonya Vrunsky feels the "fire of worship" burning in her while she is interviewing a famous philanthropist, John Manning, for a Jewish newspaper, *Ghetto News*. The language Yezierska uses to describe the young woman's feelings is styled after the tone of a devout prayer. Referring to one of his charity appearances, Sonya tells Manning passionately: " 'Never before did a born American talk out to them so prophetically—what means it America!' " Nevertheless, "in spite of the emotional stimulus she gave him, his frosty blue eyes failed to kindle." Even though her "whole face was alight" and her "personality, femininity, flamed through [her] unrevealing uniform," Sonya's ardent worship is directed toward a god who does not seem capable of comprehending her fiery admiration: "Through a tear-dimmed mist she saw his tall slenderness, the shoulders slightly stooped as though by a head too heavy for his frail strength. The premature grayness of his hair was to her a nimbus—a cloud of white light, adding the final touch of divinity to the luminous features."[39] In this passage John Manning is portrayed as a frail and almost handicapped figure. This image of an impotent deity provides a contrast with the fiery "Oriental" heroine. Yezierska's character thus builds her image of an idolized American Protestant and develops her desire for what he represents around the disembodied vision of a vulnerable saint who inspires feelings of tenderness and protectiveness but who does not possess a healthy and passionate body.

Such a portrayal of Sonya's ideal clashes with the love and physical attraction she conceives for him later and with her mad desire to inspire reciprocal affection. Yet Yezierska stops short of a tearful melodrama about unrequited love by presenting her character as a driven, ruthless, exotic Salome, who would not be diverted from pursuing her goal. In this way, Sonya may give grounds to her anti-Semitic detractors to see her as cunning and double-faced. By employing the Old Testament myth, the author juxtaposes two other stereotypes—the archetypal Jewish temptress and the chaste Christian saint—and thus seems to suggest right away who is going to be the winner in this meeting of extremes, whose head will appear "on the plate" at the end. However, the sexual tension building up between the two lovers is counter-balanced by the young woman's idolization of her love object. Sonya's bold resolution is to "get him," to marry the rich man and show everybody that she, a poor Jewish immigrant, can in cold blood "catch on to" the biggest match in town. But Yezierska complicates this portrait of Sonya by making her turn Manning into a demigod father figure for whom she falls. When Sonya remembers her conversation with Manning, the scene is evoked in the tone of religious revelation: "'My child! You have been a revelation to me!' she repeated. . . . His presence, so ethereal, yet so vivid, still breathed over her. . . . The very air was pungent with his spirit—the light of his smile still enveloped her" (12).

Sonya-Salome's passion for the saintly and disembodied father-god is not wholly in tune with the conventional immigrant Cinderella story. The heroine is too bold and too cunning; the affair touches on sacrilege and incest. As Schoen suggests, Yezierska was consciously writing an antimyth, and she set out to dispel the romantic notions that some readers had about ghetto life and ghetto people.[40] But she also seems to want to make it clear that a mixed marriage was mostly an unattainable dream in the era when rich men often went into the ghetto's brothels to buy sex. As a reformer, Manning is one of those middle-class men who, like the real-life individuals described by John D'Emilio and Estelle B. Freedman, "did enter the red-light district, whether as customers or as reformers, [and] confronted the reality of sexual values that differed from their own."[41] Sonya's shameless scheming to seduce him, to make him lose his Puritan poise and to reciprocate her passion, suggests deeper social undertones. It makes clear that Manning does not fit the anti-Cinderella story either, for it is impossible to seduce the impotent god and father figure. And whether he is viewed as unmanly, weak, and frail or as secretly devious and exploitative of ethnic women's sexuality, a potential red-light district patron is a dubious prospect as the native-born husband of a model immigrant woman.

Therefore, Yezierska's text functions as two antistories: it unmakes the mythical one about Salome and John the Baptist as well as another one about an immigrant Cinderella's intermarriage. It portrays a confused Jewish temptress caught between her passion for and devotion to the American Christian "saint" who falls prey to this confusion. On the other hand, it challenges the myth of miscegenation with Yezierska's depiction of marriage as an economic agreement, one that entraps two strangers representing alien sexual conducts. With an openness rare in her time, Yezierska presents Sonya's expectations concerning her sexual union with John Manning as unreal. The scene describing their first sexual encounter, an unabashed premarital affair confirming high society's worst suspicions, takes place in the pastoral setting of one of Manning's estates and is a highly ambivalent depiction of a carnal union between an immigrant female and a native-born male.[42]

Not only is the scene presented within the imagery of a dream allegory so that we are not sure whether it actually takes place, but it is also described in such sacred, overblown terms that it may be just a fantasy—if not a vision—resulting from Sonya's passionate worship of her saint. After all, Manning has been a very restrained and repressed Puritan, and it seems impossible to suddenly imagine him rolling in the grass with his fiancée. It is also true that Sonya is a confused young woman, and she would rather worship her beloved than seduce him. Her projections about the inevitable "seduction" that marriage entails are akin to a religious ritual. In such a context, the reader has reason to suspect the author of parodying the heroine's manipulation of events in the Cinderella story. Yezierska ironically comments on the impossibility of this idyllic fusion of two "others" by using fairy tale imagery: "They opened their eyes and saw how forest and meadow palpitated with the Miracle" (ST 173). The dissonance implied in the difference between the main characters' dispositions and their implied sexual acts calls into question the propriety of the mixed-race romance, on the one hand, and subverts even the simple antimyth of the Cinderella story that Schoen proposes in her reading, on the other.

Contrary to what prevailing criticism of this book suggests, Yezierska's text clearly harbors a deeper message beneath its seemingly melodramatic, Hollywoodlike script.[43] On the surface, we read a story of Sonya's ruthless conquest of John Manning and of the failure of their marriage, which does not withstand Manning's wrath when he finds out that Sonya has borrowed money from a loan shark in order to entrap him. In this failure, it would seem that the man is punished for his "ungentlemanly" desire for a lowly immigrant, as Sonya leaves him for a Jewish designer, Hollins, and jeopardizes his reputation with the scandal of divorce. The woman, however, lives happily ever after with her "own kind" and finds fulfillment in the art of dressmaking—a happy ending for her. Nevertheless, in her subtext Yezierska "unmakes" this surface narrative, which provoked the critics and resulted in an unpopular movie, by suggesting that Sonya fails rather than triumphs in her intrigues. It is she who is truly vanquished, whose "head is served on the platter" as a result of the frustrating play between the sexual identities of an immigrant woman and a native-born male. As with the stories discussed earlier, the key to this message can be found in and beyond the novel's ending.

The final scene of *Salome* brings Sonya and Manning together for the last time in her new lover's fashion store. Henriksen mentions that this scene was rewritten after a suggestion by Yezierska's editor, who was offended by Sonya's undeserved triumph (*AY* 177–78).[44] This rewritten moral, "Revelation," has Sonya brooding after the outburst of her ex-husband's passion, a violent scene that almost ended in rape: "She saw how men and women helplessly and unknowingly destroy themselves and each other in the blind uprising of brute passion which lies like a sleeping dog within the consciousness of the divine soul" (*ST* 289). Nevertheless, the crucial part of this chapter, the true revelation, is not this didactic discovery of the conflict between the "darker side" of human nature and the Emersonian divine, but Sonya's contemplation of the fact that, for the first time in the novel, the demigod WASP reveals his violent and sexual nature. Out of his upper-class element, he appears unrestrained by the conventional sexual conduct that seemed to guide his behavior even in their marriage bed. The scene depicting Manning gripping Sonya with untamed desire and attempting to force himself on her is the most powerful encounter in the whole novel. In this moment the tables turn, and the fiery heroine is terrified and flees from the god who has suddenly become flesh and raging libido. This scene contains the only true "miracle" in the novel, and in its violence and graphic realism it undermines further the premarital pastoral consummation of Sonya's and Manning's love.

The fact that she is surprised at Manning's ability to be so violent and his capacity for treating her openly as a sexual object brings into question their whole relationship (289). Supposedly, she has left him because he is a "pale-blooded Puritan" who did not respond to her sexual needs. Yet when he reveals his passion at the end, it is in circumstances hardly conducive to making love. Suddenly she sees him for the first time as a "naked savage" (290). Thus Yezierska has Sonya discovering the American male as a dichotomy—at once a restrained Puritan and a violent "savage."

Sonya's realization that, in her desire to deify America as male, she has constructed an idealistic and deceptive image of Manning is parallel to her confrontation with her own confused sexuality. The conflict between the Oriental and the American—the Jew and the Christian—is thus played not only between Sonya and Manning but also within the young woman who sees herself trapped between the two incompatible identities. Sonya's story is an allegory of acculturation—because of the conflict with Manning she discovers the contradictory desires fighting within her new striving-to-be-American identity. As the ultimate schemer and plotter, the young woman thus writes not only Manning but also herself; she builds an intrigue of the story around fictitious projections of herself in the new country.

The reader glimpses this underlying conflict in the way Yezierska allows her heroine to enter the deep-structure subtext. We can see interesting examples of this hidden authorial commentary in two scenes when Sonya looks into the mirror and contemplates her face in response to the feelings Manning arouses in her. In the first scene, after having parted from her idol at their first encounter, the heroine rushes to her looking glass. What she sees is an exalted vision of a saintly face: "She gave herself a passionately critical scrutiny. With hands pressed against her cheeks she studied the reflection of herself. *Luminous black eyes flashed back at her—keen-edged swords of desire*. 'He—he is for me as the sun is for the earth—light—life. He is the breath of all that is beautiful. Ach! How I could love him! I'd wrap *my soul* around him like a *living flame*'" (13, emphasis mine). Her countenance is lit with the "fire of worship," with love that speaks about the soul and not the body. The "swords of desire" and the "living flame" touch on the imagery of Christian martyrdom, but the mirror conspicuously captures only Sonya's head and not Manning's—John the Baptist's. In this scene Sonya is in love with the idea of her god and, unconsciously at this point, with the idea of "sacrificing" her body to be with him—in love with herself as a prospective American woman. She frames her face in her hands, as if detaching it from the rest of her body in an anticipation of martyrdom. Her subliminal union with her saint is meant to be a communion of the two beautiful spirits and a perfect mingling of the races they represent, a mythical merging of celestial bodies rather than earthly ones.

Sonya's hidden fear of sexuality in her idol and in herself, represented here in the imagery of pain and torture, surfaces in another mirror scene, at the point in the novel when she feels close to attaining her goal. Realizing what their eventual nuptials would involve, she grows suddenly frightened; in her room next to Manning's she listens to the sounds he is making, while he, on the other side of the wall, feels her eyes following him and spying on every movement of his undressing. In this voyeuristic scene, Sonya—the sexual aggressor—realizes that achieving her dream will mean sexual consummation, and she simultaneously rejects and desires it:

> She picked up the mirror nearly to drop it at the *reflection that stared at her*—blood-shot eyes—swollen lips—cheeks aflame as if the blood had run riot, twisting, distorting her features. She flung the offending mirror on the couch. This minute she would go to him—put an end to all the intrusions—the unrealities that stood between them. A thought, big, daring, wonderful, slipped into her mind. . . . "I am not ready for fulfillment," she told herself with chastened humility. "Something in me shuts me out from the light of my own soul. . . . I have to get away to save my soul." (159–61)

She feels like a trespasser into the other gender role and like a shameless voyeur, not to mention a sinful fallen woman. The artifice of her marriage—based on deceit—implies false faith in the ideal marriage with her new country. And yet she yields to that female "Jekyll/Hyde" reflection that she sees staring at her, to this ambivalent Sonya who is first a chaste virgin and next a ruthless "blood-thirsty" (or just sexually unfulfilled) monster she does not recognize. In this scene she is lost. She does not understand her desires and fears them instead of controlling them. For this reason, the suspicion that she is a flesh-and-blood female "crazy for a man" terrifies her; her own sexual desire is something to be afraid of, something that makes her vulnerable and weak, like those other women she has always wanted to be superior to. Yet her resolve to go through with the union proves that she also realizes the inevitability of coming to terms with her sexuality—the martyrdom—from which she was hoping to escape into the happy ending of an idealistic, mythical American marriage.

Hence it is also Sonya's frustrations that ruin her marriage, not only Manning's frigidity or Puritan repression in the American male. Although she accuses him of coldness and restraint in their final confrontation—"You didn't want me when I was burning up for you"—she also "had lain beside him night after night, sleepless, nerves unstrung, hungering in vain," without giving any sign of her longing, bound by her desire not to offend with her insatiability, not to prove that she was indeed the oversexed ethnic female (287). What is actually revealed at the end of the novel, then, is that both male and female have not faced their carnality. Thus the ethnic heroine and her American lover are incompatible. Manning can only say, "I didn't know, I didn't understand," as if he did not indeed realize what marriage entailed. On the one hand, this scene presents a clichéd immigrant scenario, one that Yezierska employed frequently, of the passionate ethnic woman who confronts her temperamental inferior in the native-born male. On the other hand, it suggests that Sonya never made clear what she wanted from her husband because she was never sure of her own desires. The stereotype of the exotic other's superior sexuality is thus debunked. Through these two people, who superficially fit the clichéd model of the intercultural marriage, Yezierska shows how such a union implies a clash between complete strangers rather than guaranteeing their successful merging. No union, no melting, no "two in one" are possible in Yezierska's antiromance.

That is why the novel's ending unmakes the clichés of the "romance" with which Sonya justifies her story in her final deceptive "triumph." *Salome* is about the immigrant woman's inability to come to terms with her sexuality in the new country, which victimizes her through ethnic stereotypes of femininity. Yezierska makes it obvious that the promise of a happy ending through marriage also holds in store a disillusionment with the woman's own desires and their object.[45] The newcomer female rejects a carnal union with an American male other because it destroys her myth of America as a disembodied male and of herself as an antithesis to the stereotypes of ethnic female sexuality. All the same, she cannot stop craving the new culture and longing for it to accept and embrace her for what she is—even in her confusion. In this respect, Sonya's marriage with Hollins, an American-born Jew, does not resolve anything. It implies suspending her confusion and choosing a compromise, a "half-way" intercultural solution.

Thus, by ending with Sonya pondering her fate, Yezierska gives the reader a chance to read the young woman's desperation. If she wants to succeed in her work as a designer, Sonya needs a man, a "native-born" Jew, who understands her alien side and can translate it for America, one who can mediate her into the world of business. Although she is a first-generation Jewish American just as he is, she cannot as a lower-class female be accepted for what she is and wants. For the New World has her categorized as a Salome, in an image and a myth that has little to do with her humanity, sexual identity, intelligence, and ambitions.[46] That is why, in the end, Yezierska has Sonya choose work as a fashion designer over passion and romance; her marriage to Hollins is a sensible choice and guarantees her a secure future. As long as she dresses others, instead of offering her charms as a temptation for native men, she can exist as a part of the alien ethnic enclave adopted by the dominant culture.[47] Moreover, as a female married to a man of her own ethnicity, she will no longer be a threat to American "racial purity." Thus the social order is restored. Like the heroines in the short stories, like Yezierska herself, Sonya wants the impossible and ends up turning against herself in her conflicting desires. But she finally has to settle down to a compromise, both with the dominant culture and with her own frustrated and often incomprehensible identity.[48]

### Unbridgeable Gap

In *Bread Givers, Arrogant Beggar,* and *All I Could Never Be,* the novels following *Salome of the Tenements* during the precarious rise and fall of Yezierska's popularity, the theme of an immigrant woman's search for a happy ending, despite the conflict involved in becoming American, is developed further and with greater insistence. The heroines of these texts find their new country more and more ambiguous and their place in it more and more uncertain. Work and creativity become their remedies for the frustrating trials of acculturation; the story of their struggles to attain education and to become intellectuals often overshadows the romance stories in which they would appear in more traditional gender roles as mothers and lovers.

For Sara Smolinsky, the heroine of *Bread Givers,* the way to success leads through education and self-reliance. However, pursuing her ambitions involves the denial of her rabbi-father and of the tradition and religion that he represents. The tension and conflict between the young woman and her parent are the reasons for the book's subtitle: "A struggle between the father of the Old World and a daughter of the New," a telling suggestion that, perhaps, Reb Smolinsky "fathered" the tradition of the Old World whereas his daughter has been really conceived by another father—the New World. Nevertheless, Sara faces a more complex problem than just challenging her father's conservative views on the position of women in Judaism and Jewish culture and on their subsequent adjustment to America. Aside from her personal struggle to escape the patriarchal bonds of Judaism, she insists on being independent of any man and on defying patriarchal domination over all women. Like Shenah and Sophie in the short stories, Sara, too, sets as her goal becoming an educated American woman through self-reliant struggle. Like these young girls, she understands that she has to pursue her task alone because yielding to the desire for a man—for sexual gratification, support, and the security of marriage—would mean a betrayal of her "duty to herself" as an individual.[49] Thus, just like Sonya-Salome, Sara learns to fear her sexuality; she realizes that a "respectable" scenario prescribed for her by both the Old and the New Worlds is marriage to a man who can ensure the continuation of her faith and provide her with economic security but who can also thwart her dream of becoming an American teacher. The gender roles she is expected to fit into as a Jewish female collide with her individual desire to become independent and emancipated.

As Doris Weatherford stresses, immigrant women learned how to question their domestic roles from American feminists and followed their teachings in demanding liberation from the Old World patriarchies.[50] In her desire to be a New (American) Woman, Sara rejects the traditional female roles of mother and wife, and she tries not to be "oversexed," in the sense Charlotte Perkins Gilman understood immigrant women to be. She refuses the advances of a wealthy Jewish suitor to whom she is very attracted sexually and "sacrifices" her body on the altar of education. As if to deny her femininity—an obstacle to the development of the mind in a culture that cannot have a woman possessing both beauty and intelligence—she wastes her looks in the sweatshops and in poring over her books late at night. In resisting the advances of Max Goldstein, a rich Jewish entrepreneur from California, Sara chooses intellect over carnality:

> I touched the hand he had touched, my face, my neck. . . . I knew now the meaning of a certain inner smile that I used to see in certain women's eyes. I felt that same smile in me. . . . I was thrilled. Flattered. Ripened for love. Then why did I let him go? . . . Slowly, one piece of a broken thought began to weave itself together with another. If I'd let myself love him, I'd end by hating him. He only excited me. But that wasn't enough. . . . I looked at the books on my table that had stared at me like enemies a little while before. They were again a life of my life. . . . I seized my books and hugged them to my breast as though they were living things.[51]

Although Sara seems to have enjoyed her affair with Max Goldstein, she decides against being the lover of any man who would want her to be just his wife—an object of support and of sexual desire rewarded for her services with his "gold." To accept the gender roles designed for her by both the Jewish and American cultures means she would have to trade in her sexuality. To refuse to accept them, she has to repress it.

On the way to becoming her own person, an American "teacherin," according to her father, Yezierska's heroine consciously defies the stereotypical narrative of miscegenation prescribed for her ethnicity and gender, as well as the makers and supporters of this narrative in both cultures. Her choice results from intellectual judgment, as she observes how her father's tyranny ruins her three sisters' lives with unhappy arranged marriages and how (which infuriates her even more) the women succumb to their fate meekly, without rebellion or attempted escape. Ironically, to her broken and traditional sisters Sara is a strange creature because they cannot comprehend renouncing for the sake of "books" the prestige and security that the institution of marriage guarantees. Even to her mother, the choice is simple: "I'd be happier to see you get married. What's a school teacher? Old maids—all of them. It's good enough for *Goyim*, but not for you" (172). At that time one was either a wife or a schoolteacher. Therefore, Yezierska has Sara fight not only her sexuality but also other women in her family for whom the development of the mind and the liberation from the bonds of Judaic domesticity, from the poverty of the ghetto even, mean a denial of femininity and Jewishness rather than American success.

In Sara Smolinsky, Yezierska creates the New Jewish Woman who defies the sexual stereotypes through which the dominant culture sees immigrant females from this ethnic group—the promiscuous woman, the inferior Eastern Jew, the Other driven by animalistic sexual instincts.[52] At the same time, she challenges the religious and cultural models of womanhood held by traditional Jewish immigrants who wanted to hold on to Old World values against the influence of the progressive groups with which their children came into contact in the New World. Sara is thus successful both in obtaining an education and repressing her unwanted ethnic sexuality—the first action directed toward the New World and the second against the Old. Yet she has to pay the price for taking this ambivalent stand between two "fathers." As Alice Kessler-Harris stresses, Yezierska "offers independent and self-willed women, and she does not hide the psychic pain of their sacrifice."[53]

Having graduated and having found both a job and a "room of her own," Sara meets a mate who complements her achievements—her superior at the immigrant school where she is employed. It is as if Yezierska were afraid to leave the reader with Sara as a single professional woman. Despite the emphasis on their instant love and understanding as compatriots—"*Landsleute*"—the union between an idealistically open-minded Americanized Jewish male and his educated and sensible bride that concludes the narrative seems more like an inevitable social contract than the passionate love Sara has always desired. Instead the conclusion of *Bread Givers* presents a happy Hollywood-style reward featuring love and reconciliation with Sara's ailing and widowed father, whom the couple take in. But we should read it as the ethnic woman's punishment for "making it" in America, for although Sara initially fled from her father and renounced what he stood for, she now consents to take care of him because her American husband tells her to, and, possibly, because Yezierska had to resolve the family conflict in order to appease her audience.[54] Furthermore, the benign optimism of the conclusion is undermined by images of Yezierska's heroine and of her lover that clearly convey his physical control over her, images that are heightened by the first-person narrative voice. When he hears her mispronounce a word in a class, he walks in with all the authority and power of the principal and corrects her, "the tips of his fingers on my throat" (272). He takes "hold of both my hands" when they first have tea together in her room and his "grip tighten[s] on my arm" as they leave her father's apartment after their final reconciliation (279, 297).[55]

The much-discussed conclusion of *Bread Givers* shows that an emancipated Jewish woman has to be "tamed" by a male who is superior to her. The seemingly happy ending to Yezierska's clearly feminist novel questions and disrupts the single woman's triumphant progress and jolts the reader, already used to Sara's independence, with her submission to a traditional marriage. Clearly, after her experience with Max Goldstein and her lonely years in college, when she envied the American kids their beautiful and love-centered life, Sara simply cannot succumb to a sensuous and exciting male. As was true for Sonya at the end of *Salome*, Sara's choice is an Americanized Jew—level-headed, educated, and intelligent, one who will be a father-mentor figure for the successful ethnic woman now alienated from her Jewish background. In this way, Hugo Seelig represents her New World father, with his features "all fineness and strength," "a Jewish face, and yet none of the greedy eagerness of Hester Street any more" (273). The irony of this happy ending is that it emphasizes the price Sara has to pay for a few years of feminist freedom. Having been her own person, she has to settle at the end for a life controlled by her husband-father, a man who subtly combines the repressive energies of both worlds. As Thomas J. Ferraro notes, "What is most provocative about Yezierska's interrogation is not that she identifies a psychologically operative patriarchy, but that she shows how a specifically Jewish and feminine socialization allows patriarchy to catch up with even the most rebellious of daughters."[56] To everybody's great relief, Sara's marriage frees her from being "the daughter of Babylon." Although clearly suggesting her love for Hugo, the ending destroys her independence by showing that she needs a man to affirm her femininity after the years of repressing and sacrificing it to free herself from the Old World and to prove her intellectual abilities in the New. In the end she loses; she is neither a Jew—she refuses to have her clothes cut at her mother's funeral—nor an American—she comes back to her repressive Judaic roots through her Americanized Jewish husband, who uses her to explore his "heritage." Thus suspended between two cultures, Sara is like the heroine of "Children of Loneliness": "I am one of the millions of the immigrant children, children of loneliness, wandering between the worlds that are at once too old and too new to live in" (OC 163).

### Home for the Girls with Grit

A similar feeling of loss and confusion is the lot of Adele Lindner in *Arrogant Beggar*. Like Sara, she identifies successful Americanization with sexual repression and feels that, in the eyes of the dominant culture, she is predominantly a stereotyped Jewish female. Once again, the identity conflict in this immigrant female Bildungsroman involves the heroine's turning against her own sexuality in her attempts to defy the dominant stereotype. Although her struggle is lost from the very beginning, as became clear in Sara's case, it nevertheless teaches Adele, the arrogant beggar of the title, about the reasons for her otherness within the dominant culture. Yezierska's heroines come to identify being an American with education and success, and being a Jewish other with carnality and physical suffering. Because of their lower-class backgrounds and tough struggles with poverty and hunger, they are constantly reminded of their class and ethnic inferiority. And in the midst of this conflict, the women search for an impossible solution, for an ending to a journey of self-discovery that is as implausible as those Yezierska pastes onto her novels.

As an orphan, the heroine of *Arrogant Beggar* does not have to combat a conservative father the way Sara does. Her problem is that she must make a decision about what she wants to do with her life in America. Yet her choices are again limited by the roles she can play as a lower-class, ethnic female: a domestic servant, a cook, or a social worker. While in these roles, she can also hope to marry rich and thus end her economic struggle; in one way or another she has to rely on others to solve her problems for her. She must depend on the charitable institutions symbolized by the upper-class "ladies bountiful" to teach her a trade fitting her social position, or she must rely upon a man to save her from the drudgery of manual labor.

The novel begins when Adele enters Mrs. Hellman's Home for Working Girls and, rather predictably, dreams about a man unlike any she has known so far in the ghetto, one who embodies the higher life she expects from America-Arcadia. It is the familiar dream in Yezierska's fiction of a male intercultural mediator. In this respect, Adele willingly begins enacting the scene that the charity women prescribe for single immigrant girls who are being trained as "domestic scientists"—servants—and who then will be placed in the care of suitable husbands. The home organizes social events so that the young women can meet their suitors and so fulfill the narrative of their Americanization. Yet every girl's desire is to "catch on" to a wealthy man, not so much because she dreams of "real love," but because he can take her away from the stifling formality of the house. Typically for Yezierska's time, romance is based on the economic realities of the "market."

Superficially, the conflict in *Arrogant Beggar* involves the male of the Old World and that of the New, as Adele has to choose one or the other and thus decide her future according to the miscegenation narrative. Initially, a fascination with her rich benefactor, Mrs. Hellman, makes her fall in love with the woman's son, Arthur, who is a native-born, upper-class Jew. Arthur, then, represents an unattainable combination of physical attractiveness (he does not look "typically" Jewish), class, and Americanized ethnicity. Adele worships the cultured and immaculately dressed youth and compares this idealized image of success in America to her unkempt ghetto suitor, Schlomoh. After her first encounter with Arthur Adele thinks: "Unapproachable. A god, standing in a museum, with the sign, 'Don't touch.' Looking out with his cool gaze at the crowd around him. . . . 'Sea-gray eyes,' I whispered to myself. . . . 'Not dark, but those queer, gray-green glints of colour, more distinguished than dark.' . . . The first man of the other world. The first man I must know. But how can I open that shut door? How make him see me the next time we meet?"[57] In contrast to the religiously ardent desire that Arthur's aloofness inspires in her, she dismisses Schlomoh's effusiveness; she is disgusted with his loyalty, submissive love, and physical longing for her: "He jerked out his hand to grasp mine. What a hand! The damp skin clinging to my fingers like a limp fish wriggling against my palm. . . . His touch turned me to ice. . . . He seized my hand. Before I knew it, he kissed my fingers. Hungrily. Ravenously. Devouring lips that would eat me up if I let them. I broke away, fled" (95–100). The juxtaposition of the two men reveals a religious fascination with the American male deity, on the one hand, and a clear sense of revulsion toward the earthly qualities of the ethnic male, on the other.

The comparison between Arthur and Schlomoh pits the disembodied, "all-for-the-eyes" image of Apollolike Arthur against the pathetic body, "all-hands" Schlomoh. What Adele dreams of is the cool world of Anglo-Saxons, perfumed and detached from the bodily functions that she identifies with the lower-class people from the ghetto. She is inspired by the statuesque qualities of well-groomed Arthur, while Schlomoh's common humanity, the imprint of the ghetto's poverty on him, repels her. The contrast between the two men's names speaks for itself as a lofty Arthurian image is juxtaposed with that of a lowly fish peddler.

Nevertheless, her longing for Arthur and her frustration with Schlomoh's desire derive from sources inside Adele rather than in the two men themselves. For the more significant issue in Yezierska's book is Adele's search for her own sexual identity and her inability to find it with an American man, or with any man for that matter. She mistakenly perceives her problem in terms of Arthur and Schlomoh, in terms of the choice implied by the two. But the two men simply reflect her own duality, one that propels her frustration. It is this frustration—this confusion about her sexual identity in a culture that encourages her to choose a man by insisting on traditional gender roles—that she tries to escape. After Adele delivers a defiant speech attacking the heartless ladies of the girls' home, a scandal erupts that causes her to flee desperately into the alien city. Thus she must forgo the only "respectable" way she has for "making from herself a person." There is no doubt that Adele despises the patronizing and hypocrisy of the wealthy women who play philanthropists for their amusement. Nevertheless, it is also true that she is running away from herself, after realizing the duality bred into her by the dominant culture. She is both the earthly female—a partner for Schlomoh—and an idealistic dreamer—a worshiper of Arthur. She has to start her life over again if she is to find an Adele she would rather be.

Yezierska's feisty heroine finds a job as a dishwasher and is taken in by a poor old woman, Muhmenkeh. To Arthur Hellman, who disliked her admiration at first, Adele's actions prove that she "has the grit," that she has "more spunk than I thought any girl could have" (158–59). He decides to pursue Adele into the ghetto because her anger and revolt have suddenly made her a desirable and fascinating other for him. Once she stops acting like a model immigrant girl, once she reveals her pride, beauty, and anger, she becomes an interesting and exciting object of desire.

However, at this point Adele turns her back on the man who used to be the embodiment of her dreams. This decision is key to the conflict Adele finds in herself; it explains the unreal and artificial ending of the novel. Her greatest disillusionment occurs when she realizes that it is due to Arthur's initial rejection that she makes her speech and begins to hate the charity she used to be so grateful for. Thus she runs away as much from the hypocrisy of the ladies bountiful as from the humiliating realization that a man's rejection made her reevaluate her life. It does not matter that he offers her marriage later, having found her in the ghetto and having nursed her back to health after a rather severe melodramatic illness. She refuses him because she now realizes that

Arthur desires to possess her as much as Schlomoh did, that the two men want her to be an object of their desire while all she wants is to be her own person—a subject in her own story. Adele fears this male possessiveness and thus appears to reject completely her past dream of finding America through a union with a man.

Nevertheless, the novel's conclusion surprisingly disrupts this resolve and shows us Adele finally happy with an ideal man who suits all her needs and dispels all her fears. The man is Jean Rachmansky, a Jewish piano player from Poland who, like herself, escaped from the humiliation of being a Hellman protégé. Adele's meeting of Rachmansky, and the unexpected eradication of her fears concerning sexuality that results, are not very convincing unless we approach the ending as irony on Yezierska's part. Like Schoen, I believe that the ending is "the most obvious and least acceptable form of manipulation" and that it robs the novel of "its potentially powerful statement about the trials and joys of a woman finding and making her own life."[58]

Adele does make her own life when she rejects Arthur and the easy, "Americanized" life he offers. Her return to Muhmenkeh's is a decision to make it on her own and to forgo men for the sake of a self-reliant single life. When she chooses that over marriage, she also chooses the company of women; she finds a perfect companion-mother-girlfriend in the old woman who loves her unconditionally.[59] Nevertheless, as soon as the now contented Adele begins dreaming about what could become her true vocation—writing—Muhmenkeh's death deprives her of the only friendly soul she has had in the whole world. Muhmenkeh, who has been telling Adele the story of her life and who has inspired her to write it down, leaves the story at the very moment when the young woman has found the possibility of fulfillment in authorship. Her death deprives Adele both of love and of the subject she wanted to describe. Significantly, the passage in the novel where Adele begins to "write" Muhmenkeh's interesting past in her thoughts precedes the old woman's demise. We can read this passage as Adele's lesson in the elusive power of fiction. In a sense, as soon as she has been turned into a story in Adele's mind, Muhmenkeh has to disappear, perhaps in order to make room for a happy ending featuring the inevitable male savior of the single woman.

According to this "risky" reading, we can interpret everything that happens from that moment on as Adele's "fiction" because, after Muhmenkeh's death, the story becomes odd and discordant against the rest of Yezierska's novel. It seems as if Adele were writing a "draft" of her future, an unexpected happy ending that will miraculously resolve her desperate situation after Muhmenkeh's death leaves her penniless and without a place to live.

Adele's rebuilding of Muhmenkeh's place into Muhmenkeh's Coffee Shop, which becomes a hip meeting place for artists and intellectuals, and, finally, Adele's unexpected meeting with Rachmansky and their idyllic love are all presented in the dreamlike sequence of unreal and implausible events.

Thus Adele's story really ends in the silence at Muhmenkeh's deathbed and the girl's desperate situation. We can only wonder what she can do in America without a job, with no money, and with no friends. Perhaps she could become a prostitute—an occupation that many lower-class women turned to in economic desperation.[60] It is not surprising, then, that Yezierska felt compelled to follow with a pasted-on, fleeting dream of the character's possible future, which she gives to the reader because she does not want to resolve her text at this point. She is not yet ready to write about the dangers that beset a lower-class female or about authorship and the trials this vocation brings to a woman's life. That is why Adele's fantasy results in her subject's death—writing something up often "kills" reality, but it also makes unreal things happen. Adele's and Jean's passionate consummation of their love is thus a fictional resolution to that which they "fought and feared" but could never resolve in reality (AB 262). Such an ideal union and happy ending are possible only in Adele's "fiction," her unresolved dream, which she creates in lieu of coming to terms with her sexual identity. In the end, the novel leaves the reader with another anticlimactic union of two bewildered immigrant artists; it shows the impossibility of intercultural miscegenation, and it suggests as well the unresolved sexual and authorial crisis in its heroine.

### "My Children Were the People I Wrote About": Turning Woman into Text in *All I Could Never Be* and *Red Ribbon on a White Horse*

Yezierska's two last books, *All I Could Never Be* and *Red Ribbon on a White Horse* (1950), separated by eighteen years of painful authorial silence, continue the themes depicted in her earlier texts, but from the more mature perspective of a middle-aged woman and experienced writer who no longer cares to hide her disillusionment. During that time Yezierska had to adjust to her own suddenly changed Cinderella story, when, after being the glittering celebrity, she became a poor and obscure literary orphan no longer noticed and sought by the literary market. As Vivian Gornick remarks, "The slightly hallucinated cry of Yezierska's immigrant anguish did not mesh readily with Depression realism. The words continued to pour from her pen, this time for the drawer alone. Now began her true exile."[61] Although separated by so many years and changes both in America and in the author's life, the two novels engage in an interesting dialogue around the themes that haunted Yezierska's earlier texts. Between these two books, the immigrant woman's struggle to come to terms with her sexuality while pursuing creativity and freedom in the new country is discussed with renewed vigor. It seems that the questions posed by *All I Could Never Be* are answered in *Red Ribbon on a White Horse*; the last conspicuously clichéd and awkward happy ending of the first book is beautifully redeemed in the second.

### Rewriting One's Story

Superficially, both these novels by Yezierska can be characterized as very similar works. A critic who disliked *All I Could Never Be* wrote: "This last book of hers . . . is no more a new book than a new edition of a previous publication."[62] But while it is true that both texts tell the same story of the writer's experiences and career, the very fact of their repetitiveness is interesting as a statement about authorship, fiction making, and autobiography writing as forever reshaping the actual events of one's life. Yezierska never hid from anybody the fact that she kept rewriting her experiences in America—all her characters were versions of her own family, herself, her friends, and her acquaintances.[63] Nevertheless, in thus rewriting reality she freely fictionalized the actual events and changed the real-life characters according to what suited her narrative. This often caused confusion among critics who either took her every word for truth, or blamed her for being drained of interesting ideas because they saw her rewriting the same fiction and the same characters over and over.

The disparity between critical interpretations and demands and what actually happened to Yezierska, or what she actually wrote, seemed never to bother her. In fact, in reading the study of the mother written by the daughter, and especially in looking at the writer's novels and stories, it becomes clear that Yezierska's whole literary career was an attempt to rewrite the life narrative prescribed for her as an immigrant woman writer in a new language. As Henriksen points out many times, her mother never knew exactly when she was born, and hence kept inventing her age according to the circumstances; that is why critical confusion exists over this particular issue. Moreover, the writer delighted in feeding the journalists diverse rags-to-riches stories in which she inventively played with her own and her family's history. She was pleased with the headlines hailing her as a "sweatshop Cinderella" who miraculously made it to Hollywood overnight; she allegedly perpetuated such dramatic anecdotes herself. Yezierska also openly referred to her relationship with John Dewey and made it into a melodramatic part of virtually every novel, where she freely used and rewrote genuine letters and poems she had once received from the famous educator. In both cases, she fictionalized her own history by either concealing or fantasizing about it. Being a believer in packaging her books well, she tried to be in control of her publications and came up with ideas for covers, advertising, and marketing.

The insistence on fictionalizing her life is clearly visible in the title and content of *All I Could Never Be*, where Fanya Ivanovna, an aspiring writer, engages in a long struggle to publish her texts and become popular. Fanya's need for love and acceptance in America results in her relationship with a male mentor, Henry Scott, who helps her gain recognition as an author.[64] In the novel's concentration on the woman's writing career, we see Yezierska fictionalizing her own story as a continuation of Adele's struggle in *Arrogant Beggar* to work out a creative life. Fanya's life is a picture of what Adele's could have been had she followed her dream of making stories and had she found a mentor to deliver her into the world of letters. The novel lays out the sacrifices and frustration that are in store for a female who desires "a room of her own" and wants to devote her whole life to her vocation. As Fanya finds out, and as the first-person narrator confirms later in *Red Ribbon*, in America at that time a woman had to choose either to be "oversexed" or to be a writer.

At the beginning of her story Fanya attends Henry Scott's lecture. While looking at him, she realizes that "[her] fanatic idealism made him the symbol of all she could never be."[65] Her identification with a male is significant because men provide the models by which an aspiring female author would have to define herself. In "Mostly about Myself" Yezierska makes it clear that she is aware of her otherness as a woman writer: "Writing is ordinarily the least part of a man. It is all there is of me. I want to write with every pulse of my blood and every breath of my spirit. . . . I burn up in this all-consuming desire my family, my friends, my loves, my clothes, my food, my very life" (*ChL* 14). This authorial restlessness and insatiability pervade the narrative voice in the lecture scene. While participating in it, Fanya is presented as simultaneously observing and writing it, as she immediately engages in self-criticism and editing of her "fanatic" idealism. Brooding about the Higher Life of the native-born Americans whom she envies so much, she begins to fantasize about Henry Scott, to fictionalize him even before they meet. While, self-consciously, "her swift imagination went on creating him in the image of her own desire," she compares him to Moses and Isaiah—the Old Testament leaders of her people (*All* 28). She is already exercising her powers as a writer and remaking the man into her fiction; she is celebrating her first willing subject to be turned into a story in which the two incompatible cultures cross-breed to produce her dream father-mentor. It is no accident that Scott's speech about prejudice against strangers gives her a chance to engage in a silent dialogue with him. Her experiences of xenophobia and prejudice complement his calls for tolerance in America. Therefore, from the very beginning Fanya consciously projects the ideal of America as embodied in a man, who is a creation combining her own immigrant experience and her feminine literary fantasy. Consequently, the later awkward termination of their friendship is largely of her own making because she has written their story so far away from its realities that she loses her grip on it.

When Fanya's god becomes a male, when Henry approaches her sexually during a walk following months of study and work together on a project in Philadelphia's Polish immigrant community, she realizes that "she wanted from him vision—revelation—not this—not this" (*All* 101). But her disillusionment is with her own creation and her own impossible desires. Her having written Henry Scott as an asexual body proves to be a failure of *her* vision to include in the story of their relationship not only his sexuality but also her own attraction to him. The shock primarily discloses Fanya's frustration with and, possibly, repression of her sexuality, which she has been trying to drown in her work. In a scene reminiscent of *Salome*, she confronts her body:

> She went and looked at herself in the mirror. This was the face and the body she had to live with day by day—the image of herself she longed to be rid of, because it stood between her and her work, impalpable and menacing. . . . her face—tired and lined and white, the face of a woman who has come to middle age before her time; her body, splendid and vital; body betraying face and face betraying body. With her mind she denied love—except the bitter memory of it, and that she would have denied if she could; but her body had ripened for it year by year, against her will; and today this discrepancy seemed more than ever grotesque. (*All* 123–24) [66]

Fanya sees herself as a hybrid of a much-feared sexual body and the prematurely old "face" of an intellectual—a combination attesting to her duality and fragmentation as a woman and a writer. Her sexuality is a source of anxiety because its secret workings attracted Henry and gave him wrong ideas about her feelings toward him. She also confronts the ensuing failure of her control over how others see her because her body—unyielding to her authorial powers—betrays her. She imagines that her face has become a page in which everybody can read her disillusionment with her unfulfilled life, empty of love and devoid of the stunning success that would have justified the sacrifice. Instead of proving to be a saving force, her desire to write has turned her into an alien to herself.

Realizing this, Fanya attempts to run away from writing and applies for various kinds of "honest work," work in which she would be just "a hand among hands" instead of "turning herself inside out into words . . . forcing people out of air" (125). Her desire for manual labor marks an interesting reversal of earlier heroines' desires to be more than sweatshop "hands." She considers her writing unnatural and blames it for distancing her from other people and their realistic everydayness. However, the remedy of "honest work" does not last long and she decides to see Henry again, hoping that, after so many years, she will be able to find her literary inspiration with him again. Their meeting is a complete disaster, "a meeting of ghosts," except for the fact that Fanya realizes fully the failure of her youthful fiction about their relationship: "He knew he was a Yankee puritan. And therein lay his strength. She sought escape from what she was. Therein lay her weakness. . . . Dreaming of love that never was!" (203). As she leaves her old dream behind, she sees, too, that the America represented by Henry Scott has no intention of changing to accommodate her alien frustrations and demands. It will never live up to the fiction she has been writing about it.

This discovery leads to the ending of the novel, in which Fanya leaves New York and settles down in a small New England town, Oakdale, where she hopes to find refuge and a peaceful place to write. In the epilogue the inevitable man (a Russian of unclear ethnicity) appears to save her from loneliness. Predictably enough, this fairy tale prince, a handsome compatriot artist, is sent to her rescue, since any other resolution would have to feature a single woman critically predisposed toward her place in the new country—a violation of the convention Yezierska simply could not afford. As Henriksen remembers the revisions of *All I Could Never Be*, Yezierska was chastised by her publisher for suggesting that a casual meeting between the free-thinking heroine and her male compatriot evolved right away into a sexual encounter.[67] Apparently, even an educated immigrant Cinderella was not supposed to have brought her body into the American culture, where women, and especially sexually suspect immigrant women, were expected to express their sexuality only within the bonds of marriage.

But beyond this ironically happy closure, an alternative and more intriguing ending occurs earlier, when Fanya befriends old Jane, a local rebel against "soap and water." Again, Yezierska hints at the possibility of female bonds and companionship as an alternative to the miscegenation scenario. Jane is a "foremother" of the sixties' generation, who never pays attention to social conventions, and she inspires Fanya's admiration with her simple and fulfilling life on a farm from which she excitedly follows the world's events. It never occurs to self-confident Jane that she is seen as a pathetic local "freak," that she is not the center of the universe—a trait Fanya respects and wants to emulate. The closuring of *All I Could Never Be* takes place when Fanya finds peace in comprehending that she is not the only strange and alienated person in the world. Her writing appears to be like Jane's queerness and like her refusal to follow the town's conventional rules. She realizes that what she has been running from—her otherness as a woman and a writer—is precisely the source of her greatest happiness. Thus, in the final lines of the epilogue, after the unrealistic romantic encounter with a prince charming, her fragmentation is revealed as something to be accepted and affirmed. The "romance" ending of *All I Could Never Be* should be read as another of Fanya's literary exercises in inventing a different ending to her story; she seems to be waking from a dream about the mysterious stranger she has taken in, and she finds herself amid a "tremendous stillness, a tremendous peace [that] held her excitement in an ocean of quiet. All she had ever longed to be, had been secretly, silently growing and ripening in her breast" (255–56). It is in herself, in embracing her predicament, that Yezierska's heroine finds a haven from the conflicts perpetuating her life. Although this is not a solution to her problems and does not eradicate her pain, Fanya learns to find satisfaction in what she is, a sexual woman, an inspired writer, a Wandering Jew—an immigrant.

### "Deformities Struggling to Be Gods": Woman Writing America

The existentially hopeful conclusion of *All I Could Never Be*, in which Yezierska's heroine reconciles with her complex immigrant identity, is confirmed in *Red Ribbon on a White Horse*, which ends with the narrator talking about "creating and recreating [herself] out of [her] defeats."[68] Over the gap of eighteen years Yezierska seems to respond to emotional traumas presented in the previous novel, explaining them with the quiet certainty of an older woman. In this, her last text, we follow her life story once again: the novel is a mosaic of the familiar events fictionalized in her previous texts. But despite the first-person autobiographical voice, the author is explicitly aware here that she is making up just another story about herself. She finally admits that she willingly took part in turning herself into a paper heroine when she was famous; transforming oneself into fiction is part and parcel of being a writer. In Hollywood, having found her "place in the sun," she looks at the front-page news that her success has made: "There was a picture of me above those captions, but I couldn't recognize myself in it, any more than I could recognize my own life in the newspapers' stories of my 'success'" (*RR* 40).

The price of fame and recognition is alienation, and the narrator of *Red Ribbon* pities her old self in its continuous estrangement from her environment. When she was still a part of the ghetto, struggling to become a writer despite her family's and friends' discouragement, she was considered a crazy woman whom no man would ever take seriously: "'Marry her? . . . That *meshugeneh*? That redheaded witch? Her head is on wheels, riding on air. She's not a woman. She has a *dybbuk*, a devil, a book for a heart'" (30). The very fact that a woman wanted to be her own person, that she dreamed of a career and education made her suspect to other Jews, especially males. In a sense, her own people deprived her of womanhood, just as she, like the strong-headed females from other novels, has destroyed their traditional image of a subservient female with her unheard-of intellectual desires.

Her orthodox Old World father, reminiscent of Reb Smolinsky in *Bread Givers*, considers the narrator a "daughter of Babylon," "an *Americanerin*" who refuses to serve him and thus to fulfill the filial duties prescribed by Judaism. The father's curses follow her throughout her lonely life: "You've polluted your inheritance. . . . You'll wander in darkness and none shall be there to save you" (33). The narrator's emancipated aspirations are perceived in terms of sexual impurity; to her father, an educated woman is like a prostitute because she trades her body—which should belong to a man and his children—for intangible ambition and learning. Her father sketches her future for her: "Run! Where? For what? To get a higher place in the Tower of Babel? To make more money out of your ignorance? Poverty becomes a Jew like a red ribbon on a white horse. But you are no longer a Jew. You're a *meshumeides*, an apostate, an enemy of your own people. And even the Christians will hate you" (*RR* 217). As with Stern's heroine in *I Am a Woman—and a Jew*, the paternal curse only propels the narrator of *Red Ribbon* to pursue her American Dream further, even though it means forsaking her father and the tradition he stands for: "His old God could not save me in a new world. . . . Why did we come to America, if not to achieve all that had been denied us for centuries in Europe? Fear and poverty were behind me. I was going into a new world of plenty. I would learn to live in the now . . . not in the next world" (*RR* 33). However, living in the now proves to be as difficult as cutting herself off from the oppressive tradition. To her father, becoming a writing woman in America is equal to being a whore. Nevertheless, the New World itself is not free of the ambivalence related to her position as a Jewish woman and a writer either. Although she can live alone and be her own person, she is still a stranger, a symbol of that exotic ghetto that she evokes in her writing because that is the only way the dominant culture wants to see her. As Mary Dearborn stresses, Yezierska was undone by her Cinderella public image, since the critics condemned the person they themselves had helped to create.[69]

In this respect, Yezierska's entrance into the New World can be seen as warranted by her consenting to become a creation of publicity. To be an author who sells her books, she allows herself to be remade into somebody she does not identify with but has to accept and internalize. This double alienation, being neither Jewish nor American, neither real nor fictional, suspends the writer in an identity limbo. The realization that she can never be a Hollywood Cinderella makes the narrator call herself "not a woman—not a writer"; after an unsuccessful lunch with Samuel Goldwyn she realizes that she does not belong to Hollywood and its sex-and-money-driven elite. She knows that she "wanted the impossible of life, of love. And so I stood empty, homeless—outside of life" (*RR* 74).

However, her feeling of alienation—of being an outsider in both worlds—gives the narrator a chance to use her precarious position to observe others and to engage in self-discovery through writing. The premonition of this conviction can be found in "Mostly about Myself," which compares the act of writing America with a woman writing to another woman or writing herself: "The moment I understood America well enough *to tell her about herself as I saw her*—the moment I began to express myself—America accepted by self-expression as a gift from me . . . hands reached out to help me" (*ChL* 28–29). The newcomer woman can be her own audience and rewrite her "America" for herself. Although she feels that her occupation is a handicap and deprives her of femininity—she compares herself to a crippled Zalmon, the fish peddler–artist—she also feels it opens the worlds of intellect and humanism to a representative of the "generations clamoring for expression" (*RR* 103). She "taste[s] the bread and wine of equality" while working for John Morrow, another incarnation of Dewey (107). In this way, because she is an outsider, she nevertheless takes some part in both worlds and experiences the incompatible extremes of Judaism and Christianity—she partakes of "Bread and Wine in the Wilderness"—in an America written by the immigrant and the native-born. Thus, although she is an alien, she can use her writings to challenge both cultures created by men. She adds her share to an alternative version of these cultures as created by women.

In addition to revealing the sexual oppression of a woman in a narrative caught between two cultures, Yezierska's novels sketch a portrait of an immigrant woman writer, who, even as author, cannot escape the conflicts that other heroines experience in the new culture. Unlike these earlier portrayals, though, *Red Ribbon on a White Horse* concludes completely differently, with a lonely woman brooding over her life of work, her successes, and her frequent failures.[70] This unexpectedly "unhappy ending" is an affirmation of otherness by a woman who chose to live alone in heightened and ever-increasing awareness so that she would be able to write. The writer never has her narrator, or any other character in her autobiographical texts, mention Yezierska's own two failed marriages and her daughter. Speaking on the pages of her last book, she writes of the fictionalized version of herself: "My children were the people I wrote about. I gave my children, born of loneliness, as much of my life as my married sisters did in bringing their children into the world" (216).

Yezierska closes her own story with a confession that seems as far from reality as all her fairy tale conclusions do but that nevertheless rings truest among her ambivalent messages about acculturation, gender, authorship, and the politics of immigrant female identity. Although she conceals the existence of her live daughter, the writer admits that her work could be more important to a woman than her biological motherhood. She says in "Mostly about Myself": "With me, the end and the middle and the beginning of my story whirl before me in a mad blur. . . . I jot down any fragments of a thought that I can get hold of. And then I gather these fragments, words, phrases, sentences, and I paste them together with my own blood" (*ChL* 10). In Yezierska's texts, writing as a vocation and a career—or any artistic activity, for that matter— implies a repression of sexuality or deferred gratification. Yet precisely because of her female otherness, a woman can find fulfillment in her solitude and in "giving birth" to her texts. Such a predicament may seem oppressive and unjust, yet Yezierska makes the best of it in the America of her time; she registers the pain and explains the mechanisms of repression as played between the dominant center and its ethnic margin.

By persisting in her defiance of the official narrative inscribing her as a woman, a Jew, and a writer, she opened a possibility of happier endings for the women writers to come after her. Her most feminist achievement is that she never abandoned her desire to question the construction of the immigrant woman by the dominant culture. She preserved her spirit in her texts, which to some may still seem melodramatic and overblown, but which for others carry an enduring faith in being oneself despite all odds, in embracing the conflicting identities that result from the pursuit of the dream of one's "America" beyond the superficiality of the happy endings prescribed for us by others. At the end of *Red Ribbon* Yezierska writes: "Yesterday I was a bungler, an idiot, a blind destroyer of myself, reaching for I knew not what and only pushing it from me in my ignorance. Today the knowledge of a thousand failures cannot keep me from this light born of my darkness, here, now" (220).

This peaceful celebration of self-reliance anticipates the writings of Eva Hoffman and Vivian Gornick—two more recent Polish American Jewish writers. As the latter comments on Yezierska, "She is an essence of the alienated immigrant, and of the alienating, independent woman." To Gornick, the author of *Red Ribbon* is "one of the great refusniks of the world" in her passionate denial of "life's meanness and littleness," in her demands on the reader and on "America"—in all its possible meanings. I can only agree with Gornick's assessment of Yezierska: "The performance is astonishing."[71]

# 5 In Alien Worlds

TRANSCENDING THE BOUNDARIES OF
EXILE IN THE WORKS OF MARIA KUNCEWICZ

Objections are raised against fiction writers dipping their
pens in the blood and sweat of foreigners. Some critics
would like to confine novelists to their own provinces, as
if fiction were not a free-for-all country. An even stronger
outcry is heard when authors resort in their work to a language which their own national readers do not currently
understand, while foreigners consider it their exclusive
property. . . . I took the chance in spite of the reservations.
I took it, for I do not think that human understanding is a
geographical notion.—Maria Kuncewicz, *The Olive Grove*

## You Can Be an Immigrant Twice

**A**nzia Yezierska's desire to build bridges of intercultural understanding between America and its newcomers brought her in touch with Maria Kuncewicz, an expatriate Polish writer whose historical novel, *The Forester*, Yezierska reviewed for the *New York Times* in 1954.[1] Although the two women were from the same country, this meeting between an author and a reviewer was an encounter of perfect strangers representing different ethnic and religious groups as well as two separate stages of American immigrant history. Yezierska was a Jewish immigrant of the late nineteenth and early twentieth centuries—the period of the "huddled masses"—whereas Kuncewicz, a Catholic, arrived with the political refugees and intellectual émigrés of World War II and the Cold War—the "displaced persons" and the "dissident" wave fleeing the Nazis and the communist regimes in East and Central Europe. Even a brief look at Kuncewicz's biography suggests that she shared with Yezierska little more than her origin in Poland and her knowledge of its language.

Maria (Szczepańska) Kuncewicz was born on October 30, 1897, in Samara, Russia. She was a child of exiled Polish parents—her father was a school principal and her mother a violinist. Her father had been expelled from his country for political activities, but he was able to return there with his family in 1899. As a young woman, Maria Szczepańska studied philology in Nancy, at the Jagiellonian University in Cracow, and at the University of Warsaw. She also pursued concert singing at the conservatories of Warsaw and Paris. Although she considered a musical career, the desire to express herself through writing was stronger, and her literary debut took place in the Polish journal *Pro Arte et Studio* in 1918. Szczepańska married Jerzy Kuncewicz, a populist activist and a writer, and had a son. In 1924 she started working for the Polish Pen-Club and, once she had left Poland in 1939, she worked for the P.E.N. centers in England and the United States. She emigrated to this country in

1955 and lectured on Polish literature and culture at the University of Chicago from 1963 to 1971. She received numerous awards in Poland and abroad for her novels, which were translated into many languages; she was a nominee for the Nobel Prize in literature.[2] She died in 1989 in her beloved home in Kazimierz, Poland, where she kept returning as an American citizen after over thirty years of exile. Her son, Witold Kuncewicz, lives in the United States.

Like the details of their lives, Yezierska's and Kuncewicz's individual journeys to the United States also seem beyond comparison. Both saw America as a haven, but for different reasons and from the perspective of different backgrounds. As a Jew in the Diaspora, Yezierska was already a minority and an exile in her home country, which was under Russian occupation and had been erased from the map of Europe. In the 1890s, when her impoverished family left for the Promised Land in search of religious tolerance and better economic opportunity, they were escaping double oppression—the czarist persecution of the Jews and the occupation of partitioned Poland. In contrast, Kuncewicz was born into an environment of comfortable, middle-class intelligentsia, and she came of age during the time when Poland regained its independence in 1918. When she saw her country lose its freedom and sovereignty—in 1939 and in 1945—she chose to remain abroad, especially after the Yalta agreement had placed East and Central Europe under the Soviet Union's sphere of influence. Unlike nineteenth-century immigrants, Kuncewicz and her fellow refugees during the Cold War came to the United States not because it was the only place that would give them jobs and shelter, but because it was a part of the anticommunist West, where one fled from the Soviet and Nazi invasions in 1939 and from the postwar terrors and intolerance of the communist regimes in the East.

Once Yezierska—a lower-class East European Jew among millions of similar nineteenth-century immigrants—arrived in the United States, she had to confront anti-Semitism and xenophobia and she had to fight the poverty, sexism, and classism of early twentieth-century America. Kuncewicz, in contrast, crossed the Atlantic at a time when the United States favored white educated political refugees from the Eastern bloc and often made them lecturers and professors at American universities.[3] A mature middle-class intellectual arriving in the 1950s, endowed with university degrees and fluent in English, French, Russian, and German, was spared much of the humiliation and pain that a young ghetto girl had to go through just a few decades earlier as she acquired a new language and struggled hard to escape the drudgery of the sweatshop through education. Representing two distinct periods in immigration history, Yezierska and Kuncewicz were also perceived as two different types of East European newcomers by the dominant culture. To Americans of her time, Yezierska was first and foremost a lower-class Jew, a ghetto prodigy who briefly shone as a celebrity; she was defined by her ethnicity and class rather than her nationality. Maria Kuncewicz, a citizen of an enigmatic country in the Other Europe of communism, was defined through Cold War politics rather than primarily through her ethnicity or nationality.

Nevertheless, despite their religious, cultural, historical, and political differences, Yezierska and Kuncewicz met through the latter's novel, as if to prove that literature is indeed a terrain where unexpected encounters and strange dialogues are always possible. In fact, their divergent receptions in the United States—through cultural narratives that described them both as immigrants or émigré females—provide the reader with clues to their shared otherness as representatives of the heterogeneous tradition of East European women's writings. Although seemingly incomparable, the careers of Yezierska and Kuncewicz nevertheless illustrate an important tradition as it undergoes a transition from works by earlier immigrant women to those written at the time when the world had broken into ideologically hostile empires. It was a time when familiar Ellis Island immigrants were turning into political refugees from fascist and communist regimes. With the added dimension of political exile, in the historical and political context of the Cold War, the immigrant woman's otherness became even more complex. The condition of being a foreign female and an ethnic minority in the dominant culture that informed the writings of Antin, Yezierska, and Stern thus gained a new ideological perspective in Maria Kuncewicz. For these reasons, Kuncewicz and Yezierska—and the historical and political periods they represent—not only *can* be read together but, in fact, *should* be read together as two distinct voices in a literary discourse that refuses to be divided by the fall of the Iron Curtain. Their meeting, recorded in Yezierska's *New York Times* review of Kuncewicz's *The Forester*, can be easily missed, but it still establishes an important bridge between the two generations of East European immigrant and exiled women writers in America.

Despite the unique historical and political circumstances of Maria Kuncewicz's journey to the United States after World War II, it was still a little like the traditional immigrant crossing into a Promised Land. "America" in the 1940s and 1950s retained much of the ideological appeal that Lazarus described so enthusiastically in "The New Colossus." As a distant place, where the rulings of the Yalta agreement did not apply, it promised freedom of speech and cultural openness for disillusioned exiles and refugees. Kuncewicz writes about her journey to New York: "When one is travelling to New York, on board a ship, or a plane, or in a car, one has to be a poet a little. . . . Because New York is a collection of dreams of infinite numbers of people from different classes and nationalities of our time. . . . This city was created not so much as an anti-thesis of British York, but as an anti-thesis of all that had ever been. And even today it is certain that fewer people would want to fly to the Moon from New York than come to New York from, for example, Kielce, Châlons sur Marne or perhaps even from enchanting Taormina."[4] America-Arcadia, the dream land of "infinite numbers of people," still lures with promises, no matter what the United States government and its allies decide about the postwar East Europe. As Werner Sollors stresses, the rhetoric of "a 'refuge for the oppressed' [Psalms 9:9], is part of a providential view of American history as fulfillment" (*BE* 43). To Kuncewicz, a trip to New York surpasses space travel in attractiveness, although her comparison can be read as somewhat ironic in that, for some people, a trip to America could be even less possible and harder to undertake than the one to the moon.

Kuncewicz's writings oscillate between direct messages and subtle ironies similar to the ones implied in the passage describing a trip to New York. In recording the rupture with Poland and her mother tongue, her novels and notebooks rely on metaphors of travel, emigration, exile, and cross-cultural trespassing. Metaphors of exile are especially suited to Kuncewicz's geographic and literary journeys, which often seem more far-flung and more daring than trips to the moon. Although her writings record a personal story of separation and removal from her home country, they also map a larger refugee story—they "speak for the millions," as Mary Antin's did—about others who fled the totalitarian rules of Hitler and Stalin with her. As a writer who is simultaneously an immigrant, an exile, and a "visitor" in America and in other countries, Kuncewicz thus inherits and develops the tradition of earlier immigrant texts amid the complex historical and political scenarios of the second half of the twentieth century.

Kuncewicz's "American chapter"—the texts describing her immigration and naturalization in the United States—is an especially interesting part of her story, as it brings a writer who embodies and describes exile into the literary tradition that has always harbored outsiders. Kuncewicz is an "American" author because she does not have a fixed nationality after her emigration, because in the United States she is an immigrant fleeing ideological persecution like the Pilgrims or the nineteenth-century Jews did before her. As a refugee in a world separated by hostile "isms," where internal exile from dominant ideologies has become a normal condition, she is a sum of her outsider's qualities—nationality, languages, passports, citizenships—and thus she fits in well with her new country's cultural diversity, a multiplicity that is perpetuated by otherness. Yet Kuncewicz's American chapter ends unexpectedly, even though the United States was the only country whose citizenship she took and the one in which she lived the longest. She revises the predictable ending of the immigrant narrative by daring to answer the question that Yezierska posed: "But from America where can you go?" In the late 1960s, Kuncewicz's answer was a return to Poland, from which she continued to travel as a naturalized American.[5]

This double immigrant passage—first to the New World and then back to the Old World—is the answer of a writer who creates her own Promised Land in her texts and who boldly claims citizenship in the whole world. In this way, Kuncewicz's career and texts spin still another bridge between the cultures of America and East Europe, one that allows for a two-way intercultural translation and a further rewriting of the typical newcomer woman's narrative. The unusual ending of Kuncewicz's story thus develops the narrative of woman's acculturation beyond the endings described by Antin, Stern, and Yezierska. She shows that the story of Americanization does not have to end in the United States and that as a writer she can take her "America" wherever she goes. It is precisely in her inverted immigrant passage and her desire to keep "finding" her Promised Land through cosmopolitan writings that she remains an American citizen and an American writer.

Because this is so, I discuss Kuncewicz's major texts, mostly novels available in English, and her preoccupation with the themes of female exile, with crossing and playing on the borders between cultures and among genres— documentary, autobiography, and fiction. I place my readings within a context that emphasizes the external categories defining Kuncewicz's status as a Polish woman writer living abroad and writing as a refugee in English, French, and Polish during the Cold War. I argue that her focus on signification—a fascination with writing as a subject and with being written as an object in the narratives of others—arises from her political biography as an author and "character" constructed in reviews, immigration documents, and English translations. I show that her life story and texts are similarly affected by "cutting" or "crossing out" by translators, by censorship in her own country, and by émigrés abroad who did not want to forgive her for her return to Poland.

I also examine Kuncewicz's "American chapter" and her passage over diverse boundaries into her American and cosmopolitan "nature." By exploring her publishing history and reception in the West, I demonstrate how she creates her artistic "world citizenship." I argue that Kuncewicz's texts and career are an indispensable contribution to the cultural dialogue between East Europe and the United States. They propose a rereading and reevaluation of this dialogue by showing the dependence of the postwar intercultural discourses on the earlier tradition begun by immigrant women writers and by questioning the male-dominated dissident model of the Other Europe in the United States.[6]

### "As a Woman, I Have No Country"

The emergence of the communist states in East and Central Europe after World War II changed international political configurations and affected cultures and literatures by introducing a new type of international artist—the dissident. This new artist changed the image of an East European immigrant from that of a lower-class laborer to that of a middle- or upper-class intellectual. Without and within the development of dissident writing, the distinct tradition of intercultural bridge building begun by immigrant women at the end of the nineteenth century continued its dialogic course.[7] Maria Kuncewicz's texts contribute to this tradition by exploring dominant scenarios that reflect changing historical and political configurations: those external narratives that inscribe women's positions in the private and the public spheres, their authorship, and their subjectivity. By moving the themes surrounding female acculturation beyond those of the "huddled masses" tradition, Kuncewicz's writings point both to the historical continuity in newcomer and exiled women's literature and to their ability to work out a polyphonous voice that still preserves the historical, ethnic, religious, and political differences of its authors. After Antin's subversive subtexts, Stern's descriptions of her acute cultural splitting, and Yezierska's ambivalent endings, the strategies of Kuncewicz's career and writings illustrate how the condition of exile influences a writing subject who is a woman and, at the same time, how this gendered focus also evokes a larger human predicament in modern culture.

As Virginia Woolf writes in *Three Guineas*, a woman has no country, as she is already an outsider—the other—to the whole world: "'For,' the outsider will say, 'in fact, as a woman, I have no country. As a woman I want no country. As a woman my country is the whole world.' And if . . . some obstinate emotion remains, some love of England dropped into a child's ears by the cawing of rooks in an elm tree, by the splash of waves on a beach, or by English voices murmuring nursery rhymes, this drop of pure, if irrational, emotion she will make serve her to give to England first what she desires of peace and freedom for the whole world."[8] Woolf's concept of a woman writer, especially powerfully presented in *A Room of One's Own*, calls for exile as necessary in the process of writing. In order to produce texts and be an independent artist, the woman has to retire to her secluded "room" and leave behind the external world, which has written a number of gendered roles for her but which has not accommodated her desire to be an author.[9] Woolf's idea of the female exile focuses on the specificity of woman's writing experience and is geographically confined to one country and one language.[10] In contrast to Woolf and in response to a different historical and cultural context, Maria Kuncewicz's writings map a more complex geography of the female outsider—not only as a writer but also as a refugee, or even a trespasser, into foreign cultures, idioms, and political systems.

This new perspective on exile in Kuncewicz complicates the immigrant woman's otherness in the dominant culture, as we have seen it described in Antin or Yezierska, by adding to it still another dimension of identity. Because she chooses or is forced to live among many different peoples, the refugee or exiled woman is now written as a sum of her alien documents and papers. She is positioned in between nationalities, idioms, and ideologies much more precariously than immigrants before the war because of the world's ideological polarization between capitalism and communism. She is a foreign subject in terms of visas and passports, nationality, ethnic background, language, and foreign customs, but she is also an object written as a character in political narratives that feature her as a female refugee from a country that became (or was made into) a satellite of the Soviet Union, a writer who has to depend on international refugee organizations, a displaced person who wants to continue her artistic occupation despite having lost her native context.

Being an alien woman from the communist East, she also represents a different cultural concept of femininity and sexual conduct, both of which obtain political meaning in the capitalist West. Her way of dressing, her accent, her marital status, the kind of work she can do, all become additional factors to be tested against stereotypical images of females from East Europe. As a woman, she is also marginalized further as the "other" type of an émigré, one who does not fit the dominant heroic model of a male dissident hero from the Other Europe.[11] According to Julia Kristeva's "A New Type of Intellectual: The Dissident," sexual difference, being a woman, is a form of dissidence in itself: "A woman is trapped within the frontiers of her body and even of her species, and consequently always feels *exiled* both by the general clichés that make up a common consensus and by the very powers of generalization intrinsic to language." Being an exiled intellectual herself, Kristeva knows what it is like to be writing from the male-dominated academe of Western Europe.

She emphasizes that the woman "is always singular, to the point where she comes to represent the singularity of the singular—the fragmentation, the drive, the unnameable."[12] Maria Kuncewicz explores such meaning of female exile by disguising her "other dissident" voice and by coding her messages to the reader. In close reading, the "unnameable" becomes tangible and the fragmented woman turns into flesh-and-blood characters on the pages of her books.

The theme of female exile that pervades Kuncewicz's writings is illustrated astutely in her futuristic short story "Dom. Wizja Przyszłego Fin de Siècle'u" (Home: A Vision of a Future Fin de Siècle). In this 1944 text, written in England where she spent most of the war, Kuncewicz ponders the fate of the postwar world and envisions a "Global Republic," where "everybody lives everywhere," and where unconscious exile becomes a normal condition. The utopian society she imagines existing after "war number three" profits from annual compulsory moving from place to place, from regularly changing sexual partners, and from renouncing any family ties, because people have been trained not to crave having a home or loving just one or only a few persons. There are no traditions to fall back on, no sentiments to nurse or be aggravated about. Without knowing it, people of this new world live in a blissful exile from any tangible values of the past and from the memories that would make them vulnerable and attached to other people and objects. Nevertheless, this state of willful ignorance can become an obstacle to one's well-being; it can threaten one's happiness as soon as one has realized the existence of the past preceding the present, seemingly perfect reality.

Amid the almost science-fiction-like setting of Kuncewicz's story, two aspects of exile come into confrontation in a conversation between two women protagonists: Wanda, the "old European" who remembers the prewar times, and Priscilla, the "new woman of the Global Republic" who cannot remember but wants to learn about the past she came from. Priscilla asks Wanda about the meaning of "home," as she needs that explanation for her job as an "interpreter of texts." She is very intrigued by Mrs. Dalloway's and Antonina Buddenbrook's attachment to and gratitude for the walls and collections of objects constituting their homes. Nevertheless, because of her "scientific" involvement with "old world" literature, she is beginning to question the new world's policies; she wants to know how it felt for Wanda to have had a permanent place to live and a group of people called a family. Priscilla desires knowledge and explanation for the sake of her personal "well-being" within the order that has gotten rid of outdated sentimental values. However, the answer given by Wanda—knowledgeable of both exiles, a futuristic immigrant time traveler—is not satisfying. " 'What should I do to achieve a complete well-being?' " Priscilla asks. But Wanda remains silent. "A very old smile played on her smooth face, the smile of Eve, the oldest of the earthly 'refugees.' 'What should you do?' she repeated. 'Forget! Forget about the little tree in Créssy, about Marco's hands, about the unpleasant voices, and about having borne children. If you don't forget, nothing in the world will be able to mend your 'well-being.' " Contrary to this good advice, Priscilla decides to explore the pain of loss and nostalgia embedded in the home. She wants to live in Wanda's former house, which still stands in a European village as a material witness to the old times. She finds the answer herself—it is not possible to achieve well-being without having experienced "fear, despair, and thankfulness" at home."[13]

In the Global Republic, choosing home means choosing exile from the external world and expulsion from the society of happy ignorant people who live everywhere without taking roots. Yet Priscilla decides to explore exile-home for two reasons: because of a temptation arising from reading novels and as a necessary rite of passage to becoming an "interpreter of texts." She wants to learn and experience the meanings of forbidden words; perhaps she wants to write her own story in a world that has imposed a uniform narrative on everybody's life. Her envy of Wanda's wisdom and of her "strangeness"— her accent, antique accessories, vivid facial expressions, and the timbre of voice, in short, her "other exile" as a female from another era—has a source in the desire of Eve, who risked eternal banishment to the Earth for the sake of an uncovered secret. Priscilla renounces the safety of a carefree life in the world without families and moves into Wanda's old house to experience its "growing into her," to collect memories and sentiments. She chooses refugee status for the sake of painful knowledge. The older woman follows her, to resume arranging flower bouquets for her home. The story's end suggests that the two women establish a miniature family—the mother and daughter— who will inhabit the mysterious home. Their stepping over the threshold into the domestic sphere, embedded in the forgotten mythologies but still alive in the symbolic old building, means committing an "original sin" against the futuristic Eden where people live in the public sphere only and where having houses and loving others is strictly forbidden.

The story of Wanda and Priscilla suggests that Kuncewicz sees women as natural refugees—Others—who carry on Eve's decision to risk Paradise for knowledge and who welcome the literal and symbolic pain of creation— childbirth and death—in return for fulfilling their desire. Priscilla voluntarily decides to experience being an Eve; she leaves the Global Republic and renounces the futuristic Eden in an act of free will. Her actions prove the continuity of the lineage begun by the first earthly mother and translate Eve's defiance against the authority of paternal God into an expression of woman's authorial desire. Priscilla's decision can be seen as a woman writer's resolution to pursue the dream of writing a "home" despite being homeless, to insist on reconstructing the past even though the present has decided to erase it. Kuncewicz's other texts explore this concept of exile in which the desire to write one's own story is an act of rebellion and entails becoming a "stranger" and "foreigner" in a world that obliterates individual expression in the name of political consensus.

As we have seen in Antin's and Yezierska's texts, one price an immigrant woman writer often has to pay for her Americanization is estrangement from her sexual identity as a foreign other. In times of Cold War migrations, which inspired Kuncewicz's short story about exile, a similar problem exists for a foreign woman whose gender makes her more vulnerable than a man's. Coming from one patriarchal culture into another, she is seen as asking for protection from the host country, which, just like a "stepfatherland," should see to her safety and comfort but which, while protecting, can also attempt to control her foreign female otherness. The loss of home for women exiles is more acute than for men because they leave not only their homeland but also the familiar domestic sphere that has defined their gender roles. Although men lose a home, too, they are nevertheless more welcomed in the New World as public-sphere participants. For example, immigration rules against admitting single women, pregnant girls, and unattended wives and fiancées prove that rebuilding "home" in the United States was made legally easier for men.

Julia Kristeva analyzes the specificity of the female exile in her discussion of the Danaïdes—"the first foreigners to emerge at the dawn of our civilization . . . foreign women"—who challenged the courting customs of their host culture. Kristeva emphasizes the foreign female's sexual appeal as the exotic other who attracts attention with her difference: "Your awkwardness has its charm, they say, it is even erotic, according to womanizers, not to be outdone." Nevertheless, this very attractiveness invites detestation and xenophobia: "No one in this country can either defend or avenge you. You do not count for anyone, you should be grateful for being tolerated among us. Civilized people need not be gentle with foreigners. 'That's it, and if you don't like it why don't you go back where you came from!'"[14]

According to Kristeva, the foreigner stirs the native's anger because his or her unwelcome otherness disrupts the dominant culture's belief in its own superiority and self-righteousness, and points to its own sense of inherent strangeness.[15] This clash of two alien personalities confronting each other's strangeness is especially visible in mixed couples and marriages. For any newcomer, "the humiliation that disparages the foreigner endows his master with . . . petty grandeur," and for a woman it can mean being treated like a "bought bride." Kristeva recalls a French-Polish couple she used to know: "I wonder if Wanda's husband would have dared to act as brazenly like a Don Juan, to discover libertine bents in himself, to flaunt the girlfriends she, alas, did not have the sense of humor to appreciate—if his wife had not come from Poland, *that is from nowhere*, without the family or friends that constitute, in spite of what people say, a shelter against narcissism and a rampart against paranoid persecutions." The myth of attaining America through miscegenation can also be understood in this way because, as Kristeva suggests, no successful mediation is possible unless the mutual otherness between the foreigner in exile and her host country can be reconciled.[16] With the added complication of political separatism, of "us" versus "them," marriage as cultural mediation—Pocahontas's myth—becomes an ambivalent metaphor in cases where it is a means to attaining a citizenship. Referring to Poland as a "nowhere," Kristeva recalls Alfred Jarry's parodies in *Ubu Roi* and implies an ironic hierarchy among refugees and exiles. This hierarchy of otherness works according to the ranking of the place one came from; those from "nowhere," especially women, are at its very bottom.

The complex position of the female exile in postwar times also arises because the war and subsequent population changes forced many male roles upon women, thus complicating the definitions of the feminine and the masculine. Mary Anne Schofield notes that, during a war, "gender lines are redrawn, re-defined, and re-marked with a writing that re-inscribes femininity during this volatile, chaotic period." Similarly, women writing during the Cold War have to face a challenge of not only redrawing and readjusting gender roles in their texts, but also of rewriting themselves as female authors. Schofield emphasizes that these postwar redefinitions of gender and authorship inspire an emergence of female diaries and notebooks—"the exilic literature in its purest form"—which analyze both the "self writing" and the "hidden self being explored—in exile." The autobiographical trait that has been so prominent in the texts by earlier immigrant women remains important in wartime and postwar writings, because translating lives into texts helps one understand and map the vicissitudes of individual existence in the increasingly chaotic world. Schofield stresses that "diaries are kept individually yet are to speak to the group" because of the authorial desire to connect with other people amid the new historical and political circumstances that impose alienation, separation, and hostility. Schofield notes that in Maria Kuncewicz's war memoir, *The Keys: A Journey through Europe at War* (1943, 1946), this desire to communicate with others is related to the author's need to redefine herself as a woman and a writer lost within new historical circumstances: " 'Not sure that I understand their true meaning, I began to keep a diary, in the hope that someone might explain the things I was witnessing.' "[17]

Like all other writers and artists, like everybody after the war, Kuncewicz had to find that "someone" within herself and search for explanation in her own writing. In her texts the complex lack of freedom resulting from exile, the state of "being written" in diverse external narratives, gives the writer a chance, even compels her, to construct an alternative, defensive version of herself—in Schofield's terminology, the "self writing."[18] Such an approach to authorship suggests a split into the "deep structure" writer—a subject exiled from her own text—and the "surface structure" writer—one who explores her position as an object "written" by others. The interaction between the two resulting texts, those written by and those written for the woman, results in a depiction of exile in works that document self-making and, particularly, in autobiographical novels that intertwine fiction with history. Thus, to seek reasons why these texts by an author such as Kuncewicz are "exiled" from the mainstream canon in the United States reveals a larger problem that involves the specific cultural narratives this country creates for ethnic and "visitor" women writers.

As a female author and a political refugee, Kuncewicz is necessarily defined in opposition to other writers, mostly male, who comprise the new type of an artist—the East European dissident—and whose fame attests to the preferences of American publishers, editors, and translators.[19] She finds herself on the outskirts of a specific canon that the texts of these writers establish in the dominant culture. For example, whenever postwar Polish literature is mentioned in the United States, the names of Czesław Miłosz, Stanisław Barańczak, or Zbigniew Herbert are usually cited. Those who are acquainted with Philip Roth's Penguin series, Writers from the Other Europe, may also remember Tadeusz Borowski, Jerzy Andrzejewski, Tadeusz Konwicki, or Bruno Schulz. However, when asked about any Polish women authors, an American reader who claims an interest in East European literature would probably be at a loss. Because the vast majority of the available literature denouncing communist evils comes from male pens, it is not surprising that women writers from Poland have been relegated to obscurity. A seemingly outdated division between the public-political and intimate-domestic, between male and female spheres, still influences the particular canon of Polish literature in America.[20]

However, reasons for the relative obscurity of writers such as Kuncewicz can be found not only in the traditional division between public and private spheres, which corresponds to the ideological preferences of American publishers and audiences, but also in an American narrative that has gendered the reading of literary exile and expatriation. Shari Benstock describes the relationship between a male exile's "patria" and a female exile's "matria": "For women, the definition of patriarchy already assumes the reality of expatriate *in patria*; for women, this expatriation is internalized, experienced as an exclusion imposed from the outside and lived from the inside in such a way that the separation of outside from inside, patriarchal dicta from female decorum, cannot be easily distinguished. . . . *[M]atria* . . . [is] an 'internal exclusion' within the entire conceptual and definitional framework, the 'other' by and through which *patria* is defined. *Patria* can exist only by excluding, banishing *matria*; *matria* is always ex*patriated*."[21] Taking Benstock's argument a step further, there is no room for the "matria" in the patriarchal dominant culture; the only purpose women's writing serves, then, is to become exiled as the other, to provide space and exposure for men's. Unless they can connect with the male "canon" in its emphasis on the politicized "heroic narrative" of the dissident expatriate, immigrant and exiled women's texts are necessarily marginalized and excluded from public discourse as the other experience of exile and emigration. As Hilary Radner stresses, exile is a metaphor describing the "status of femininity in the dominant intellectual discourse of Western European culture," where "the feminine voice is exiled from the public place—the political assembly, the court of law, the corporate boardroom—and seeks refuge in the private spaces of the home."[22]

Nevertheless, it is due to this exiled position between the politicized public and the domesticated private spheres that some Polish women's writings may seem especially interesting to us nowadays, after the failure of the communist state and after the dismantling of the "curtain" that used to segregate international texts according to their political and ideological value. The works of Maria Kuncewicz are particularly intriguing to study at a time when, after the failure of the communist regimes, the "posttotalitarian mind" can be appreciated openly and without the political constraints that would often acknowledge dissidents or "collaborators with the regime," but hardly ever those men and women who wrote simply about their lives.[23]

## Writing Exile

All of Maria Kuncewicz's novels, even those written before her immigration and after her return to Poland as an American citizen, explore the ambivalences of exile and otherness—what she calls "the commonness of the human condition" (*N* 32). A search for freedom and self-fulfillment, for an idea of nationhood, and for an understanding of a woman writer's position in history written from the feminine perspective of "ex patria" are the major themes of her fictions. Kuncewicz's texts investigate the meaning of exile in fictitious and factual characters, while she herself is a subject inscribed in terms of an alien other—a woman, a writer, an expatriate, a foreigner, and, finally, a Pole who returns home from her overseas refuge. By recreating in her writings her own perceptions of the complex state of exile in herself and others, Kuncewicz not only describes her own position as the externally and internally expatriated other, but also affirms it as a literary inspiration. As she explains in *Fantomy* (Phantoms), writing helps her come to terms with her own intangible identity: "I consider my life to be mostly all that happens in the state of unconsciousness—spinning head, loss of breath, blindness, flight, forgetfulness . . . speed, love trance, vulnerability. I write to bring myself down to earth, to stop the motion I force upon myself: to regain consciousness from un-being. . . . [I]n the slow rhythm of writing a self-knowledge emerges, I clutch onto an alien element . . . and begin to exist as a separate being. That is the reason for and an aim of my writing—a purely private matter."[24] Kuncewicz's authorship actually enables her to exist and to draw contours around the otherwise incomprehensible being she is—a "phantom"—unless written down and read by others. Because she is not sure who she is, as her phantasmagoric reality is always in the making/writing, she gives herself over to be observed as a stranger whom others can see and classify as a set of qualities. (In this respect Kuncewicz's writing herself is reminiscent of Yezierska's coming to terms with her ambivalences as a woman and writer in *Red Ribbon on a White Horse*.)

Viewed chronologically, Kuncewicz's texts disclose the growing awareness of this "purely private matter" in her art. The desire to grasp who she is and the joy of sharing this dynamic process with her readers intertwine into fascinating texts about people who "could have been themselves, if they weren't me" (*Fant* 200). This approach to fiction and autobiography suggests the author's affirmation of being constantly exiled from herself, of being able to become a tangible person only on the pages of her books. In this way her writing and living mingle and, though complicated by exile, provide her with a means for being independent of external oppression as a subject.[25]

### Absent Spaces in History: Writing the Other "National Time"

Kuncewicz's ability to turn what could have been lifelong misery and resignation into creativity arises, she suggests, from a hereditary obligation to her mother, an unfulfilled violin virtuoso: "My art of writing results from an infinite sympathy for the suffering of my mother, and from an illumination that somebody can agonize so much because her art did not come true. This type of human tragedy has engaged me very much, it has enchanted me for my whole life."[26] Kuncewicz's lifelong fascination with exile began with an experience that was only partially her own—her mother's story of unfulfilled art. Kuncewicz used this material for her first novel, *Cudzoziemka* (The Stranger, 1936).[27] The German-Russian-Polish origins of Kuncewicz's heroine made it impossible for her to belong to just one culture and resulted in her self-imposed tragic refusal of fulfillment and happiness.

Her mother's lonely life is most probably the reason why the writer is so preoccupied with the meaning of having a home. Being removed from a beloved "nest of generations" is one of the chronic pains for a displaced person. Kuncewicz has an awareness of losing identity, of being uprooted from an almost Arcadia-like environment. The remembrance of home refers not only to "things past" but also those present, even to attempts to "remember" the future as the mingling together of present and past. Vivid memory and imagination are the major components of the complex state of exile. If one cannot remember, one cannot feel estranged or question one's condition. Thus losing home—that definite space identifying an individual as a native and providing her a sense of belonging to a country, society, culture, family, and even to the material objects that bear some personal mark—constitutes one of the major perspectives in Kuncewicz's complex vision.

As Andrew Gurr stresses, "Deracination, exile, and alienation in varying forms are the conditions of existence for the modern writer the world over," and "home has no identity except through self-knowledge."[28] The concept of home arises immediately from the concept of exile; the writer actually creates his or her home through the act of self-making, which, as an exercise in rewriting and renaming reality, presupposes being estranged from a familiar environment. Maria Kuncewicz's texts explore this condition in France, England, and the United States, where she stayed after she had fled the war in Poland. As we have seen in her short story about Wanda and Priscilla, self-knowledge indeed arises from the experience of home, while homelessness inspires authorship and fiction-making. In *The Keys* (1943, 1946), a remarkable blend of reportage, fiction, and autobiography subtitled *A Journey through Europe at War*, Kuncewicz narrates her experiences as a homeless wanderer. The book relates her flight from Poland and her first decade as a refugee in England. Her next novel, *The Conspiracy of the Absent* (1946), is in turn concerned with the lives of those who stayed in the country and died for the home which the author had fled in 1939. *The Conspiracy* was followed by *The Forester*, which appeared in Paris in 1952 and which seemingly marks a break from war themes, with its nineteenth-century setting and nostalgic sentiment for the past and people long gone.

When read consecutively, these three novels move from an intensely immediate autobiographical experience, through fictionalized autobiography, to historical fiction. The experience of the first-person narrator–refugee abroad in *The Keys* turns into guilt-filled speculations about the fictitious characters' lives in war-torn Poland in *The Conspiracy* and then transforms into an exploration of Poland's past under Russian occupation in the nineteenth-century setting of *The Forester*. In the wartime *The Keys* and *The Conspiracy*, the writer moves from an intense autobiographical trauma into a fiction about what could have happened and what she could have seen and done had she stayed in her country. The transition between the two modes of writing is not very smooth; it gives the reader the impression that an intense feeling had to be "written out" or released from the author's mind. However, it is precisely because of the dissonance between the two texts that we can read them as parts of the same story. They complement each other and intertwine into a complex soundtrack left by the woman writing her life as it was and as it could have been. Kuncewicz's later shift to events of the last century in *The Forester* can also be read in relation to that movement in contemporaneous history reflected in *The Keys* and *The Conspiracy*. From an intense mode of registering the factual-fictitious present, the author turns to her family's past and reconstructs their lives, which, despite their historical remoteness, strikingly reflect the postwar divisions of the world by politics and ideology.

**"Keys to a Void."** *The Keys* begins with a journal entry in which the narrator attempts to recall past signs of the approaching war. She thinks back to the invasion of Prague in 1938 and imagines it disappearing, along with its intellectuals. She sees it as a circus vanishing act. No one, least of all the artists and intellectuals, was prepared for 1 September 1939, the invasion of Poland, either. The writer remembers her struggle with words while trying to convey the simultaneity of feelings and events, yet she cannot help being left outside the mysterious current of history happening to her rather than within her. The suddenness of war turns everything upside down; people vanish, the favorite family bibelots she saw as signifying material eternity evaporate, and the word "forever" becomes a cruel joke.

The war finds the narrator between her summer house in Kazimierz—a small Renaissance town on the Vistula river—and her apartment in Warsaw. The suddenness and cruelty of the Nazi invasion transform her into an Alice in Wonderland, or a Peter Pan, both of whom wake up and fly in a world so strange that even their stories could not predict it. Yet when she looks around, the sun is shining and the trees seem more beautiful than ever in the bright September light. Nature is oblivious to war and decorates the scenes of atrocities with cruel and indifferent beauty; its narrative has not been disturbed. Under the indifferently shining sun people throng the highways and railway stations to escape the Nazi bombers. They are fleeing the country where the enemy planes "took their sky away" and where the soil under their feet may defy the laws of gravity at any moment. The narrator seems to be writing in the midst of the crowds hurrying to leave a dangerous Warsaw deprived of its sky and pavements. Jews, like their Old Testament predecessors running from oppression, are preparing for another descent into their metaphorical arc of the twentieth century—ghettos, woods, remote villages—to escape the Nazi flood and the death it brings to them under the name of racial purification. Kuncewicz is trying to understand why 1 September 1939 has happened and why no one believed that "the good right to live of the benign Polish nation" was a myth—a blindness in all those who did not want to open their eyes to the reality of contemporary history.[29] The only answers the narrator has are symbolized by the keys to various places in Europe where she lives throughout the war. In Paris she thinks: "All my keys are keys to a void."[30]

The first bunch of keys that Kuncewicz's narrator looks at locks her past in Poland and opens the life of an expatriate. Metaphorically, she is always holding on to these objects that open the past, from which she has been extracted by historical events. There is a key to her house in Kazimierz and there are three others: to the gate, to the elevator, and to the door of her Warsaw apartment. This time she has them all in her hand and does not have to call the sleepy concierge to open the gate for her because her apartment vanished with the whole building. With her superfluous keys in hand, she joins the refugees fleeing doorless Warsaw. She realizes that these men, women, and children running away from their homes are becoming a tribe, a race of their own, and that she is one of them:

Many, many evil things have been said about refugees. In every language this word is colored with contempt. Blocking the highways they hindered military operations. . . . and later the enemy took advantage of this. They ate out so many villages, they littered so many parks, they terrified so many neutral hearts! And in the end, the British "country" is appalled with the Londoners, who—paying no heed to tidiness and privacy—crowd the tunnels of the underground stations where being English loses its nobility because it is placed side by side with being a rat.

One day some of the contempt underlying mercy for refugees will be removed. One day a philosopher or a poet will appear and will establish the date of September 1, 1939 as the day of the angels' moving from heaven to another dimension; . . . a doctor will come who will classify the psychosis of "skylessness," and a patriotic writer will absolve the cosmic patriots. (*K*, Polish, 36–37) [31]

In this passage, the crowd that the narrator joins and describes in her notebook is not composed of Poles only. Already it blends into a collage with the images of Londoners filling up the underground during nightly air raids, whom she will observe many months later. Chronology is not important here, for the writer is concerned more with conveying her immediate impressions through language than with composing an elaborate cause-and-effect account. To the reader, her writing seems to be channeling thoughts onto paper spontaneously, while the arranging is done by intuition rather than by careful planning.

In effect, the beginning of the war in Poland and the Battle of Britain merge in her text and result in an international dimension of human suffering in a "skyless" twofold city—Warsaw-London. This perspective is broadened even more in the last sentences of the quoted passage, where the narrator looks at the global implications of being exiled from one's home and sky. Perhaps she realizes that history is, to some extent, a narrative about the tribes of exiles always running away and always being compared to rats, a narrative about a race despised for its inexact numbers, improper manners, and infinite despair.

However, despite her preoccupation with the cosmic dimension of war, the narrator does not lose sight of a woman's singular perceptions. In fact, the whole text is a play of outlooks between the cosmic crowd and the individual, who tries to place herself within some tangible perspective of history. One in the crowd, she sees herself vividly as becoming somebody else when she is given her refugee passport, and when she is told in Romania, at a time of moral terror, "What an artist should do to save his art." (An elderly film director advises her that ideological "prostitution" is the only "safe" choice in case Germany wins the war). In Paris she takes part in a matinee that the French organize at the Comédie Française to express solidarity with her nation. During the performance she discovers she is somebody else again, for the citizens of Paris worship an abstract "sublime et héroique martyre" who does not have much to do with the living Poland that the narrator knows has been reduced to the quivering flesh of the corpses killed by Nazi bombs.

Unlike the narrator, the French audience understands better the "universal" symbolism of Proserpine and Demeter's story, which is used as a metaphor, and they love Polish-French Chopin. They do not know the name of the river on which Warsaw was built and do not care that the twenty-year period between the world wars was one of amazing artistic and intellectual activity in a free country. Because they believe in the validity of the classical analogue, the time of darkness, of Proserpine's imprisonment in Hades, did not stop for a moment. During the performance of a pilot's "Letter from a Burning City," history becomes theater:

> The French rose in their seats. Demeter, the goddess of fulfil[l]ment, had not deceived them! The harvest had been reaped. Proserpine, her refractory daughter, enamoured of shades, had indeed descended into the underworld. The solemn-looking gentleman in snuff-coloured clothes calmed the audience with one impressive gesture. After a theatrical pause he went on reading: "On September 25th I was entrusted with an important mission." . . . The actor ended. . . . Applause broke out. Applause so frenzied that it was impossible to distinguish the hands. . . . Then the lights began to fade out one by one. . . . In the cloakroom a General and a civilian—their coats and hats on—stared down at the floor. "*Et cet envol de l'aviateur d'une ville en flammes—tel un phénix s'élévant du brassier*," the General muttered, straightened himself, his eyes sparkled. He smiled faintly. "*Une belle métaphore*," said the civilian." And now to tell the story behind that metaphor. (*K*, English 67)

Despite her irony, however, the narrator does not blame the French; she simply realizes that they have to write their own story about her and her country, or she would be invisible to them. That is also why she immediately puts her observations about France on paper, before they disappear from her, too, within the acute sense of unreality enveloping the displaced person.[32]

A similar event of estranged narration depicting a Polish woman abroad happens in London. After church, a woman casually asks Maria the narrator about her family in Poland, and the narrator answers: "They are still alive, thank you." To the puzzled inquiries she says that no, they are not sick, they simply live in Warsaw. The sympathetic but terrified woman asks her to tea, and the narrator immediately sketches in her imagination that perfect English five-o'clock which will take place at the woman's house. All is there—furniture and pictures, china, cakes, and the ritual of questions—to prevent Maria from talking about that terrible Warsaw again. Foreseeing that future afternoon, when the British woman will defend the English story about Poland, the narrator realizes that she is stigmatized with death. To those who are aesthetically and temperamentally far from contemplating it the way she does, she "stinks of blood and hunger." Despite her dress from Harrod's and her Cornwall shell necklace, she spreads a stench of "Polish spring" in the pure English air. No wonder those she sees as others in her exile—the natives of her adopted countries—write a narrative about her in lieu of the one she could offer as someone "from there." For the English it is a desire to make things pure and simple, and for the French it is their love of symbolism and sublime art. In the midst of these versions, while attempting to write herself, the narrator faces the other she is to her hosts abroad—"une belle métaphore" and an abject body exuding death.[33]

Thus the key to her "true" identity cannot be found during a "journey through Europe at war." The narrator exits from her diary-story with the puzzled feeling that there are no keys to unlock human mysteries in the world of displaced individuals and mythologized nations. All she can do is write about events and people, without ever hoping to solve the secret of why they happen or are so. Nevertheless, this task of writing-witnessing brings her closest to approximating an identity in transition that inspires artistic expression. At least she is able to see the other in herself, thanks to being an alien metaphor or an abject body to people she meets abroad. By situating herself outside of the identity she cannot fully grasp, by absenting her subject position, Kuncewicz constructs the woman simultaneously writing her story and participating in it as the other that her observers construct to suit their own versions.[34]

Kuncewicz develops this approach to subjectivity and authorial identity within her next novel written in exile, *The Conspiracy of the Absent*. In this multilayered text, the fiction about the war in Poland that she could not have seen becomes an alternative to the estranging autobiography-story she narrated in *The Keys*. By shifting action between wartime Poland and England—the isolated territories where her fictitious characters move—she develops a concept of "national time" or "Time," which envelops the other in herself and in those around her and which she has already sketched in the previous book.[35] As *The Keys* make clear, all peoples share a certain cultural affinity and can superficially understand and sympathize with one another within the shared myths—they organize matinees and invite one another to tea.[36] In this superficial sense, geographical borders between countries do not eliminate human comprehension; they are only artificial obstacles hindering territorial contacts. However, despite their ability to visit foreign terrains, people can never enter the specific time zone built around every nation by history and its particular cultural and socioeconomic developments.

This exclusive bubble surrounding each country—"national time" or "Time"—is subtly and trivially present in flowers and colors symbolizing things differently for Poles and for the English, but it also creates invisible barriers segregating peoples as others to one another, no matter what their "common cultural heritage." After a meeting with an elderly couple and their grandson, the narrator thinks: "Dear old folk, dear little Peter, and all you calm and tolerant people of England, what is it that stands between you and me? Certainly not your pride and not mine. Between us is the Time of your country. Time, begun in the early morning of history, untroubled by neighboring emanations, slow and separate, caressed by the Gulf Stream, fed by the most nourishing fruits of peace. A Time of happiness" (*K*, English 141). She realizes that individual characteristics and national history cannot be fully explained or translated through cosmopolitan culture and shared languages. Being molded by Time, people are all different; they are bound to be strangers to one another, regardless of how much they subscribe to their "common Western heritage." For an exiled writer such estrangement is doubly alienating. Once uprooted from the place where her own "national time" protects her from strangers, she becomes an enigma to herself as a foreigner who is always defined by her alien host-culture observers. As Kristeva argues, without her own culture to shelter her abroad, to provide her with a protective cocoon of national time, a woman is doubly exposed to be misread by others. She is externally alienated in her new home as a foreigner, while being exiled internally from her country and the "national time" she has left behind as an expatriate and a woman. Therefore, as previously mentioned, writing herself into this doubly estranged reality—constructing a "matria" between her internal and external otherness—requires that she absent the subject position. For a woman, to create a text that can grasp the "self writing" and communicate with the outside world despite the insurmountable differences of nationality and gender, she has to remove herself from the misread central subject position and confront her otherness as an outsider.

In Maria Kuncewicz's terminology, this state of decentered subjectivity is called being a "phantom" and involves a lifelong process of writing herself in different times and spaces. Kuncewicz recounts this process in *Fantomy*:

> At the beginning I wanted to be a boy, then a non-material being, finally a flat-chested blond—all that so as to deny myself, to destroy myself in the only dimension that was uniquely mine—my imagination. In contrast to Gombrowicz and other slaves of society, I never let anybody "make my face" for me; I made it for me myself and only for myself—in order to be able to live with myself. . . . In my contacts with people, I pretended I did not exist. . . . I felt I was not there for them in their favored, substantial dimension. . . . Now I am listening to a girl's sandals clanking on the road between the gardens and I run along with this indestructible girl. (*Fant* 94)[37]

The phantom identity that Kuncewicz works out of her complex otherness in exile allows her to fluctuate between the impossible inner self she keeps erasing and the external one that her environment makes for her but that she refuses to accept. Being thus outside herself, writing her subjectivity for herself in her texts but never inhabiting it permanently allows her to move in time and space as an ever-changing subject in the making. Thus she can simultaneously be a "flat-chested blond" and a girl with "clanking sandals." Moreover, since her writing is always set against a particular national time and place abroad, it becomes an exercise in playing on the borders between internal and external otherness, an attempt at partial translation across the boundaries of incomprehension.

**Under the Burden of Presence.** Kuncewicz's acute awareness of the time barrier is very clear in *The Conspiracy of the Absent*, where Sophie, a famous Polish concert singer and a refugee in London, is desperately trying to get news about her family struggling under the Nazi occupation in Poland. At one of the meetings in a small hotel where exiles from many countries talk about Shakespeare and politics, she hears a speech about the "conspiracy of the absent," who prevent one from taking on the "burden of presence." The speech is delivered by a Spanish-looking English lord, who argues for defying the negative influence that their "absent ones"—people they have left behind in their countries—have on the refugees. He suggests forming an international organization of intellectuals who would work on affecting the "fate of the world." Sophie looks at the empty chairs next to hers and immediately thinks of those whom she has left in Poland. Why would they conspire against her? Why should she be afraid of the absent ones she loved and for whose safety she feared? On the other side of the time zone, in Warsaw, Susan and Kira, Sophie's nieces, become involved in the underground movement. Their lives are very "present" in a time that is always threatening death and torture. For these young women, Sophie is the absent one; to people in Poland, London means almost a different planet. For the nieces, Sophie acquires mythological meaning as their favorite aunt and a magnetic personality around whom the artistic life of their prewar paradise used to be centered. In England and in Poland—both touched by the war but touched very differently—Sophie and her nieces build their own idealized versions of the absent loved ones to cherish and dream of.

However, in the course of the novel the lives of the three women, immersed in two different national times and within the larger "Time of War," come slowly to the point where they see their utopias turning against them. While in a restroom attempting to divest herself of some compromising documents, Susan throws away an unread letter from Sophie that reached her illegally. She does so not only to protect herself from being searched by a Nazi who is guarding her but also to defile the absent past and herself in it—ideals that will never return to the reality of death and poverty. She discovers the psychological power behind Sophie's writing, which represents remote and alien London—the place where people flee to, choosing sporadic bombings over the methodically planned genocide of Jews and Poles. Susan feels guilty that she cannot be the girl her aunt remembers and to whom she writes. She fears her own weakness and realizes the cowardice of her vulnerable body, threatened by pain and death.

On the other end of the time zone, Sophie brings herself to the brink of suicide after losing a boyfriend, torn to pieces by a bomb during an air raid. Having been left without news from home for a long time, she cannot bear the loneliness and uncertainty. She suddenly wants death to end the waiting for some turn of events or for someone to tell her what to do after her last jewel has been pawned.

Kira, Sophie's other niece in Poland, is also not sure who she is and what she should do with herself in a suddenly absurd world. Raped and nearly beaten to death by a German officer from whom she was supposed to "buy out" the life of a little boy taken to Auschwitz, she is miraculously saved by a guerrilla squad. One day she sees herself in the mirror for the first time in months and cannot recognize the woman in front of her. That other looking at her from the glass is some "absent" Kira she has never noticed before. In London Sophie recalls a similar confrontation in her childhood when, startled by her reflection in a suddenly lit room, she exclaimed, "It's not me!" The absent others whom Kuncewicz's heroines encounter in *The Conspiracy* are the versions of themselves spread in the historical narratives of memory.

Thus the "conspiracy of the absent" is each woman's inability to accept the stranger in herself; they deny their connection to the alien and abject people whom each of them carries hidden inside. That is why Kuncewicz ends her novel on an ambiguous note. In Poland pregnant Susan is killed during a resistance mission, whereas Kira remains with the guerrillas and falls in love with her aunt's former lover, who has killed her Nazi rapist. In London, on the last pages of Kuncewicz's text, the reader follows Sophie's suicidal thoughts and a decision to welcome the "burden of presence." We never learn how she will do this—in life or death—or what will happen to Kira, her lover, and other characters in the two countries.

The open-ended conclusion of *The Conspiracy* may be the only way to close a story about the "burden of presence," for which each of the characters has to take responsibility. Kuncewicz suggests that, although we may live consciously and fully, we are never totally sure who we are; our existence means being eternally exiled from self-knowledge. The suspended closure is Kuncewicz's answer to Dr. Johnson, whose words she has chosen for the ambivalent motto to her novel: "Whatever withdraws us from the power of our senses: whatever makes the past, the distant or the future predominant over the present, advances us in the dignity of thinking beings." [38]

**History Revisited.** Knowing that there are no keys to our internal mysteries and that it is not possible to escape from living in the present, Kuncewicz makes her characters inhabit both the places in history she herself visited and the ones she dared to visit only by means of writing fiction. Nevertheless, *The Forester*, with its nineteenth-century focus and its Lithuanian and Polish settings, marks a shift from the course taken by the writer in her wartime journey through *The Keys* and *The Conspiracy*. The story reconstructed in this short novel is based on Kuncewicz's father's diary and his family history and takes the reader into the depths of Lithuanian forests and to a Warsaw occupied by the czar's invisible yet palpable presence. The nineteenth-century world of *The Forester* is completely different from the image of the Victorian age of scientific discovery, the flowering of the novel, industrial expansion, and the rapid economic growth that an average European would identify with that era.

The epigram that opens *The Forester* is from Hermon Ould and is one of the first indications that Kuncewicz is still pursuing her search for the meanings of otherness: "We are not real, we crave reality." In the author's preface, designed for her English-speaking readers, Kuncewicz acknowledges that her theme is not a new one: "The fact that people are neither what they think they are, nor what anybody else believes them to be, is the book's theme; an ageless problem much alive in modern fiction."[39] Yet she also warns the readers about her "unorthodox" perspective, which takes them into the "unpleasant" foreign past, to the "crossroads of Eastern Europe" marked by perpetual revolt of the suffering Polish people and by the plight of other minorities living side by side with them under Russian rule. In this way, the author uses a familiar theme in an unfamiliar setting to show that "evocations of the past naturally invite analogies with the present" (6).

However, while revealing that her historical novel is a commentary on the present, she also cautions the reader against drawing oversimplistic analogies between the political meaning of czarist rule in the past and that of the postwar Soviet domination of East Europe: "Organized violence is still breeding violence, but in the liberal period an imperialistic power had fewer means and less desire to assert its claim to human souls. Under the totalitarian régime Caesar will not be appeased with the face of the coin; and were young Casimir, my hero, to fight his life's battle in our days, neither the forest, nor his mother could afford him a refuge" (6). Her story is not about mere political analogies but rather about how historical events affect people and set in motion narratives that write whole generations. Rather than simply read Casimir's story as a direct metaphor for totalitarian oppression, we should see it as anticipating people's lives under communism and as showing the way in which the mechanisms of control have been developed by political regimes since the nineteenth century.

*The Forester* recounts crucial stages in the life of Casimir, a young Pole who comes to an understanding of his national identity by making connections between present and past events, between his mixed ethnic background and the ruthless russification of the region he comes from, between his passionate love for a woman and his patriotic love for his country. Despite the author's warning in the preface, the reader cannot help juxtaposing Casimir's story with the well-known facts of people's lives under Stalin. A close reading of Kuncewicz's text suggests that the author has subtly disguised her dissident voice in a narrative that claims to be free of analogies that it cannot escape. Its wealth of historical detail and its emphasis on the themes of nationhood and political oppression practically force readers of *The Forester* to make their own judgments about the historical frame of Kuncewicz's novel and the political one in which it is received and interpreted. It seems, then, that *The Forester* invites our reading of the present through the past, but only while we are engaged in pursuing Casimir's story. Therefore, Kuncewicz's preface discourages our interpretation of his life as a disguised commentary on totalitarianism, not because the two are unrelated but because she wants to prevent us from making hasty generalizations about her political message before we actually start reading her text and begin to interpret it on our own.

Superficially, *The Forester* supplies us with Kuncewicz's exiled vision of a woman writing about her family's past—the voice of one absent, in a foreign land, enclosed in a foreign translation, and addressing foreign readers. Yet the author emerging from this text about the inevitable cross-sectioning of politics, history, and individual identity is a phantom who pretends that she can only dwell in the past and in the familiar realm of historical romance, the "feminine" authorial space. However, by exposing her goals and her literary technique in the preface, Kuncewicz invites an alternative reading of her text and of her authorship. On the one hand, she tells us what we ought and ought not to look for and, on the other, she signals that there may be no way for us to determine whether what we have read is anything more than our own "craving" for reality, a fiction spun by our imagination. This warning is about the contagious image-making involved in the process of writing, reading, and interpreting. Before we enter the "alien world," we are thus prepared for a self-conscious theme writing out its author's otherness from still another place in history, one she would like to inhabit.

Czesław Miłosz calls *The Forester* Kuncewicz's best psychological novel written abroad by reason of the book's references to the Polish uprising against Russia in 1863 and its general concern with historical detail. On the other hand, he terms the author the "most Western" of the Polish women writers who are her contemporaries, due to her "focusing upon the individual." Thus this famous émigré attributes Kuncewicz's success to a combination of "foreign" themes and her intimate background in national history. He stresses the fact that *The Forester* was written from abroad but about Poland, which "throws some light on the Polish writer's predicament."[40]

This opinion is justified as far as the progression of Kuncewicz's texts is concerned and their culmination in *The Forester*. However, with the publication of *The Olive Grove* (1963) and *Tristan* (1975), the two novels written both in English and Polish, Kuncewicz proved not only that she could render Polish estrangement in history but that she was also skilled in using an entirely foreign otherness as her topic. In these novels, writing as an exile from her decentered subject position, she explores the theme of national time among the English, the French, and the Americans. She also uses their languages to show the illusion of penetrability of these cultures to the modern version of the "impecunious invader."

**Passions in the Olive Grove.** In her introduction to *The Olive Grove*, Kuncewicz describes her "trespassing" in the realms of foreign language and character in an attempt to write a story of prejudice and nationalistic hatred. In this novel, the first text she ever wrote originally in English, she fictionalizes the famous case of Sir Jack Drummond, his wife Anne, and their daughter Elizabeth, who were murdered by the villagers of Lurs in southern France while on a camping vacation. However, she is not simply recounting a tragedy of a particular family but rather searching for the reasons that made a person commit such an atrocious act: "In 1952 only seven years separated us from World War II. But that little girl who had run, under the lovely stars of Provence, from a man who wished to smash her skull, that child's lonely flight through darkness in a strange country, led deeper into human mystery than war itself. Fascinated with this force that can change ordinary breadeaters into murderers, I travelled back home . . . looking attentively at people; the force throbbed under their skins, it worked inside their brains."[41] In what can be read as an almost allegorical tale about a fight between good and evil, Kuncewicz crosses the "boundaries of human understanding," which she hopes are not drawn according to "geographical notions." She plunges into a French-English episode from her perspective as an outsider-participant and shows that ethnic hatred has not ended with the war.

In this truly "foreign" novel, Kuncewicz also juxtaposes the narrative about authorship, which she has begun in her previous texts, with a larger story about exile as a human condition. A stranger writing self-consciously about other strangers continues to prove that all people are alien "others" to one another within a world torn apart by political, religious, and ideological divisions. Having explored this theme in the familiar settings of Polish history and within her own life, she turns in *The Olive Grove* to still another mode— that of fictionalizing the factual. This time, the exiled author disguises her mature perspective in the character of a little English girl, Pat Monroe, whose imagination and perceptions become the main focus of the story. This device shows the reader, with even greater clarity than any "adult" perspective could, that a human life is no more than a passing episode in a larger historical and political narrative on which we have no influence.

Although written as yet another reaction to the war, *The Olive Grove* does not, however, blame a particular ideology or political system for the crime in the novel. Instead, it explains how an individual can be manipulated and conditioned by tradition, religion, and prejudice and how these factors often conjure up a demagogic rhetoric that justifies the worst crimes. Kuncewicz's Baptiste Varioli is such an individual—an average French farmer who commits murder for no apparent reason other than the centuries-old hatred for the "Anglais" and his personal sexual and moral obsessions. After the murder he explains his compulsion to commit it with the cool logic of a religious fanatic. The Englishwoman offended him with her red hair and by calling him a "shadow" on his own land. The man was no more than a malicious English "vampire," a communist who came to destroy France, and the girl was "une petite diablesse" Protestant who made his grandson give her the Holy Communion (*OG* 237). Filtered through this mind, a quiet British family become demons because Pat's mother has red hair just like a woman Baptiste used to desire but could never have. The girl's father symbolizes a threat through his memory of the Resistance and his knowledge of the petty crimes that the Variolis committed to buy more land, and the girl "bedevils" Baptiste's grandson with her foreign imagination and a sacrilegious wish to suffer like Jesus Christ or Joan of Arc. These are the reasons why the old man goes berserk one night and strangles the woman, shoots the man, and smashes the child's head with a rifle butt.

And yet the author does not pass judgment on him. Her task is to show how Baptiste is slowly driven to the madness of a murderer, how his Christian nature permits and justifies such an act against the three alien Protestants because some unexplainable force, responsible for crimes against humanity all over the world, lurks beneath his ordinary façade. Although some critics accuse Kuncewicz's characters in *The Olive Grove* of being unconvincing or too complex psychologically, she constructs them as if they were actors in a fairy tale—"believable" humans on the one hand and mythical types embodying the forces of good and evil on the other.[42]

As the author admits in the introduction, however, her aim is not simply to condemn anybody or to divide the world into black and white characters. She wants to show instead that, although the war had been over for several years, an innocent child was not safe in her sleep and what the little girl had to be afraid of was ordinary people and their isolated minds rather than organized political extermination. Pat Monroe is modeled on an English girl, Vivi, whom the writer knew personally and came to love for her sensitivity and imagination. Kuncewicz shows the absurdity of the hatred that makes a grown-up man kill a child or a woman:

> The time had long passed when I divided humanity into victims and criminals. In two world wars I have seen how History was taking charge of indi-

vidual responsibilities, how Race, Nation, and Church were used to cover up personal obsessions, how the wrong people were slain for the wrong reasons, because love seemed too difficult a solution to human problems.

The murder at Lurs did not strike me as more brutal than many such crimes happening daily all over the world. I reacted so strongly because of Vivi. But as I set out on my search for motives which could induce people to kill any of her kind, I soon discovered that her life was merely a bubble on the surface of a deep bog. And the bog was made of layer upon layer of national prejudice, class hatred and personal misunderstanding. Into that bog, as a novelist, I felt impelled to probe. (*OG* x–xi) [43]

However, Kuncewicz's disillusionment with the supposedly "most civilized" nations of Europe is not the most intriguing part of the story. What truly strikes the reader in *The Olive Grove* is the writer's horror at people's minds and her authorial compulsion to explore this horror through fiction. Amid the cultural achievements of the Western world, a murderous thirst for blood still persists. Even the Christian faith, with its call for love and forgiveness, is based on human sacrifice. But the irony of Christianity in our era is that human sacrifice has become so common that it does not move anyone anymore. Kuncewicz's novel suggests that no civilization has ever saved people from hatred; Hitler could have been born anywhere, not only in the country of Goethe.

Apart from its clear religious and historical connotations, Kuncewicz's novel is also a collection of diverse myths and symbols that enable it to present a more general, cross-cultural view in its criticism of international animosities. The Protestant aloofness of the English and the passionate faith of French Roman Catholics are juxtaposed as hostile stereotypes, the crucifixion of Christ arises in relation to ancient pagan customs of human sacrifice, medieval legends echo in modern philosophical disputes, and the naive Marxism of Pat's idealistic father is confronted with the ignorant opulence of his American relatives, who come to spend summers at their French estate. The olive grove—the title metaphor—becomes an almost ironic synecdoche for fading humanistic values. From the holy place of Christ's painful meditation, in which God-man accepted his mission to redeem others, the grove is transformed into a piece of property that can unearth family feuds and evoke greed and hatred strong enough to incite murder. After little Pat's death, Baptiste's grandson sets the grove on fire in an outburst of impotent anger against the cruel world of the adults who killed his friend; symbolically, he also rebels against the world of "fathers" who are deaf to their children's pleas for mercy and who sacrifice them to redeem others. The novel ends on a bitter and ironic note—even justice and compassion are dead, or have turned "terrible," as Vivi would put it, in a decadent world. Old Baptiste Varioli will most likely be protected from persecution for his crime by the local tradition of loyalty and by his son's fear that his own dishonesties might be uncovered if he denounces his father. (In this respect Kuncewicz's fiction reiterates what really happened in the Drummond case.) The burning grove, with which the book closes, consumes any hopes for a better world order, one that cannot be achieved amid pervasive hatred. Only a few years after the war, what Kuncewicz's novel seems to be saying is that love is impossible in the era of totalitarianism, when national times are set apart even further than before.

**Brangien's Narrative.** The discovery that love has never been, and will never become, a "solution to human problems" led the writer to another novel, *Tristan*, which concerns the myth of romance and exile. This text tells another international story, as its action takes place in England, Poland, and the United States, and its characters come from even more diverse cultures. That Kuncewicz conceived her novel in British Columbia, Canada, many years after the actual events that inspired the work had taken place, adds to the large geographical frame of reference in which to consider the work.[44] The novel tells the story of a Polish submarine officer, Michael, and an Irish student-model-actress, Kathleen. As with most of Kuncewicz's fiction, *Tristan* was inspired by real-life traumas—the author draws on her own experiences as a Polish mother living in England and awaiting news about her nineteen-year-old son, who is off fighting the war on a submarine. In addition to fictionalizing her family's story, Kuncewicz also reconstructs a medieval Celtic myth of chivalric love—another tale about exiles—around an affair of the Polish marine with the Irish girl.

*Tristan* required the writer—identified with the main narrator, tellingly named "Brangien"—to cross many borders before she was finally able to capture the story in words.[45] She remembers the paradoxical indifference she had to the myth of Tristan and Yseult while living in their land:

> For three years in Cornwall, although I had been walking around the hill and the ruins that were still called Ristormel Castle, I did not think about King Mark, Tristan, and Yseult the Fair. . . . I would be looking into the emptiness of the sea, at the cove called Mark's Gate and I could not see Mark, but only primroses and sheep. . . . I would be watching gulls and

swallows and I did not see in any bird's beak a golden hair of Yseult's. Neither did the river Fowey evoke associations with a white or a black sail of Tristan's. . . . Only when I was immersed in the Canadian woods at the lake . . . did I start seeing Tristan and Yseult. (N 263–64)

Gaining distance—that is, placing a few borders between herself and the places she describes—seems essential for dealing with mythologized autobiography in Kuncewicz's prose. What triggers the story is precisely the remoteness in time and space from the actual events, their fading away and becoming fiction as memories and impressions. Still another form of exile—the woman writer positioned on the last North American frontier and reaching back into her past and into the ancient myth—makes it possible to encompass a startling number of national times. Thus the romance and the lovers' drama are depicted by Wanda, a mother-narrator who reads her own story of exile from love and fulfillment into that of her son and his girlfriend. The young couple's inevitable mythical trip away from each other leads to America, the country of exiles.

The mother-narrator-writer, a Brangien who survives to tell the story, presents the Promised Land as a prison of passions and a refuge from feelings. Seeing New York for the first time, she says: "Too narrow, too tall, too steep—the city did not enchant me. I could sense the short breath of the walls as they squeezed into coexistence on the rocky island, straining upwards so as not to tumble into the water. People seemed half-strangled, too, by fumes and concupiscence. Women were made up to excess; men showed over-tension in their faces. I sat down on a bench near the Hudson and watched the water flow, turning my head now and again to admire the lacy bridge, so light, so wondrously spanning the two banks of the powerful river. . . . I felt a sudden pang of nostalgia for Warsaw."[46] The first of Kuncewicz's heroines to set foot in America is afraid of the suppressed feelings she senses in people and their close environment. In this respect she echoes Yezierska's first impressions, in "Mostly about Myself," of the inhabitants of the New World, who seemed aloof, tense, and indifferent to the newcomer. Nonetheless, the view of the bridge connecting the banks of the Hudson suddenly reminds Kuncewicz's narrator of that true home—Warsaw—and of the Vistula and that other bridge thrown over that other river in Poland. Although she can connect the visions of the two rivers and bridges—and thus constructs a metaphorical bridge between the two cultures—she cannot go back to the country where people such as her son are imprisoned for having fought on the "right" instead of the "left" in the war. She returns to Pensallos in Cornwall and from there looks over the sea toward some unrealized dream, into an unknown and lonely future; in this vigil she is very much like another mythical figure in American literature—Scott Fitzgerald's Gatsby trying to discern the green light in the darkness over Daisy's dock.

Wanda's gaze into space over the sea in Pensallos evokes the author's looking over the sea in a similar place in Cornwall, where she tried to "see" the legend of Tristan and Yseult. As if bridging the gap between fact and fiction, these two gazes meet, joining the writer's and her exiled heroine's narratives. The author could not envision *Tristan* until many years after she had left Cornwall, whereas Wanda kept observing "her unreal Truro across the cove," searching for a reason why the myth had died. As a metaphorical author of the modern story of Tristan and Yseult, Wanda-Brangien serves as an illustration of the artistic dilemmas that Kuncewicz confronted as a displaced writer. Kuncewicz's coming to terms with the myth of love in *Tristan*, which illustrates the impossibility of such a utopia after two world wars, is also an attempt to approach the general devaluation of the myth of the artist in postmodern reality. In the narration of Wanda-Brangien, she thus constructs a disillusioned author who discards both the medieval story, which can no longer accommodate the vicissitudes of modern love, and the privileged position of the writer as a godlike "arranger" who can no longer understand the world from the remote heights of his ivory tower (male pronoun intended). By focusing on the story of Wanda the narrator rather than on the proverbial lovers, and by highlighting her own creative progress, Kuncewicz emphasizes the novel as process. In this respect, she writes what Hilary Radner calls the "woman's novel"—"a narrative structure that emphasizes process [and] is often associated with feminine discourse." The "woman's novel" produces a "discourse which is both public and private" and "stubbornly rejects the status of high art." Thus in its implied critique of the male-dominated literary tradition of high art, Kuncewicz's "woman's novel" positions the female writer as an exile within and as an outsider—the other disrupting the man-made ivory tower of authorship—from without.[47]

As the next section will show, Kuncewicz's transition from fiction to autobiography records her coming to terms with the external narratives defining her as a writer and a woman. Kuncewicz's artistic creed about writing as a process of self-creation, implied by her novels and examined in detail in her autobiographical notebooks, arises from the confrontation of her fictional and self-reflective narratives with the ones that write her political biography. As a writer and a P.E.N. activist, she becomes a character in reviews and criticism, in translation and under censorship; she is written into stories that she cannot control and that construct her both as a female exile and as an ambivalent returned immigrant. Thus the bridge between America and Europe that she has built in her texts also brings together the author and her artistic otherness, a topic which she now confronts openly as a subject in her autobiographical writings. Kuncewicz's notebooks describe her actual and metaphorical "naturalization" as an American and a world citizen who engages in a "two-way" cross-cultural shuffling as a public persona and who comes to terms with her "phantom" identity as a female author permanently in exile because of her gender.

## Written by Exile

### *Writing Herself*

In her triptych of diary-notebooks, *Fantomy* (Phantoms, 1971), *Natura* (Nature, 1975), and *Przeźrocza* (Slides, 1985), Kuncewicz continues to focus on the construction of her authorship and moves between fiction and autobiography even more openly than in her novels. She sees her art as arising from a secret space within herself, as an expression of someone who does not possess a voice:

> Two days ago, in Kazimierz on the Vistula, Radio Warsaw reminded us that Maria Kuncewicz was born in this or that year. I felt my duality more sharply than ever. Somewhere, over the so-called waves of ether, exists a Maria Kuncewicz, begotten by letters and voices, and here, in this square house, I am standing, I, born of the mother Róża and the father Józef, a person not to be deciphered, a person without a voice.
>
> I am currently reading the second volume of a French woman writer's autobiography and am astonished by the foreignness of the being named Simone de Beauvoir, by her passionate effort to decipher herself and the world, while I reconcile myself to mysteries.[48]

However, in thus reconciling to "mysteries," Kuncewicz affirms her art as fiction, but, like de Beauvoir, she also embraces autobiography as her inspiration. Her texts record her life, but they also construct "the person not to be deciphered"—a fictitious character—who appears in seemingly autobiographical narratives.

Significantly, the place where this crossbreeding between two genres happens especially poignantly is the United States. For example, the way in which New York is shown in *Tristan* echoes Kuncewicz's own impressions when she, like Wanda, came to this country after her son had decided to stay here and become a citizen. The bridge linking the Polish and the American rivers in her novel is also a metaphor for the writer's own journey across the Atlantic. Even Kuncewicz's return to Poland as an American citizen, described in *Natura* and *Fantomy*, is presented as drawing a bridge between the only true "citizen of the world"—a cosmopolitan artist—and a lucky holder of American citizenship—a returned "naturalized" immigrant—who can triumphantly defy the travel constraints enforced by her country's government.

As was *Tristan*, Kuncewicz's autobiographical writings were influenced by her stays in the United States between 1955 and 1984 but, especially, by the political implications of her double citizenship. Her focus on authorship in exile and on genre-crossing is heightened by her positioning between East and West, whereas her personal experience as a refugee contributes to her debunking of the traditional view of writing as a sublime vocation positioned above the pedestrian lives of average citizens. When she talks about her art in the notebooks, she defies any stylistic camouflage and resorts to telling her readers, as Flaubert did with his "Mme Bovary, c'est moi," that she is and always has been her own characters. By using historical and factual material to construct the most interesting fiction—autobiography—she is reducing the art of writing to a life function, proclaiming authorship as an essential "biological necessity" arising from the conditions of living:

> That "splendid isolation" of a writer or an artist has been always ridiculous to me. For the same reason, I have considered the didacticism of Belles-Lettres artificial. Writers don't have to know more than others. . . . In fact I write because of my lack of trust in any other medium of expression; because of my conviction that I cannot communicate with the world directly and authentically; I write from my awareness of this communicative handicap. . . . I don't have any artistic creed . . . *writing is my biological necessity and not a realization of any previously predetermined philosophical or theoretical goals.*[49]

By confiding in her readers so much, by disclosing her intimate links with every character and pronouncing her autobiography and biology as sources of her art, Kuncewicz is obviously making herself vulnerable to the kinds of accusations always directed at women's writing. Like Antin or Yezierska, she is overtly "feminine" because, unable to disengage art from life, she is incapable of concentrating on the "abstract" or "transcendent" topics that should constitute serious literature.

Kuncewicz's claim that it is her physiology rather than her mind that authors her books echoes Yezierska's metaphor about writing as giving birth to books. In her last text, *Listy do Jerzego* (Letters to George, 1988), Kuncewicz describes the experience of labor and giving birth through biblical analogies. She emphasizes the change of perspective afterwards, when she has "authored" another human being:

> We danced. Like two lunatics, in a completely empty space, we danced a fiery mazurka to get warm. . . . I felt marvelous. And wet. . . . A nurse appeared, from the clinic where I was to go to give birth. She said: "Your waters broke."
>
> Where did the waters come from? Why did they break? Where did the flood come from? Why did it withdraw from Noah? Something brimmed up and something subsided, back to normal. A boy was born fit as a fiddle, only the little vessels in my eyes broke. For a few weeks I lost the whites in my eyes, and stared at you and the world with two black holes.[50]

This passage about giving birth to her son, Witold, appears between sections in which Kuncewicz describes her writing as inseparable from living. Using the metaphors of dance with her artistic alter-ego—a phantom girl who appears in her dreams—she presents her art as the "hateful look-alike" who "speaks for me, when I'm silent, who acts, when I'm asleep, who leads me onto roads of no return" (110).

As I previously argued, a woman writer is always defined by her gender and body and is thus the other in exile from the masterpieces written in celebration of the disembodied male mind.[51] As Jane Marcus claims, "Estrangement seems built into the female condition." Always writing "elsewhere," the woman writer produces a "*triologue*"—"a triple-tongued discourse with her culture"—because she is already in exile speaking "*his* tongue, [and] so further conditions of exile simply multiply the number of her 'veils' and complicate the problem of exegesis."[52] Read through feminist theory, Kuncewicz's writing explores this feminine authorial estrangement and tears down the veils around a woman writer that not only envelop her in the patriarchal culture but that also separate her from herself as a product of that culture. Kuncewicz confronts her version of otherness and shows how it crossbreeds the fleeting "phantom" existence of a refugee caught between diverse national time zones with a female immigrant writer who is obsessed with signification. The site where this obsession is played out is her body-authorship engaged in the continuous process of writing her feminine identity.

As Judith Kegan Gardiner sees this problem, writing woman's identity is a dynamic, "fluid and flexible," process rather than a state:

> One reflection of this fluidity is that women's writing often does not conform to the generic prescriptions of the male canon. Recent scholars conclude that autobiographies by women tend to be less linear, unified, and chronological than men's autobiographies. Women's novels are often called autobiographical, women's autobiographies, novelistic. . . . Because of the continual crossing of self and other, women's writing may blur the public and private and defy completion. . . . The model of the integrated individual was predominantly male, and women writers show that this model of characterization is inappropriate to their experience.[53]

Kuncewicz's constant self-creation and writing relate her life between America and Poland as a composition of bits and pieces of impressions and fictions. She not only defies but even rejects completion in her insistence on boundary-crossing and trespassing into forbidden territories. Hence, Gardiner's feminist analysis coincides clearly with Kuncewicz's views on her own art and on a woman's life, where "the borderline between one's interior and the external world is extremely blurry."[54] However, it is important to note that even in fluidity and fragmentation, the author of *Tristan* preserves her exiled independence—her decentered subject position. She absents herself even from a specific feminist classification, for she was never a feminist by organizational affiliation, as in the sense of doing something other than writing what she thought. In fact, while abroad, she was often surprised by the reactionary manifestations and pronouncements of some female groups; she did not trust crowds and slogans.

Still, it is precisely this aloofness from and suspicion of any organized doctrine that makes her views on women's writings interesting to the contemporary reader literate in feminist theory. Kuncewicz sees women's literature as unique and absolutely necessary for constructing a fair view of human experience, but she perceives it as encompassing both female and male elements. She believes that such literary androgyny is inherent in all texts, regardless of an author's gender. Her refusal to be associated with any philosophy or ideology signifies a desire to represent herself exclusively—even in exile from other women. This approach seems to support Gardiner's views on female identity in the making: Kuncewicz's refusal to participate in any ideology or to declare any philosophy as her driving force confirms the focus in her texts on the dynamic process of writing as becoming herself. However, at the historical moment that Kuncewicz terms the "age of Ideology," it is inevitable that, despite her resolve to avoid definitions, she is carefully studied and classified in the texts written by others. As a "heroine" of reviews and literary criticism, she is thus fictionalized and pigeonholed; the "phantom" she is to herself is beyond definitions, but the woman projected in her texts can be pinned down and analyzed in her reader's critical texts.[55] Kuncewicz's career and reception abroad construct her external otherness, the public persona that arises from the political and historical circumstances of her life and that may help explain her lack of popularity as a Polish woman writer in the United States.

### "The Nature of Things" Abroad

In 1954 the International P.E.N. Club Centre For Writers in Exile published an anthology, *The Pen in Exile*, edited by Paul Tabori and issued in Great Britain. Among the introductions is the short "Exile without Tears" by Maria Kuncewicz, in which she recapitulates the émigré writers' struggle for their own organization abroad. She compares unwanted, stateless persons to "white elephants" rejected by the "human zoo": "no one wanted them; humanity would not waste charity, imagination, creative energy upon an object of social luxury."[56] As in her novels depicting estranged characters, Kuncewicz's own life and writings reflect the ironically "luxurious" status of an alien and expatriate, one who is blown through the world by external political and historical circumstances.

When she was fleeing the advent of World War II in Poland in 1939, Maria Kuncewicz did not realize that she would not be able to go back "home" until 1958, and that even that trip would be just the visit of an exiled author holding U.S. citizenship. Traumatic historical and political scenarios made her into a temporary wanderer, into a character in some larger story that was being plotted independently of her own writing. From Romania to France, from Bordeaux to England, from there to America, and later back and forth between Europe, "thawed" communist Poland, and the United States, she lived a story shared by many displaced writers. She was to find out that, as Margaret Storm Jameson writes in the introduction to the English edition of Kuncewicz's *The Stranger* (1945), being a refugee means being expelled from two countries simultaneously: one's homeland and one's literature.[57] Kuncewicz's concept of writing as one's only true country and homeland across national time zones—no matter how illusory and intangible—arose from her efforts to help other stateless persons cope with the predicament of exile.

After the war had ended, Kuncewicz and a group of other stateless writers in London were looking for support to be able to work and survive abroad. The world was recovering from the atrocities of the Nazi reign, and people were sending letters to the P.E.N. Centre condemning its efforts to aid stateless authors. *The Pen in Exile* quotes some of these letters: "How can you care whether a writer is able to write his book or not? What do you think anyone's books have to say to a world full of hungry or frightened people?"[58] Comparing himself or herself to a foreigner looking for a place to write, an average citizen felt superior, having been a direct witness and victim of the "reality" that the "literati" merely tried to imagine and translate into words. Having beheld the political turmoil that tore the world apart, readers doubted whether the books written from exile could bring them any help in understanding the political paradoxes pervading their everydayness. This hostility toward foreign writers was one of the reasons why Maria Kuncewicz conceived the idea of, and later designed, her appeal to the United Nations for a "world citizenship."

The appeal was Kuncewicz's initiative taken against the "white elephant" stigma she and so many other writers bore at the time. She hoped that the United Nations would privilege the stateless authors and give them an opportunity to travel without forcing them to declare political and territorial loyalties: "Let the refugees have a say in the cultural reconstruction of the world . . . do not force stateless people, by obstructing their liberty of travel, education, and employment, to apply for new nationalities. By sheer force of events they have acquired the feeling of belonging to a community larger than one nation. . . . [H]istory made them citizens of the world, and they should be treated as such."[59] However, despite its publication in the world press, accompanied by the signatures of such celebrities as Einstein, Russell, Huxley, Shaw, and others, the appeal was ignored. Eventually, the "refugees of the pen" managed to form the International P.E.N. Club (later the P.E.N. Centre for Writers in Exile but often referred to simply as the Pen Club). With Maria Kuncewicz as its honorary president, the organization provided these writers with some political leverage, even though it did not succeed in obtaining for them the world citizenship status that Kuncewicz envisioned. The P.E.N. institution came into existence because many intellectuals believed that Margaret Storm Jameson was right in stressing the special meaning of the exiled authors for the Free World: "They understand, as we do not yet, the real meaning of the struggle going on in the world, the real nature of the choice which is being forced on us. They understand it by having lived it. . . . But what we merely know, they feel: what we reason about they have in their nerves. . . . A short pamphlet by the Polish writer . . . says more, and says it more sharply, about the moral and psychological position of the intellectual in Eastern Europe than could a million words of speculation or warning by the most intelligent of English liberals."[60] Storm Jameson sees the intellectual life in exile as the only reliable source of information about the "Unfree World." She appreciates the outsider-participants' perspective on the "Free World" and its insights, which go beyond any westerner's one-sided understanding.[61]

However, despite the worldly importance of their artistic task, the displaced writers were meant to become "citizens" of very specific countries; the world felt awkward about the crowd of stateless people who could freely comment on both sides of the Iron Curtain. The International Refugee Organisation, which was "handling" their cases, worked hard to incorporate them into particular societies and linguistic traditions. Kuncewicz called that process "a liquidation as rapid as possible of that awkward monster—the stateless."[62] In such a context, Storm Jameson's words about the mission of the exiled writers sound almost ironic; why would the exiles want to create texts full of understanding if they could not be understood themselves?

The echo of Storm Jameson's words could still be heard in the 1970s and 1980s, when the West would see writers from the Other Europe exiled "internally" in their own homelands, which were ruled by ideological terror and ruthless censorship. Thirty years after Storm Jameson, Stanisław Barańczak called for reading novels by East European authors in order to stop the "continental drift" taking America away from other nations and their cultures. Like Storm Jameson, he stressed the indispensability of art in communicating cultural messages otherwise untranslatable into news and media commentaries.[63] In a similar tone, Margaret O'Brien Steinfels called for increased reading of the books about the totalitarian rule in East Europe before it is too late, before "the story . . . [slips] away . . . [because] of the quotidian character of so much that is happening now" and before we forget how long the struggle for democracy has gone on there.[64]

Not surprisingly, the appeal of contemporary critics for more regard toward the exiled writers and their work brings to mind Kuncewicz's pleas from her invocation to the United Nations in 1949. Considering how little we know about those times and lives, we can look at the thirty years that elapsed between Storm Jameson's and Barańczak's words and recognize the ever-present stigma of the "white elephant" still making interesting East European authors obscure to western readers. Perhaps Maria Kuncewicz realized that she would never be able to become a "citizen of the world," and that was why in 1960 she decided to become naturalized in the United States, which she saw as one of the nations reflecting the world's diversity most clearly. However, even here she has been virtually unknown, due to her "difficult" and "ethnic" imagery and, possibly, due to her failure to write decisively against the communist state and thus to fulfill the popular image of a dissident. Because she was more interested in writing about how politics and history influence people, instead of declaring her ideological loyalties, her texts could not be used to strengthen the image of freedom in this country by providing condemning contrasts with the lack of freedom in East Europe. In the country of immigrants and exiles, which some Americans of the sixties, fleeing to Europe, would see as oppressive and parochial, she remained a "foreigner," a newcomer who would not melt or blend and who kept exploring the condition defining her as a "resident alien" and then as a "citizen."

Kuncewicz describes the moment of becoming an American in her autobiographical *Natura* as taking on the "nature" of the new country. This fragment seems a clear continuation of the ideas Antin expressed at the end of *The Promised Land*, when Mary deliberates upon her revival within the Natural History Club and upon her "American jar of specimen." Both examples suggest that the immigrant woman perceives her naturalization as an entrance into both the ideological and the physical "nature" of the new culture. Kuncewicz comments on her naturalization: "But whose nature was supposed to become adapted to whom? Mine to the new country's? Or the new country's to mine? . . . Before my naturalization in America, a long time ago, Poland had naturalized my ancestors. America wasn't new on Earth either. Long before Columbus it had been naturalized by the native tribes, whose names are dying on maps and on hotels' neon-signs. Apparently that is the natural sequence of things. . . . The thing I decided to adapt to was: life" (N 164). The "nature of things" Kuncewicz ponders in *Natura* indicates clearly the complexity of her position as one more person, name, and nationality entering the host culture, which, in its effort to "melt them," absorbs and erases individual stories.

Because Kuncewicz is already a sort of a naturalized Pole due to her Russian-German-Polish parentage, being an expatriate and taking on U.S. citizenship only heightens her sense of internal and external exile. In America she discovers that the very nature of the country she has entered is an ambiguous concept in itself, that its history and ideology are full of paradoxes. Therefore, neither she herself nor the new country has an established "nature"— a ready-made identity—that one could simply put on like a new coat. In the context of its ambivalent "discovery" and the historical injustices from which it benefited, both America and Americanness appear to Kuncewicz as even more fictional than her own writings. Getting used to life in the United States, then, implies living a narrative over which she does not have much control, as her new citizenship and her "American" character are as elusive as her ever-changing phantom identity.

### Reading the Alien

Maria Kuncewicz's fate as an expatriate drove her to the United States in 1955, sailing "with a tightened throat of an immigrant" (*N* 27). Although she decided to adopt the "nature" of her new country, she never became its true "citizen," never entered America as a writer who made a lasting impression on its letters. Ironically, she adopted America with all its paradoxes, but America never adopted her and her otherness as an exiled woman writer. The lack of wider interest in Kuncewicz's novels that are available in this country, two of them written in English—*The Olive Grove* and *Tristan*—and four others translated from Polish—*The Stranger* (1945), *The Keys* (1946), *The Conspiracy of the Absent* (1950), and *The Forester* (1954)—might have been a consequence of this writer's characteristically complex "foreign" style and of her philosophy concerning the role of exiled writers in the postwar world.[65] Since she rebelled against being inscribed onto the model of an expatriate who is defined by just one country and political system, because she demanded "world citizenship" for refugee writers, artists, and intellectuals, she was hard to categorize and explain to an American audience unfamiliar with the subtleties of East European literature in exile. Despite the failure of her United Nations appeal, Kuncewicz's writings pursued her individual version of world citizenship and often projected textual complexity that reviewers found hard to deal with—it was termed "not pleasant," "for a limited audience at best," and "slightly depressing." Paradoxically, in the country of exiles Kuncewicz was often considered a trespasser by critics who misread her focus on cultural otherness as a foreigner's arrogance.[66]

In response to the publication of *The Olive Grove*, O. K. Burger wrote in the *New York Times Book Review*: "It is a pity that so much of this novel is on the odd side, that the author's search for the ultimates leads her into so much murky symbolism. . . . In the end, one concludes that it is one thing for a foreigner to write English—and quite another to understand the English."[67] In this review Kuncewicz was condemned for trespassing: she not only had crossed the clear-cut linguistic boundaries as a nonnative writer of English but also had challenged the insider's privilege of defining English or American mentalities from her vantage point as a nosy foreigner. Although the reviewers did not like it, she peered into the affairs of other nations insistently; as a novelist she felt it her obligation to try to understand even those who might have liked to remain "aliens" to her inquiring Polish pen.

Her desire to pry into the "nature" of other countries arises directly from Kuncewicz's inquiries into her own cosmopolitan identity and from her sense of being always scrutinized by the gaze of observers to whom she is a stranger and a foreign "specimen." In *Przeźrocza*, she writes about her first trip back to Poland, which made her realize how uprooted she was as a "citizen of the world":

> Finally, in the year '58, I returned to Kazimierz . . . to my house, which, even before the war, I had started thinking of as the "anchor of generations." A strange miracle! During all the post-war times on the Vistula, in the house which was "my own," newly inhabited, warmed up, and loved, not even for a day did I feel as at home as in the rented apartments where I had also lived before the war. These days I always sense some intruder behind my back. And I share this sensation with the natives in Rome, in England, in America, wherever fate drives me. . . . nobody, after all, lives by themselves any more. (*Przeźrocza* 90)

The "intruder behind my back" inhabiting Kuncewicz's house in Poland is a metaphor for the public gaze scrutinizing her as a foreigner and a writer no matter where she lives. Her sense of homelessness seeps into her texts, which are often considered opaque and complex because they are haunted by the ghosts of places and cultures in which she trespassed as an alien person.

Nevertheless, although exposed to the gaze of the international public, Kuncewicz insists on writing about difficult themes, which, not surprisingly, prompted opinions such as Warren Miller's about *The Olive Grove*: "Not language but plot is this book's undoing; like a detective novel, it is complicated without being complex. Lacking in depth, and with no walls to contain it, the plot spreads and spreads. And the author is self-indulgent; *too much is there which does nothing to advance the novel*. . . . I was often reminded of Sybille Bedford's work . . . but Mrs. Bedford has a way of converting history and literary ideas into *good gossip* . . . her asides are always a delight."[68] Apparently, Miller sees Kuncewicz's "strangeness" in her inability to convert "history and literary ideas" into "good gossip." She should not venture to write complicated novels and ought to abandon "too much" analysis for the sake of "advancing" the action. (With all due respect to Bedford, hailing "good gossip" as "a delight" in a woman writer may not be a compliment in this context.) Miller praises Kuncewicz's English, though, and, oddly enough, her contribution to "illuminat[ing] French foreign policy and delusion of grandeur," even though the author explicitly pleads ignorance about such themes in the introduction. Most interestingly, however, the critic seems to object to the "no-walls" quality of Kuncewicz's novel, which can be read as advocating an idea of open nationhood, of crossing the boundaries and trespassing into other countries' otherness. Such a concept could seem threatening to a conservative critic who would rather subscribe to the clear separation of the western democracies and literatures from the threats of "communist egalitarianism." Miller's superficial dislike for nontraditional plots turns eventually into a tirade against the Evil Empire, which shows how much discourse about literature reflected political discourse in Kuncewicz's time.

Although not concerned with chasing the "reds" in texts and authors, the reviews generally sympathetic to Kuncewicz also tend to emphasize her talent for writing about "strange" phenomena. An anonymous review of *The Forester*, published in the *Times Literary Supplement*, calls the novel "a convincing reconstruction of an alien world" and classifies its hero as "a suspect foreigner." Anzia Yezierska's response to the same novel praises the "folktale of divided loyalties," but worries about the book not "quite coming through" because the author "tells *about* her people instead of letting them speak, think, and act for themselves."[69] Apparently, even to the critic, who was herself an immigrant, the writer's absence from her story seemed a natural thing. (It is interesting to note how in this respect Yezierska the reviewer is completely divorced from Yezierska the novelist.) The authorial presence only spoils the "folkloristic" authenticity of the foreign tale. Contrary to this opinion, a review of *The Conspiracy of the Absent*, although commending the "skillful contrast of life in war-time Poland and England," complains about the author's minimized textual presence. Kuncewicz's detached narrative in this novel, achieved by means of creating a filmlike chronicle of different settings, "weakens the narrative," and the book's symbolism "remains somewhat obscure."[70] According to this reviewer, the author should inhabit her text more conspicuously to guide the reader through her exotic narrative.

In a complimentary reaction to the controversial *The Stranger*, Ruth Page recognizes a "real novelist" in the "foreigner" and praises her ability to construct a world independent of "our personal faith in the political clichés of the moment." Page's most illuminating remark, however, is her brilliant insight into the novel's key theme—"the psychology of exile"—which she sees in Kuncewicz's heroine's desire to turn inward in an act of conscious alienation from her milieu. Nevertheless, Page does not go beyond this and fails to apply her insight consistently to the whole novel, which, at one point, she finds "comic in essence" because it takes the heroine her whole life to find out about her paradoxical delusions.[71] Obviously, Kuncewicz does not lack "ironic imagination" and a sense of humor, but a novel featuring a woman struggling between internal and external exile is not very comical (as we have seen, trivial delusions result in tragedies in *Tristan* and *The Olive Grove*). Like Page, all Kuncewicz's critics were, of course, fully justified in having had doubts about an unknown foreign woman writer. However, it is significant that they all built their interpretations around Kuncewicz's "strangeness." And in order to "tame" this strangeness for their audience, they were writing her into still another script as an object of inquiry, as a character in their critical "fictions."[72]

A fairer view of Kuncewicz's novel-memoir-documentary, *The Keys*—which sympathizes with her flight into exile—is presented in a *Times Literary Supplement* review. Its author admires Kuncewicz's unusual mode of writing, "differ[ent] from the normal type of record of war-time flight or travel," and her ability to convey sympathy for the refugees "deprived of the sky over their heads" all over the world. This is one of a very few critical responses that actually attempt to see Kuncewicz's text as a witness to unique experiences in history. The reviewer senses her desire to express her "painful sense of unreality" in Paris and sympathizes with the "routine of refugee existence," which oftentimes turns into invisible but acute malaise.[73] In *Natura* Kuncewicz calls this malaise her "schizophrenia, medically—imperceptible, in daily life—obvious" (*N* 27).However, what this review commends in Kuncewicz's art—her bold trespassing onto foreign territories and literally living *on* other cultures and languages—makes the writer into a stranger to herself. She slowly becomes her own story, a permanent foreigner who disguises herself in order to observe others but who, in the process, cannot control being surveyed and misread as an author. In such a double perspective, the exiled writer is both the observer and the observed, classified by her papers, visas, political views, accent, tastes, appearance, even by her ability to be an authentic specimen of "a Polish female writer," of a displaced person from East Europe. As a result of this double role, she lives by crossing borders, by encroaching on foreign territories, for which she pays with estrangement from the critical versions of herself that undertake to translate her for native audiences. In this context, the failure of her "world citizenship" is paradoxically productive because, as a failure of the international utopia for writers, suspended over geographical and political divides, it gives her a chance to establish an alternative "free-for-all" country in her texts, where she can move freely all over the globe. Although as a woman she may "have no country," Kuncewicz creates her whole private world in her books.

## Translations and Crosscultural Misreadings

Although it helped her defy the Polish regime's restrictions on foreign travel, Maria Kuncewicz's U.S. citizenship—her "blue passport" to world citizenship—was not able to protect her from being exiled from her own texts in her own country. If she wanted her books to appear there after 1956, she had, at least theoretically, to comply with communist censorship. Furthermore, consenting to her books' publication in Poland meant a violation of International Pen Club policy, which prohibited its members from maintaining any contacts with the regimes. Suspended between the United States and Poland, she had to accommodate the rules set for exiled writers by both cultures: she had to risk censorial intrusion into her texts if she wanted them read in her country, while her very desire to communicate with her Polish audience, many of whom still remembered her prewar publications, was considered a betrayal by the émigré community.

On the one hand, Kuncewicz's decision to return to Poland—her reversed immigrant passage—liberated her from the constraints of the typical, one-way newcomer narrative. On the other hand, it alienated her from the community of exiles abroad, and even from some of her audience in Poland, because she violated the dissident narrative in which returns into communist East Europe meant practically announcing one's collaboration with the regime. In light of these two factors, I propose to examine the reception of Kuncewicz's re-published texts in Poland and her response to being expelled from the Pen Club. While giving us a defensive version of her exile and return, Kuncewicz offers interesting insights into émigré politics that confirm her commitment to writing her own narrative despite its misreadings and misinterpretations by others. By pointing out how she has been "erased" and "cut" from her own texts by censors in Poland and by translators in the West, I also want to show that she has been perceived as a political writer whose message had to be controlled regardless of the culture in which she was published.

Kuncewicz's agreements in 1956 with PAX and Czytelnik—two major publishing houses of Poland who promised to "respect the integrity of her texts" —caused her resignation from the position of the honorary president of the International P.E.N. Club: "The title of honorary president was abolished to get rid of me . . . in the face of such a clear vote of non-confidence, I decided to leave" (*N* 159). As she writes in *Natura*, not without bitterness, some of her colleagues interpreted her decision as unforgivable disloyalty and an act of collaboration with the communists, whereas she saw it as an attempt to restore at least some of the normality ravaged by politics:

> [Since] I had not signed the Polish writers' London manifesto against being printed in Poland, I went to the American officials with a statement that I just had decided to publish there. An American with whom I had a discussion about this over lunch did not seem either shaken or eager to protest. But the so called Polish Desk [at Radio Free Europe] rang a big alarm. . . . the demise of "Kowalscy" [Kuncewicz's radio novel] was suddenly announced and any collaboration with me was immediately dissolved. The latter was implemented so zealously that even two tapes [of the radio novel], already recorded by the actors, were destroyed. (*N* 158)

Because of her desire to reconnect with her home and readers, the community of exiles saw Kuncewicz as a "stranger" to their values and subsequently expelled her from their formal ranks. The destruction of the tapes with Kuncewicz's radio novel seems especially ironic in light of what censorship was doing to texts and art in East Europe—in the name of ideology and loyalty as well.[74]

It is hard to determine whether Kuncewicz's publications in the People's Poland meant any compromise with the authorities or how much her textual integrity was actually respected. At that time, publishers were usually not allowed to mark places in the text where cuts or censorship-enforced revisions occurred. However, the privilege of doing so was granted to PAX, which issued the first edition of Kuncewicz's autobiographical *Przeźrocza*. Possibly due to its political connections with a Catholic lobby honored by the government, which at that time was engaged in "appeasing the Vatican," PAX could print an abbreviated code of the law restricting freedom of speech in these places in the text where censored excerpts were deleted from the original. The readers of Kuncewicz's book, whose subtitle, "Notatki włoskie" (Italian Notebooks), does not imply any political references, nevertheless found the following string of mysterious abbreviations in places where Kuncewicz began discussing nationhood, prisons, and the then new phenomenon of Lech Wałęsa: "[Ustawa z dn. 31 VII 81 r. O kontroli publikacji i widowisk art. 2 pkt. 1, 2 (Dz.U. nr 20, poz. 99; zm. 1983 Dz.U. nr 44, poz 204)]" (61, 120, 128).[75]

Although her name had never been directly connected with any radical dissident and antiparty movements, Kuncewicz's views were "dangerous" enough to be "edited" before publication. In this way she was still exiled from her readers and from her own language at home, where her writing was deemed alien to the dominant ideology, while being also estranged from the émigré circles in America, where her return to Poland signaled a strangely similar kind of ideological betrayal. However, her decision to write and publish for her native readers, despite the regime's control, can be seen as even more risky than remaining abroad within the safety of émigré circles where one could write without coding the messages. Kuncewicz's texts defend themselves best, and close readings of them reveal this writer's subtext of resistance against the oppressive reality that she smuggles under her deceptively private, feminine texts.

In a letter to an American friend, she writes: "I never strove, never strive, to become a national monument; my work is strictly personal."[76] Her focus on personal feelings and intimate perceptions enables her to reach out to her readers and to tell them the story of a double refugee caught between the private and the public, between the individual and the political, between East and West. In *Natura* she writes about her bitter experience of this double refugee status:

As soon as I regain freedom of speech in my country, I claimed, *as a writer*, I cease to be a refugee. . . . This argument did not convince the humanists, whose humanism worked exclusively within the borders of their own nation. One also had to deal with a phenomenon that with the years became a form of psychological paralysis: to defend by all means the stance once taken, without paying heed to the changes in one's own and the other worlds. It was considered a betrayal to disrupt such thinking addictions and—last but not least—the source of glamour and income. As a result, beside the true idealists, there appeared a kind of a professional refugee, a person who made his/her handicap into a career, and who condemned people striving for normalization of life as opportunists.

Discussions with professional refugees are dull and I never engaged in them. As far as "bona fide" refugees are concerned, I distinguish two kinds: missionaries and neurasthenics. The first kind kill nostalgia with political activity, the second with fear of the ruined scene of their youth and of emptiness in the place where there once were home and loved ones. And there is one more kind: world citizens, or—for now—phantoms. (*N* 159–60)

In the censored text of *Przeźrocza*, Kuncewicz illustrates how this ambivalent refugee status of a phantom-world citizen influences her authorship.

Although this book, the third in the series of autobiographical notebooks, is seemingly about her prolonged visits to Italy in the late 1970s and early 1980s, it actually describes her exile from the contemporary history of her country.

*Przeźrocza* reads like a journal, a writer's notebook, reportage. It recounts Kuncewicz's prolonged visits to Rome between 1978 and 1981 and, among other events, describes the then famous kidnapping and murder by the Red Brigades of Aldo Moro, party chairman of the Christian Democrats. Interestingly, Kuncewicz's detailed account of what this event meant politically and morally coincides with important happenings in Poland—the turbulent late 1970s, the founding of Solidarity, Lech Wałęsa's talks with the newly elected Polish pope, the introduction of martial law, and the imprisonment of political dissidents. Although in *Przeźrocza* she is writing down her life, Kuncewicz inhabits an absent space in her country's immediate history as a writer who cannot speak directly about what is happening there—her memoirs have to be an exercise in disguise. Already marked by the intrusion of the censor, *Przeźrocza* shows the writer's struggle to compose her message by absenting herself from Poland and her failure to do so successfully in the parts that still have been cut out by the vigilant servants of the regime. Kuncewicz's text thus conveys her alienation from the historical and political present twice— by her own writing method and by censorship, which erases some parts of her already disguised message.

A careful reader of *Przeźrocza* sees the analogies and painful comparisons that Kuncewicz is making between the situation in Poland, where the workers risked being confronted by Russian tanks, and the case of Aldo Moro in Italy, which showed the indifference of the state toward the individual. By criticizing those policies of the Italian government which sacrificed its faithful servant to the terrorists, Kuncewicz is expressing her disillusionment with the politics of the state in her own country, which later on sacrificed its own people during the period of martial law. She describes the strategy of such literary disguise in a letter to her American friend, a letter written and mailed in the United States and thus free from censorship: "Poland is ruled by communists and nationalists, Hugo, but above all by Russia, and this is not, as everybody knows, the fault of the Polish people so much as of the Yalta agreement. Polish writers have been trained though generations in the art of allusive writing, and the code is clear to every Pole at home and abroad."[77]

However, although it develops her subtle dissident voice and, with it, the tradition of "internally exiled" Polish political writing "between the lines," Kuncewicz's allusions in *Przeźrocza* also serve a larger purpose. In criticizing the policies of the Italian government and by commenting on the implications of the outcome of Moro's case, she shows her disillusionment as a world citizen with the politics of any state. She looks at her own life and sees the juxtaposition of two concepts—the state and the homeland—as a larger pattern perpetuating both individual and national histories: "The time of my youth, a short epoch between the first and the second world war, that time did not manage to enlighten me politically: I was too busy realizing my own being, personal impressions, and perspectives in separation from that alien body called society. My immigrant period, 1939–1958, did not bring about an apotheosis of the state either, despite the anthem's announcement of an apotheosis of the army: 'We'll cross the Vistula, we'll cross the Warta, we'll be Poles.' The state was ceding itself for the sake of a homeland" (*Przeźrocza* 61). After the word "homeland," the text is censored. However, based on the fragment following this textual "wound"—internal authorial erasure in the text imposed externally—we can infer Kuncewicz's rejection of the official conception of the state in favor of her own concept of homeland. She translates the larger political crisis caused by the state into "human conflicts" and thus manages to explain what homeland means to her despite the censorial cut:

> But in Italy, new liberations from the rule of foreign powers were not called off by current development of history. The kidnapping of Aldo Moro belonged then to such category of human conflicts as settling accounts within the mafia and camorra or to family dramas such as adultery, incest, or fratricide. . . . The conflict . . . was based on a difference of dispositions: Moro represented those who didn't lose hope, and the kidnapers were taking revenge on him because they had lost theirs.
>
> In this somber early Italian spring of 1978, I pushed the newspapers off. . . . How difficult it is to reconcile the law of the state with the law of the heart! (*Przeźrocza* 61–62)

Kuncewicz's accusation of the state in this fragment combines a political statement with a comment arising from a woman writer's otherness. One's country should be like one's home, which cares for its inhabitants and follows the traditionally feminine heart rather than the stereotypically masculine head in its political dealings. As *Przeźrocza* emphasizes, Aldo Moro's love for his homeland was not reciprocated or appreciated by the state, which sacrificed him as a mere human life that would go unnoticed in historical statistics. In the man-made state, there is no place for the heart and for the homeland—for the "feminine" and "sentimental" constructs of patriotism and nationhood.

She accuses the state of terrorism and indifference equal to that of Aldo Moro's kidnappers: "But isn't the state a terrorist organization that craves the death of its opponents? What citizen and what country can withstand the terror of the state, if they won't recognize force as the highest tribunal, which some will call God, others civilization, and still others conscience? The names aren't important" (*Przeźrocza* 126). Her passionate rhetorical questions to the reader communicate her anger and feelings of helplessness. However, in her call for solidarity against the ruthlessness of the state, Kuncewicz also demonstrates the power of her texts, which construct their own "homeland."

Kuncewicz's appeal to the reader is one of the most important features of her female dissident voice. Unlike male émigrés abroad, she could not formulate her message openly and hope that it would be heroically smuggled to Poland to "lift up the hearts." However, she came up with a specific poetics of writing through absences—the parts of *Przeźrocza* that were censored, the erased ones, speak louder than many open, clearly anticommunist texts written abroad. Kuncewicz's letter about the art of allusive writing states plainly what any careful reading of *Przeźrocza* and other Kuncewicz works makes clear and what she articulates herself in referring to the ideological content of her texts: "I don't think I owe anybody an explanation; a printed text must defend itself; if it doesn't, the more the pity."[78]

Kuncewicz's works defend themselves very well in Polish, but they have a harder time doing so in translation, which can be seen as a subtle form of censorship. Except for *The Olive Grove*, originally written in English, and *Tristan*, rewritten in English by Kuncewicz, the rest of Kuncewicz's novels were translated by others and, for the most part, not very well.[79] The critics of Kuncewicz's English editions point to the weaknesses of these renderings or praise them unjustly. In both cases the author is made even "stranger" and harder to understand to her audience than she actually is. For example, a review of *The Conspiracy of the Absent*, translated by Maurice Michael and Harry Stevens, terms this version "not outstanding."[80] And in another review Polish-speaking Virgilia Sapieha's response to a translation of *The Stranger* points to "stiff" English rendering and faulty word choices.[81] Yet, a review of *The Conspiracy* in *Kirkus* praises it unjustly as "[a] good translation, perhaps more English than American, [which] has a particular interest for Polish people and is more feminine in cast."[82] However, a look at the very last pages of this edition, where a crucial scene resolving the heroine's life in London takes place, reveals an omission of over half a page. Did the reviewer read the whole novel? Did the interpreters-translators "cut" what looked to be too long a passage, too complicated an ending? Or did it matter to readers of the English translation that its Chapter 1 is really Chapter 2, with the initial seven-page chapter of the original version deleted? Again, there is no way to determine exactly how much of the "translation editing" was done behind the author's back and how much with her consent, but it is striking to see such an abbreviated version without any explanation.

Obviously, no translation can be more than an attempt to approximate the original meaning, but cutting or changing the meaning is another matter. Yet, as if to prove that an imitation, rendering, or an approximation is as good as the original, the United States did not consider Kuncewicz's writing truer to the reality of her nation and culture than James A. Michener's best-seller *Poland*. Kuncewicz comments on this ironic fact in *Listy do Jerzego*, a collection of epistolary "conversations" with her late husband, a writer and a pursuer of exiled reality: "Michener's Poland is simply a piece called Queen on the chessboard of history. Her [Poland's] 'facts and gestures' were designed in such a way so as not to make the price of the book exceed the interest of the American reader. Thanks to that, in the year of your death, George, the romance about Poland remained on the *New York Times* best-seller list for thirty eight weeks. Neither you nor I had ever dreamed about such a success, although we had known its heroine personally" (75). Again, Kuncewicz appears as exiled, precisely for the reason of her hard-to-represent nationality. This time she is alienated by the laws of the publishing market, which promotes the American version of her country by Michener. In this way, where she comes from and, consequently, who she is, become a commercialized story, which is selling widely—"reaching the masses"—all over the country. Thus Michener's *Poland*, printed in thousands of paperbacks, replaces the "untranslatable" original and achieves successful sales without having to mention the "unpronounceable" names of its native writers.

### The Foreigner Reads America

Taking into consideration the difficulties involved in advocating such an author as Maria Kuncewicz, there may be as many reasons to rediscover and tell her story at the crossroads of the world—America—as to dismiss her as a mere visitor who just did not succeed in capturing an audience. Because America is an important place and concept in Kuncewicz's cosmopolitan writing, because she often regards the United States as a point of reference and juxtaposes its history with that of the rest of the world, because she cared to teach American students about "exotic" Poland and its literature, and, finally, because she wrote her books and lived some of her life here, she should be given another chance to tell her American story.[83] Once again, it is not that we are supposed to "rescue" a "forgotten voice"—Kuncewicz "wrote" her right to be included in American literature. Our task is to acknowledge this right rather than grant it as a privilege.

In recognizing Kuncewicz's contribution, we are also stepping onto the bridge that she has built between America and Poland. Her desire to engage in intercultural translation was largely a result of her predicament as a writer in exile; it also arises from the "textual yearnings" to be accepted, to find an audience in the new country that we have seen in early immigrant women. The insistence of Mary Antin and Anzia Yezierska on "teaching" America about their ethnic group, on making the dominant culture confront its own oppressiveness, develops into Kuncewicz's investigation of exile as a larger political predicament, on the one hand, and as an individual and artistic condition, on the other. In her introduction to *The Stranger*, Margaret Storm Jameson emphasizes the importance of the West's acquaintance with its "strangers" from East Europe: "It is Poland, a distorted mirror in which history is reflected as a succession of cruelties, deportations, massacres. . . . It is that Eastern Europe of whose existence we English complain, without understanding, without for a moment understanding what a country loses with its loss of certainty, of permanent addresses, of unbroken family traditions. Or what it gains—in hatreds erected as defense against memories of defeat and weakness."[84] Storm Jameson suggests embracing the East European "other" in order to acknowledge and show solidarity with the cultures which, to a certain extent, became a barometer for the postmodern history. She indicates that there is a lesson that the West can learn by reading East European literature: texts are witnesses to people's lives, and ideas are ambassadors between isolated political systems.

In this context, the unique depiction of the individual and collective experience of exile in Kuncewicz's writings can be seen as reflecting a postmodern authorial condition in a world segregated by ideologies. Kuncewicz's decision to become an American was the first step toward practical world citizenship and, at the same time, one more exercise in self-alienation. She was celebrating her freedom to move all over the continents, but she also realized the more acutely that her happiness was not available to the millions of people trapped within the borders of East and Central Europe; she felt guilty for abandoning them many years ago. Therefore, the symbol of America that she had seen in Disneyland, Uncle Sam, once appeared to her as Henry David Thoreau—with his ideals of individual freedom and resistance to the external social forces—and another time as the black primadonna from Gian Carlo

Menotti's opera *The Consul* who represents the "absent" left behind the Iron Curtain: "This wife separated from her husband in the epoch when the post-war borders slammed closed; this madwoman crazy with pain, tearing up the forms in the consulate and howling 'papers . . . papers . . . papers!' . . . she was looking into my eyes, and through her were gazing the millions of eyes fading behind the barbed wires, the homeless eyes, the hopeless eyes. I turned my head away. I said: 'I know I should have died'" (*N* 165). Nightmarish immigrant guilt often destroys the utopian dream of world citizenship, which is now cheaply symbolized in the mere passport of a superpower—a "paper" symbolizing the writer's individual freedom and its unavailability to those who are left behind. The cruel and self-destructive aspect of individual exile comes into play within the larger political context—citizenship and refuge are granted because of, and "thanks to," the oppression of those who did not make it abroad and who remained within the nations exiled from democracy.

It is interesting how this awareness visits Kuncewicz's memory of the day when she was naturalized in the United States: "But what has made it possible that I, I especially—a utopianist and a believer in myths—took the defeat of the world citizenship for the nature of things that is called life? Did I take for it the defeat of my own dream? On what could my optimism be based now that it has been supplied with a passport of the superpower?" (*N* 165). Becoming American means freedom to "pursue happiness" individually and opens up the world. It also marks the end of the writer's dream about ever being able to live unbound by territorial allegiances. This émigré conflict results from the fact that, as Julia Kristeva notes, "being" has to be considered first in relation to the place where one is and then in relation to the state; "Where am I?" conditions "Who am I?"[85]

For Kuncewicz, American citizenship is a source of guilt and anxiety in its political dimension, which inscribes her as a citizen of a superpower and which thus erases her Polishness to those who remained under communism. However, becoming one of many minorities in this country affirms the writer's ethnic awareness of being a Pole—the conflict of identities and the resulting absence of any definite subject position becomes a source of expiation and an impulse to renewed creativity. A walk through the corridors of the University of Chicago, where she developed courses on Polish literature, is a journey back to her own learning about the world and to the longest homework she has ever had to do—that is, writing down her phantom identity in exile: "I was wandering through the high-ceilinged rooms filled with school furniture, I was awaking echoes in the corridors. I was inhaling the smell of books and touching the pieces of chalk that were still warm from the touch of some-body's fingers, which had drawn some important signs on the blackboard. And I felt that I came back. Where? Well, to Nancy in France, to Cracow and Warsaw, that is, to youth, to this lost home of all wanderers through time" (*N* 228). Facing her new American nature, Kuncewicz realizes that a part of her will always remain attached to those young days of being a student in Poland and France, of being young in the wide, wide world. From her "America," it is actually possible to go back home, because in this country everybody's nationality becomes included in the myth of intercultural multiplicity and di-versity. Thus the ethnic heritage she embodies is already a part of a larger one and will be passed on to her American grandson. To this young boy, Kunce-wicz's and her son's Poland will inevitably turn into a legendary place, a name on the map to which he can trace his descent. The writer's inverted immi-grant passage does not mean going back to "belong," but rather to retrace the steps in her own intimate country, which has already become the "free-for-all" domain of writing that transcends geographical boundaries.

Through her defiance of and fascination with external narratives and domi-nant plots, Kuncewicz has carried the East European female immigrant dis-course into a phase in which the otherness of an immigrant woman gains a new dimension with the political and authorial experiences of the Cold War female refugee and exile. In Kuncewicz's fiction, America is the crossroads of the world—an anticipation of the fragmented culture about which Eva Hoffman writes in *Lost in Translation*. Kuncewicz's idea of the national time also anticipates Julia Kristeva's perception of its American version: "Ameri-can time must always be deciphered on a double register: On the one hand, the *universal*—but within it, memory forgets and is resolved in the present, the efficacity, the synchronic structure of the moment; on the other hand, the *specific*, but which dissolves in the particular continuity of civilizations." Maria Kuncewicz's textual trespassing into time goes even further than establish-ing its double register in America. As her texts and theory of fiction prove, the Polish exile was able to construe a time of her own, which could en-velop America and unmake its double status into the unique experience of a phantom-woman writer. For her America becomes as much a part of the "nature" she investigates as all the other places on earth she loves. She shows her readers that, although there will always be boundaries and differences, it is possible to look beyond them into the specific cultures and minds of other peoples. It is true that we are "each [a] group of women [and men] in the specific time" of its country and history, but as "phantoms" we also share a common existence in the larger scenario written for us by the indestructible external forces of politics, history, and cultural prejudice.[86] That is why we should read the works of women such as Kuncewicz—which reach *from* other countries *toward* America—instead of handing them our authorized versions of their stories from the center of the world we believe ourselves to occupy.

# Eva Hoffman's Observing Consciousness

## TRANSLATING THE CULTURE
## OF STRANGERS

Strangely, the foreigner lives within us: he is the hidden force of our identity, the space that wrecks our abode, the time in which understanding and affinity founder. By recognizing him within ourselves, we are spared detesting him in himself. . . . The foreigner comes in when the consciousness of my difference arises, and he disappears when we all acknowledge ourselves as foreigners, unamenable to bonds and communities.—Julia Kristeva, *Strangers to Ourselves*

## Love Thy Foreigner

**M**aria Kuncewicz's return to Poland, where she continued her travels and writing as a "world citizen," can be seen as part of a paradigm most recently described by Eva Hoffman in *Exit into History: A Journey through the New Eastern Europe* (1993). Relating her travels through the region she came from, Hoffman writes that for modern East Europeans their countries are like fate—those born in that part of Europe are inextricably connected to it. She compares this East European predicament to Hester Prynne's story in Nathaniel Hawthorne's *The Scarlet Letter*, which ends with the heroine's return to Boston, the place where she suffered and loved: "I think of Hester Prynne, and her desire to live out her life where her fate was; for so many Eastern Europeans their countries have been something like fate."[1] Maria Kuncewicz's return to Poland and to her home in Kazimierz can be seen as one of such instances of fate, similar to the one described by Hawthorne, who fictionalized an early female immigrant in Hester. Hoffman's own visits back to Poland, from which she emigrated in 1959 at the age of thirteen with her family and other Polish Jews, mark out a fate that seems a combination of those created by Hawthorne and lived by Kuncewicz.

As if to crossbreed Hawthorne's fictional story of Hester and Kuncewicz's real biography, Hoffman positions her narrative about going back to East Europe between fiction and reality. She contemplates upon her trip to Poland right after the "revolution" of 1989: "Every immigrant has a second, spectral autobiography, and in my revision of my own history I would have stayed in Poland long enough to become involved in the oppositional politics of my generation" (*EH* 41). Hoffman's "spectral autobiography" is an imagined narrative about the past that she could have lived as a citizen of just one country, completely immersed in the fate and national time of her native Poland, which she left for Canada and the United States as a young girl.

In her attempts to write down this imaginary life in Poland in her autobiographical novel *Lost in Translation: A Life in a New Language* (1989), Hoffman clearly echoes Maria Kuncewicz's literary pursuit of woman's "phantom identity" in flight through different cultures, languages, and historical periods. As I have previously stated, life in Kuncewicz's autobiographical *Fantomy* consists largely in events that happen in a "state of unconsciousness"—in dreams, flashes of feelings, sparks of emotions, and the abandonment of love—and these happen to a phantom-woman floating through the world, one never defined, never pinned down, never familiar even to herself. Unless she writes down the events, they do not exist; until she describes them on paper, her own life is just a fleeting story. But even as she records it, her life becomes a narrative about somebody else, an "experience dressed up in make-believe names." In this constant pursuit of her own otherness, Kuncewicz plays a game with the other—a kind of foreigner-observer in herself—whom she calls the "Witness": "I am behaving the way I do because of the Witness, who hates idleness, but mounts difficulties while praising ambition. I ask: Why do you order me to examine my life publicly in my old age? The Witness is silent. His cruelty consists precisely in the fact that his very presence forces me to look for the answers to my own questions inside myself. . . . I have been fighting against the shame of being and the fear of self-identification forever. Why should I spare my neighbors in this our shared commedia dell' arte?" (*Fant* 282–83). The stranger-Witness confronted by Kuncewicz in herself is an internalization of what all people are, a crowd of foreigners desiring communication, trying desperately to express their otherness privately and publicly. As a writer-translator of this desire, Kuncewicz describes everybody's individual strangeness to themselves as a part of a general predicament in the "age of ideology."

Kuncewicz's individual discourses with the Witness in *Fantomy* anticipate a larger cultural situation in which Hoffman finds herself as she records what gets "lost in translation" between East Europe and the United States after the Cold War. In fact, *Lost in Translation* and the wanderings through Eastern Europe that the author describes in *Exit into History* prove that the "neighbor" has not been "spared" and that Kuncewicz's "commedia dell' arte" of intercultural communication is still going on. After all, although the "walls are crumbling" and the world is becoming smaller in the "international triumph of liberal democracy" proclaimed by the media, it is still hard to say that nations and people know much more about one another than they did a decade ago. What Kuncewicz anticipated in her intimate dialogues with the Witness in the 1970s Hoffman has been exploring further in her Polish

American literary journeys through history and autobiography, journeys that describe an individual caught amid the world community of strangers and aliens in the late 1980s and 1990s. Her vision of the Americanization of a Polish-Jewish woman emphasizes her own acceptance of the mixed blessings of foreignness: "I've now gained the status of an exotic stranger. . . . I'm excited by my own otherness, which surrounds me like a bright, somewhat inflated bubble. After a while, this will become a treacherous condition, for it will be difficult to break out of my difference and reclaim a state of ordinariness in which, after all, we want to live."[2] Hoffman's text progresses through the tangled paths that an identity in crosscultural transition has to travel, but the journey of her autobiographical narrator maps the pursuit of otherness that engages individuals and whole nations.

Discussing a multinational France at the end of this century, Julia Kristeva suggests how living by such an affirmation of every individual's intrinsic otherness works on a national level: "A paradoxical community is emerging, made up of foreigners who are reconciled with themselves to the extent that they recognize themselves as foreigners. The multinational society would thus be the consequence of an extreme individualism, but conscious of its discontents and limits, knowing only indomitable people ready-to-help-themselves in their weakness, a weakness whose other name is our radical strangeness."[3] Kristeva suggests that an affirmation of shared otherness— "strangeness to ourselves"—is the only way to learn about and accept other cultures and peoples in an age when exile and homelessness are the lot of so many. The cultural and social model that she proposes transcends Kristeva's French-centered outlook. A similar growth of "foreign consciousness" can be discerned in the revival of multiculturalism in the United States, in post-totalitarian Europe, and perhaps even in the global society, where people are constantly on the move among nations and continents.

In *Strangers to Ourselves*, Kristeva argues that such individual affirmation of otherness will conquer the fear of and prejudice toward the other from foreign nations and alien cultures. Only then is dialogue between any interlocutors possible; only then can one write and communicate with others on the common, "foreign" wavelength. An ability to promote such communication arises out of Kristeva's own in-between position as an expatriate Bulgarian in France—an East European woman scholar in the somewhat hermetic world of the western academe.[4] However, while advising individuals and countries to welcome otherness—what in *Nations without Nationalism* she terms "esprit général"—she also warns that the price to pay for it will be the constant presence of the difference embodied in the internal and external "stranger." Yet it is precisely this acute awareness and recognition of difference that should cause people's hatred for the external foreigner to lessen after they have embraced those they have internalized. The memory of the "strange within us" will always remain—otherness is an inescapable weight each person has to shoulder. But he or she can "lighten that otherness by constantly coming back to it."[5] The only way is to "escape its hatred, its burden, fleeing them not through leveling and forgetting, but through the *harmonious repetition of the differences* it implies and spreads" (*SO* 1, 2, 3, emphasis mine). Therefore, a healthy balance between the inherent otherness within the individual and that within each culture of the world can be attained through their repeated affirmation and reenactment. What an individual should strive to achieve, whole nations should engage in, too.

Maria Kuncewicz's discourses with the Witness and her relentless pursuit of woman's phantom identities anticipate this approach to otherness very clearly through the "harmonious repetition" of the metaphorics of exile in all her novels, especially in the autobiographical *Natura* and *Fantomy*. And Kristeva's suggestion that individuals should revel in their inner strangeness also provides an interesting intertext in which to read the Polish American journeys recorded in Hoffman's more recent novelistically autobiographical and autobiographically journalistic texts. In their emphasis on the impossibility of completely successful assimilation and cultural translation, Hoffman's *Lost in Translation* and *Exit into History* engage Kristeva's question—"Should one recognize that one becomes a foreigner in another country; because one is already a foreigner from within?" (*SO* 14). Hoffman's works also provide a literary illustration of Kristeva's idea that an insatiable desire for the foreigner and the exile drives all people. This "passion for another land, always a promised one, that of an occupation, a love, a child, a glory" inspires in Hoffman a relentless pursuit of meanings in the space between her Polish and American promised lands (*SO* 10).

Although *Lost in Translation* records her progression from Poland to a successful career in the United States, Hoffman's search for identity in this transitional space defies traditional immigrant narrative structure. The work is a passionate exploration of the state of "being lost" utterly in the process of mapping a transition between cultures rather than a simple immigrant success story. It does not end with any kind of arrival that suggests permanence, acceptance by the dominant culture, and complete fulfillment and satisfaction. In its openness to the voices exploring otherness around her, Hoffman's works provide a literary terrain where many texts and authors can engage in dialogic encounters. Representing two generations of expatriate Polish women in the

United States, Kuncewicz and Hoffman talk to one another through their writings, which describe what Hoffman refers to as the "utterly nomadic" world, and construct what Maria Kuncewicz calls the "free-for-all country" of fiction (*EH* 408). They also share, although not to the same degree, the position of the outsider-participant straddling multiple borders. Similarly to Kuncewicz, who found herself between historical eras, countries, and languages, Hoffman shuttles back and forth between the West and the East in her travels as an international journalist, between religions and ethnic traditions as a Jew who grew up "next door" to Catholicism and between national identities as an expatriate for whom Poland is "always a here, a fully real place" despite her cultural identification with the United States (*EH* 185). Like Kuncewicz, Hoffman is a transitional figure in the tradition of East European women's writings. Her life and career fall on the borders, too, between a world war and peace, between the Cold War and the present era of yet clearly undefined postrevolution and postcommunism.

Hoffman's inquiry into the two worlds to which she belongs as a Jewish Polish American brings back the themes preoccupying Antin, Stern, Yezierska, and all the other writers of the "huddled masses" at the beginning of the century. The author of *Lost in Translation* shares her Jewishness with these forerunners, although this part of her background does not have as profound an effect on her identity as it did on the daughters of orthodox rabbis like Yezierska or Stern half a century earlier. In engaging a discourse of acculturation, ethnicity, identity, and authorship in the late twentieth century, Hoffman openly interweaves the earlier tradition with her own and opens up the future for new East European women's narratives. She comments on the nature of such connections between the past and present by juxtaposing her narrator's Polish-Jewish origins with her American present and future in *Lost in Translation*: "While my American friends, after undergoing the normal disillusionments of adult life, gradually temper their optimism, I try to slough off the excess darkness that is false to my condition. Paradoxically, it's not an easy adjustment to make; our first knowledge is the most powerful, and the shadows cast by it upon the imagination can be more potent than the solid evidence of our own experience" (*LT* 253). The "first knowledge" in Hoffman's text refers to her early experience of acculturation and, necessarily, to her preoccupation with the past and the East European Jewish immigrant tradition from which she comes and in many ways tries to relive. The contrast between the proverbial optimism of America and the dark broodings of its marginalized cultural others pervades the first impressions of all newcomers from the East, no matter what their ethnicity, class, and religious denomination.

Nevertheless, arriving in North America at a time when the governments of Canada and the United States made immigration for political dissidents and minorities from East Europe easy, the author of *Lost in Translation* goes through a passage from the Old into the New World that is very different from that of lower-class Jews fleeing the *shtetl* in the nineteenth century. Although her parents had to struggle with poverty and a language barrier, there was never any doubt that she and her sister would go to school and would not have to work to support the family. A child of educated and cosmopolitan parents, Hoffman was able to continue her music lessons and was encouraged to read and pursue intellectual activities upon her arrival in Vancouver, British Columbia. In this respect, her story of "making it" in America as a writer is slightly less glamorous than Yezierska's, who had to struggle much harder and who could thus present a more poignant contrast between her bleak past and glittering success. However, despite many differences between Antin or Yezierska and herself, Hoffman clearly arises from their tradition and draws her own story along the themes of linguistic identity, gender roles, and foreign authorship that preoccupied these writers. Her narrative proves that, aware of historical and class differences, she is rewriting these women's past stories because they continue to "cast shadows" not only upon her hungry imagination as a newcomer writer, but also upon the imaginations of readers of East Europe in the West, those for whom East Europe is still "an imagined 'other'—either a glimmering, craved, idealized other, or an other that is dark, savage, and threatening" (*EH* x).

In this chapter I examine the "solid evidence" of Hoffman's experience in *Lost in Translation* and *Exit into History* as it reflects her exploration of immigrant otherness during and after the Cold War. In order to emphasize how *Lost in Translation* arises from and is a rewriting of the earlier texts by immigrant women, I chose to concentrate on a close reading of Hoffman's work rather than on the critical reception of her books. As a borderline writer, Hoffman faces the challenge of both responding to a long tradition and remaking it to suit the different public and personal forces molding and dictating her narrative. I argue that, by successfully unmaking and reshaping the models passed down to her by earlier authors, Hoffman creates her own genre of immigrant-expatriate woman's writing, one in which male and female voices can engage in literary dialogues through diverse narrative models, historical periods, immigrant generations, gendered life stories, cultural idioms, and concepts of identity that celebrate the "strange within." While opening her text up to such discourses with diverse others, Hoffman also emphasizes the intimate nature of the individual case study of woman's otherness in her crosscultural Bildungsroman. Her map of her journey through language not only records her linguistic rites of passage but reveals as well an inward movement of self-discovery. In thus constructing herself through the crossbreeding of two linguistic and cultural identities, on the borders between historical periods, political systems, and immigrant generations, Hoffman is also rewriting the dominant culture and "founding" her unique "America" of strangers. Just as her narrator learns gradually to accept the ambivalent "losing" of herself in "translation" between Polish and English, she also masters ways to enact a complex recovery of her identity amid the joys and terrors of intercultural writing.

### The Joys and Perils of Intercultural Translation: Eva Hoffman's Immigrant Tale for the Fin de Siècle

*Lost in Translation* is an excellent example of how the "observing consciousness" works in a foreigner confronting the other in herself and in the new culture around her. This text shows very clearly that the tradition of female immigrant writing begun by Antin and Yezierska is still evolving in the different historical and political context of our time. It also poignantly illustrates the complex condition of conscious otherness in which all modern cultures find themselves, the condition which makes possible exchanges within the dialogic terrain of literature that engage whole nations and individuals. Unsure of the "shape of her story," Hoffman takes the immigrant narrative to its limits by mixing autobiography, memoir, reportage, and confession with the stuff of fiction. Through such putting together the "splinters and fragments" of intimate literary matter, she creates a textual collage that reflects the "blessings and terrors of multiplicity" in the world around her:

> And what is the shape of my story, the story my time tells me to tell? . . . A hundred years ago, I might have written a success story, without much self-doubt or equivocation. A hundred years ago, I might have felt the benefits of a steady, self-assured ego, the sturdy energy of forward movement, and the excitement of being swept up into a greater national purpose. But I have come to a different America, and instead of a central ethos, I have been given the blessings and the terrors of multiplicity. Once I step off that airplane . . . I step into a culture that splinters, fragments, and re-forms itself as if it were a jigsaw puzzle dancing in a quantum space. . . . Perhaps a successful immigrant is an exaggerated version of the native. From now on,

I'll be made, like a mosaic, of fragments—and my consciousness of them. *It is only in that observing consciousness that I remain, after all, an immigrant.* (*LT* 164, emphasis mine)

Hoffman's novel retells the story of the Americanization of the female from the perspective of an expatriate woman reassessing her life at the end of the 1980s, after she has achieved an American Dream of sorts: a successful career as a writer and a journalist and the enviable position of a professional New York City woman. Like Antin's, hers, too, is the Cinderella tale about fairy god-mothers—wealthy benefactresses who help a poor immigrant from Poland become a model Canadian teenager. She is told how to move, what to wear, how to speak to the opposite sex. There are also charming princes who are drawn to her foreign exoticism and need for acceptance. Having fallen in love with language, she marries an extraordinarily talented conversationalist and thus enters the dominant culture through a traditional union with a native-born. All throughout her adolescence and youth she is thus mediated into America by others: as the nonnative speaker of English she marries *into* the new language, and as the foreign sexual body she is legitimized as the wife of an American male.

However, apart from reiterating the familiar plot of the female rites of passage—flight from oppression, linguistic struggle, education, marriage to a native-born man, career—Hoffman's text revises the tale of woman's ac-culturation and self-consciously, even openly, challenges earlier models of gendered crosscultural journeys. Instead of ending her narrative with marital bliss, she admits to the failure of her union with a native-born and informs the reader about her divorce and therapy. Although successful as a student at Rice and Harvard and then as a teacher and writer, she presents the way to these accomplishments as a process of painful self-inquiry and ever-growing confusion, one in which she is expected to conform to the superior norms of the host country and give up fighting in defense of her foreign identity. As an adult in the land of optimistic promise, she presents her Americanized side with the irony of a seasoned traveler of the margins: "We live in a post-tragic condition. If you marry the wrong man, you can get divorced; if you start out on a wrong career, you can retrack and start another one; in this country you can pick yourself up from bankruptcy, and a stint in jail. . . . There is no ultimate failure here. . . . I hold on to this view as gingerly, as delicately, as if it were a rope that might snap if I tug at it too hard. . . . Think positive, an assertiveness-training voice in my head exhorts me" (*LT* 249).

In her sincere account of the ambivalence in the Americanization of the female, Hoffman converses with many external and internal voices—her own and those belonging to other writers—and she points out the fragmentation and crises inherent in this experience for both men and women. She composes the bits and pieces of male and female stories already told, recalls the immigrant women who came before her, and voices both admiration and criticism for prominent male writers from East Europe who have dominated literary exchange west of the Iron Curtain.[6] In its preoccupation with the past, the present, and the future, all mingling and shifting, "dancing in the quantum space," *Lost in Translation* is a dialogic text that claims the heritage of all East European newcomers who dreamt of and "found" their "America" before Hoffman. It is a moving document registering the ways a female "observing consciousness" is now able to engage openly in the fragmented discourses of the other—language, the body, sexuality, and ideological oppression, all of which forms the immigrant experience.

### "I Might Have Written a Success Story"

It is easy to recognize familiar elements of the female immigrant narrative in *Lost in Translation* while reading about Hoffman's childhood in Poland, her removal to North America, and her later maturation and growth between Canada and the United States. The novel consists of three parts, "Paradise," "Exile," and "The New World," and is told by a first-person narrator who recalls her life from the mature perspective of a well-established New Yorker. Like Mary Antin's *The Promised Land*, *Lost in Translation* opens with a vivid description of the Old World, which is left behind for the promises of the New. However, unlike the grim visions presented by Antin and Yezierska, Hoffman's Old World is described in the chapter entitled "Paradise."[7] The reader learns about growing up Jewish in postwar Poland (which could be a happy place despite economic hardships, communist oppression, and anti-Semitism), the beauty of Cracow, where the narrator, Eva, lived with her family, the little girl's love for her country and her playmates, and her favorite Gentile neighbors, from whom she picked up such Catholic behaviors as crossing herself when passing churches. All these beloved people and places are inevitably lost when Eva's parents decide to immigrate to Canada in search of better economic opportunities after the Polish government opens the borders to postwar Jewish emigration in 1956. The narrator's love for the country of her childhood is the reason that Hoffman's book opens not with a view of the Statue of Liberty but with the acute memory of her pain of loss when the ship to Montreal sailed away from the port of Gdynia.

On board the *Batory*, the narrator feels the first pangs of nostalgia, or *tęsknota*—"a visitation from a whole new geography of emotions"—which teaches her an early lesson in "how much an absence can hurt." The absence that hurt the narrator at thirteen has multiple meanings. It is the absence of the places and people she loves, the loss of language, tradition, and national identity. But it is also her own absence in Poland, among people she left behind, within the "happy, safe enclosures of Eden." Instead of joy and anticipation at the miracles of America, the narrator feels that her "life is ending" (3–5). Looking back at her adolescent nostalgia from the vantage point of a mature American woman, the narrator ponders the degree to which her story is intertwined with those of others while it retains its uniqueness: "There are models for immigrant fates, as for all others, though I doubt that any of them feels entirely natural to those who live them" (95).

In constructing the story of the passage through the perspective of an adult narrator reaching back to comfort her unhappy adolescent incarnation, Hoffman clearly distances herself from these "models of immigrant fates" that separate Old World and New World identities. She frames the first part of the book with images of herself at thirteen, on board ship, staring into the water and experiencing the pain of nostalgia. And yet she makes it clear that the transatlantic passage connects the young girl with the mature woman who writes her story some thirty years later in the United States. By emphasizing this connection, Hoffman debunks the myth of "cultural death" and of "shedding" the Old World identity upon arrival in the New. The person whose story Eva "has to tell" is the same as herself; in contrast to Antin's narrative, the character and narrator coexist openly and complement each other. They thus produce a text that records their simultaneous realization of the vitality of this connection. The last part of the book recovers the unbreakable bond between the narrator's Polish and American cultural identities that collaborate to produce her "new language" of immigrant experience, although it is impossible to convey this new language "in translation." Hoffman's rites of passage are ongoing, not a one-time crosscultural journey. The movement of the narrative from memories of Poland and the crossing, through education and acculturation in the "New World," to its peculiar, indefinite conclusion emphasizes both the cyclical and continuous nature of *Lost in Translation*.

After the story of the crossing, which is intertwined with flashbacks into the past, the reader follows the heroine-narrator from her idealized Polish childhood into the ordeals of acculturation and linguistic struggle in Canada and later in the United States. Crossing Canada on the train from Montreal to Vancouver, she feels that the journey into the new continent and country marks an end to her childhood: "The train cuts . . . like scissors cutting a three-thousand-mile rip through my life" (100). However, the "rip" is an inherent part of the fabric of her life; it divides it "into two parts" that compose a whole instead of splitting it apart. Eva suffers from nostalgia throughout her youth, but she also attains an education, wins scholarships, continues to play the piano successfully, and finally becomes a writer. Superficially, her rites of passage seem to reflect those in the works of Mary Antin, Elizabeth Stern, or Anzia Yezierska; the story of her education and decision to pursue writing over music recalls Maria Kuncewicz's choice to become an author. Nevertheless, despite its many surface similarities with earlier texts, the story that unfolds in Hoffman's text differs from those by earlier immigrant women. What strikes the reader is not the familiarity of the narrative pattern, which we scarcely notice any more, but the repeated emphasis on the lost Eden of the Old World, on the narrator's struggle with her immigrant otherness and with that of her new North American milieu. There is not much of the proverbial newcomer enthusiasm for the new country and its ideology; instead there is the pain of loss and the suffering of the girl who resists starting a "life in a new language." Hoffman does not have to pretend optimism or to worry about the demands of the public in the same way that Antin or Yezierska had to in their time.[8]

When Eva and her sister enter school and are given new English names, their scorn for this "careless baptism" is clear:

> Nothing much has happened, except a small, seismic mental shift. The twist in our names takes them a tiny distance from us—but it's a gap into which the infinite hobgoblin of abstraction enters. Our Polish names didn't *refer* to us; they *were* as surely us as our eyes or hands. These new appellations, which we ourselves can't yet pronounce, are not us. They are identification tags, disembodied signs pointing to objects that happen to be my sister and myself. We walk to our seats, into a roomful of unknown faces, with *names that make us strangers to ourselves.*
>
> When the school day is over, the teacher hands us a file card on which she has written, "I'm a newcomer. I'm lost. I live at 1785 Granville Street. Will you kindly show me how to get there? Thank you." (105)

The loss of their Polish names is equated here with the loss of a stable national identity, even with the loss of the familiar body identified with the name. It is not a long-awaited ritual marking the rites of passage into an American paradise anymore, but an act of cultural deprivation and denudement. Eva rebels against being subordinated to the dominant culture, which not only requires her to change her name so that the natives can pronounce it, but which also forces its standards of acceptable behavior on her. Unlike earlier narratives, which were expected to openly worship native-born ways, Hoffman's expresses the narrator's "immigrant rage" at the "false persona I'm being stuffed into, as into some clumsy and overblown astronaut suit" (119).

Although she was old enough to understand the oppressive reality of the communist rule in Poland at the time of her departure, the narrator openly admits that her Americanization is a lonely and painful ordeal rather than a glorious passage into unquestionable democratic freedom and economic opportunity. In fact, she is ironic about the successful immigrant women who perpetuate the traditional narrative of progressivist material achievement: "They have attained within a few years what it took their Jewish predecessors on the Lower East Side at least two generations to achieve. . . . Theirs is an immigrant success story, and that's the story of their own lives that they accept. . . . Sitting upright in their cars, in their immaculately pressed dresses, keeping their houses more spotlessly neat than the natives, they say to each other, 'I'm fine, everything is fine,' and they almost believe that they are" (143). Instead of emulating these women who are the envy of the neighborhood, Eva decides to carve a space for herself as an outsider—an "observer" of the "reality that I feel so very out of" (131).

The second part of her story, which describes the clash of two worlds, a part conventionally entitled "The Promised Land" in other texts, is called "Exile" in Hoffman. Nevertheless, Hoffman's narrator does not simply lament the loss of the country of her idealized childhood and reject the new alien culture around her in this section. She emphasizes instead her growing away from herself, her becoming Kristeva's other in both cultures.[9]

Eva's removal to Canada marks a separation from the "stranger"—the individualistic other—she used to be in the familiar environment of Poland. It calls for a creation of a new "strange self" to fit her new environment and her role as an outsider-observer straddling two cultures. "Exile" is a detailed study of the feminine nostalgia—*tęsknota*—that connects the stories of a young girl and mature woman through the metaphorics of language and the body. While being forced into her new North American persona, the role of a teenager with crinoline, coiffed hair, high heels and all, the narrator continues to miss her natural and unself-conscious growing up in Poland acutely, despite the lack of freedom and the oppression that her country's political system inflicted on its citizens:

Nostalgia is a source of poetry, and a form of fidelity. It is also a species of melancholia, which used to be thought of as illness. As I walk the streets of

Vancouver, I am pregnant with the images of Poland, pregnant and sick. *Tęsknota* throws a film over everything around me, and directs my vision inward. The largest presence within me is the welling up of absence, of what I have lost. This pregnancy is also a phantom pain. I don't know what to do with this private heaviness, this pregnancy without the possibility of birth. (115)

Eva misses the familiarity of the "stranger" she was while living in her home-land. While walking the streets of Vancouver, she is pregnant with the loss of her Polish self and body and dressed up in the new strangeness of somebody who is a foreigner twice: Ewa, an immigrant who cannot ever go back, and Eva, a renamed newcomer, "a disembodied sign," who cannot and does not want to enter the new culture either.

The narrator's *tęsknota* in the above passage is comparable to that described in Nabokov's *Speak Memory*. Hoffman points out how much Nabokov's ideal-ized Russia is a product of "retrospective maneuvers to compensate for fate." Nostalgia has the power to "crystallize around . . . images like amber." "Loss is a magical preservative," for it makes the past clear and beautiful in its petrified permanence (115). But unlike Nabokov, Hoffman does not want her past "crys-tallized" within the "amber" of memory.[10] She does not want to cut herself off from it or exorcise it either. Instead, she has her narrator create a perpetual present, a fiction in which time does not move and the past is continuously being relived within the present. Teenage Eva even lies in her letters to her Polish friend in order to create an impossibly seamless chronology, welding a past, present, and future, in which she controls her manifold otherness. In this maneuver she both repudiates and perpetuates the traditional newcomer suc-cess story: "I am repeating a ritual performed by countless immigrants who have sent letters back home meant to impress and convince their friends and relatives—and probably even themselves—that their lives have changed for the better" (116). Unable to free herself from the burden of the past and not ready yet to face the pressures of the present, Eva consciously creates fictions about herself. Consequently, utilizing the poetics of exile and otherness, she constructs a unique narrative framework to accommodate her complex sub-ject matter. Instead of attempting cohesion and recording a heart-warming progression of achievements, her story traces a painful process of adaptation to displacement, of learning that "being 'an immigrant' . . . is considered a sort of location in itself" (132–33). The new location she inhabits teaches her, however, that the advantages of observation have to be paid for through acceptance of her marginalization.

Kristeva writes that the foreigner should be happy to be free from ties to his or her own people. Yet the "consummate name of such a freedom is solitude" (*SO* 12). For the immigrant woman in Hoffman's time, this solitude, being stuck with one's *tęsknota*, is perceived as "pregnancy without the possibility of birth." In Hoffman's text the body is openly, painfully connected to the experience of a foreign woman in her new milieu; it is pregnant with the past that it cannot abort or bring into the new homeland.[11] The narrator responds to the good advice of her new friends: "But everyone encourages me to forget what I left behind. It wasn't any good back there, our Jewish acquaintances say, why would you even want to visit, they didn't want you there anyway. I hang my head stubbornly under the lash of this wisdom. Can I really *extract what I've been from myself* so easily? Can I jump continents as if skipping rope?" (*LT* 115, emphasis mine). In the passage about Nabokov's *Speak Memory*, Hoffman beautifully shows that she can appropriate Nabokov's "sensual impressions" and engage them in a dialogue with her own much more bodily female longing. Juxtaposing Nabokov's masculine interpretation of the past as magically "arrested" within memory and her own perception of nostalgia as a "phantom pain" impregnating the body, she is playing with the experience of otherness in males and females. She rewrites these experiences as her own dialogic encounter with the strangers within and without herself. Thus she is able to "give birth" at least to the expression of her inability to merge with her new environment, to the discovery that in a "splintered society" one can perhaps only "assimilate to" the "very splintering itself" (197). By opening up her text to discourses with other authors, she elicits not only the splintering of the immigrant experience, but also the instability of the genre used for describing this condition.

Another dialogic encounter with a writer who came before her takes place at the end of "Exile." It happens on the threshold between the section describing the hardships of Americanization and the one entitled "The New World," which presents Eva's adult life and successful career. From her mature perspective Hoffman looks back at Mary Antin's *The Promised Land*, that "gospel of immigration." Although she openly denies writing a "success story," Hoffman sees herself as a heir of Mary Antin's legacy, because the latter's life "so closely resembles my own, that its author seems to be some amusing poltergeist, come to show me that whatever belief in my singularity I may possess is nothing more than a comical vanity" (162). *Lost in Translation* and *The Promised Land* can indeed be read as the same story passed from generation to generation of immigrant Jewish women.[12] In this sense, both Hoffman and Antin write success stories—whether they want to or not, for both these writers and their texts are inscribed in a narrative pattern determined by the history of reading and interpreting.

However, Hoffman struggles and comes to terms with the stranger inside and outside of herself, with the woman writer represented by Antin, the other's life and writings, and the other historical period, even though this struggle ends only superficially, with resigned acknowledgment that "she, like I, was affected by the sentiments of her time." Antin had to write a success story because "the America of her time gave her certain categories within which to see herself—a belief in self-improvement, in perfectibility of the species, in moral uplift." Conversely, Hoffman has to write the story that "her time is telling her to tell," a fragmented, sometimes puzzling, and ambivalent tale determined by the confused outlook of the end of the twentieth century. This realization that her time requires a different narrative model arises from Hoffman's growing familiarity with the "multiple perspectives and their constant shifting" in the America she has come to know: "Who, among my peers, is sure of what is success and what failure? Who would want to be sure? Who is sure of purposes, meanings, national goals?" (163–64).

Her inability to answer these questions is the reason why Hoffman ends the section "Exile" with a statement about the perils of immigrant authorship: "I cannot conceive of my story as one of simple progress, or simple woe. Any confidently thrusting story line would be a sentimentality, an excess, an exaggeration, an untruth." She admits to consciously making her tale into a mosaic of fragments in order to avoid similarities with the earlier versions, and yet she brings in Antin's seemingly clear tale to disrupt these efforts at the turning point in her narrative. "Perhaps it is in my misfittings that I fit," she writes, summarizing this strategy very well. Like the other strangers and the culture around her, Hoffman makes sense because she does not want to, because she feels overwhelmed by the realm of otherness, wants to resist it, and yet cannot avoid confronting it: "We slip between definitions with such acrobatic ease that straight narrative becomes impossible" (164).

Hoffman's "observing consciousness" works out the ambivalent immigrant woman's narrative in *Lost in Translation*. Her narrator knows she cannot escape being a product of her time—a character in the narratives being written independently of her—a phantom existing outside of herself in the way described so aptly by Maria Kuncewicz. Nevertheless, she learns to translate at least the outline of her predicament and to share it with others by engaging her individual strangeness with those around her. Through writing she succeeds in constructing a dialogue that simultaneously continues and debunks the contributions of the writers who came before her. The past stories, the glowing achievements, and the latent messages about oppression make sense together as a choral discourse that a writer can now both record and challenge openly. Hoffman makes the best of her postmodern predicament, in which one is "faint from excess, paralyzed by [the] choice" of available options in the culture, a predicament in which every newcomer is "a quantum particle trying to locate [herself] within a swirl of atoms" (160). Hoffman's search for identity in *Lost in Translation* records a journey inward, through language and across borders between the past and present, and it proves that although "exile is the archetypal condition of contemporary lives," crosscultural texts provide a home for many marginalized others (197).

### "Between Two Languages Your Realm Is Silence"

Julia Kristeva claims that the foreigner's position between two languages— neither of which he or she fully inhabits—usually means being reduced to and imprisoned within silence. However, she does not suggest that those who have experienced the traps and freedoms of bicultural shuttling should remain voiceless (*SO* 15). As her own writings show, one ought to engage in speaking about the "strange within us," explore other cultures, and subject foreign literatures and peoples to the inquiring pen of the foreign outsider-observer. Hoffman's journey of self-discovery between Poland and America explores Kristeva's realm of linguistic limbo in which all immigrants find themselves, having lost touch with the everyday ease of the mother tongue and being unable to enter the hermetic idiom of the native. As Hoffman's narrator recalls in "Exile": "I know that language will be a crucial instrument, that I can overcome the stigma of marginality, the weight of presumption against me, only if the reassuringly right sounds come out of my mouth" (*LT* 123). She seems to state the obvious, and yet she also voices the impossibility of a perfect linguistic crossing for those who come to a new country too late to lose their foreign accents and word sensibilities. In *Lost in Translation*, language is not so much a traditional tool for self-expression and communication, but a foremost marker of ethnic identity and class that gives strangers away and exposes them to humiliation and scrutiny as nonnative speakers and foreign bodies.

Teenage Eva has brought from Poland the knowledge that "better" people speak "better" language, and she is deeply ashamed of being unable to eradicate her conspicuous Polish accent: "Some of my high school peers accuse me of putting it on in order to appear more 'interesting.' In fact, I'd do anything to get rid of it, and when I'm alone, I practice sounds for which my speech organs have no intuitions, such as 'th'" (122). Accused of excessive individualism, which, according to a narcissistic reading of American culture, should actually make her more interestingly American, the narrator craves conformity and desires to melt with the crowd. For the teenage girl her accent is an unforgivable difference, her English never "good" enough to qualify her as one of the "better" people. In her efforts, however, she becomes "a living avatar of structuralist wisdom," as the new language and the new persona it requires her to acquire confuse her judgment. When she learns new words and expressions, she is often attracted by their sound and repelled by the artifice of meaningless convention in some utterances, such as "You're welcome." She feels trapped by "cultural distances" when her mother accuses her of becoming "English," of taking on the mannerisms of restraint that come with speaking the new language and that separate Eva from the "storminess of emotion" prevailing in her family. She is thus trapped between trying to sound good to her peers and alienating herself linguistically from her parents.

Eva's linguistic rites of passage parallel her cultural ones and, not surprisingly, provide another lesson in estrangement and alienation. In English the "signifier has become severed from the signified" and thus "does not evoke," whereas in Polish after a while the words have "atrophied, shriveled from sheer uselessness" (106–7). Such linguistic estrangement pervades her inner world and exiles her from it, too. She realizes, "I have no interior language, and without it, interior images—those images through which we assimilate the external world, through which we take it in, love it, make it our own— become blurred, too. . . . The words float in an uncertain space. . . . I'm not filled with language anymore, and I have only a memory of fullness to anguish me with the knowledge that, in this dark and empty state, I don't really exist" (108). Such extinguishing, or suppression, of her inner world makes the narrator realize the temporal nature and fragility of her native language, which she has always taken for granted, and the stubborn impenetrability of the new one, which requires not only a fitting external identity but also a brand new internal identity.

In the attempt to adjust her external and internal languages to the new environment and the new rules of communication in English, Hoffman's narrator fears becoming invisible not only to herself but to others. "Because I'm not heard, I feel I'm not seen," she admits, as she discovers that the artifice of the new idiom makes any direct contact between her and her native interlocutors impossible (147). Moreover, in addition to making her opaque to them, the linguistic inadequacy bars her from penetrating, from reading beneath the "surfaces" of those interlocutors, from getting to know them just as much as she would like to be known by them. A way out of this situation is suggested by her fellow students, who define identity in their culture as a self-invention. Since "you are who you think you are," Eva faces a plethora of possibilities and, again, is paralyzed by choices offered by her imagination and by the commercialized environment around her. Her truly consumerist "shopping" for a fitting linguistic and cultural identity—she compares it to selecting a brand of toothpaste—goes hand in hand with the narrator's bodily metamorphosis into a self-conscious teenager. She realizes that the price exacted by new language acquisition is a new "look," as preconceived and rigid as the rules of grammar. Through connecting language and the body in the process of creating Eva's bicultural identity, Hoffman points to the necessity, if not tyranny, of the right body image, which a nonnative speaker is expected to adopt in order to be accepted and understood. For Eva, learning English means acquiring a new "resident alien" body—the experience Mary Antin knew about, although could not admit to openly in *The Promised Land*.

As a "green" arrival eager to fit in, the narrator readily agrees to the before-and-after beauty experiments that her Canadian benefactresses want to perform on her in order to transform the immigrant Cinderella into a domestic princess. She lets herself be coiffed, shaven, and put into a brassiere; she acquires a whole new vocabulary of cosmetic rituals, beauty regimens, and outfits and accessories. "Alienation is beginning to be inscribed in my flesh and face," the narrator remarks, recalling one of Eva's "after" photographs. The new body image fits the girl in the picture as uncomfortably as the new language and causes her an almost physical pain: "My shoulders stoop, I nod frantically to indicate my agreement with others, I smile sweetly at people to show I mean well, and my chest recedes inward so that I don't take too much space—mannerisms of a marginal, off-centered person who wants both to be taken in and to fend off the threatening others" (110).[13] Paradoxically, her superficially disappearing foreignness makes the narrator less secure and self-confident instead of happy with her New Worldliness; its disappearance strips her bare of the protective cocoon of her familiar physicality. While becoming more and more like her peers as a well-groomed and properly attired body, she feels more and more threatened and rejected as an individual, as that inner Kristevan stranger whom no one can see and appreciate but who projects "the light-footed dancer [she] really is" (119). She confesses that she hates to pretend and yet lets herself be made over into a "pretend teenager." She realizes that, until she can consciously and independently choose "from the Babel of American language, the style of wit that fits," she will continue to be taken for the "elephantine creature" who may look the part when she doesn't say anything but who "sounds as if she's making pronouncements" every time she opens her mouth (118–19).

However, even the creation of her own "body of language" later on does not bring about the narrator's liberation from being misread by the dominant culture. Even after she arrives at what she calls the "sum of my languages" in the third part of the novel, "The New World," she still feels alienated. Perhaps Spivak clarifies this phenomenon when she argues that the crucial question a minority should ask before speaking is: "Who will listen?" In listeners' decisions about whom they will hear, the speaker "speaking as" counts most in whether one is read by others. In particular, if a marginal individual confronts a dominant culture, it does not matter so much who this individual truly is but rather whom the audience choose to read as him or her. Spivak explains that "for the person who does the 'speaking as' something, it is a problem of distancing from one's self, whatever that self might be." Being heard automatically implies alienation from one's innermost identity, both in one's decision to represent a group or an idea and in being perceived by the audience as a member of that group or a supporter of that idea.[14] Fear of such "homogenization" of perceptions and identities pervades the world in *Lost in Translation* and makes its radar-sensitive narrator scan her innate and perceived identities with vigilance. When she rebels against the artifice of her teenage persona, she rebels against being read as a replica of her Canadian peers instead of as her unique self. While acquiring the new language she feels alienated as much by the necessity to imitate others in order to express herself as by her peers' insistence on hearing a pretentious posturing of an "interesting" foreigner in her mistakes and mispronunciations. In defense against this alienating "homogenization" taking place outside her, Eva develops a multitude of interlocutors within. She creates voices that collaborate to express her two competing, incongruous, and yet inseparable cultural identities.

While struggling with her English and her *tęsknota*, the teenaged Eva holds conversations with herself, as if to avoid speaking as Eva only. She splits into two voices: the first one, anonymous and talking about "Ewa"—the spectral Polish incarnation—and the second, Eva—her yet undefined North American version: "You prefer her, the Cracow Eva. Yes, I prefer her. But I can't be her. I'm losing track of her. In a few years, I'll have no idea what her hairdo would have been like. But she's more real, anyway" (120). Interestingly, the comparison between these two versions of the narrator involves mostly their physical appearance. As long as the interrogating voice can imagine Polish

Ewa's hairdo, the two girls can be compared; they can coexist as bodies. However, as the narrator learns from writing in her diary—an activity that requires a choice between languages—using her native Polish would be like trying to translate the present through the "untranslatable past." Similarly, making the past—and now "spectral"—Polish identity inhabit the increasingly English body in the present is an act of self-misrepresentation. To resolve this paradoxical conflict between her desire to retain both her mother tongue and her Polish body, and the pressure of her "time and place" to discard them, Eva chooses the "language of the present, even if it's not the language of the self" for the diary. The decision represents "an earnest attempt to create a part of my persona that I imagine I would have grown into in Polish" (121).

This early exercise in autobiographical fiction-making has positive results, though, for it enables Eva to achieve an identity in writing—"the truest thing about me." While engaged in the "solitude of this most private act," she realizes that her writing is "beginning to invent another me." Almost as if she were illustrating Spivak's theory, Hoffman has Eva withdraw into her written self and pursue "speaking as Ewa" there, in the "public language" of her new culture. In her diary, then, she plays both the speaker—who speaks as herself, "Ewa"—and the audience—the Eva who hears herself speaking as the other. Henceforth she attests to the fact that even the innermost self is a battleground of the strained interactions between the self and other—what in Hoffman translates into the contention between "Ewa" and Eva. One is never free from speaking as somebody else, and this is especially true of speaking to oneself because, as Kristeva stresses, the "strange within us" is always there and, like the unconscious, will resurface and have to be dealt with. Yet for Hoffman's narrator writing also fosters and brings back her Old World love for language, despite the argumentative nature of the inner voices that it creates in the Hoffman's narrator. Its intense privacy makes her feel a powerful user of the new idiom—"I claim every territorial prerogative"—and simultaneously vulnerable in her desire to claim this power in the public sphere of interactions with her peers (217–19). As Eva continues to mature into a woman, she realizes that the precarious connection between language and the body is taking on a new dimension—she confronts her intimate inner voices with the seductive voices of the natives.

When she falls in love, she "falls in love with otherness" and is "seduced by language." She even marries "a master of the riff," hoping that his "bebop speech can carry me right into the heart of America." But she realizes that it is "a tricky contract," one that makes her confuse her husband and his eloquence (186, 219). This confusion significantly links the male and the idiom as competitors and seducers; it suggests that they can both be seen in almost sexual terms. It also echoes the earlier immigrant fairy tale featuring a prince who carries the passive heroine off into the happily-ever-after of successful assimilation. However, the failure of her marriage proves to Eva that the fairy-tale language acquisition model does not work and that she has to create a discourse of her own to meet and comprehend the prince's. While thus venturing into the world of sex and the world of external voices, she realizes that she has to add a "bottom" to the language she has learned "from the top down"; that is, she has to build a bridge between her eloquent literary inner otherness and her tongue-tied colloquial outer one. This realization means, too, that her body's "competence" is so much ahead of her linguistic "performance" that this inequality marks still another identity splintering. While using the public language intimately, she has grown a public body that remained Polish under its Canadian American surface and is thus untranslatable for the new culture; it cannot engage in discourses with interlocutors and lovers as an equal. In order to be able to communicate, she has to invent a linguistic identity that will serve as a go-between.

Instead of demanding that the culture around her finally begin to understand her, as Yezierska did to some extent, Hoffman shows the more "realistic" Eva determined to penetrate the opaqueness of her "American Friend." She portrays her as sort of a "Witness" embodying her adopted home: "I think if I could enter the subjectivity of that face, then I could encompass both myself and my American Friend within it. . . . I want a language that will express what that face knows, a calm and simple language that will subsume the clangor of specialized jargons and of partial visions, a language old enough to plow under the superficial differences between signs, to the deeper strata of significance" (212). While diving into the "strata of significance" deeper and deeper, she discovers that mastering the "riff" is not enough; she cannot simply imitate the seductive natives but must create a linguistic identity of her own, capable of "triangulating" from her inner voices toward her American Friend and carrying messages back. Triangulation is a larger metaphor and a key image in *Lost in Translation*, one that illustrates the progress and nature of the narrator's journeys on the textual, authorial, linguistic, and identity levels. While attempting to construct her own voice, Eva finds herself "invaded" by the attractive voices of others: "They ricochet within me, carrying on conversations, lending me their modulations, intonations, rhythms." Triangulating among them, hoping to make them her own, she feels like "a silent ventriloquist." This patient and seemingly peaceful tug of war between the desire to imitate and the necessity to create her own expression results in the narrator's remaking in a new language. The speaker who emerges from this remaking feels like coming back to the very souce of language:

> I could not have found this true axis, could not have made my way through the maze, if I had not assimilated and mastered the *voices of my time and place*—the only language through which we can learn to think and speak. The silence that comes out of inarticulateness is the inchoate and desperate silence of chaos. The silence that comes after words is the fullness from which the truth of our perceptions can crystallize. It's only after I've taken in disparate bits of cultural matter, after I've accepted its seductions and its snares, that I can make my way through the medium of language to distill my own meanings; and it's only coming from the ground up that I can hit the tenor of my own sensibility, hit home. (276, emphasis mine) [15]

Out of Eva's linguistic triangulation emerges an ability to make the voices of others her own, to compose her choral linguistic identity out of them, to create an idiom capable of describing both her old and her new life. In doing this, she discovers the source of all languages, her "home," in herself.

Hoffman illustrates this process of linguistic self-creation through a metaphor involving manual labor, thus implying the body. The metaphor emphasizes the feminine nature of the new language and the relationship between its production and woman's craft: "I am being remade, fragment by fragment, like a patchwork quilt; there are no more colors in the world than I ever knew" (220). Hoffman uses the image of the quilt not only to elicit the narrator's linguistic identity as a carefully constructed design, but also to show how the final product will connect her two linguistic spheres without erasing differences between them. On the one hand, the audience—the interlocutors—will be able to read the quilt and admire its singularity and "strangeness." On the other, the narrator-author will preserve the secret of its making, its otherness, while partaking in the joy of sharing it. Through the metaphor of the quilt, the narrator proves that an artifact designed and executed very carefully can attain a life of its own, even the magic of true art. The voices that become Eva's and communicate with others emerge from her as a part of her body; they are no longer ripped away from her physical presence. This new body language—marking a sort of "life in a new language"—delights instead of causing pain and brings pleasure to the speaker while never erasing the memory of her suffering. When she falls in love again, the artifice is gone and the language and the body "translate" in unison: "We speak, my lover and I, until words tumble out without obstacle, until they deliquesce into pure flow, until they become the air we breathe, until they merge with our flesh" (246). Just as the narrator initially felt that "linguistic dispossession is a sufficient motive for violence," she now realizes that she can move between her languages "without being split by the difference" (124, 274).

In this way, her inner voices—"Ewa" and Eva—can subside, embrace each other, and be translated into a dialogue with the external world. Once again, Hoffman presents this realization as "coming home," through feminine images of procreation and fertility. In these fragments of the novel, in which the authorial voice talks over the narrator's, as if to prove the dialogic character of the text even further, Hoffman comments on her own translingual author-ship: "Experience creates style, and style, in turn creates a new woman. . . . When I speak Polish now it is infiltrated, permeated, and inflected by the English in my head. Each language modifies the other, crossbreeds with it, fertilizes it." Just as she did with her lover, the speaker has learned to merge with the flesh and the spirit of her speech. She realizes that she has been "on both sides" of her story and that it is time to write it down. Her authorship is compared to "crawling back" into her Polish childhood, to engendering herself through her text (272–73). One cannot help recalling here Yezierska's insistence that the characters in her books were her only children. From her different cultural predicament, Hoffman admits to not only "giving birth" to her text but also to herself: "It's only when I retell my whole story, back to the beginning, and from the beginning onward, in one language, that I can reconcile the voices within me with each other; it is only then that the per-son who judges the voices and tells the stories begins to emerge" (272). Like Yezierska, the narrator-author is proud of her textual motherhood; unlike her, she emphasizes much more clearly that female authorship entails not only engendering books but also oneself. Interestingly, Hoffman complicates the logical sequence of author-book, by pointing out that the "emerging" of the person happens only after the story has been told—the text begets the author.

The new East European immigrant woman author created in *Lost in Trans-lation* absorbs and joins the choral discourse of the diverse writers who came before her and of those who will write their stories after having read Hoff-man's in the future. Hoffman is living proof that the "observing conscious-ness" of the foreigner is often the best tool to communicate cultural predica-ments and literary histories. The in-between gap she will always occupy as an immigrant actually makes possible her "translation therapy," her writing in order to make sense of things in her America here and now and her Poland "then and now." [16] "Like everybody, I am the sum of my languages," she ad-mits, meaning the different idioms we acquire in different stages of our lives as well as her bilingual nature (273). Although recalling that her English voice is often a "highly unreliable instrument" (217), Hoffman writes her way toward a very intimate, unique part of herself. The linguistic journey that originated in the self, reaching out to others, draws a trajectory back inward into the self again. At the end of her novel-memoir-notebook, the narrator reaches her innermost otherness, a place in herself that she calls "ground zero" and that can be reached by means of "triangulation," or by reaching both out and into oneself. This place is her intrinsic voice, born of silence, an "even voice . . . capable of saying things straight, without exaggeration or triviality" (276). And it is in this voice that Hoffman expresses her message about the foreignness we all share, about her individual otherness, which saves her from, but which is also a function of, the general cultural predicament—the Kristevan "strange within us."

Hoffman's bilingual and bicultural journey should be theoretically different from those that natives of one language and one land might experience. Yet her search for the meanings "lost in translation," her success and failure in recovering these meanings, can be read as shorthand for anybody's desire for his or her intangible "true" voice and identity. As she muses on her predicament, Hoffman may very well be the "exaggerated version of the native." Her "America"—found in and founded on language and the body—is an invaluable gift both to those who think they made and own the country and its ideas and to those who still come to it as exiles seeking refuge.

## On the Borders

In the shadow world of refugees, all exiles and immigrants of the world are united in their search for a new home, as Bharati Mukherjee's *Jasmine* so poignantly describes:

> There are national airlines flying the world that don't appear in any directory. There are charters who've lost their way and now just fly, improvising crews and destinations. . . . There is a shadow world of aircraft permanently aloft that share air lines and radio frequencies with Pan Am and British Air and Air India, portaging people who coexist with tourists and businessmen. But we are refugees and mercenaries and guest workers. . . . We are the outcasts and deportees, strange pilgrims visiting outlandish shrines, landing at the end of tarmacs. . . . We are dressed in shreds of national costumes, out of season, the wilted plumage of intercontinental vagabondage. . . . What country? What continent? We pass through wars, through plagues.[17]

National identities, borders between countries, and racial and ethnic differences disappear in the face of shared experiences of dislocation. Like Mukherjee, Hoffman sees the modern world as pulled apart by migrations and uprooting of whole cultures and single individuals. On the border between the second part of *Lost in Translation*, "Exile," and the third, "The New World," Hoffman reflects on the challenges of multiplicity that American culture and a world filled with refugees pose for any newcomer, for every individual. She sees the modern immigrant as a replica of the native, a reflection that blows out of proportion the inherent Kristevan strangeness of both the dominant culture and its minorities.

Just as Hoffman's narrator sees herself as a version of the native-born, the America of her time is an "exaggerated version" of the world in which exile and uprootedness have become everydayness: "Dislocation is the norm rather than the aberration in our time . . . the fabulous diverseness with which we live reminds us constantly that we are no longer the norm or the center, that there is no one geographic center pulling the world together and glowing with the allure of the real thing; there are, instead, scattered nodules competing for our attention. New York, Warsaw, Tehran, Tokyo, Kabul—they all make claims on our imagination, all remind us that in a decentered world we are always simultaneously in the center and on the periphery, that every competing center makes us marginal" (274–75). All people are immigrants, and all countries places of exile in the world where the "center does not hold." Especially in the United States—founded on the "dream"—reality, as Kristeva argues, "seems to remain distant from the generous wishes that the laws of the Union nevertheless aspire to fulfill" because "America as a land of immigrants . . . [nevertheless] asserts itself as being more and more turned in on itself and practices protectionism when confronting the demographic, political, and economic currents (Cuba, Vietnam, Latin America) that the international situation produces."[18] From her outsider-participant vantage point between Poland and North America, Hoffman responds to and records this American situation as well as the splintered and fragmented global culture by shuffling between narrative structures, by erasing boundaries between language and the body, and by boldly crossing the borders between past and present.

In its mapping of a journey through language and self-discovery, *Lost in Translation* is a text both describing and positioned on the borders itself. Its three-part structure—"Paradise," "Exile," "The New World"—seems to be constructed according to the traditional sequence of the passage from Old World to New World. However, Hoffman's autobiography revolves around the axis of the middle part, "Exile," which emphasizes dislocation between two cultures and stretches from the East to the West in a way suggesting a never-ending process of passage and arrival rather than an act of permanently settling down. Hoffman's "triangulating" narrative technique suggests the cartographic mapping of a territory—the creation of a topography of her literary lands—and projects an illusion of almost scientific control over them. Yet neither the novel's structure nor its narrative movement is subordinated to the key geometrical metaphors of triangulation, axis, center, and margin. Instead, having created a framework of relative order to guide the reader, Hoffman uses it to explore her narrator's complex and unstable position on the borders between the past and present traditions of East European women's writing, the Cold War and the posttotalitarian age, and between Eva's growing up in the past of her parents and her attempt to fit into the North American present. The resulting text is a patchwork quilt similar to Eva's new language, composed of "patterns" and "patches" making up a whole in which order is deceptive and can be appreciated only in its complexity.

Similarly, Eva's otherness in *Lost in Translation* is a cross-stitching of the painful past inherited from her mother and father, for whom the war is their "second birthplace," and the difficult present she has to figure out in a new language and a new place. The narrator's exploration of the influence of her parents' Jewishness, their memories of the Nazi occupation, and their shared lessons in Polish history, economics, and politics makes the border between immigrant generations the ultimate location for Hoffman's intercultural observer-participant. Written from such a vantage point, *Lost in Translation*, itself published on the border between the Cold War and posttotalitarian eras, creates a voice for the wanderer-journalist in *Exit into History*, who abandons the world of autobiographical fiction to venture into a travel documentary subtitled *A Journey through the New Eastern Europe*. Crossing physical borders into Poland, the Czech Republic, Hungary, Bulgaria, and Romania, Hoffman's second book explores the cultural realities of and fictions about that "lifeless, monochrome realm where people walked bent under the leaden weight of an awful System," that "repository of utopian ideological hopes," and that "region struggling against a demonic dystopia" (*EH* xiii). *Exit into History* composes a textual, journalistic quilt of sorts, too, as Hoffman ventures into different countries and tries very hard to present their uniqueness and differences in order to refute the myth of an East European monolith. Her book ends up creating a whole composed of fragments that join the personal impressions collected by her bicultural observing consciousness.

At the beginning of *Exit into History*, Hoffman defines her trips through the countries of East and Central Europe as excursions into the "idealized landscape of the mind," as an attempt to see and write down her Poland and the region around it before they disappear (ix–x). Setting out on her journey, she also entrusts herself with the mission of revisiting not only the region, but also the fiction that it has always been to the West. In this respect, the narrator of *Exit into History* continues the task of remembering and preserving the past that was Eva's inspiration for writing in *Lost in Translation*: "To some extent, one has to rewrite the past in order to understand it. . . . It is the price of emigration, as of any radical discontinuity that it makes such reviews and readings difficult; being cut off from one part of one's own story is apt to veil it in the haze of nostalgia, which is an ineffectual relationship to the past, and the haze of alienation, which is an ineffectual relationship to the present" (*LT* 242). Hoffman's journalistic travels through the new East Europe are a field trip taken in order to write down the Other Europe, which is already receding into the past in its rapid disappearance under consumerist and political westernization.

Saving her Poland from oblivion, before it turns into another westernized country overrun with McDonald's restaurants and Exxon gas stations, is related to preserving her parents' tragic war memories—the "awful story" of persecution and the mass destruction of Jews, tales of betrayal and heroism, accounts of death and survival, hardships and hopelessness in the Stalinist terror. In *Lost in Translation* writing is a bridge connecting what could have been "frightening fairy tales" in her childhood and what now are stories she must know and preserve in order to "do justice" to her parents (252–53). "My mother wants me to know what happened," confesses the narrator, "and I keep every detail of what she tells me in my memory like black beads." Knowing the past is a "matter of honor," just like affirming one's Jewishness, and Eva feels that she should relive the pain of the past with her mother and father; she wants to "atone" for their suffering. Her father's tale about carrying his sick wife for many kilometers through endless snow and into hiding from the Nazis makes her realize that she "comes from" their pain, that "it is useless to try to get away" from still another image of the past, "another sharp black bead added to the rest" (24–25).

The "black beads" of memory are like a rosary through which Hoffman's narrator runs her fingers; each bead prompts a prayer-reflection about the past and connects the two immigrant generations and two national histories. As a recorder of her parents' past and a writer of her own life, Hoffman finds herself between the Jewish and Christian traditions of her country, between two powerful influences with which she grew up in Poland. She is aware of her difference as a Jew but, having been raised with Catholic children and in a culture infused with this tradition, she shows how the influences of Judaism and Catholicism in her past engage in a dialogue. Therefore, she views posttotalitarian Poland in *Exit into History* from the vantage point of an emigrant whose history is defined in terms of both the enchanting but "hermetic otherness" of Judaism and the redeeming suffering but repressive self-sacrifice of Catholicism. Caught between these two perspectives, Hoffman is very well equipped to be a chronicler of the new East Europe. Because "the chronicle always comes before fiction; imagination, inventive reworking, will have to wait till later" (*EH* 17). In *Exit into History* she wants to record rather than interpret her country's past, just as in *Lost in Translation* she lovingly pictured her family's celebrations of both the High Holidays and Christmas, her love of Judaism and her inescapable growing up within a predominantly Catholic culture.

As in the autobiographical novel, the past of her region, which evolves in a new and confusing posttotalitarian present in *Exit into History*, has to be exorcised through a "complicated doubleness," too (*EH* 388). Hoffman's return to East Europe is a journey back to Poland both familiar and new, and an actual discovery of the unknown countries with which hers has been always identified and stereotyped. Without being "split by the difference," she arrives simultaneously as a Pole equipped with childhood memories of her homeland and with the knowledge of the Other Europe she has acquired as a sophisticated American. However, the material for her account comes from the conversations and interviews with people she meets in her travels and is necessarily filtered through their own sense of dislocation, the proverbial East European "internal exile," and a sense of not fitting into the new reality. To a certain extent, what they offer are memories and impressions comparable to the "black beads" she has inherited from her mother. Moreover, like her own story, theirs are often split by paradoxes and do not make sense to her "American" side. While in Romania, she befriends an eminent scholar and activist whose life has been divided into two periods: one in which he is a staunch Stalinist and, after the shock of finding himself and the party wrong, another in which he is a dissident taking part in underground activities. Pavel is "a lapsed Communist who yet still likes to think of himself as 'a man on the left,' and . . . doesn't fit comfortably anywhere in the new Romanian puzzle." In relating his dilemmas, Hoffman uses her American "slight observer's distance" to talk about Pavel's life as an "experience that might prove instructive in thinking about the future" (*EH* 327). How can he still be a leftist after having learned about the atrocities of Stalinism? Why would the new Romania reject him now instead of inviting to join the government? As Hoffman suggests, Pavel's experience and all the disturbing questions it evokes should teach us to see East Europe and its people as impossible to categorize according to our clear-cut western standards.

Yet what she sees as "a fragment of a usable past" in Pavel's story is also the "stuff of consciousness and conscience." It is a personal tragedy to which she responds with compassion and the sympathy of a native to a region that has bred so many who can say now: "'I don't know if you can imagine . . . how difficult it is to say that the thing you've been devoted to—the essence and core of your life—has been a mistake'" (326–27). Pavel's case is one of those which seem impossible to translate for Hoffman's American audience. He not only fits perfectly both categories of the oppressor and the oppressed as a former communist and a dissident but also stands in between them as a thinker and an activist who still believes in the leftist ideals that first attracted him to Stalinism. Hoffman is fascinated by Pavel's case and describes his dropping out of the party as an almost religious crisis, as the "despair of losing his faith" and as the "feeling of sin" (324).

In Romania, which her traveler's persona terms a "Bermuda Triangle of the mind, a place that concentrates all one's anxieties about unnameable dangers and the darkness of the unknown," Hoffman experiences even more shocking encounters than the one revealed in Pavel's life story, experiences that put her double perspective as insider and observer on trial (262). While visiting a Romanian orphanage, she confesses her fear at the sight of "faces distorted by mental illness and retardation." Her horror increases when she learns that many of the children brought up in such institutions were used by the secret police—the Securitate—because they would "'be loyal as a dog.'" In Hoffman, this discovery evokes a conflict between her task as a detached observer-chronicler and her emotional reaction as a private person who has embarked on this experience out of her "sense of duty." But at the end of her visit she realizes, "Instead of a sense of duty fulfilled, I feel a strange guilt for having seen what I did, the guilt of an uninvolved witness at a tragedy" (327–30). Much like Eva in *Lost in Translation*, who tried to atone for and relive her parents' suffering by writing it down, Hoffman's chronicler in *Exit into History* sees herself as recording the pain of the people she meets rather than purely analyzing events in a journalistic fashion.

This intense combination of emotional and detached perspectives pervades Hoffman's visit to Poland and, especially, her encounters with the emerging nationalism and xenophobia of her country and the region around it. When she encounters an anti-Semitic taxi driver, she debates with herself: "I haven't had my morning coffee, I'm groggy and thick-headed . . . Do I really have to take this on? I guess I do. On this matter, I have my Historical Obligations. So I start from the basics" (98). She engages in a drive-through conversation about the history of Polish Jews, in which her well-educated American side lectures on the facts and sympathizes with the ignorant young man who simply was not taught the truth in school and was left to thrive on anti-Semitic stereotypes because "ethnicity was supposed to evaporate under Communism." Yet this is an occasion for Hoffman as narrator to realize that "the Polish and Jewish parts of my history, my identity—my loyalties—refuse either to separate or to reconcile." She thus lives through this experience as a chronicler and commentator and as a writer of intimate memoirs who cannot help inscribing it into her autobiography. She realizes that in these confusing matters that intertwine politics, ideology, and personal history, she needs the "benefits of sanity rather badly." In attempting to live up to her Historical Obligations she is both a defender of Poland, which is often reductively and stereotypically branded as an anti-Semitic country, and a vigilant accuser of its ignorance on the Jewish question. Her parents, after all, "survived the Holocaust in awful circumstances" there (101).

She remembers encounters with Polish anti-Semitism in Romania while talking with Pavel. She realizes then that the national and ethnic identities in East Europe may be even more complex than she thought. Pavel, who is a Jew, identifies himself as a Romanian first, but also cautions her not to jump to conclusions: "'Rationally, it's much more interesting to be a Jew than to be a Romanian, but it's not really a choice. Some people tried to impose on me the quality of being a foreigner. This is one form of anti-Semitic coercion— forcing a person to take on a Jewish identity that he may not have. I've never submitted to this coercion'" (323). Pavel's obligation is to himself first, and he will resist any attempts by others to classify him against his will. But he cannot help being an outsider precisely for the reason of his individuality and resistance to political and ethnic stereotypes. Hoffman is as unable as Pavel is to resolve the "Jewish question" on either the private or the public level.

This inability arises from the fact that, like Pavel, she is caught between being a victim, a member of the group that has been and continues to be used as a scapegoat, and being an individual who refuses to submit to this victimization, an other who chooses her identity for herself. Once again, Kristeva's theory of otherness helps explain this conflict:

> The complex relationships between cause and effect that govern social groups obviously do not coincide with the laws of the unconscious regarding a subject, but these unconscious determinations remain a constituent part, an essential one, of social and therefore national dynamics. . . . [I]n the long run, only a thorough investigation of our remarkable relationship with both the *other* and *strangeness within ourselves* can lead people to give up hunting for the scapegoat outside their group, a search that allows them to withdraw into their own "sanctum" thus purified: is not the worship of one's "very own," of which the "national" is the collective configuration, the *common denominator* that we imagine we have as "our own," precisely, along with the other "own and proper" people like us? (*NN* 50–51)

Both Pavel and Hoffman recognize that, as Jewish others to their environment, they are rejected and stereotyped by it. Yet, while recognizing their externally defined Jewishness, they also embrace their inner "strangers" and thus emerge as individuals who are independent of the scapegoated other constructed by their hostile environment. However, as Kristeva stresses, the hostility against them will not subside until those guilty of it do as Pavel and Hoffman did—that is, until they embrace their own "strangeness within" and thus learn to accept the otherness of people outside themselves, people whom they used to reject in order to define themselves. Although she does not believe that a reconciliation like this will soon happen in East Europe, Hoffman admires the fervor and emotional commitment of those who fight xenophobia and anti-Semitism there. While watching a television debate on Polish-Jewish relations, she is impressed with the "sheer intensity" of the speech by one of the participants who vehemently attacks a right-wing nationalist. This prompts a reflection on how such heated issues are discussed in the United States, where "nobody on the cooler medium of American television would speak with such uncontrolled movements, or such naked fervor" (102). Once again, she confronts the East European cultural other from her American perspective, yet she is also able to detect how this other views the United States and the West thanks to her vigilance as an emigrant.[19]

### An Experiment in Reality

Engaged in writing *Exit into History* as a chronicle for her American audience, Hoffman concentrates on the otherness of East and Central Europe as perceived by the West, which still wants to see this region as an exotic and back-ward part of the otherwise "civilized" continent. Even after the recent political and economic changes, "There's been a sort of assumption in the West that post-Communist Eastern Europe is in an adolescent phase, from which it'll have to grow into 'our ways' awkwardly and slowly." Hoffman is bothered by such culturally imperialist attitudes and asserts that "the ways of the West aren't that mysterious after all, and Eastern Europe isn't made up of bumbling teenagers" (*EH* 19). Just as she used to argue with her prototypical Ameri-can Friend in *Lost in Translation*, she now stands up to defend her birthplace, which is "only a long plane ride away from the East Coast" but which is also beyond a "distended, uncrossable, otherworldly distance," the "immeasurable length of loss and longing: a distance of the imagination" (*LT* 241). Yet Hoff-man's leap from constructing her idealized Poland—"Paradise"—in *Lost in Translation* to recording it as a part of the mysterious Other Europe in *Exit into History* is an authorial leap from one autobiographical mode to another.

As a visitor with divided allegiances, Hoffman feels protective of her re-gion's difference and wants to save it from misunderstanding by her adopted country and the rest of the world. While in Budapest, she reflects on the re-fusal of the West to include its East and Central European cousins, who are "so much a part of Europe, and yet so excised from the European conscious-ness." This is the personal statement of an emigrant, one who understands the displacement of the Other Europe through her own life story. As a natural-ized American, Hoffman feels "a certain sense of loss—from the part of me that has become Western—and perhaps even a touch of anger from the other side." In other words, she regrets the disappearance of the myth of East Euro-pean uniformity that was so convenient to the West but is angry that such perverse nostalgia ever enters her Polish mind (*EH* 209). Just as Eva did in *Lost in Translation*, she has to shuffle between her allegiances to both cultures and perform the difficult balancing act of explaining their strangeness to each other and to herself—her "customary and highly uncomfortable position" (*EH* 220).

Yet after her return to New York, where she composes her book, Hoff-man identifies with the time and place where she has to live her life. "Be here now," she also tells herself at the end of *Lost in Translation*, and this com-mand marks her coming home at the end of her journey of self-discovery. At the same time, this arrival is the starting point for her journalistic-autobio-graphical travels through the new East Europe as a naturalized American. In contrast to the first book, which moved from the Old World and into the ethnic self immersed in the New, the second departs from America and returns to the authors' roots in the Other Europe, to her closeted Polishness, which is viewed by a traveler. However, as if to erase the effects of this reversed immigrant journey, Hoffman finishes *Exit into History* in the clear voice of an American insider confronting the East European other. "They're coming, the Eastern Europeans are coming, to inspect us from close up as we can now inspect them," she remarks walking through the streets of New York, filled with multilingual crowds. This sudden identification with her western other, after her journeys recording a divided perspective, may be seen as arising from her realization of the "dangers of [intercultural] travel." While in Poland, she recalls Thomas Mann's *Death in Venice* and identifies her and his protagonist's trips as "travel toward Otherness." Unlike Aschenbach, she is "pursuing the essence of the familiar," but like Mann, she is aware that to travel toward any otherness is "to risk disintegration; it is to lose the firm certainties of yourself" (78). She can oscillate between her two perspectives during her travels, but she has to retain a firm cultural location from which to maintain her split identity.

In this context, the ending of *Exit into History* affirms Hoffman's vantage point as an American while also emphasizing its inherent Polish-Jewish otherness. She uses a larger national perspective to illustrate such a positioning of her subjectivity:

> From *our* side, the temptation to continue seeing Eastern Europe as a screen for *our* projections—a wild region still, or a sort of moral wilderness reservation which ought to be innocent of the deeper corruptions of the West—remains powerful. The Iron Curtain has lifted, but imaginative curtains take longer to remove, and *I* would not be surprised if we became prone to Cold War nostalgia just for that reason, if we felt secretly disappointed should Eastern Europeans turn out to resemble us too closely. But at best *I* think that Eastern Europe should be an occasion not for projection, but for its reverse—for self-reflection. Insofar as it is trying to become more like us, Eastern Europe is partly a test of what we stand for. (409, emphasis mine)

This passage shows how, by employing alternating first-person plural and first-person singular pronouns, Hoffman manages to retain her double perspective. As if to weld her individual experience with the collective approach echoing Kristeva's "esprit général," she gives advice to the western "us" as a Polish American "I." In this respect, Hoffman's book can be also read as performing the task of shifting the ideological perspective on East Europe from the traditional, "masculine" one of patronizing "projection" to the "feminine" one of "self-reflection," one involving a dialogue between the other and the "strangeness within." Kristeva defines the task of women in times of struggle against nationalism as especially important because of their "luck and the responsibility of being boundary-subjects: body and thought, biology and language, personal identity and dissemination during childhood, origin and judgment, nation and world—more dramatically so than men are" (*NN* 35). Hoffman's narrative position on the borders and between cultures is thus both complicated and enhanced further by writing a woman's story.

In addition to marking her gendered vantage point, Hoffman's insistent reminders about her double perspective in *Exit into History* emphasize also the impossibility of writing an unambivalent linear narrative about the new East Europe she visits on several occasions. She sees the present in such countries as the Czech Republic, Poland, Romania, Bulgaria, and Hungary as an "experiment in reality" that neither the East nor the West can comprehend. As a writer of this incomprehension, she actually rejoices in the historical uncertainty, as if she takes pleasure in the temptation to fictionalize that it might inspire. She ends her account by saying, "It is possible that Eastern Europe might be in the vanguard of *something*: a 'third way' different from what we have yet conceived. . . . [T]he grand, complex Eastern European experiment is both determined and utterly fluid; its results can only be shown in time, and they can—perhaps fortunately—never be finally declared" (410). Speaking from the position of a female writer who chooses to be placed between the West and its other as well as between East Europe and its other, Hoffman may fail in constructing a uniform and clearly focused narrative about politics, history, and economics. But she succeeds in recreating the conflicts and tensions of her indefinable region through the ones perpetuating her fluid text.

In her unresolved shuffling between autobiography and journalistic objectivism, Hoffman echoes Antin's attempts to write both a personal account and a story of her people in *The Promised Land*. Like Yezierska in *Red Ribbon on a White Horse*, she struggles with her parents' past and is conscious of writing her intensely personal account in the shadow of the "generations clamoring for expression" and in between two patriarchal cultures. As in Stern's *My Mother and I*, she continues the matrilineal heritage first described in *Lost in Translation* through collecting the black beads of her mother's and other people's stories. While continuing the tradition begun by these writers, Hoffman also revises it and shows its complexities for the contemporary reader. In this respect, she brings to mind Kuncewicz's *Witness*, whose vigilant gaze always scrutinizes the observer engaged in appraising others. As witnesses of woman's self-discovery and recorders of East European otherness, Hoffman's *Lost in Translation* and *Exit into History* enter American literature as invaluable documents of how both individual and national consciousness are made in a world that is becoming "utterly nomadic and interpenetrated, even while it becomes more separatist" (*EH* 408).

# 7 The Untold Story

## VLADIMIR NABOKOV'S *PNIN*
## AS AN IMMIGRANT NARRATIVE

Some people—and I am one of them—hate
happy ends. We feel cheated. Harm is the norm.
Doom should not jam. The avalanche stopping
in its tracks a few feet above the cowering village
behaves not only unnaturally but unethically.
—Vladimir Nabokov, *Pnin*

## Reading Male through Female

Occurring at the beginning of *Pnin*, this comment by Nabokov's narrator Sirin foreshadows the conclusion of the
title character's career at Weindell College. In the last
scene, pathetic and endearing Timofey Pahlich, who has always made the
reader laugh and often evoked genuine sympathy throughout the whole novel,
is "lighting out for the territory," seemingly in a very American, if not Americanized, way. Yet Pnin has to leave and drive off into the proverbial sunset
(sunrise in the final scene) not as a hero, but as a loser, having been ousted
by his clever and enterprising compatriot, Sirin, who will replace him as professor of Russian. In such an ending "doom does not jam" and indeed "harm
is the norm." The sentimental lover of squirrels and bad poetry by cruel ex-
wives flees, while the no-nonsense political careerist Sirin takes over. Apart
from illustrating the realities of college politics, tenure reviews, and promotions, this unfortunate outcome to Pnin's career at Weindell marks also an
unhappy resolution to the narrative of acculturation that he lives through as
a Russian émigré in the United States in the 1950s.[1]

Although Timofey's story inspires compassion, a sympathetic reader sometimes feels overwhelmed with Nabokov's textual artifice, which surrounds and
overshadows the protagonist's characterization. For example, when Eva Hoffman compares her story in *Lost in Translation* to those inscribed in other East
European writers' texts, she also describes Nabokov's characters as "aesthetic
objects." They are beautifully crafted and attractive. We feel for them. But they
always are attesting foremost to their own artificiality and to their author's
preoccupation with his craft. Hoffman both admires and rejects Nabokov's
authorial narcissism: "I wish I could define myself—as Nabokov defines both
himself and his characters—by the telling detail . . . I wish I could live in a
world of prismatic refractions, carefully distinguished colors of sunsets and
English scarves. . . . Characters, in Nabokov's fiction, being perfectly them-

selves, attain the *graced amorality of aesthetic objects*. How trite and tedious, in contrast, to see oneself as a creature formed by historic events and defined by sociological categories" (*LT* 197–98, emphasis mine). It is easy for any reader to lose himself or herself in Nabokovian detail and love of artifice and to approach *Pnin*, for example, as merely a brilliant exercise in craftsmanship.[2] Hoffman calls such approach to literature "graced amorality" because it rejects history and social turmoil as necessary contexts for human experience. As Hoffman notes, it is undoubtedly true that the preoccupation of Nabokov's texts with their own aesthetics distracts the reader and can discourage exploration of the writer's characters outside the aesthetic realm.[3] The story of Timofey Pahlich Pnin, for instance, can be read as no more than a crafty, hilarious joke about academic America.

But if such a reductive reading is justified to a certain extent, it also results from a long tradition that pigeonholes Nabokov into the role of the great, if not the greatest, male Russian American writer of the twentieth century. Even before readers open his novel, they expect to find confirmation of Nabokov's fame on the pages of his work. As a "great white male writer," he is expected to be above the "trite" details of everyday life; his position in the literary pantheon and his gender seem miraculously to absolve him from dealing with, and his readers from searching for, the "marginal" themes pervading writings by minorities and women. As he himself proudly announces, his America, even the one described in *Lolita* and *Pnin*, is an artificial construct: "I have invented in America my America and just as fantastic as any inventor's America."[4] Yet although the "prismatic refractions" and "English scarves" indeed do not lend themselves to analyses emphasizing gender, class, and ethnicity, that ought not stop a careful reader from looking beyond the predictable endings of Nabokov's texts, endings always critical of the happy resolution. Instead of seeing him as the unique and indefinable literary phenomenon that he will always remain to some critics, he should be approached as a member of the heterogeneous crowd of newcomers from East Europe. In the gracefully amoral *Pnin*, after all, he presents a story of a Russian immigrant that ends unhappily and thus suggests that the narratives of acculturation which serve as the context for Timofey's unfortunate Americanization are often the tales of failure.

Using its ending as a springboard, I propose to reread Nabokov's seemingly "American" novel as an immigrant narrative, one that employs and revises the traditional narrative models of male and female Americanization. I have chosen to examine a prominent male novel in the conclusion of this study on immigrant women writers to demonstrate how the female tradition I have explored in these pages actually revises and engages in a dialogue with the "canonical" male texts that still marginalize it. Looking at gendered narrative roles through Nabokov's famous double—Sirin and Pnin—yields a reading of *Pnin* as a dialogic text that explores the intersection of the traditional masculine and feminine immigrant plots. Such a reading arises from Nabokov's playful reversal of roles between male and female characters, a reversal that results in an interesting, and "seductive," subplot ensnaring not only Timofey, Liza, and Sirin but the reader as well.

### An "Other" Ending

Vladimir Nabokov's distaste for happy endings may seem strange considering his brilliant career and global success as a celebrated Russian American novelist. What happier conclusion could a writer conceive for his own story than, in Brian Boyd's words, "wealth and fame that would allow him to devote himself solely to writing, to cross the Atlantic again in triumph, to regain Europe, to retain America, to carry his words around the world"?[5] Unlike female immigrant writers such as Mary Antin or Anzia Yezierska, Nabokov was actually able to have the best of both worlds. After twenty years of hard work as a teacher, scholar, scientist, and writer, he realized the newcomer's dream of having the means to flourish on both ends of the crosscultural bridge spanning North America and Europe. The stories about his exile, described in a plethora of diverse critical studies and narrated in numerous interviews and memoirs, as well as in such novels as *Pnin* and *Lolita* (1959), echo the male immigrant version of the rags-to-riches tale. The author of *Pale Fire* "made it" in postwar America both economically and artistically; his books sold and won praises and awards and turned the little-known author into a celebrity practically overnight, after the stunning international coup of *Lolita*.[6] Nabokov's success was so sudden and complete that, to some of his critics and readers, it overshadowed the tough struggle that had brought it about. However, beyond his extraordinary achievement and beyond other possible interpretations of his career, we can also read a male story of Americanization in which a hardworking Russian émigré reaches the artistic and economic top in the competitive Promised Land.[7]

Nabokov's aristocratic origins, superior education, and multilingual background should not make his readers forget that he too was an immigrant like those writers of the "huddled masses" period. Although his work seems to have little in common with Maria Kuncewicz's and Eva Hoffman's more contemporaneous tales of female exile in a world divided into the hostile East and West, he still belongs to the dissident tradition that they challenge and redefine in their writings. Obviously, in comparison with the lives of these women, Nabokov's story is the happiest, and its ending most enviable. While it is only recently that the texts of Yezierska and Stern have been resurrected and while attempts to retranslate Maria Kuncewicz may still have to wait, the author of *Lolita* has been the unquestioned representative of successful mediation between the literatures of East Europe and America since the late 1950s.[8]

Nevertheless, it is interesting to go back to the traditionally dominant male texts and explore them using the themes derived from studying the other gender, themes we have come to understand only by examining writings by women in the immigrant tradition. Reading women as makers of the East-West dialogue changes the "balance of power" between male and female texts. It actually invites reconsideration of the male émigrés—Vladimir Nabokov, Jerzy Kosiński, Janusz Głowacki, Joseph Brodsky, and others—as the marginal others to the female tradition. Such a change of perspective inspires new readings, ones that question the established interpretation of the male story and, by employing new themes derived from the female writings, open up interesting exchanges between both gendered narratives of acculturation. For example, we can reread Nabokov's "American" novels as reflecting the themes of sexual ambivalence introduced by women writers. Humbert Humbert's tragic love affair with Lolita can be seen as a metaphor for a male immigrant's inability to enter the new culture, America itself, on its sexual terms. Only as a pervert and a criminal is he able to merge with the Promised Land, this epitome of feminized landscape and sensuous wilderness, this adolescent and fascinating culture, but also this vulnerable and violence-marked body.[9]

Without looking back at the established, canonical male writers like Nabokov, this study would have concluded with another "happy ending." It might have achieved its goal of resuscitating the "forgotten voices" but it would have also kept the female versions of the immigrant narrative from speaking in an interesting dialogue with their others, the male tradition that they challenge and revise. Rereading the male authors in the light of the themes derived from the writings by women makes possible an encounter involving both genders, a dialogue which takes place within the larger discourse between the cultures of East Europe and America. Even in criticism and animosity the two stories, male and female, comment on and provide interesting contexts for each other.[10]

The reading of *Pnin* proposed in this chapter spotlights Nabokov's novel as a male text that nevertheless succeeds in telling a feminine story.[11] It shows the possibility of trading places within the male-female movement of narrative discourse as defined by Teresa De Lauretis and other feminist critics. This discourse maps the narrative as a theater where gendered roles and sexual identities are reflected and played. *Pnin* revises the traditional masculine immigrant tale by interacting with and parodying typically feminine plots and themes. Although it is impossible to forget the advantages that the author of *Lolita* has over any woman writer—the unbridgeable abyss of gender, economic, and class difference—it is important to reconsider his contribution to the dialogue begun by the immigrant women writers. Reading Nabokov as "one of the crowd" would probably offend his aristocratic sense of individuality and aloof refinement; it would at least produce a dissonance with the culturally constructed image of this writer that most of his readers and critics are used to. In fact, a reading debunking this traditional image of Nabokov can be seen as a revision of the rather reductive "happy endings" that the literary criticism of this writer has already predetermined for him as the "great writer." The anticlimactic ending that this study proposes will actually place Vladimir Vladimirovich's text among those by "scribbling women," the descendants of "Jane," of whom he wrote in his famous misogynist letter to Edmund Wilson: "I dislike Jane, and am prejudiced, in fact, against any women writers. They are in another class. Could never see anything in *Pride and Prejudice*." [12] What better ending, what better proof that dialogue is possible despite difference, than to show that a Nabokov text can be read as an encounter with writings by women of "another class"?

## The New Cinderella: Feminine Plots and Male Narratives

Superficially, Timofey's story in *Pnin* is a brilliant and hilarious joke about America's newcomers, in this case an archetypal professor from Russia, with his "mythopoeic" English and exceedingly funny foreign ways.[13] But beyond humor, the tale about Pnin is also a story about an exile who has been brutally uprooted from his milieu by historical and political events. Having left his homeland and after years of living on a Nansen Passport in Europe, Timofey crosses the ocean and is dumped into a strange America without much linguistic or cultural preparation.[14] Pnin's prerevolutionary Russia—the childhood paradise comparable to Hoffman's—is an alien and extinct environment, one that practically vanished after political and ideological changes had forced people such as Pnin, and Nabokov, out of their country. In this respect, Pnin comes from an almost mythical and legendary place no longer identifiable as a part of the Old World. He is an orphaned citizen who has to confront a strange culture, who has to try "melting" into a nation that cannot comprehend his alien and complex nature. In describing Pnin's tragicomic rites of passage, Nabokov's novel is a late-1950s version of male Americanization in which the male and female stories are skillfully combined to construct a truly complex protagonist.

Timofey's position between genders and narrative models can be seen in the crucial scene at the end of the novel, when he has just found out that he is about to lose his job at Weindell College. He is contemplating his sad situation in what could be called a typically feminine setting.[15] Pnin is washing the dishes—performing "housewifely" duties—after the "house-heating" party he threw to celebrate his decision to settle down in Waindellville, to buy a house, and to finally put down roots after years of émigré homelessness. But, ironically, he is crying over his fate in this scene, for he finds out that he has to leave in search of another job and place to live at the very moment when he thought he had finally found a permanent home. To make his anguish even worse, he suddenly drops a utensil into his dishwashing and becomes terrified, thinking that he has just broken a precious gift from his young friend Victor: "Pnin hurled the towel into a corner and, turning away, stood for a moment staring at the blackness beyond the threshold of the open back door. A quiet, lacy-winged little green insect circled in the glare of a strong naked lamp above Pnin's glossy bald head. He looked very old, with his toothless mouth half open and a film of tears dimming his blank, unblinking eyes. Then, with a moan of anguished anticipation, he went back to the sink and, bracing himself, dipped his hand deep into the foam. . . . The beautiful bowl was intact" (172). The crisis with the bowl, a beautiful and precious gift from the son of Pnin's ex-wife and her psychiatrist-husband, breaks the housekeeping routine and freezes Pnin in momentary immobility. He abandons his chores and reflects on his homelessness and solitude; he cries over what he thinks is the irretrievable loss of the only token of love he has received in America. The bowl is a gift, metaphorically, from a young man who could have been his son. This moment of reflection projects a sentimental and emotional mood; the reader might feel sorry for pathetic Pnin and be moved by his tragicomic predicament. But as soon as we are ready to sympathize with his character, Nabokov triumphantly recreates the bowl. The beautiful gift is intact; it was only an insignificant goblet that broke.

The intricate design and possible symbolic meanings of this particular scene from *Pnin* remind one of another bowl and another American expatriate novel. In Henry James's *The Golden Bowl* a precious vessel is crushed to pieces, revealing its imperfect nature—what was supposed to be gold turns out to be merely gilt and cracked crystal—thus helping the reader understand the layers of intrigue and the subtleties of James's complex narration. In Nabokov's Russian American text the bowl remains intact and in its original state; it is miraculously resurrected to prove the unbreakability and value of the friendship between Pnin and Victor. On the other hand, it also brings together two typically female narratives: Pnin's search for a home (domestic) and his Cinderella tale (romantic), for the color of its glass reminds Pnin's guests of Cinderella's slippers.[16] As in James's novel, the bowl in *Pnin* is a magnet drawing the elements of the plot together—Pnin's yearning for a place to settle down is underlined by a Cinderella-like longing for deliverance from oppression and loneliness. Even though he cannot have a permanent home, Timofey has found someone to be his metaphorical son, to give him a sense of having a family, someone who sees through his pathetic exterior.[17] Similarly, Victor finds a metaphorical parent in his mother's ex-husband and keeps indulging in fantasies about this mysterious scholar and gentleman, whom he envisions as a fugitive king from the great lost kingdom of Russia.[18] In his acceptance and appreciation of the boy, Pnin performs the role of a mother. The bowl representing their relationship withstands the crisis and symbolizes Pnin's little domestic triumph in the trials of his Americanization. It also represents Pnin's scintillating nature and depth of personality that lie behind the mask of the clown he wears to the eyes of the dominant culture.

With its comical rendering of the protagonist and his predicament in the world of American academics, Nabokov's text is a parody of a typical male immigrant tale, such as Abraham Cahan's *The Rise of David Levinsky* (1917). Cahan's novel depicts a Russian newcomer and his economic rise; it is a story of masculine conquest and ruthless struggle for status in the process of becoming an American. The narrator of Nabokov's novel—successful Sirin, who bears the pen name of the author—fits this model well. But Pnin's search for home and family brings to mind the tale of female acculturation through marriage and homemaking—the story of mediation through miscegenation. Moreover, his affair with an American university unravels along the lines of the immigrant Cinderella fairy tale in which Pnin's Cinderella side pertains to his hidden qualities, which are as indiscernible to the eye of a superficial observer as the true beauty of Victor's bowl. For example, Timofey's incessant parodist Cockerell and his indifferent compatriot Komarov can see only a fool and a clown in their colleague, but the Clementses, at whose house Timofey boards for a while, learn to appreciate his joviality, humor, and warmth. Pnin's intellect and erudition are also revealed in the scenes depicting a reunion of Russian émigrés at the Pines, where he is welcomed as a cherished compatriot and recognized as an eloquent conversationalist. The novel implies that, in the public sphere of American academe, Timofey is a superficial type to be ridiculed, while in more intimate, almost "domestic" settings of his own or his friends' houses, he is a complex and interesting character. Just like Victor's bowl, which reveals its true value only to those who can appreciate it, Pnin's true worth and depth have to be deciphered beyond appearances.

Therefore, Pnin's final escape from Weindell, after he has proclaimed that he would never work under triumphant Sirin, should not be read as the simple retreat of a loser. In Pnin's flight from Sirin, Nabokov has his character escape a particular type of the immigrant scenario that his adversary represents and that Pnin rejects. While Sirin represents success and fits comfortably into the world of American academe and its political workings, Pnin stands for failure in his lack of tenure and in his inability to read the interpersonal mechanisms governing Waindell College. This comparison between the two characters is drawn along the lines of the male versus the female roles within the narrative: in the pursuit of his academic success Sirin represents the hero, whereas Timofey is an obstacle in this pursuit (Sirin gets Pnin's job) and is thus placed in the feminized position. The way the two characters are constructed by Nabokov elicits this contrast by juxtaposing the public and the domestic spheres, the masculine and the feminine. Sirin is hard-nosed, mysterious, and opaque; we learn about him through his actions and from other characters; he represents the external world of dynamic movement and adventure. On the other hand, Pnin is vulnerable and static; he is presented largely through his inner life—the feminine realm of the sentimental—and thus appeals to the reader's emotions; his yearning for a domestic space represents the female sphere within the home.

The contrasting pair, Pnin and Sirin, remain written forever, side by side, into the life of a small American campus in Nabokov's fictitious America. Although the antithesis of each other, they both constitute the same immigrant tale, in which they become what Pnin's "staunch protector," Dr. Hagen, calls "a delicate imported article worth paying for in domestic cash"—a foreign academic (11). Despite their staggering differences, the two characters are indispensable to each other, as Pnin's singular humanity can be appreciated even more against the smugness of self-assured Sirin, who, in turn, can be condemned for complacency because Pnin is constantly an underdog and an easy target for his ruthless compatriot's wrongdoings.[19]

Such coupling of personalities is very typical in Nabokov, who is famous for his doubles and who uses them with great skill and humor in *The Real Life of Sebastian Knight*, *Lolita*, and *Pale Fire*, with their Sebastian Knight and his half-brother–biographer, Humbert Humbert and Quilty, Kinbote and Shade.

In the case of *Pnin*, the juxtaposition of characters not only brings about the two versions of a Russian professor in America, but also stresses the ambivalence of the immigrant story that makes up Nabokov's novel. The two characters embody two versions of male Americanization according to Vladimir Nabokov: Pninian—through pain and failure, the heart-wrenching sentimental and "feminine" version—and Sirinian-Nabokovian—through success and assimilation into the dominant culture, the no-nonsense masculine conquest. In thus complementing and intertwining with each other, these two versions reveal their artifice as narrative devices.

Just as the author needs his self-conscious craft, Pnin needs Sirin to be the carrier and the interpreter of his message; the female story needs the contrast of the male one in order to be appreciated in its difference. That is why Sirin has to represent the somewhat clichéd narrative of male Americanization in order to provide contrast for Pnin's complex position between the masculine and feminine plots. The story of a Russian immigrant in *Pnin* elicits the complexities of male Americanization, which has to be read through gender just as its female other. In Nabokov's text the double-tracked, male-female acculturation of Timofey includes both the emotional and pathetic narrative of Pnin's pain *and* the "heroic" scenario of successful Sirin, who takes advantage of his more sensitive compatriots. *Pnin* thus tells the newcomer's story twice: along the lines of a somewhat "feminine" sequence of Pnin's search for home and family, and along Sirin's victorious trajectory of a rising author and a marketable academic.[20] In this context, which also includes women characters, such as Pnin's ex-wife Liza, Timofey plays the female lead in the story of his own Americanization.

### The Only Female in Pnin

Pnin's feminine qualities are introduced on the very first pages of the novel, where he is described sitting on the railway coach heading for Cremona, somewhere in New England. Although he possesses a "strong-man torso," his shoulders are "unnecessarily robust" and his legs are "disappointingly" spindly, ending in "almost feminine feet," which are clad in shoes always "curiously small." Pnin's body begins "rather impressively, with the "great brown dome" of his bald head, but his heavy glasses mask an "infantile absence of eyebrows." He is sitting with his legs crossed, "po-amerikanski," displaying his bare shins (7, 61, 35).[21]

When the narration focuses on Pnin's teaching abilities, they are presented in contrast to those of "stupendous Russian ladies . . . who . . . by dint of intuition, loquacity, and a kind of maternal bounce . . . infuse a magic knowledge of their beautiful and difficult tongue into a group of innocent-eyed students." Although not in the same category with the "stupendous ladies," Pnin does not fit into the "ascetic fraternity of phonemes," or the modern linguists either (10). He is in between, beyond classification, an other among familiar categories, a curious hybrid that does not fit either of the genders. "[P]oor Pnin, poor albino porcupine!" the narrator calls him (44).

Another clue to Pnin's feminine qualities is his heart condition, which, in the first chapter, renders him semiconscious on a park bench and sends him into something like a dream allegory, a journey back into his childhood. When the "tingle of unreality" overpowers him, Timofey feels "porous and pregnable," as if melting into the landscape. The narrator warns us right away that such a state means a destruction of the ego, since "*man* exists only insofar as he is separated from his surroundings. . . . Stay inside or you perish" (20, emphasis mine).[22] Keeping apart from the landscape is especially important in America, where nature is forcibly feminine and sensuous. Pnin does not heed this advice and keeps giving thirsty squirrels water, swimming at the Pines, and being haunted by dreamy Russian woods and pastures.

Moreover, Pnin is not decisively masculine and is, possibly, impotent; he never fathers a child while married to Liza, who begins sleeping with another man soon after their nuptials and who keeps writing poems about other lovers. Timofey is also somewhat "outside" the typical male body. His fascination with sunlamps and the meticulous care he takes with his appearance are rather stereotypically effeminate traits. As an unheard-of oddity in town, sunlamp-browned Pnin is taken for a Catholic saint by a charwoman and for a Buddha by Betty Bliss, who has seen his effusive performance in a film on Russian gestures, in which he sports a "Gioconda smile." Both are very chaste and desexualized figures. An innocent "crush" that Pnin has on Betty, "a plump maternal girl of some twenty-nine summers," his most gifted student, is completely desexualized, as he can only visualize "a serene senility" with her (40, 42, 43).

Pnin's antimasculinity is explained by his tragic unrequited love for Liza Bogolepov, his unfaithful and rather common "poetess" ex-wife. After the sad end of their marriage, he is unable to love or to be a man again, an explanation quite self-consciously ironic. When Liza comes to visit him, Timofey exhibits awkward, adolescent excitement and cannot control his nervousness. He still nurses hopes that she might want to come back to him and is destroyed by her cruel declamation of a new poem about a new lover and by her blunt disregard for his feelings. In this respect, Pnin is a Russian Don Quixote, a reader of romances and a failed reader of reality, because he loves his idealized fantasy rather than the real woman. The style describing Pnin's emotions often evokes romance and sentimental plots: "To hold her, to keep her . . . with her cruelty, with her vulgarity, with her blinding blue eyes, with her miserable poetry, with her fat feet, with her impure, dry, sordid, infantile soul" (57–58).[23] In contrast, Sirin's version of Liza is mocking and ironic, that of a tough ex-lover. He sees her as a cunning plotter who takes advantage of men and rather enjoys breaking their hearts. In this context, Liza's affair with Sirin, her marriage to Pnin, and her subsequent infidelities are all parts of a "seduction" scenario in which Pnin is the innocent and naive party to be taken advantage of; he plays the exploited innocent, ruined and abandoned by the modern version of a "rake," "une femme fatale." This role reversal between Liza and Timofey suggests that we can read *Pnin* as a parody of an immigrant romance in America—the land where, as one of Yezierska's stories proclaims, "the lovers dream."

### A Sentimental Dissident

The mock "tale of seduction and betrayal" in which Liza and Pnin play the reversed roles of the seducer and the seduced can be read in relation to an actual sentimental text, Susanna Rowson's *Charlotte Temple* (1791).[24] Rowson's didactic novel tells the story of a young innocent English girl who is persuaded to accept letters and advances from a rake, a British officer named Montraville. As a result of her typically sentimental misreading of reality and due to the evil plotting between Montraville and Charlotte's chaperone, a woman bearing the telling name of Mademoiselle La Rue, the girl agrees to elope to America. Once there, she is exploited and abandoned in New York during the American Revolution. The wages of sin are Charlotte's death in childbirth, a typical ending for a fallen woman, while Montraville marries a rich and beautiful aristocrat and enjoys life for a while before his conscience makes him repent and die, providing the cathartic ending.

Both stories, Rowson's and Nabokov's, begin in Europe, where a young innocent is getting an education. The romance is brought about by means of a letter, which in Rowson's story is written by the rake to the virgin and which in Nabokov's is Pnin's epistolary marriage proposal to his beloved Liza. This ruthless young woman shows Pnin's love confession to Sirin, her first choice, behind Timofey's back. However, Sirin sees Liza for what she is and refuses her advances. As a result, Liza marries virtuous and trusting Pnin, a move recommended by her therapeutically minded psychiatrist friends, who are concerned about her suicide attempt over Sirin's rejection and who order "Pnin—and a baby at once" (45). Pnin is thus "seduced" into matrimony by a woman who uses him and does not love him. He is exploited, and then left alone and broken, as heartless Liza, like Rowson's Montraville, falls in love with a more attractive object.

In both stories America is the place where the final crisis and punishment are staged after a long transatlantic voyage. Both innocents are thus immigrants who come to a sorry end in the New World because they cannot read others and the codes governing gender relations. In *Charlotte Temple* the girl agrees to live in sin with her seducer, is then abandoned, bears a child, and dies in poverty, having reconciled on her deathbed with her heart-broken parents. In *Pnin*, although it is obviously Liza who gets pregnant, it is really poor Timofey who is taken advantage of. Having abandoned him, his unfaithful wife pretends to reconcile with him temporarily and then returns, pregnant with another man's child. But this is only a ruse, performed to secure her passage to the Promised Land where she is going to marry another man, Dr. Eric Wind, a psychiatrist who understands her "organic ego." Like Rowson's, Nabokov's version of the "tale of seduction and betrayal" ends in the New World, where Pnin is dumped once again, heartbroken, possibly impotent, and unable to love any more. His destroyer continues to haunt him—the "wages of sin" are Pnin's responsibility for Victor, and keeping score of his former wife's lovers and husbands over the years. Later on, Timofey even has to take over the mothering of Victor, as Liza practically abandons her son to his care in order to marry her newest lover.

As a parody of both the masculine and the feminine immigrant tales and of the sentimental plot, *Pnin* employs the gender-related betrayals awaiting an inexperienced newcomer in America. Its paradoxical link with a text such as *Charlotte Temple* occurs through the immigrant narrative, too. Rowson's text is perhaps one of the first novels about an Old World female crossing the ocean to reach America, while Nabokov's arises from the specific East European tradition that flourished a century later. Charlotte is thus one of the first immigrant women characters who experience the oppression of their sexuality in the Promised Land, a theme developed later in the texts of Mary Antin or Anzia Yezierska. In a parody of this theme, *Pnin* depicts Timofey losing his masculinity in the New World and being branded with the stigmatization of the other. In his faithful love for ruthless Liza, in his "motherly" affection for Victor, and in his preoccupation with other people's pain and suffering, Pnin occupies a feminized space in Nabokov's novel. Of course, he is "seduced" and betrayed as a fictitious character—an artifice concealing human emotions—so that the reader can laugh and the narrator can preserve his aloof power over the plot.[25]

As an innocent exploited for his sentiments in America, Timofey is also a parody of an East European dissident, a figure for whom Nabokov had a lot of sympathy and affection. *Pnin* reveals subtly that Nabokov was well aware of anti-Soviet, Cold War sentiment in America, which would alienate his protagonist still further. At Timofey's housewarming party, Senator Joseph McCarthy's name is casually mentioned, as is Cuba, where the double-named "Twynn"-Thomas is going to do "research," having obtained a miraculously implausible grant. In their conversation after the party, Hagen mentions that "political trends in America discourage interests in things Russian," which is meant as an apology for firing Timofey (169). The narrator also points to a letter that Pnin wrote, "with [his] help, to the *New York Times* in 1945 anent the Yalta conference" (16). This document possibly referred to the selling out of East Europe to the Soviet Union by the western allies. Right before he learns that he is going to have to leave, Pnin proposes new courses he and Hagen should teach: "'On Tyranny. On the Boot. On Nicholas the First. On all the precursors of modern atrocity. . . . when we speak of injustice, we forget Armenian massacres, tortures which Tibet invented, colonists in Africa. . . . The history of man is the history of pain!'" In his invocation, poor Timofey is a hopeless romantic, and even Hagen feels briefly sorry for him, "'*Der Arme Kerl*, . . . At least I have sweetened the pill'" (168–70). In the no-nonsense world of tenure, appointments, and political intrigue, there is no room for Timofey's tears over long-lost lives, over long-forgotten pain of past generations. Yet by being there, pathetic, feminine Pnin serves as a repository of his author's unequivocal sentimentality for the old Russia, squirrels, accented English, and all underdogs—feelings to which Nabokov would not openly admit.

### Rereading the Author

While discussing any of Nabokov's texts, a critic has to cope with Nabokovian paradoxes, his literary "impertinences," and arrogance toward whatever and whomever he dislikes.[26] In her tribute to Nabokov's genius in *Lolita*, Joyce Carol Oates also writes: "Yet when Nabokov talks of the work *[Lolita]*, we are disappointed, for there is an arrogant, contemptuous side of his nature that tends to distract us from his genuine accomplishments—'Nothing is more exhilarating than philistine vulgarity,' he says, in explaining his use of 'North American sets' for the work. And he needed this stimulus, this 'exhilarating milieu,' or he could not have written the novel."[27] Oates makes her point brilliantly by showing how Nabokov thrived on things he disliked, how he was still able to turn them into beauty. Not that he would have appreciated a comment from a writing woman very much. His distaste for women novelists is widely known, and so is his disdain for sentiment, happy endings, and pathos.[28] Nevertheless, his subject in *Pnin* is pathetic, sentimental, and heartbreaking, as he writes a story of a lonely Russian exile, as he creates a man who is the butt of ethnic jokes, a cuckolded husband, and an unfulfilled father—a male character who ends up playing the female lead in his own story.

Because the author identifies himself so strongly with Sirin, the unreliable writer-narrator in *Pnin*, Nabokov's presence in the novel contributes to the male narrative that undermines Timofey's accomplishments and brings about the unhappy ending to his story. Obviously, Vladimir Nabokov the author is responsible for the conclusion, as he willingly enters into his novel under his real pen name, Sirin. Yet there is still Vladimir Nabokov the exile, the man behind the celebrity, the aching Russian soul experiencing *tęsknota*—homesickness—for the country and people he has lost forever. "We are all Pnins!" exclaims a Russian colleague of Nabokov's at Cornell and one of the possible models for Timofey, perhaps a spokesperson for Nabokov's own suppressed feelings of nostalgia.[29] Nabokov is as much Sirin as he is Pnin. Although this latter incarnation of the author—an anxious, insecure, and always-on-the-run person—is carefully hidden behind numerous fictions, we can glimpse it in Boyd's excellent biography, in the letters and other documents left by Nabokov, and, if we read beyond the joke and the parody, in Pnin's "feminine" story of Americanization. Seduced by the Promised Land, unable to enter it because he cannot learn its language, lonely, and ridiculed, betrayed by the laws of the academy, Timofey can be seen as a tribute to those Russian immigrants about whom America has never heard, to those whose alien "virtues" were never truly rewarded in the Promised Land.[30]

Read from such a feminine perspective, *Pnin* reflects the cultural, linguistic, and artistic split in its author—the many-layered Nabokovian story of a multicultural, bilingual, and several-times-exiled writer who was also a lepidopterist and a scholar.[31] It enables the reader to see past the craftsmanship of the artist and to imagine the anxieties and fears of a person. In this respect, the reader uncovers the sentimental and romantic themes in the writer who would never admit that any such "poshlost" could be found in his texts. Pnin, leaving the novel boldly and driving off into the never-ending American road at the end, is a loner in search of home, a parody of a Cinderella who flees from the reality of the day after the night of magic. What remains is the joke and the narrator's forced laughter—the clichéd male story. But what remains is also questioned by the open closure of Nabokov's text, in which Timofey's feminine side opens up an interesting reading of the male immigrant narrative described and lived by his maker. Like the immigrant women's stories, which challenge and revise the male East European canon, Timofey's otherness questions traditional readings of Nabokov and shows that his novel should be read as part of the gendered dialogue engaging male and female narratives within the literary discourse of East Europe and America.

# Conclusion:
# Where Do You Emigrate to Now?

"You used to be able to emigrate to America," a Polish friend, who has been here several years, quips. "Now where do you emigrate to?" For her the world is too small to sustain the fabulous America of people's dreams; there is no America any longer, no place the mind can turn to for fantastic hope.—Hoffman, *Lost in Translation*

**W**hen I first read this fragment in Eva Hoffman's *Lost in Translation*, I had two reactions, both related to my work on this project and my somewhat complex position as a Polish scholar working in the field of American literature in the United States. The first one was "Where did I read this before?" This reaction lead me to reread Anzia Yezierska's "How I Found America," which poses a similar question in an almost identical situation. In this short story, discussed in Chapter 4, a disillusioned East European Jewish immigrant woman asks another: "But from America where can you go?" But my second, more complex reaction united me with Hoffman and Yezierska. It made me realize that I am like that "Polish friend, who has been here several years." And this reaction gave me the answer to that loaded question so often asked me: "Do you think you will ever go back?" In reacting to Hoffman's passage, I recognized that there is no "going back." Once you leave your country for long enough, there is no other "America" beyond this present one to emigrate to. Once here, you are stuck in the Promised Land. This raises questions: How can an immigrant withstand the loss of his dream? How does she reconcile herself to everyday reality, which refuses to sustain her desire for vision and "discovery" by offering America here and now? It is a real place, not one the mind can "turn to" in its hunger for new frontiers and stimulations.

The insistent repetition of these themes and questions about "emigration" in the work of two different writers I have studied kept resurfacing during my revisions of this study. I became self-conscious about what I was doing and constructed a critical fiction of sorts, a version of an "America" I was hoping to "discover" for my readers. I found myself trying to establish my own finished and complete Promised Land in this book, although my argument had been designed to prove from the start that Yezierska and Hoffman are right, that the search for it should go on, that it can never be "found." Does my confession suggest that I have arrived at my "America," despite believing that this could never be possible? Or does it suggest only that I have constructed a transitory "America," one from which I will keep "emigrating" to seek still new ones? After all, Yezierska's and Hoffman's narrators keep pursuing their "fantastic hope" and "fabulous dreams" contrary to the commonsense advice to settle for reality.

The purpose of this epilogue is to show that Hoffman's and Yezierska's immigrant inquiries and answers about where one might "go" *from* America provide a metaphor for critical readings of their particular tradition and for relating them to the larger discourse on multicultural literature. These writers' continual "emigrating" suggests the need to pursue the only "Americas" that will never disappoint—creativity, imagination, and self-expression. Their passing down of this approach from one generation of immigrant authors to another attests to the historical continuity and shared experiences of otherness among women of different classes and cultural backgrounds. So, as critics approaching their writings within the larger arena of multicultural literary studies, we should follow their advice to "emigrate," seek out, and acknowledge connections among traditions rather than to settle down in our separate, specialized Americas. Critics like myself, especially those who are personally related to their field of study, should find these connections even while resurrecting or defining various marginalized traditions of female writing.

For example, as I analyze my own scholarly and theoretical position and my situation as a foreign scholar writing this book, I find myself echoing some of the critical strategies developed by African American scholars.[1] In particular, I feel like a "shadow" of the black female feminist critics, who created methodologies for reading writings by African American women just as I have had to do for the immigrant women from East Europe. Obviously, what I have in common with such scholars as Deborah E. McDowell, Barbara Christian, or Valerie Smith is a focus on the marginalized female participants in American literature and a desire to make their presence acknowledged and their writings accessible. In recognizing this similarity, as well as in emphasizing that it does not erase very basic differences of race as the historical and political contexts of our subjects, I see us shuttling along the same routes between the centers of critical and academic power and the relative marginality of our fields. While doing our scholarship, we also share the pleasures and dangers of identifying too closely with our topics. Such proximity affects how we read the literature we later "translate" through criticism.

In proposing that we "emigrate" from our fields and among them, that we compare, juggle, and crossbreed diverse literary Americas more openly, I hope to offer East European immigrant women's writings as another inspiration for critical journeys. As a little-known field that deserves more attention and inspires enticing comparative and risky readings, it offers interesting perspectives on the constructions of authorship, literary theory, gender, class, sexuality, and ethnicity. In handing it to the readers of this study, I am inviting them to my temporary "America." Although necessarily bound to be a finished product, this book also opens a critical space from which, I hope, my readers will "emigrate" enriched and more interested in learning about others as they pursue the patterns in the infinite patchwork of strangeness that is literature.

### Imaginary Americas

When the disillusioned émigré in the fragment from Hoffman's *Lost in Translation* asks "Now where do you *emigrate to*?" she displays a lack of imagination, for the question suggests a belief that "the world is too small to sustain the fabulous America of people's dreams" (261, emphasis mine). Hoffman's narrator distances herself from this view and from the advice to give up the "fantastic hope" it implies, by emphasizing that the world is too small only "for her"—the anonymous interlocutor, the "Polish friend, who has been here several years." As in Hoffman's account, Yezierska's narrator in "How I Found America" is advised by a friend with the same background as herself to abandon hope of ever finding the "land of milk and honey," the Promised Land that has failed to live up to its promises: "But from America where can you *go*?" (*HH* 277). Yet Yezierska's narrator, like Hoffman's, insists on looking for some other "America" beyond the immediate one in which the narrator and other immigrants live.

By juxtaposing skeptical interrogators with the first-person heroine-narrators who refuse to listen to them, Hoffman and Yezierska point out the need for, the desirability of, and the timeliness of the fantastic journey to "find America." The intimacy of the autobiographical narrative voices in both texts, and the present tense of the verbs "emigrate" and "go" in the two questions, stress this journey's urgency and attractiveness even in the eyes of those skeptics who advise not to undertake it. In *Lost in Translation* and "How I Found America," immigrants—and all people in the Kristevan understanding of our shared foreignness—are divided into those who keep inventing their private Promised Lands and those who lack imagination and thus forsake the challenge to produce and sustain the imaginary Americas to which one should keep "emigrating."

I emphasize this comparative example because it shows the complexity of the writers presented in this study and elicits both imaginative and unimaginative critical readings that are possible in response to them. The collection of texts I examine in these pages both establishes and debunks an "America." The ongoing tradition in which Hoffman and Yezierska participate and from which they speak, and which I have "contained" within the physical covers of this book, inscribes no definite "America," but, rather, it suggests where and how one ought to look for it. The Promised Land sought by these writers in their texts can never be "found" either as a place and an idea lost or as a fulfillment of desire constructed on the frontier of the mind. It is "still [and always] in the making," Yezierska insists. In "Mostly about Myself," she transforms Waldo Frank's ideological cliché about the continued search for America into her own artistic creed. She realizes that it is the very impossibility of ever finding the Promised Land, the "death" of her idealistic American Dream, that inspires her writing. Therefore, she defines true New World artists through a paradox—as "vitalized by the killing things which had failed to kill them" (*ChL* 30).

Just as Yezierska derives the power to write her imaginary and elusive Promised Land from her inability to find it in the real place, Hoffman turns the unbridgeable "gap" between her Polish and American cultural identities into a vantage point, the "window through which [she] can observe the diversity of the world" (*LT* 274). Instead of settling down to disillusionment with the American Dream, which all immigrants seem to experience in the United States, these writers appropriate, reanimate, and fictionalize the concept behind the American ideology of individual freedom. They create and reinvent *their own* Americas every time they write.

Like Yezierska and Hoffman, I see other East European newcomer writers engaged in the process of charting a whole new geography of female and male experience of immigration and exile, a whole "New World" of literature, and a unique cultural dialogue that engages many different and individual Americas. The women, in particular, explore and take to its limits the concept that Bercovitch calls the American "ideology of consensus" and Kristeva the "radical strangeness" across cultures. These explorations inspire new imaginative readings of traditional immigrant journeys and gendered narratives. Elizabeth Stern's and Mary Antin's narratives of acculturation highlight the newcomer woman's desire to rewrite her gender and ethnic identities and to challenge the unimaginative roles that she has been assigned by the dominant culture, which refuses to acknowledge its own otherness in those it marginalizes. Maria Kuncewicz's Cold War exile in different "national times" and her fight for "world citizenship" as an international activist and writer suggest that the borders between cultures, languages, political systems, literatures, and narrative models are there to be crossed in constructing a "free-for-all" country of fiction. Reconsidered in the context of these women's "findings," Vladimir Nabokov's employment of the male and female immigrant narratives to construct an "American academic" novel suggests that the boundaries between marginal and canonical texts are as fluid and imaginary as the ones between the gendered spaces in the novelistic discourse.

Thanks to the inspiration for redefining the theory of immigrant literature that all these writers' texts provide, a bicultural critic such as myself can participate in the textual "contact zones" between East Europe and the United States.[2] It is this experience of propagating and contributing to the cultural work of the writers I study that allows me to confront my own critical "America" as the author of this study and as a foreign academic in the United States. In particular, it helps me to realize the theoretical and methodological concerns that unite me with and separate me from other critics. It leads me to understand more fully from whom I differ and with whom I can establish surprising "cultural bridges."

### Critic as Other

For a critic approaching any collectively rewritten "America," such as the one presented in this study, the task of reading and interpreting that America necessitates a reinvention of all the individual versions of the Promised Land it contains. Realizing this, that literary criticism is always a translation, a reinvention, or even a rewriting of literature, I want to emphasize that my own readings in this study have been consciously constructing an "America" of sorts. Although it was obviously inspired by the texts of the writers I discuss, in many ways my critical Promised Land is a work of imagination similar to their fictions. By "finding" the Americas of Antin or Nabokov, for instance, I have "found" my own; my "findings" about their visions of it construct a basis for the version I hereby offer to my readers. This critical stance is both attractive and dangerous to one confronting a tradition that she herself belongs to or feels connected with through, gender, ethnicity, nationality, race, and class. The attraction comes from the pleasure of interweaving one's critical and personal narratives with the literary ones; the danger arises from being tempted to "read too much" into the literature in order to tell and write one's personal narrative.

As a scholar of American literature from Poland, I am both an insider and a stranger. Because I live and work in this country and have been accepted as an American academic, I can enjoy the pleasures of building intercultural bridges as an outsider participant, as an agent of Hoffman's "multivalent consciousness." However, as a Pole, as a woman defined by the strange oxymoron "resident alien," I am the Kristevan foreigner as well as an actual foreigner trespassing into another culture and its language. Because I, like those I write about, am suspended between America and East Europe, I can be seen as being tempted, even beyond the usual critical desire, to inscribe a version of my own story into those I study. And I am certainly open to being read as doing so, even while quoting other critics and insisting, like any stereotypical nosy foreigner "who knows better," on my unique take on the Promised Land. Caught among my literary and critical narratives, as well as those defining me in terms of passports, visas, and my "desirability" as a foreign national, scholar, and immigrant, I may seem to be performing a tightrope walk from my own otherness to that of the writers I study, and from them into that of my new culture.

In its continuous shuttling among the external and internal narratives of my topic, my own story, academia, the myths of immigration, and so on, this study stems from and celebrates becoming a "foreigner" to oneself in writing, once one puts pen to paper. As Kristeva emphasizes, literature "is written as a defense of the dignity of the strange." Consequently, its study entails confronting the foreignness of ourselves and others—in Kristeva's terminology, the thorough realization and investigation of "our remarkable relationship with both the *other* and *strangeness within ourselves*." [3] When applied to literary criticism, this approach suggests that a study will contain its author's and its subject's strangeness and that it will both address and engage external literary and critical others. It implies another invitation to a dialogue, not only with the literary traditions that provide the "other" to the one under scrutiny, but also with scholars, no matter how different, who investigate these traditions. [4]

### More (Strange) Dialogues

What is the literary "other" of the immigrant writings? The answer is simple and also very complex, even confusing. Because, according to Oscar Handlin's much-quoted "premulticulturalist" statement, "immigrants are American history." [5] This question, then, could be rephrased to read: Who is the other in "proto-American literature"—that is, in the literature created by white European newcomers? Toni Morrison provides a current historical explanation for the genesis of early American writings: "Cultural identities are formed and informed by a nation's literature . . . what seemed to be on the 'mind' of the literature of the United States was the self-conscious but highly problematic construction of the American as the new white man." In Morrison's reasoning, the other needed for the defining construction of "whiteness" in America was "blackness," the "Africanist persona," which emerged from black slavery and "enriched the country's creative possibilities." She claims that "in that construction of blackness and enslavement could be found not only the not-free but also, with the dramatic polarity created by skin color, the projection of the not-me. The result was a playground for imagination."[6] As Morrison argues, there is no possibility of studying canonical American literature—written by European immigrants to establish both the whiteness of the writer and the reader in the new culture—without analyzing the presence of the blackness that made their construction possible.[7]

However, Morrison does not emphasize enough that the immigrants who shaped the American Dream, that "much fondled" term and ideology, were men. Nor does she pursue the knowledge that, although they were bound to follow and be read through male models, immigrant women were not included equally in the process of creating the "new white man." Morrison's focus on the larger racial dichotomy underlying American literature makes the issues of class and gender inherent in both "blackness" and "whiteness" subordinate to the politics of race. As she says about her goal, "My project is an effort to avert the critical gaze from the racial object to the racial subject; from the described and imagined to the describers and imaginers; from the serving to the served." In fulfilling this goal, however, she herself becomes a "describer" and "imaginer" of a specific "America," which lends itself to comparisons with other such constructs. For a "describer" of the immigrant tradition, then, Morrison's concept of the American as "new, white, and male," defined against "blackness," works well to explain the dominant vision of the Promised Land that was created by upper-class North European men. But it fails to explain how lower-class newcomers, and especially East European women, fit into the concept of whiteness and how their specific "America" arises as defined against blackness. In other words, how can we read these women's whiteness through gender and class? Who is their literary other?[8]

Although it will not help much to say that the women I study contributed instead to the creation of the white immigrant female writer, such a statement will at least allow for comparisons between critical approaches used to define these women's tradition and that of their logical other in this context—African American female writers. I realize that what I propose here is a thematic leap almost impossible to justify, but I reserve the freedom to take it within what Morrison calls "a sharable world and an endlessly flexible language" of readers, writers, and critics.[9] While pointing to African American women's writings, which white immigrant women engage as their other, I also hope to highlight the otherness of these white immigrant women in relation to currently more widely known literatures by the groups that are being scrutinized under the label of multiculturalism.

In his historical review of "literary ethnicity" in American literature, Thomas S. Gladsky explains the difficulties that preclude the recognition of "Polish literary selves": "Current academic interest in ethnicity . . . confines [it] once again within narrow borders. In addition, university curricula and professional conferences continue to define ethnicity with a parochial adherence to exclusivity and insiderism and insist on descent rather than the more expansive notion of literary ethnicity as a way to approach texts that may not necessarily be 'by, for, or about' a particular group."[10] Instead of studying specific groups defined strictly by descent, Gladsky proposes looking at ethnicity as a literary construct, in which Polishness, for example, can be read in texts produced by immigrant writers, their descendants, and by "Americans" (e.g., William Styron's *Sophie's Choice*). In supporting Gladsky's view that literary multiculturalism would benefit from a more creative engaging of literary traditions other than mostly "African, Asian, Hispanic, and Native American," I want to stress, too, that I agree with Toni Morrison's emphasis on interactions among cultural and racial constructs that define one another's otherness. Ideally, I would like to see articles about reading strategies that could be applied to Harriet Jacobs *and* Mary Antin, to James Baldwin *and* Jerzy Kosiński.[11] Perhaps, if the writers and cultures they belong to cannot yet talk to one another directly, we, their critics, could initiate theoretical and methodological dialogues and be the mediums ushering in their more complex intertextual encounters.

This desire to "emigrate" into other fields may result from fatigue with my own, but it also issues from my rethinking of the strategies I used while working on this study. I remember one day when, while preparing a lecture on slave narratives, I realized that what I was trying to do in recovering the Other Europe written by women was exactly what such critics as Valerie Smith, Henry Louis Gates, Jr., Hazel V. Carby, and many others had done already in recovering and putting into literary-historical frameworks texts by African Americans. I understood that, like them, I had to write a historical and theoretical narrative for my field, a narrative that necessarily arose from my own perspective and position as a contemporary critic and bicultural scholar; like theirs, my narrative was both scholarly and personal. I remember specifically looking through Smith's introduction to Harriet Jacobs's *Incidents in the Life of a Slave Girl*, which made me think whether or not she could indeed read Jacobs as "manipulating" the complex narrative models that provided the context for her work in 1861. Could that woman writer, whom Smith recovers for American literature, indeed have planned to consciously interrogate the two genres in the way Smith claims she did? Or is it only Smith's verbalization of what *she*, as a critic today, reads Jacobs as doing? [12]

This shock of recognition—definitely not the first and probably not last—that as critics we always impose our readings and discourses on the texts we study to produce the interpretations we can understand sent me into a momentary panic over my work. I felt not only that I was perhaps reading too much into the East European tradition, but that I was working very hard to recreate what other scholars had discovered a long time ago. What was, then, the exact contribution of my work to American literature? Smith's essay on Jacobs, which had inspired my question, also provided the answer. Looking at how seamlessly Smith's interpretation incorporated a reference to Elaine Showalter's formulation about the "subversive plot of empowerment beneath the more orthodox, public plot of vulnerability," I reconsidered my fears and decided that my goal would be to incorporate into my study this very instance of learning about critical dialogism from Smith. [13] As critics of literature we keep doing the "same thing," especially in recovering traditions that have been marginalized by the canon. Yet every time we realize how repetitive our task is, we also create opportunities for dialogues with one another as "authors" of literary-historical narratives describing these traditions. To borrow from Showalter, too, I believe that seeking connections with other critics and traditions, even very remote ones (e.g., immigrant and African American), provides exactly the "subversive plots" of critical "empowerment" that we need in order to study literary otherness more openly. Conversely, shying away from acknowledging shared critical strangeness across our respective fields, traditions, and even disciplines means submitting to the "public plots of vulnerability" and prevents our seeking imaginative intertextual Americas.

Of course, it is always possible to read too much, to be carried away on risky readings while trying to prove the uniqueness of our approach. [14] Yet it is even worse not to try such readings at all. For example, Audre Lorde's "Notes from a Trip to Russia," which reads often like a diary of a rather naive American tourist, succeeds in presenting an interesting view of the Soviet Union precisely by being aware and self-conscious about having to explain Russia through the familiar references to American culture. Lorde locates her essay-diary within the playfields of the imagination, even of imaginary Americas, as she does at the very beginning when she describes her first impressions of Moscow, which she keeps confusing with and defining through images of New York. She also keeps dreaming about Moscow every night for a long time after having returned to the United States. As she says about her hectic two weeks, filled with an African-Asian conference and a very structured tour through the Soviet Union, "It will take a while and a lot of dreams to metabolize all I've seen and felt."[15] Therefore, she frames her account as giving the "true" impressions of the trip as they came, without the theoretical distance of scholarly analysis, and thus opens herself up to criticism for presenting "undigested," perhaps even naive, images of the Soviet Union. As an American whose otherness in Russia is complicated further by her race, gender, and sexual orientation, Lorde deliberately creates a version of the Soviet Union that reflects her position of an observer. By emphasizing her individual limitations and biases, she creates a dialogic account in which the voices representing various aspects of her identity clearly inform what she sees and thus become part of her vision of Russia.

Because she relies on the East-West referential framework and analyzes both Russia and America through their cultural and political others, the reader of Lorde's text can forgive her for not always realizing that almost everything she saw on her trip was only what the carefully supervised tour for a foreign visitor had allowed her to see. For instance, while praising the peaceful coexistence of ethnic minorities in the countries annexed as Soviet republics, Lorde reads too much optimism, or peers too little, into the political oppression that allows such happy ethnic symbiosis. Neither does she seem to fully understand that the conflict between the workers and intellectuals, which her government-approved translator points to rather cryptically, is fueled by carefully steered communist propaganda. Despite, however, praising the collectives and communist harmony in the country rather naively at times, Lorde has moments when she thinks she is not getting the whole story: "I felt that there were many things we were not seeing. . . . I also feel a stony rigidity, a resistance to questioning that frightens me, saddens me, because it feels destructive of progress and process."[16] By warning herself against easy admiration, she also reminds her readers that her account reflects only a partial view of reality. Her story is thus also about herself as a reader of "Russia," who is located within and speaks from not only a certain construction of America but also through the constructions of the "Evil Empire" or the noncapitalist other that this America has taught her.

To understand all the subtleties of Lorde's reading of Russia, we should study not only American and the particular African American traditions from which she speaks but also Soviet and Russian cultures and their own explications of themselves and of the United States. Lorde's text cannot obviously do all this for its readers, but it can certainly inspire them to see the complexities of seemingly remote intercultural dialogues thanks to her authorial perspective. "Notes from a Trip to Russia" can also make us realize that we can reach for very different authors and nontraditional sources to acquire a more comprehensive perspective on the literary and critical relations between East and West.

As Lorde's account shows, the subject of our studies of other cultures is also inevitably ourselves; in reading others we always come back to reread our own vantage points. Similarly, while engaged in the study of East European tradition in the United States, we are not simply recovering an other that is separate from a "generic" us, but we are studying ourselves and our own strangeness. For example, while reading immigrant women's texts, we learn not only about how these women "found" their alternative Americas but also about how their texts reproduce and revise the dominant cultural narratives about the America they "find" in the real place. And whether their texts explicitly acknowledge it or not, the America of the "real place," like all its readers, is the complex stranger in itself; it is permeated by Morrison's "blackness" and "whiteness," it is complicated by gender relations and class struggles, and it is full of translinguistic interpretations and multicultural visions. That is why reading these women should inspire our analyses of their others—e.g., African American women, WASP men, East European dissidents—and should teach us that there is no limit to critical dialogues about ourselves.

### East and West the Morning After

In her 1993 study of the "demilitarization" in the post–Cold War world, Cynthia Enloe emphasizes the need to interrogate gender dynamics before and during the revolutions in East Europe in order to understand the cultural changes happening in that region right now. She argues that the Cold War should be understood "as involving not simply a contest between two superpowers . . . but also a series of contests within each of those societies over the definitions of masculinity and femininity that would sustain or dilute that rivalry."[17] She claims further that gender tensions not only reflect a binary opposition between men's and women's situations but also determine the concepts of women's activism in the West and in East Europe. At one point she refers in particular to the antithetical images of the "East European woman" and the "western feminist" that have been used extensively by the media in both cultures to present negative views of their political other:

> The 1989 revolutions in Eastern Europe brought about the dismantling of the Warsaw Pact and a surge of demilitarization. But although Polish, Czech, Hungarian, East German, and Romanian women played central roles in the grass-roots organizing that made the eventual upheavals possible, this demilitarization was not guided by feminist insights into the causes of militarization. In a mirror image of Western anti-Communist regimes' needing the symbol of the overworked, "unfeminine" Soviet or Polish woman to justify their Cold War policies, the Communist regimes had depended on feminism's being so tainted by its association with Western bourgeois individualism that no woman in their own nations would be inspired by feminist analyses or aspirations. Without the image of the self-absorbed, materialistic, man-hating Western feminist to combat, the restlessness of women in Eastern Europe might have translated into gender-conscious political action much earlier. Olga Havel might have become famous in her own right rather than as an imprisoned playwright's loyal wife.[18]

Although I find Enloe's argument fascinating, her approach in this fragment is a bit oversimplified. Can we truly believe that it was mainly a fear of the "man-hating Western feminist" that caused the East Europeans to distrust and fear the women's movements in capitalist countries? Did the women in Poland hate that image as much as those in Hungary? What about those who bought the glamour of their western counterparts but rejected their liberation? In trying to show the tensions between the superpowers and their impact on gender politics, Enloe risks lumping very diverse cultures under the safe umbrella of a generalization.

A reason for this oversimplification can be seen, trivially but significantly, on the cover of Enloe's book, which reproduces a photograph showing a group of Russian women sitting on the railway tracks in Moldavia and protesting ethnic Romanians' separatist tendencies. There is nothing wrong with the photograph itself, but its placement on the book's cover seems to reinforce stereotypical views of women in the communist East. The photograph shows older, worn out, typical "overworked, 'unfeminine'" females—the specimens you would see in National Geographic programs—who look exactly like the image that Enloe describes as having been used to justify the Cold War policies in the West. The placement of this picture on the book's cover, under a title that specifies Enloe's focus on "sexual politics," reinforces the stereotype of the female from a communist country because it evokes clichés about her rather than points to the complexity of Enloe's argument. In other words, the book is stamped with an image the western reader expects and will be attracted by, as it both reconfirms that "Other Woman's" exotic difference and reassures females in the West that they still have her as their antithesis.[19]

However, what happens between the book's cover and Enloe's argument is also indicative of the problem we now face as readers and writers of the new East Europe and of the new post–Cold War world. Before we can find a new vocabulary to talk about the cultures of all the countries that used to comprise the Soviet bloc, we have to deal with the old generalizations. We have to try to talk about new things while we are still stuck in an outdated language and its attendant stereotypes. In having to rely on the images she hopes to debunk, Enloe does not commit any serious transgression; instead, she simply reflects the complexity of this transitional period in contemporary history.

At a time when some critics talk about the emergence of the "posttotalitarian mind," one that puts an end to thinking in terms of cultural oppositions and contrasts, it is very hard to devise an alternative way of representing new cultural relations.[20] For example, how are we to change our cultural codes to accommodate the surprising number of "new" nations issuing from the former Soviet bloc and asking for separate recognition? In a sense, the very disappearance of the political conglomerate, which not so long ago could be conveniently used to generalize about these nations, genders, and individuals lumped under it, now poses serious problems and challenges. The number of strangers has multiplied suddenly, and the need for cultural translators and mediators has increased.

As Stanisław Barańczak notes, culture—art, texts, film—is the best go-between in the modern world. It is better than political speeches and the scientific analyses of experts. He claims optimistically that "continental drift" can be stopped, since the "widening gulf between collective mentalities has more than once been crossed in the past and it still can be bridged by the kind of insight that culture provides." He urges America to "abandon the idea of cultural self-sufficiency and to reach deeper into other nations' minds."[21] Like Barańczak, Jeffrey Goldfarb notes in his 1982 comparative study on cultural freedom in Poland and the United States: "By situating ourselves between East and West, we can appreciate the invisible nature of constraint in the West, as well as less than apparent supports of cultural freedom in socialist societies."[22] Yet according to both these critics, the particular encounter between East and West, in the past and the present, can be perceived as America-centered. Reaching out to embrace the Other Europe, old and new, can be read as embracing a newly reconstructed America, one coming to terms with its own ethnic origins, cultural freedom, and ideological ambiguities.

In contrast to Barańczak's and Goldfarb's somewhat optimistic predictions, the writings by women I have discussed in this study, especially Kristeva's *Strangers to Ourselves* and Hoffman's *Lost in Translation*, indicate that there is no true possibility for completely bridging the gulf of otherness between cultures and individuals. We will always remain foreigners to one another, just as we will always be strangers to ourselves. But that is precisely where we can communicate, where we can work out new idioms for a dialogue, for we will always have at least our otherness in common. The task for literary and cultural critics today is not to keep the West and the East apart, perched on the extremes of incomprehension, but to explore the conflicts and misunderstandings between them, just as we explore these between the male and the female versions of the larger discourse of literary strangeness. In particular, as Enloe's book indicates, there is an especially urgent need to follow the story about women positioned between East Europe and the United States, the writers whom we can bring back from oblivion, reread, retranslate, and reinterpret as contributors to the making of our cultures. This study has been written with the hope that the texts it describes will be rescued from exile, recovered in translation where necessary, and granted a chance to express the Americas they "found" in their own otherness.

Concluding a critical work with an autobiographical mission statement, more or less pertinent to the topic, should not be seen as trite and egotistical. After all, even in theory, we come to terms with our own strangeness. In the remarks closing her study about the feminist critique of individualism, Elizabeth Fox-Genovese writes: "These fragments of autobiography carry no particular lesson, unless it be that much of our sense of richness and joy of life comes from our appreciation of the differences between men and women, our appreciation of each other."[23] In thus revealing herself to her readers, Fox-Genovese appeals to our understanding of her otherness as the one who is caught in the larger theoretical and scholarly discourses but who also struggles to remain her own individual stranger. That is where every story, literary or critical, begins, and that is where it should also end: with the particular lesson of the stranger who came upon a particular idea and felt a desire to share it with others.

What I desire to share with my readers through this study is a hope that in our future readings of East European literature in the United States we will acknowledge the full extent of its otherness, that we will not underestimate its individual makers because, as Poles, Czechs, Hungarians, or Slovaks, they are no longer attached to the monolithically constructed other, the "Evil Empire" of communism. Each and every one of them, no matter what nationality, gender, and religious denomination, should be a participant in the "free-for-all" country of fiction. Thus to the possibility of imaginative and risky dialogue among strangers I add my voice and my message suspended between Poland and the United States, my "autobiography" and "fiction," my critical "America."

# NOTES

## Preface

1. Kristeva, *Nations without Nationalism*, 16.
2. Kuncewicz, *Natura*, 289, translation mine.

## Introduction

1. Antin, *They Who Knock*, 98.
2. Gilman, *The Living of Charlotte Perkins Gilman*, 316, 324.
3. James, "Boston," *The American Scene*, 232.
4. Antin, introduction to *The Promised Land*, xix, emphasis mine.
5. Hoffman, *Lost in Translation*, 280.

## Chapter 1

1. Obviously, Yezierska had been "heard" when she became a best-selling writer in the 1920s, but as her texts, their reviews, and the decline of her career suggest, she was never fully "understood." I discuss her ambivalent success as an author in Chapter 4.

2. My underlying theoretical approach in this study is feminist. Rather than providing a bibliography of all the critics and titles that went into its formation, I want to mention names of some of the feminist scholars to whom I am most indebted: Elaine Showalter, Carolyn G. Heilbrun, Nancy Armstrong, Nina Baym, Jane P. Tompkins, Rachel Blau DuPlessis, Annette Kolodny, Susan Rubin Suleiman, Teresa de Lauretis, Susan Gubar, Sandra M. Gilbert, Julia Kristeva, Gayatri Chakravorty Spivak, and Mary V. Dearborn.

3. In the terminology of this study, the juxtaposition of East versus West means East Europe, in particular Poland and Russia, versus western capitalist countries, especially the United States. The concept of the Other Europe comes from the name of Philip Roth's Penguin series, Writers from the Other Europe. Roth introduces each of the volumes, devoted to works by such writers as Milan Kundera, Tadeusz Konwicki, Bohumil Hrabal, Bruno Schulz, and others, in this way: "The purpose of this paperback series is to bring together outstanding and influential works of fiction by Eastern European writers. In many instances they will be writers who, though recognized as powerful forces in their own cultures, are virtually unknown in the West. It is hoped that by reprinting selected Eastern European writers in this format and with introductions that place each work in its literary and historical context, the literature that has evolved in 'the other Europe,' particularly during the postwar decades, will be made more accessible to a new readership." Roth, ed., *The Polish Complex*, by Tadeusz Konwicki, v.

4. See Adamic, *A Nation of Nations*, 287–304, for an interesting speculation on Jan z Kolna's (John of Kolno's) pre-Columbian voyage to America and for a historical perspective on early nativism and xenophobia in Jamestown, where Poles, Germans, and Armenians were considered "inferior foreigners" who had no political rights: "They

were in the community, working for it, helping it to survive, fighting the hostile Indians, but they were not considered of it. . . . They were in effect little better than serfs" (287). See also Grzeloński, *Ameryka w pamiętnikach Polaków*, 6–7, who also mentions the first Poles in Jamestown. The anthology provides a rich cross-section of memoirs, letters, and diaries of Polish immigrants and visitors between the eighteenth and the early twentieth centuries. American perspectives on "Polish selves" and ethnicity in history and literature of the nineteenth and twentieth centuries can be found in Gladsky's *Princes, Peasants*.

5. Bakhtin, *The Dialogic Imagination*, 257–92. Clark and Holquist, *Mikhail Bakhtin*, 276.

6. Kristeva, *The Kristeva Reader*, 58–59. See also Kristeva, *Desire in Language*. In his discussion of the appropriation of the Bakhtinian model to literary theory, Jay Clayton, *The Pleasures*, emphasizes how Kristeva "saw in Bakhtin a chance to open linguistics to society" by seeing the sign as dialogic and intertextual (37–38).

7. Morson, introduction to "Russian Cluster," 228–29.

8. Barańczak, *Breathing under Water*, 15.

9. Kundera, *The Art of the Novel*, 27.

10. I will pursue this theme of shared individual otherness underlying cultural contacts on personal and national levels in my discussion of Julia Kristeva's *Strangers to Ourselves* in Chapter 6.

11. Clayton, *The Pleasures*, viii.

12. Clifford, *The Predicament of Culture*, 1–7.

13. For a very interesting discussion of the center-margin, the host culture–newcomer interplay, see Minh-ha, *Woman, Native, Other*.

14. In his introduction to *Princes, Peasants, and Other Polish Selves*, Gladsky presents an interesting overview of the treatment and construction of various images of Poles and Poland in American culture—in particular, "America's tendency to strip ethnicity to the bone and to interpret the Polish self to suit the historical temper, national preoccupations, and literary movements, and changing attitudes toward minorities"—as well as the modern academe's often reductive and limited approaches to ethnicity (4, 288). On the other hand, Clayton sees the "tendency of literary theorists to focus only on the dyad of domination/resistance" as limiting, since "cultural norms exclude and contain . . . but they also *empower*" (24).

15. Examples of anthologies presenting exclusively male voices are Gomori and Newman, eds., *New Writing of Eastern Europe*, and Mayewski, ed., *The Broken Mirror*. Even the selections of writings from *Kultura* perpetuate the image of the East European émigré as male. Kostrzewa, ed., *Between East and West*, does not feature any women's texts, whereas Tyrmand, ed., *Explorations in Freedom*, includes only one woman writer. In 1981 Twayne's World Author Series included only one female among writers from Poland and Russia, and none among its Hungarian and Romanian writers. Levine, *Contemporary Polish Poetry 1925–1975*, includes only a token woman, Wislawa Szymborska. Davie, *Slavic Excursions*, concentrates solely on male authors of both traditions to present the "literature of *witness*" (12). For more recent examples promoting Polish literature as primarily male, see also Carpenter, *Monumenta Polonica*, and Kott, ed., *Four Decades of the Polish Essay*.

A fairer look at Polish and East European literature, in which male and female voices engage in a dialogue, can be found in Kuncewicz, ed., *The Modern Polish Mind*, Wisniewska, ed., *Polish Writing Today*, and Holton and Vangelisti, eds., *The New Polish Poetry*. See also Bassnett and Kuhiwczak, trans. and eds., *Ariadne's Thread*, Miłosz, ed., *Postwar Polish Poetry*, Weissbort, ed., *The Poetry of Survival*, and Barańczak and Cavanagh, eds. and trans., *Spoiling Cannibals' Fun*.

16. Philip Roth explained some of the reasons why he excluded women writers from his series in a brief note of 22 May 1991 that he sent me in answer to my inquiry: "I chose from the books already translated into English those that I thought were the strongest. I didn't care if they were by men, women, transvestites, or eunechs [*sic*]. I am a liberal spirit. The series is now kaput. For obvious reasons." Any Slavic scholar knows that there were many strong texts by women at the time when Writers from the Other Europe was put together. I am still puzzled by the "obvious reasons" why the series is now "kaput." Does Roth mean that the end of communism in East Europe removed the need to study the literature of its "satellites"? Or does "kaput" imply that the series ended when all the good writers (male) had been covered? The term "Other Europe" is very ironic in that it suggests that the male authors included in the prestigous series are the others, with women being the assumed dominant.

17. I develop this theme further in subsequent chapters.

18. The reason for such portrayals of women may be due to the fact that considerably fewer women than men wrote under communism. Some critics blame harsh every-dayness under the regime and the party's incorporation of "socialist feminism" for silencing women's literary voices in East Europe (see also Enloe, *The Morning After*). Others, such as Nanette Funk, claim that there is no common discourse between the women of East Europe and those of the West because "women's issues in the former Communist countries usually involved topics with which I had not had to deal as a Western feminist" (Funk, "The Fate of Feminism in Eastern Europe," B1). Interest-ingly, Funk's title promises to supply us with answers to the questions concerning the future of East European feminism, whereas the content of her article suggests that such movement has yet to emerge in that part of the world. Note also interesting re-sponses by Polish feminists: a review of the "woman's question" in postwar Poland in Barbara Limanowska, "Dlaczego w Polsce nie ma feminizmu," Magdalena Środa, "Feministki, kobiety, wiedźmy," and Grażyna Borkowska, "Dlaczego skrywamy prag-nienie wolności? Kobiecym Piórem," as well as Halina Filipowicz, "Przeciw 'literaturze kobiecej.'"

19. Such readings of male newcomer experiences as representing a generic immi-grant story go against the data, which prove that from the year 1930 on more immigrant women than men entered the United States. See Weinberg, "The Treatment of Women in Immigration History," 3–5.

20. The conference was held at St. Mary's College in Orchard Lake, Michigan, on 1–3 Oct. 1993. I am aware that one-gender models of immigrant literatures are now being successfully challenged by a variety of feminist, New Historicist, and interdis-ciplinary criticism, which I will discuss later. However, the still-prevalent reductive approaches to East European writings are especially harmful in conference programs (about which there have been formal complaints by Slavic scholars to the Modern Language Association) that aspire to be on the cutting edge of their fields. The terms "Slavic literatures" and "East European studies" have too often translated into studies on exclusively Russian or Soviet cultures—which demonstrates the paradoxical Ameri-can tendency to support the "colonization" of "minor" East-European literatures by

Big Brother. It is apparently as easy to lump the smaller, "satellite" countries in the former Soviet bloc together under a comfortable umbrella of political and cultural generalizations about the Soviet Union as it is to construct a model of East European literature on the basis of writings by men.

21. Some scholars, such as Halina Filipowicz (University of Wisconsin–Madison) and Jadwiga Maurer (University of Kansas), are promoting feminist readings of Polish literature in the United States, but we do not have more such studies coming directly from Poland, where, after the "privileges" instituted by the communists have been taken away from them, the women's movement seems to be budding into existence despite the insitutionalized sexism promoted by the state and the Catholic church. Interestingly, the studies about Poland and the role of the church during and after communism published in English are oblivious to the numbers of women affected by the "Polish paradoxes." See, for example, Monticone, *The Catholic Church in Communist Poland*, Beeson, *Discretion and Valour*, Gomolka and Polonsky, eds., *Polish Paradoxes*, Wedel, ed., *The Unplanned Society* (although Teresa Holowka's "What Goes On in Catechism Class," 193–204, contains an interesting woman's approach to teaching religion and morals to contemporary Polish youth). See also Moody and Boyes, *The Priest and the Policeman*, which is an interesting look at religion and politics in Poland as exclusively male territories, and Gladsky, *Princes, Peasants*.

22. For an example of the exclusively male version of postcommunist East Europe, see "'The Post-Communist Nightmare': An Exchange," in which Joseph Brodsky and Vaclav Havel—the dissident "Fathers"—ponder the fate of postcommunist East Europe and its relations with American culture. Even in his impressive study *Princes, Peasants, and Other Polish Selves*, Gladsky concentrates chiefly on the male models of "ethnic Polish selves" in American literature, claiming that "even to this date, no Yezierskas, Kingstons, Angelous, or Morrisons have emerged to capture the unique story of the Slavic woman" (6). See also Adamic, *A Nation of Nations*.

It is also important to note the influence of such a perspective on teaching literature. In "English after the USSR," Ohmann claims that "the end of the Cold War itself changes everything in this country" (44) because "the Cold War has confined our thinking—our sense of the culture we wish to pass on and criticize, our pedagogies and our hopes for our students, our sense of the possibilities of English—within limits so natural, so tacit, so invisible, that it will take us years to figure out what they were and to get new bearings" (46). Like me, Ohmann also proposes inventing a "new narrative" to deal with new cultural readings, so that "we and our students are . . . agents rather than the dupes in the process." (For a perspective on teaching as an "alien teacher" or the "travelling icon of culture," see also Indira Karamcheti, "Caliban in the Classroom.")

23. Neidle, *America's Immigrant Women*, 251 (emphasis mine).

24. Gardiner, "On Female Identity and Writing by Women," 185. See also Hite, *The Other Side of the Story*, especially 11–14, for an interesting polemic directed at the autobiographical feminist narrative model.

25. Seller, ed., *Immigrant Women*, 9–11.

26. This approach to immigrant writing as a source of documentary material and a subject of sociological research seems both to debunk and continue the "possessive" tradition of the 1930s and 1940s that saw immigrants as "our minorities," "problems," and "Americans in the making." See Brown and Roucek, eds., *Our Racial and*

*National Minorities*, and Seabrook, *These Foreigners*. For a retrospective look at the early twentieth-century nativism that provoked such approaches, see Higham, *Strangers in the Land*.

27. Charlotte Perkins Gilman and other ideologues of the movement feared the foreign influences of the immigrant women—in particular, their different ideologies of sexual conduct. See Gilman, *The Living of Charlotte Perkins Gilman*.

28. See Kraditor, *The Ideas of the Woman Suffrage Movement*, especially the chapter "The 'New Immigration' and Labor," 123–62. In "A Remembrance," the preface to Emma Goldman's *Living My Life*, Meridel Le Sueur comments on the racism and intolerance of the early white, upper-middle-class feminist movement in comparison with which Goldman struck a "strange cultural and ethnic figure." Le Sueur also emphasizes how shocking the famous anarchist's unrepressed sexuality was to her generation of radical American feminists, who "felt sex was a humiliating force, symbolic of their repression—of marriage and child bearing" and who, in their "neurotic fanaticism," believed that "a woman had only two choices: living her own life with a career and a calling as a radical or marriage with sex and children" (xiv–xv).

29. Spivak, *In Other Worlds*, 104–7. See also Tompkins, *Sensational Designs*, for a discussion of the canonical works as created (xii) and for an approach to the act of reading as involving political circumstances—"preferences, interests, tastes, and beliefs that are not universal but part of the particular reader's situation" (9). The approaches of Spivak and Tompkins are also similar to the theories of Fredric Jameson, whose *The Political Unconscious* argues the "priority of the political interpretation of literary texts" (17, see also 17–102).

30. In this respect, I am closer to Tompkins's suggestion that, because there is no escape from making value judgments and political choices, we should read and study noncanonical literature and thus keep revising the canon by empowering the "popular" and the "sentimental." I also think we need an even more marginal and open approach than the one Tompkins elicits in her study of sentimental fiction, because immigrant and ethnic "sentiments" are constructed as further removed from the consensus than, for example, *Uncle Tom's Cabin*, which has become a bit "canonized" recently (and so has *Sensational Designs* to a certain extent).

31. See Dearborn, *Pocahontas's Daughters*, Barańczak, *Breathing under Water*, Goldfarb, *Beyond Glasnost*, *On Cultural Freedom*, and *The Persistence of Freedom*, and Steinfels, "The Fall of the Ironic Curtain."

32. It is interesting to read how this approach developed from the works of Oscar Handlin (*The Uprooted*, *Children of the Uprooted*, *Immigration as a Factor in American History*, and *Race and Nationality in American Life*) to the recent studies on ethnicity and multiplicity by Werner Sollors (*Beyond Ethnicity*, and Sollors, ed., *The Invention of Ethnicity*).

33. In his play Zangwill introduces his famous rhetoric of the American "crucible," in which all the minorities are to melt together and create a unified ideal nation; see Zangwill, *The Melting-Pot*. It is intriguing to see how, in a modernized version, this approach surfaces in contemporary cultural and literary criticism. For example, although stressing the "invented" character of ethnicity, Sollors insists on the centralized model of America the multicultural. For Bercovitch, "The Rites of Assent," the emphasis on the issues of unity in diversity, "consensus within dissensus" and "rites of assent," arises from the myth of an American ideology of consensus—"a hundred sects and

factions . . . celebrating the same mission" (6). In her introduction to *Ideology and Classic American Literature*, Jehlen stresses that, even in defying the ideology of America, critics illuminate the "ideological dimension" of literature and of their own criticism (14–15). There may be no escape from the magnetic power of the dominant center, it is true, but an emphasis on the revisionary efforts of the marginal groups can make this model more interesting.

34. See also Brettell and deBerjeois, "Anthropology and the Study of Immigrant Women," which discusses four factors contributing to the immigrant woman's oppression in the host culture: ethnicity, gender, class, and a diminished sense of self-worth resulting from the internalization of these factors.

35. Smith, *Virgin Land*, Kolodny, *The Lay of the Land* and *The Land Before Her*.

36. See also Lewis, *The American Adam*, Marx, *The Machine in the Garden*, Slotkin, *Regeneration through Violence* and *The Fatal Environment*.

37. See also Girgus, *Desire and the Political Unconscious*, 3, and Gladsky, *Princes, Peasants*, 30.

38. For an interesting discussion of foreign women's sexuality, see Weatherford, *Foreign and Female*.

39. I am aware that my point about foreign females being the sexual other to American women parallels the well-known argument about black female slaves performing this function on Southern plantations (Cornel West sees African-American women being still the other to white women in American culture, *Race Matters*, 83–91).

40. These situations often produce conflicts between what the woman imagines him to be and what the man—even a mature mentor—really is and desires. I discuss this theme at length in the chapter on Yezierska.

41. In *The Refugee Intellectual* Donald Peterson Kent comments on the ability of immigrant women to adopt "'the American look' in dress much more rapidly than . . . the men" (211). He supports the one-gender model, nevertheless, in presenting non-gender-specific data and through dismissing the gender factor in assimilation—"There is too little difference between the adjustments made by the two sexes"—on the basis of "'impressions' rather than statistically derived conclusions" (211).

42. I make this stance general enough to include other ethnic groups of immigrant women, but I realize that there are always more or less subtle differences between how that works for an individual group and for an individual woman, such as between Gentile and Jewish female immigrants.

43. See Dearborn, *Pocahontas's Daughters*, 33–38.

44. Gubar, "'The Blank Page' and the Issues of Female Creativity," 73–89; Heilbrun, *Writing a Woman's Life*, 18–22. See also Gardiner, "On Female Identity," 177–91.

45. Izabela Filipiak's first book, a collection of short stories, *Śmierć i Spirala* (Death and the Spiral), is an interesting debut of a representative of the youngest generation of Polish women writers. Filipiak immigrated to the United States in 1986 and now lives in New York City, where she continues writing in Polish and English and pursues a career as a visual artist. I hope that her writings, which engage such interesting and controversial themes as breaking down national mythology, intertextuality between Poland and the West, homelessness, prostitution, and female sexuality and homoeroticism, will soon become available in English translation.

46. The relationship between the "law of the fathers" and women's fight for freedom is presented very interestingly in Girgus, *Desire and the Political Unconscious*.

47. Such a collective, desexualized body is especially visible in the photographs depicting Ellis Island, where the crowd seems to be a live, human river, a multilimbed organism. For example, see Weatherford, *Foreign and Female*, 204–5. See also Seabrook, *These Foreigners*, who echoes Antin in claiming that Polish immigrant heroes are "part of the bone, fiber, sinew, and soul of America" (250). A cinematic version of this approach, with a twist on the male versus the female rites of passage, can also be seen in Charlie Chaplin's classic, *The Immigrant* (1917).

48. For a classic discussion of the particular male and female "spaces" in the narrative structure, which "maps the sexual difference," see de Lauretis, *Alice Doesn't*, 118–21.

49. I will discuss the typical male immigrant narrative in greater detail later on. Examples of the male story of acculturation, often modeled after Andrew Carnegie's and Edward Bok's texts, include Abraham Cahan, *The Rise of David Levinsky*, Michael Gold, *Jews without Money*, Ole Edvart Rölvaag's *Peder Victorious*, M. E. Ravage, *An American in the Making: The Life Story of an Immigrant*, and many others. Slightly nontypical texts are Elizabeth Stern's *This Ecstasy* (a male story written by a woman) and Henry Roth's *Call It Sleep*. See also Gladsky, *Princes, Peasants*, especially 115.

50. Interestingly, in some of Yezierska's texts, in particular in the short story "A Bed for the Night," there are subtle hints at female homoeroticism, as her heroines come to the realization of the impossibility of a fulfilling sexual union with the males of either world.

51. See Gladsky, *Princes, Peasants*, 141, for a look at Kosiński's "politically inspired" novels and his rejection by Polonia, and 163–76 for "The Non-Ethnic Ethnic Novels of Jerzy Kosinski." I am aware that my approach to male émigré writings can be seen as controversial and may require more thorough support (which could be given adequately only in a separate study). However, I let it stand because I want to emphasize that even such assimilated authors as Nabokov and Kosiński were still immigrants and thus can be seen as involved in the dynamics between the gendered East European narratives. I discuss Nabokov's ironic approach to commercialized ethnicity in Chapter 7.

52. Obviously, I am aware that there are and always will be differences between male and female texts, plots, characters, and so forth. However, we can still talk about shared elements between the two stories without collapsing the boundaries separating them.

## Chapter 2

1. Handlin, *The Uprooted*, 3. I will refer to more recent criticism on ethnicity in the course of this chapter. See also Boelhower, *Through a Glass Darkly*, for a discussion of how neither "the concept of 'American' nor that of 'ethnic' is separately definable, for neither is an immediately given or individual entity in itself" (20). Boelhower presents an interesting semiotic reading of Henry James's *The American Scene* that actually glorifies James as a pursuer of the "ethnic question" rather than a xenophobe whom the superficial reading of this text yields: "There is almost no way to identify any single ethnic factor. . . . James . . . offers a corrective working hypothesis that dwells on the *production* of ethnic semiotic activity, on that unchartable non-space where a sign becomes ethnic" (31). On the other hand, in *The Rise*, Novak writes about the pressure the immigrants felt to erase their "ethnic signs," to become indistinguishable "Americans": "It is so much easier in America to forget one's ethnic past, to climb upwards into an

elite culture, to become a 'new man' without connection to the past. Who wants to become known as a 'Jewish' writer, a 'Catholic' writer, a 'Slovak' writer? Lurking in such epithets is a concession of failed generality" (xxv).

2. Sollors, *Beyond Ethnicity*, 14–15. Subsequent quotations from this work are cited in the text, abbreviated *BE*.

3. Sollors, ed., *The Invention of Ethnicity*, xiii–xiv.

4. Sollors, foreword to *Through a Glass Darkly* by Boelhower, 1–4.

5. Sollors, ed., *The Invention of Ethnicity*, ix–xx, xvi.

6. I do not think it is necessary to argue that all writing is, to a greater or lesser degree, autobiographical in its recording of the human experience. We can read Antin's text as a novel because she admits to having written fiction in her introduction and because it contains all the subgenres mentioned within hyphens. Being an immigrant and a woman, Antin was automatically classified as an author of a "documentary" and a memoir—the stuff all newcomer and female novels are supposedly based on. My approach is only one among many, and my insistence on making gender inseparable from authorship may seem far-fetched to some readers. However, as I argue throughout this study, gender, as much as ethnicity and class, is another important factor influencing the contexts in which texts get written and read.

7. Mary V. Dearborn develops this idea in *Pocahontas's Daughters*. She describes this mediation as a kind of "midwifery" necessary for the birth of an ethnic woman's text. Subsequent quotations from this work are cited in the text, abbreviated *PD*.

8. In *To Seek America*, Seller paints a vivid picture of what Americanization meant to the dominant culture during World War I: "The tactics of the Americanization crusaders were not subtle. The governor of Iowa tried to ban the use of languages other than English in all public conversations and over the telephone. Industries refused promotions, or even employment, to aliens who had not begun citizenship applications. . . . The state of California sent 'foreign language speakers' among immigrant communities to convince them to buy Liberty Bonds and give to the Red Cross because 'the time had come for every foreign-born to make his decision.' The most important duty of these state agents was to avert labor unrest and strikes, and to convince immigrant workers to stay patriotically on the job or 'they themselves would suffer in the end'" (213). See also Novak, *The Rise*, for a discussion of what "true Americanness" required from the "unmeltable ethnics": "The Poles, Italians, Greeks, and Slavs whose acronym Msgr. Geno Baroni has made to stand for all the non-English-speaking ethnic groups—pride themselves on 'fighting for America.' . . . [But] when the Poles were only four percent of the population (in 1917–19) they accounted for twelve percent of the nation's casualties in World War I. 'The Fighting Irish' won their epithet by dying in droves in the Civil War. There is, then, a blood test. 'Die for us and we'll give you a chance'" (xxxiii–xxxiv, emphasis mine).

9. In her introduction to *Immigrant Women* Seller writes: "Much of the voluminous literature on immigration has been male centered, taking men's experience as the norm and assuming that women's experience was either identical to men's or not important enough to warrant separate and serious attention" (5). A perfect example of an unambivalent male immigrant author was recognized in Ole Edvart Rölvaag, a Norwegian male writer, about whom Lincoln Colcord wrote: "In Rölvaag we have a European author *of our own*—one who writes in America, about America, whose only

aim is to tell of the contributions of his people to American life." Quoted in Handlin, *Immigration as a Factor*, 127.

10. Seller, ed., *Immigrant Women*, 6–7.

11. Yezierska, *How I Found America*, 120–21.

12. Weatherford, *Foreign and Female*, 56–57, 4. The term "oversexed" is self-consciously in quotation marks as referring to Charlotte Perkins Gilman's theories. See also Thomas, *The Unadjusted Girl*.

13. See also Theweleit, *Male Fantasies*, 2:63–90, for an interesting perspective on female sexuality as a threat to the male. Theweleit is especially concerned with showing how proletarian women and communist women came to be associated with death and castration.

14. Even the feminist approach to the Garden of Eden myth presented by Kolodny in *The Lay of the Land* and *The Land Before Her* does not acknowledge the immigrant women's participation in the making of America.

15. I develop this intriguing theme of feminine traits in male immigrant stories in Chapter 7, where I discuss Vladimir Nabokov. A separate study on this subject would include many texts, from Zangwill's, through Henry Roth's *Call It Sleep,* and even Cahan's *The Rise of David Levinsky* (where the superficial epitome of a male rags-to-riches tale disguises a subtext of sexual oppression), to Jerzy Kosiński's *Cockpit, Steps,* and *Being There,* and many others.

16. Zangwill, *The Melting-Pot*, 184, 96.

17. We can see this trait, too, in some accounts of "how pioneer women saw the beauty and bleakness of the frontier wilderness"—e.g., in Martha Gay Masterson's memoir of her emigration from Missouri to Oregon, *One Woman's West.*

18. I will discuss this theme in more detail in Chapter 4 in the close readings of Anzia Yezierska.

19. See *Women and Economics*, 147, 333, and also *The Living of Charlotte Perkins Gilman*, 108–9, for some examples of Gilman's notions concerning the hierarchy of ethnic groups and class.

20. In the years of the "new racism" and "the red scare," newcomers were deported and imprisoned for their political views. For example, Emma Goldman was deported from the United States in 1919 for her revolutionary views. For an interesting overview of this period in American history, see Seller, *To Seek America.*

21. Mary Antin, *The Promised Land*, 34. Subsequent quotations from this work are cited in the text, abbreviated *PL.*

22. See also Yezierska, *Red Ribbon on a White Horse,* in which she describes a confrontation between the "immigrants" and a Miss Howard, whose "people have been here three hundred years" and who claims: "The trouble with you foreigners, you've been given privileges you haven't earned" (184).

23. Stern, *My Mother and I,* 147. See the review "America's Possibilities for the Immigrant," *Nation,* 30 Aug. 1917, 105: "Since we are likely to have many more of those piquant narratives from our new Americans, it is perhaps worth suggesting to them that their contributions to the literature of the happy immigrant will probably gain in thoughtfulness and mellowness if they postpone the announcement of their accomplishment till their first natural elation wears off."

24. Stern's heroine, who was brought to America as an infant, cannot identify with

other immigrants and considers herself completely American. Yet as an ethnic female and a Jew, she is still constructed as an alien, and her story is relegated to the category of traditional newcomer paeans. Stern's text contains another lesson about the dominant culture assigning ethnicity to its newcomers, and about the "location" of the reader's "gaze" in predetermining the interpretation. I examine this theme in depth in Chapter 3.

25. My reasons for reading *The Promised Land* as a novel join other critical efforts to reread immigrant texts beyond the strict genre labels pasted onto them by decades of superficial readings. See also Umansky's introduction to Stern's *I Am a Woman—and a Jew* and her reasoning for approaching this work as a novel, in spite of its classification as an autobiography (vii–ix).

26. I realize that my claims about Antin's subtext may arise more from my own interpretive "obsession" than from this writer's subjectivity. However, even though Antin may not have consciously planned for a subtext to be there, I still reserve the right to look for one as a critic of her text.

27. The exact year of Antin's coming to this country is unclear. *The National Cyclopedia of American Biography* specifies the year as 1894, while Schwartz, "Mary Antin," in *American Women Writers*, refers only to the father's coming in 1891.

28. Schwartz, "Mary Antin," 61–62.

29. Zangwill, introduction to *From Polotzk to Boston*, 8.

30. Lazarus, "From Plotzk [Polotzk] to Boston," 317–18.

31. "The Immigrant," *New York Times*, 14 Apr. 1912, 228.

32. "The Promised Land," *The Independent*, 22 Aug. 1912, 445, emphasis mine. I especially like the irony we read now in the comment on Washington "winning the land for all exiles."

33. Woodbridge, "The Promised Land," 175, 176.

34. Quoted in "Miss Mary Antin Wrote Noted Book," *New York Times*, 18 May 1949, L27, emphasis mine.

35. Graff formulates the concept of readers "getting a handle on texts" through what he calls the "unofficial interpretive culture." In my emphasis on the readings and misreadings of Antin by reviewers and critics I cannot agree more with this critic's statement: "Most texts now come to us first in an unauthorized secondary version created by the way they are packaged, advertised, and talked about. The secondary text often so delimits the agendas of reading that it becomes hard finally to distinguish it from the primary text—just as, on another level, it becomes hard to distinguish between immediate experience and textualized experience." See Graff, "Narrative and the Unofficial Interpretive Culture," 5.

36. Woodbridge, "The Promised Land," 175–76.

37. See the obituary article "Miss Mary Antin Wrote Noted Book," *New York Times*, 18 May 1949, L27. For another look at Antin's "egotism," see also "America's Possibilities for the Immigrant," *Nation*, 30 Aug. 1917, 105.

38. Neidle, *America's Immigrant Women*, 256.

39. Bergland, "Ideology, Ethnicity, and the Gendered Subject," 109.

40. See Walden, ed., "Twentieth-Century American-Jewish Fiction Writers." Among Mary Antin's stories are "The Lie," "The Soundless Trumpet," "Malinke's Atonement," and "The Amulet," all published in the *Atlantic Monthly* between 1911 and 1937. In particular, "The Amulet" gives us very interesting insights into marital

sexuality in the context of Judaism, as Antin is clearly championing the modernization of traditional gender roles in such unions.

41. See also Dearborn, "Anzia Yezierska and the Making of an Ethnic American Self," 118–23, for a discussion of a "publicity-made" immigrant Cinderella.

42. Neidle, *America's Immigrant Women*, 257, emphasis mine. Bergland, "Ideology, Ethnicity, and the Gendered Subject," also stresses that it is the schoolroom—the "signifier of America"—where Mary's rites of passage take place (107).

43. See also Sollors, *Beyond Ethnicity*, 208–37, for an analysis of Hansen's "Law" of the third generation and its implications for the rhetoric of immigrant descent and consent in American culture.

44. Fowler and Fowler, eds., *Revelations of Self*, 161.

45. See also Dearborn's impressive chapter entitled "Strategies of Authorship in American Ethnic Women's Fiction: Midwiving and Mediation," *Pocahontas's Daughters*, 31–47, where she discusses Antin, Yezierska, Stern, and many others.

46. Schwartz, "Mary Antin," 61.

47. Guttman, *The Jewish Writer in America*, 25–26. The particular scenes supporting this point take place in Mary's early childhood, when she has her first thoughts on the violation of the Sabbath.

48. Homberger, "Charles Reznikoff's *Family Chronicle*," 332. Interestingly, Homberger also claims that "everywhere one looks in immigrant memoirs by women, the terms of constraint are similar," implying thus a larger tradition of the liberation-from-slavery narrative characteristic of female writing, in which the black woman and an immigrant woman are brought together by their oppression.

49. Girgus, *The New Covenant*, 14. Girgus sees the myth and antimyth tradition in Jewish writing running parallel to that of the American jeremiad (Paine, Thoreau, Emerson, Whitman, Howells, the Jameses, Fitzgerald, and others). The ability to challenge the myth of America that is already discernible in Antin can be also seen in later Jewish writers, such as Norman Mailer, because "the idealism of the myth creates its own negation or antimyth in the interests of achieving a truer form of the mythic vision."

50. For an interesting discussion of the "Eastern Jew," see Gilman, *Jewish Self-Hatred*, especially 49–50, 174, 284–85.

51. See Handlin, *Race and Nationality*, 93–138.

52. See Antin, "A Woman to Her Fellow Citizens," a speech in which she agitates the voters for the Progressive party and uses very interesting rhetorical figures to combine her insider's and outsider's voices: that of the radical outsider with that of an immigrant recently famous for her book.

53. In its attempts to use the superficial dominant idiom for reformatory purposes, Antin's work is very much in line with the didacticism of the sentimental novel, and her heroine can stand easily by the side of Ellen Montgomery, the main character of *The Wide, Wide World* by Susan Warner, whose story is also a "blueprint of survival" and an interesting document of a woman's growth in spite of the oppressive environment. (Not incidentally, Mary grows up reading Louisa M. Alcott's stories.)

54. Holte, *The Ethnic I*, 28–31.

55. Sochen, "Identities within Identity," 7–8. Sochen concentrates on Edna Ferber and Fannie Hurst, but her study also traces general patterns in female Jewish writing.

56. Nick Radel has reminded me how this dilemma "gets translated back into the Old World context in Styron's *Sophie's Choice*."

57. Antin also uses the technique of identification with the ultimate American hero —George Washington—to construct the character of a young immigrant boy in her short story "The Lie." Little David's teacher, Miss Ralston, finds out that Russian Jews are capable of "noble" lies, when it becomes clear that David's father lied about his son's age in order to be able to send him to school instead of to work. The secret comes out when David falls ill because he cannot be like faultless Washington, being a co-conspirator in his father's lie. The story can be read as a metaphor for a confrontation between the Anglo-Saxon dominant culture and the marginal lower-class Jewish immigrant who has to trick the system in order to benefit from it. It also provides a contrast—in gender terms—to the fate of Fetchke, who, as a girl, has less chance to have her father care about her education so much.

58. For Antin's heroine, according to Holte, *The Ethnic I*, "the process of Americanization was both limiting and paternal, [but] it did succeed in many instances, and Mary Antin provides an example of Americanization at its best" (31). This statement seems ironic, or at best superficial, because it dismisses many problems the critics usually omit in their discussions of *The Promised Land*—the heroine's approach to gender, the parallels between her oppression in Russia and America, and the fragmentation of her self between the two worlds.

59. It is also interesting to note that Mary's parents abandon the Old World ways completely in order to advance their children into Americanness. Although the mother and father are too old to undergo a change in themselves completely, they pretend to do so to see their desires fulfilled in their Americanized offspring.

60. As we can see in the naturalistic novels of Frank Norris (*McTeague*, for example) and in realistic depictions of city life in Theodore Dreiser's *Sister Carrie*, sex was not a taboo and could be written about by men and women alike (e.g., Gilman's *Women and Economics* and Kate Chopin's *The Awakening*).

61. Note similar mirror scenes in Anzia Yezierska's *Salome of the Tenements* and *All I Could Never Be*, discussed in Chapter 4. This preoccupation with self-examination and mirror images is obviously not restricted to female immigrant texts, but it seems worth pursuing in them and invites Lacanian readings of ethnicity and gender.

62. In this instance we can see how Antin is purging her work of sexuality so as not to hint at the controversial theme of immigrant women's alien sexual conduct and at accusations by the dominant culture that they are often loose or engage in prostitution. By making Mary disembodied and cerebral, she is fighting this sexual and class stereotype, while simultaneously showing its stifling power of textual oppression.

63. The separate theme of the repressive approach to female sexuality that is characteristic of orthodox Judaism is complex and thus broad enough for a separate study. For a depiction of that theme, see Antin's short story "The Amulet," in which she talks about "that heathen love for which there was no name in the vocabulary of the orthodox," about "the man and wife who blundered on the tricks of love neglected by the customs of their race" (34–35).

64. Bergland, "Ideology, Ethnicity, and the Gendered Subject," both blames Antin for not developing the themes related to gender and ethnicity and absolves her because at that time there were no discourses available to any writer who would want to discuss such themes.

## Chapter 3

1. I was inspired to read and research Stern by Mary V. Dearborn's comments about her in *Pocahontas's Daughters*. In particular, I was intrigued by Dearborn's remark that Stern's work contains an "interesting subtext that preserves the ethnic woman's oppositional stance to the dominant culture as it asserts the value of assimilation" (42). My reading of Stern's *My Mother and I* in these pages arises partly from a desire to answer the questions about Sterns' "subtext" that Dearborn inspired in me but did not answer, and partly from my polemics with her argument that Stern allowed the dominant culture "to prescribe modes of narration, stances toward authority, and plots and morals" for her texts.

2. Cliff, "A Journey into Speech," 59–61.

3. Although her "autobiographical" writings depict a marriage with a Gentile, Stern actually married a well-established American Jew. Interestingly, one of her pen names, Leah Morton, combined a Jewish first with a Gentile last name.

4. Stern analyzes her marriage in detail in the pages of a semi-autobiographical *I Am a Woman—and a Jew* (1926). Some critics show signs of irritation about Stern's paeans to her happy married life: "Her marriage—she is tiresomely insistent on this point—was superlatively happy" (Deutsch, "An Unimpressive Autobiography"). Stern also wrote under pen names: Eleanor Morton, Leah Morton, and E. G. Stern.

5. Stern's ambivalent approach to sex—sympathy for "free love" and liberated women on the one hand, and visible support for the temperance movement on the other—could be a topic for a separate study. It is especially poignant in *I Am a Woman—and a Jew*, *A Marriage Was Made*, and *When Love Comes to Woman*.

6. M. G. S., *New York Call*, 9 Sept. 1917, 15.

7. "America's Possibilities for the Immigrant," *Nation*, 30 Aug. 1917, 105. From a contemporary reader's response to such a critical gaze, we might ask: Why should an immigrant novel be a sociological document? Or explicit?

8. Ibid., emphasis mine. I also quoted this passage in my discussion of Antin in Chapter 2; see also Dearborn, *Pocahontas's Daughters*, 41.

9. For an interesting discussion of how even the progressive suffragists opposed immigration and voting rights for the "inferior" foreigners, see Kraditor, *The Ideas of Woman Suffrage Movement*, especially the chapter "The 'New Immigration' and Labor" (123–62).

10. Obviously, not all reviews of Stern were hostile and xenophobic. For example, Umansky writes about her popularity when she was first published, but she also stresses that Stern became unexpectedly obscure later on (introduction to *I Am a Woman—and a Jew*, v). I think that our changing tastes and different ways of reading and critiquing literature have a lot to do with Stern's absence on the course book lists and in anthologies of modern literature.

11. Just as the authors were expected to fit certain models, so were the characters representing particular nationalities or races. Oscar Handlin talks about stereotypes of nations and illustrates them with contemporaneous examples about "The Passionate Italian," and the "The Good-Natured German" in *Immigration as Factor in American History*, 135, 138. For an interesting study of the "Jewess" as "Other," who was culturally constructed in historical fiction from Scott to Cooper, see Cagidemetrio, "A Plea for Fictional Histories and Old-Time 'Jewesses.'"

12. Interestingly, the accusation that Stern turned to ghostwriting is not supported by any evidence in Dearborn's study. We know that the writer worked on a few projects with her husband; for example they wrote together *A Friend at Court* (1923), but this seems to be all the "ghostwriting" she did.

13. Bannan, "Elizabeth Gertrude Levin Stern," 166.

14. Umansky, Introduction, *I Am a Woman—and a Jew*, xii–xiii.

15. Stern, *My Mother and I*, 14. Subsequent quotations to this work are cited in the text.

16. Theodore Roosevelt's foreword to *My Mother and I* is a prime example of such a reading.

17. See also Dearborn, *Pocahontas's Daughters*, 81–83.

18. We can see a similar problem—a mother alienated from her Americanized children—in Yezierska's story "The Fat of the Land."

19. Review of *My Mother and I*, *Cleveland*, July 1917, 100.

20. To some degree, we can also see this trait in Eva Hoffman's *Lost in Translation* (1989), where "language" is considered a larger cultural construct, a specific idiom of the second generation that even the English-speaking first-generation parents cannot understand.

21. Gilman, *The Jew's Body*, 5, 18–19; see, especially, "The Jewish Voice," 10–37.

22. As previously mentioned, in *I Am a Woman—and a Jew*, this act of giving up the father is presented as a literal death of the parent. This death provides a framework for the other novel, as the text begins and ends with the narrator's realization that this fact finally liberates her from the burden of the past; she becomes the "redemptive" and redeemed member of the third generation. We will see a similar trait in Yezierska's *Bread Givers* and *Red Ribbon on a White Horse*, although this writer's texts usually attempt a compromise with the father figure.

23. The much-discussed comparisons between Jewish immigrants from East Europe and the Pilgrims via the imagery of the Old Testament are also present in Antin (especially in *They Who Knock at Our Gates*), Yezierska, Zangwill, and many others.

### Chapter 4

1. See Schoen, *Anzia Yezierska*, where the critic is disappointed that the conclusion of *Bread Givers* is marriage and love; she closes her study with a confession that she would not like to "overestimate Yezierska . . . [who] lacked the ability to create fully rounded characters" (128). See also Kessler-Harris's introduction to *Bread Givers* and to *The Open Cage*; the former draws a somewhat "guilty" comparison of the writer, who "has neither the symbolic depth . . . nor the epochal power" of Henry Roth and Abraham Cahan (xvi). For a more sympathetic view, which nevertheless discredits Yezierska's conclusions as falling prey to the cheap Hollywood scenario, see Dearborn, *Pocahontas's Daughters* and "Anzia Yezierska and the Making of an Ethnic American Self."

2. For an extensive discussion of writing women's biographies, see Heilbrun, *Writing a Woman's Life*. Heilbrun justifies recent involvement of the biographers in the relation between a woman author's life and her work: "In recent years biography as a genre has come under a good deal of close scrutiny. Roland Barthes has called biogra-

phy 'a novel that dare not speak its name,' and the understanding that biographies are fictions, constructions by the biographer of the story she or he had to tell, has become clear. . . . [Thus] the consensus about the author's relation to her work (if she is a writer) has changed. . . . [T]he picture of the author is being altered radically; and often, because of the newness of our experience with the new narratives of women's lives, our interest in the life has sharpened" (28–29).

3. Henriksen, *Anzia Yezierska*, 9, emphasis mine. Subsequent quotation from this work are cited in the text, abbreviated *AY*.

4. Quoted in Heilbrun, *Writing a Woman's Life*, 28–29.

5. Kessler-Harris, introduction to *Bread Givers*, v, vii. Subsequent quotations from this work are cited in the text, abbreviated *BG*. See also Henriksen, *Anzia Yezierska*, 13–14.

6. Levenberg, "Three Jewish Writers and the Spirit of the Thirties," 238. See also Dearborn, "Anzia Yezierska and the Making of an Ethnic American Self," 109, and Ferraro, *Ethnic Passages*, 55. As a critic who is inevitably engaging in rewriting Yezierska's story in these pages as well, I would like to suggest my theory about the writer's birthplace. Among Henriksen's "Plotsk," Kessler-Harris's "Plinsk," Dearborn's "Plöck," and Ferraro's "Ploch," it seems that Yezierska could have been born in Płock, now a city in central Poland.

7. This particular short story also contains subtle hints of female homoeroticism between the two lower-class women whom the world of men condemns to selling their bodies in order to survive in capitalist America (and thus puts heterosexual love in a highly ambivalent context). This theme of female camaraderie and solidarity should be explored in a separate study; it can also be seen in other stories, where Yezierska's heroines crave understanding and acceptance from and worship females more than males (e.g., "America and I," "How I Found America," "Wild Winter Love").

8. See Schoen, *Anzia Yezierska*, 53; Yezierska, "A Bed for the Night," *Children of Loneliness*, 175–76.

9. For examples of criticism apologizing for paying so much attention to a minor author, see note 1; for a sympathetic perspective, see Girgus, *The New Covenant*, 108–17, and his discussion of Yezierska's linguistic innovations in combining English and Yiddish into a unique and successful idiom. Girgus in fact calls Yezierska a "pioneer writer" who should have been recognized for her original contributions rather than compared with male authors (115).

10. I am drawing here on Peter Brooks's theories of narrative desire and "reading for the plot." See Brooks, *Reading for the Plot*, especially 7, 35, 216, 313–19.

11. See Holte, *The Ethnic I*, 28, for a discussion of female immigrant texts, which are juxtaposed with the typical male narratives of Carnegie and Bok (Holte concentrates on Antin's *The Promised Land*). See also Dearborn's classification of female newcomer stories as tales about acculturation through miscegenation in *Pocahontas's Daughters*.

12. Anzia Yezierska, "Mostly about Myself," *Children of Loneliness*, 19. Subsequent quotations from this work are cited in the text, abbreviated *ChL*.

13. It is worth recalling that, for example, Mary Antin's marriage fell apart, the much-publicized union of Rose Pastor and Graham Stokes ended in divorce (and thus gave Yezierska an idea for *Salome of the Tenements*), and that Elizabeth Stern, although happily married herself, explored endless cases of marital and sexual mismatches (see *When Love Comes to Woman*; for a more contemporary example, see Eva Hoffman, *Lost*

*in Translation*). Reading this theme in immigrant women and in American feminist writers, such as Kate Chopin and Charlotte Perkins Gilman, could make an interesting study in itself.

14. As DuPlessis argues in *Writing beyond the Ending*, female writers "place the critique of narrative at the center of their fiction in order to delegitimate certain plots and conventions" (x). However, DuPlessis sees this critique mostly in the twentieth-century innovative authors, such as Virginia Woolf and Doris Lessing, who defy the conventional marriage-and-romance endings of their nineteenth-century predecessors. In this context, Yezierska would be an ambivalent writer, with her outdated, nineteenth-century romantic endings, which nevertheless convey a decisively modern desire to open an alternative reading *beyond* the self-consciously used convention.

15. I am aware of only one other approach to Yezierska's texts as "erasing the patriarchal definition of female identity" in Emine Lale Demirturk's "The Female Identity in Cross-Cultural Perspective: Immigrant Women's Autobiographies," *Dissertation Abstracts*, 2584-A.

16. Wittke, *We Who Built America*, xi.

17. Yezierska, "America and I," *How I Found America*, 152. Subsequent quotations from this work are cited in the text, abbreviated *HF*.

18. It is important to note the ideology of America—as the Garden of Eden, the New Canaan, and the Promised Land reached after the Exodus—that was employed by early colonial and Puritan authors and its use of the Old Testament stories so central to Judaism. While identifying with the WASP settlers, Yezierska's character is connecting with her own ethnic history, transplanted and rewritten as the mythology of the first "Americans." See also Girgus, *The New Covenant*, 108–10, for an interesting discussion of the heroine's ideological initiation into America in this story.

19. Duffy, "You Can't Be an Immigrant Twice."

20. Yezierska, "How I Found America," in *Hungry Hearts*, 261–62. Subsequent quotations from this work are cited in the text, abbreviated *HH*.

21. Incidentally, this particular story describes an unhappy love affair between a young Jewish couple who become separated by their different social standing.

22. Although it may seem obvious, Yezierska's and her heroines' Jewishness makes them even more hopelessly stuck in America. In addition to being foreign, they are also stigmatized with their ethnicity and religion and thus can be doubly rejected and put down by the dominant culture.

23. For a similar approach to the ambivalent title of this story, see Schoen, *Anzia Yezierska*, 24, who argues that, in the two love stories "The Miracle" and "Where Lovers Dream," the writer was promoting marriage because "a woman's fulfillment, her sense of being a person could not be achieved without it," "a position in keeping with [Yezierska's] Jewish heritage." I would not agree with Schoen's view of this issue, as I think that in both stories the unreality of a perfect union, of a woman's ever finding total fulfillment in marriage, is strongly suggested. Moreover, Yezierska most fiercely attacked the notion from her "Jewish heritage" that a woman was made only to serve her man, to be an obedient wife who could eventually go to the High Heaven only *after* her husband. See also Dearborn, *Pocahontas's Daughters*, 41–42, on Yezierska's theories of miscegenation as a "shortcut to Americanization"; I would still argue with her miscegenation reading of the stories "The Miracle" and "Hunger" (109–10), too.

24. Schoen, *Anzia Yezierska*, 24. See Dearborn, "Anzia Yezierska and the Making of an Ethnic American Self," 109–21.

25. Lazarus, "The New Colossus," 307. Emma Lazarus (1849–87) came from a prominent Jewish family and, as Handlin puts it, "had early abandoned the prescribed rites and usages of Judaism which she considered obsolete and without relevance to modern life" (foreword to *The Promised Land*, ix). Emma's sister, Josephine, was a good friend of Mary Antin's and had a great influence on this young writer; it was she who infused Antin with ideas about Transcendentalism. It is interesting to note that Yezierska never had such stately and well-to-do benefactors; she could not sustain lasting friendships and ridiculed upper-class benefactors with their constant demand for gratitude in her novel *Arrogant Beggar*.

26. As much as this new dream and desire may be based on the famous relationship between Yezierska and John Dewey, I would like to concentrate on its literary representations in her texts. The biographical element is undoubtedly important for the writer's perception of America as male, mature, and intellectual—as was Dewey—but it does not seem to be the only inspiration for her remaking of the virgin-land image into a male body. I think Yezierska's writings prove that she observed a very important perspective characteristic of immigrant women who strove to create an alternative version of the myth embodying this country, a new narrative that would express their desires and working-class background. For a detailed description of Yezierska's relationship with Dewey, see Henriksen, *Anzia Yezierska*, 85–119. Boydston's edition of Dewey's poems written to Yezierska, *The Poems of John Dewey*, is also an interesting source of information, as is Dearborn's *Love in the Promised Land*.

27. See Sollors, *Beyond Ethnicity*, 71–75, 223–26, for a discussion of the American fear of intermarriage.

28. It is worth noticing that while Neidle, in *America's Immigrant Women*, 264–67, condemns Yezierska's style, calling it a "barbaric yawp," she seems not to realize that it was an effect of careful stylization to evoke the Yiddish-English dialect of the ghetto. As Henriksen explains in her afterword to *The Open Cage*, 256–57, her mother struggled to "unlearn" the educated English she had mastered at college and make alive the raw idiom of the Lower East Side. (See also Girgus, *The New Covenant*.)

29. Heilbrun, *Writing a Woman's Life*, 31.

30. The clichéd phrase about Yezierska used by virtually all critics is that she "dipped her pen in her heart." The phrase comes from Frank Crane, who devoted his column to Anzia's *Hungry Hearts* after she walked into his office unannounced and thrust her book at him. According to Henriksen, *Anzia Yezierska*, Crane "blazon[ed] Anzia's name (misspelled) and the title of her book on the front page of three hundred newspapers across the country" (148–50). We can see a connection with another cliché, "hidden hands," describing early American women writers who were rejected because of their desire to express "sentimental" feelings and "domestic" desires; see Freibert and White, eds., *Hidden Hands*.

31. See also Girgus, *The New Covenant*.

32. The emphasis on hands in Yezierska may be read as referring to woman's fragmentation, too. Unable to exist as a sexual body, she is reduced to its useful parts—its limbs—performing the manual labor. It is interesting that the idea of writing is thus also presented as manual labor—production of texts as "children." See Gabaccia, *Seeking Common Ground*, 43–44, on women as producing and reproducing agents.

33. This trait obviously echoes the tendency among American feminists of the period to reject the body; they sought "purity for women" and emphasized their intellect and independence from men as individuals. (For example, Charlotte Perkins Gilman's *Women and Economics* makes a case for liberating women from the bonds of "oversexed" gender roles as wives and mothers.)

34. See Henriksen, *Anzia Yezierska*, 214–15, 236–37, for interesting descriptions of situations in which she would have to cope with her mother's erratic ways.

35. For criticism of Yezierska's "so-called 'novels' . . . [that] all harped on the same theme," see Neidle, *America's Immigrant Women*, 264–67. Regretfully, Neidle relies too much on a single review of the writer's autobiography by Orville Prescott (*New York Times*, 23 Nov. 1970, 40:2, cited after Neidle), who uses terms such as "hysterical folly, pitiful bungling, and general bedlam" (266). See also Kamel, " 'Anzia Yezierska, Get Out of Your Own Way.' "

36. For the background of this novel and the story of Rose Pastor Stokes and her marriage to a "charity millionaire," James Graham Phelps Stokes, see Henriksen, *Anzia Yezierska*, 169–78. See also Dearborn, *Pocahontas's Daughters*, 107–9, where this novel is likened to another Cinderella story, *Pamela*, but "rewritten, with an ethnic twist," and Schoen, *Anzia Yezierska*, 39–40.

37. *Salome* was made into a silent film in 1925. It was scripted by Sonya Levien, Yezierska's friend, and featured an eminent cast of Jewish actors. However, it was not true to the text of the novel and did not depict any of the controversial issues that Yezierska intended to communicate. See Brownlow, *Behind the Mask of Innocence*, 404–5, 392–404, for a fascinating story of Yezierska's first film, *Hungry Hearts* (1921), which made her into a "sweatshop Cinderella" overnight after it had been bought by Hollywood.

38. For an exploration of prostitution as a result of female unemployment and low wages, see Kessler-Harris, *Out to Work*, 58, 103–5. See also D'Emilio and Freedman, *Intimate Matters*, 136–37, 209–15, for a discussion of ambivalent evidence that " 'It was the foreigner . . . who taught the American this dastardly business' " (215).

39. Yezierska, *Salome of the Tenements*, 7–11. Subsequent quotations from this work are cited in the text, abbreviated *ST*.

40. Schoen, *Anzia Yezierska*, 39.

41. D'Emilio and Freedman, *Intimate Matters*, 183.

42. This scene reminds one of the numerous "celebrations" we can see in contemporary cinema and television, featuring a couple making love in their new apartment or house. As early as 1922 Yezierska was cleverly exploiting the relationship between sex and real estate to show the economic motivation behind many interethnic unions.

43. In *Pocahontas's Daughters* Dearborn calls the novel "overly schematized and melodramatic" (123), while in *Anzia Yezierska* Schoen sees it as an "antimyth" of the Cinderella story and a book designed to "offend everyone" (39).

44. This reminds me of the reception of Dreiser's *Sister Carrie*, in which the heroine also succeeds against the odds of a story about a fallen woman. See also Schoen, *Anzia Yezierska*, 48, for speculation on literary influences in *Salome*.

45. See also Dearborn, *Pocahontas's Daughters*, 127, where she talks about the "centrality of ethnic female sexuality in American culture." I disagree with Dearborn's claim that Yezierska was ever fully "seduced by the metaphor, by the persuasive language of love" and that she was "unable or unwilling to forgo it, or to explore its darker and

more profound manifestations." My analysis shows that Yezierska is precisely engaging in that difficult kind of exploration and that the theme of intermarriage is for her not a "barrier beyond which [she] could not travel in her fiction," as Dearborn sees it, but an inspiration for intricate and interesting subtexts subverting the stereotype of an ethnic woman in America.

46. For an interesting discussion of the sexual stereotypes associated with immigrant women, see Weatherford, *Foreign and Female*, 3–4, 56–57, 59–65. Weatherford stresses how, by virtue of her foreignness, the newcomer woman was suspect sexually. This fear of the alien's sexuality on the part of the host culture was fed by the fact that working-class women from East Europe, for example, were much more comfortable with their bodies than the repressed women of the American upper and upper-middle classes. Therefore, immigrant women were often considered "loose" and prone to become prostitutes, simply because they knew certain facts pertaining to contraception or human anatomy. This knowledge of carnality came naturally with a life of poverty, where all family members were forced to share in every aspect of their existence because of the lack of space and privacy. (See also Craveri, "Women in Retreat," for a discussion of social class as a factor in women's sexual knowledge in Renaissance Europe.)

47. See also Weatherford, *Foreign and Female*, 96, who emphasizes how the shedding of her Old World dress symbolizes the immigrant woman's intention to become a new person. Read in this context, Sonya fails at acculturation, as her attempt to become an American through dress and money ends in a disillusionment. On the other hand, if she consents to dress the women of her new country instead, she can be accepted as a contributor to the dominant culture.

48. We can see Sonya's confusion in an ironic scene at the tenement office, where she is awaiting Manning's arrival and tries to adapt herself to the image of Mona Lisa. The scene evokes an ironic comment from Yezierska: "As the hour of Manning's arrival grew near, a tumultuous fever stormed through her. In desperate resistance she made her whole body rigid and sat down stiffly at her desk. In imitation of her new patron saint, she folded her hands and assumed a cryptic, impersonal smile. A Salome of the tenements trying to be Mona Lisa!" (138). See also Henriksen, *Anzia Yezierska*, for many instances of the writer's own struggle to be herself, on the one hand, and to defy herself as an image made by the dominant culture, on the other (note especially the ambivalent history of Yezierska's unconsummated marriage with Jacob Gordon and a subsequent union with Arnold Levitas, her daughter's father; Henriksen talks about her mother's "demon," her impossible temper, and her insistence on having things her way).

49. It is worth recalling that even Samuel Richardson's Clarissa Harlowe, although in entirely different circumstances, was trying to fulfill a "duty to herself." Yezierska is responding here to the sentimental tradition once again.

50. Weatherford, *Foreign and Female*, 56.

51. Yezierska, *Bread Givers*, 200–201. Subsequent quotations from this work are cited in the text, abbreviated *BG*.

52. See Gilman, *Jewish Self-Hatred*, especially, 49–50, 174, 284–85. (We can also see Yezierska possibly creating a smokescreen to hide her own ambivalences about this issue.)

53. Kessler-Harris, introduction to *Bread Givers*, xvi.

54. See Ferraro, *Ethnic Passages*, 53–86, for a discussion of *Bread Givers* as perpetuated by the "reproduction of patriarchy."

55. In itself, Sara's invitation to Hugo to come to her room and his acceptance of it are "loaded," as Ferraro remarks, suggesting that in that scene there are daring sexual undertones and possibly a hint at premarital sex between the lovers. He adds that such invitations were bold "among immigrant Jews in the 1920s, never mind the 1890s" (81).

56. Ferraro, *Ethnic Passages*, 83.

57. Yezierska, *Arrogant Beggar*, 52–53, 141. Subsequent quotations from this work are cited in the the text, abbreviated *AB*.

58. Schoen, *Anzia Yezierska*, 86–87.

59. This theme requires a separate study, but I would like to point out that in this novel and in some of the short stories (e.g., "A Bed for the Night") Yezierska gives female friendships homoerotic overtones. I think that she subtly hints at the possibilities for erotic attachments between women as a result of her own friendships with female writers and activists (Dorothy Canfield Fisher, Zona Gale) and as a comment on the popularity of female bonds in her time. D'Emilio and Friedman claim that for many college and professional women at that time, living together as "friends" was often an accepted and comfortable way to avoid marriage and motherhood and provided them with respected alternative "families" (*Intimate Matters*, 190–91).

60. As one of these women comments, selling one's own body oneself is preferable to working in a sweatshop as somebody else's machine: "'I don't propose to get up at 6:30 to be at work at 8 and work in a close stuffy room with people I despise, until dark, for $6.00 or $7.00 a week! When I could, just by phoning, spend an afternoon with some congenial person and in the end have more than a week's work could pay me.'" Quoted in Kessler-Harris, *Out to Work*, 104–5.

61. Gornick, introduction to *How I Found America*, ix.

62. Quoted in Henriksen, *Anzia Yezierska*, 246.

63. Obviously, fictionalizing the actual by turning autobiography into fiction is, to a certain extent, what all writers inevitably do. However, in Yezierska's case this fact has been always stressed as something that she did more than others, possibly because she was ahead of her time with her complete disregard of the literary conventions of "realism," "fact," and "fiction," which were still followed by other writers of her day. In a sense, Yezierska's writing anticipated postmodern experiments, and I think this is why she is becoming increasingly popular now, when there are more readers sympathetic to her kind of "fictionalizing." For example, Persea Books has reprinted Yezierska's *Bread Givers* and *Red Ribbon on a White Horse* and has issued several collections of her short stories—*Hungry Hearts and Other Stories*, *The Open Cage*, and *How I Found America*.

64. This particular theme is undoubtedly another reflection of the trauma that Yezierska's relationship with John Dewey proved to be for her whole life.

65. Yezierska, *All I Could Never Be*, 28. Subsequent quotations from this work are cited in the text, abbreviated *All*.

66. Interestingly, there are similar mirror scenes in Antin's *The Promised Land* (chapter 2) and in Stern's *I Am a Woman—and a Jew*. Such confrontation of an immigrant woman with her own reflection—with what she must look like to others—is a fascinating pattern in these writers. (This pattern is not, obviously, limited to women and immigrant writers.)

67. Henriksen quotes Yezierska's letters to her editor, Dorothy Canfield Fisher: "Her heroine had something of Anzia's temperament. 'A Russian Jewess could never achieve the heroic power of restraint of an Emily Dickinson. . . . The girl might have been a nobler character if she had learned restraint. But it wouldn't have been true to life. . . . Reality—the truth as I see it is to me more than art'" (*Anzia Yezierska*, 243).

68. Yezierska, *Red Ribbon on a White Horse*, 220. Subsequent quotations from this work are cited in the text, abbreviated *RR*.

69. Dearborn, "Anzia Yezierska and the Making of an Ethnic American Self," 122.

70. Such an ending is an extension of the one imbedded in the subtext of *All I Could Never Be*.

71. Gornick, introduction to *How I Found America*, xi–xii.

## Chapter 5

1. Yezierska, review of *The Forester*, 31. Kuncewicz's novel fictionalizes the life of her father's family and takes place around the time of the Polish uprising against Russia in 1863.

2. I obtained this information from Professor Hugh McLean, chair of the Department of Slavic Languages and Literatures at the University of California, Berkeley. He has kindly shared with me a copy of Kuncewicz's letter in which she thanks him for writing a recommendation for her. Kuncewicz's most important awards include the Literary Award of the City of Warsaw (1937), the Golden Laurel of the Polish Academy of Literature (1938), the W. Pietrzak Award (1966), the First Class National Award (1974), and the Medal of the Kosciuszko Foundation for outstanding contributions to Polish and American cultures (1971).

3. Obviously, not every educated East European intellectual was welcomed in the United States and granted a lucrative visiting professorship. Often one had to be the "right kind" of a foreigner—that is, one who fit the image of an émigré "saved" by the West.

4. Kuncewicz, *Natura*, 164, translation mine. Subsequent quotations from this work are cited in the text, abbreviated *N*. In quoting from Kuncewicz's works in Polish, all translations are mine unless indicated otherwise. For works that have been translated into English, I quote from those editions. (The proper spelling of the writer's name— "Kuncewiczowa"—reflects the gendered endings of Polish. For the sake of consistency I have adopted the anglicized usage throughout: Kuncewicz.)

5. As I will explain later, Kuncewicz was first able to return to Poland in 1958, and later, after 1968, the memorable year of student protests which brought about more cultural freedom, but which was also marred by anti-Semitic government policies, she regained her house in Kazimierz. Ironically, she returned when many Jews were leaving; she was allowed to come back when they were forced to emigrate.

6. In her writings Kuncewicz also engages in dialogues with French, Italian, and English cultures—a cosmopolitan contribution that deserves a separate study. I emphasize her East European–American writings because, even in her international dimension, she is positioned between the cultures and ideologies of the East and the West in the way I described theoretically in Chapter 1.

7. For a discussion of exiled and dissident writers, mostly male, see Thompson, "The Writer in Exile."

8. Woolf, *Three Guineas*, 109.

9. See also Rachel Blau DuPlessis, *Writing beyond the Ending*, 31, for a discussion of Woolf's "breaking of the sentence and of the sequence" in a woman's story.

10. For a critique of Woolf's "elitist, ethnocentric vision of both feminism and exile," see Yelin, "Exiled in and Exiled from," 396.

11. I realize that, to some extent, all these features may fit any person in exile regardless of gender. I consciously emphasize them as feminine to clarify my argument's focus on women.

12. Kristeva, "A New Type of Intellectual," 296.

13. Kuncewicz, *Nowele i bruliony prozatorskie*, 303–4, 305. See also Latawiec, "Żywy dom," 3.

14. Kristeva, *Strangers to Ourselves*, 42–46, 15, 14. (Eve's expulsion from Paradise is another example of the theme of the foreign woman.)

15. I will discuss this theme more extensively in Chapter 6.

16. Kristeva, *Strangers to Ourselves*, 14, emphasis mine. See Dearborn's discussion of the miscegenation myth in *Pocahontas's Daughters*. See also Sollors, *Beyond Ethnicity*.

17. Quoted in Schofield, "Underground Lives," 127.

18. See also ibid., 125, on "doubled subjectivity" (125) and Milbauer, *Transcending Exile*, on exile as the survival of "transplantation" and an "unnatural state of existence" (4, xi). See also Milbauer's chapter on Nabokov, "The Russian Colossus in Exile," 27–71.

19. It would take a separate bibliography to list all East European male dissident names and texts. Instead of restating what is obvious, I would like to emphasize how the stereotype of a male dissident works, using the example of Glad, ed., *Literature in Exile*. The book is based on a conference of writers in exile, held in Vienna in 1987 by the Wheatland Foundation of New York. The title suggests inclusiveness, but the book excludes, since not a single woman's text appears in the collection, nor is any woman present as a speaker in the subsequent discussions of the essays (the only female names appear in the introduction and belong to the foundation's executive director and executive secretary). The book contains the portraits of sixteen male participants, who are to represent "literature in exile." I have nothing against exclusively male gatherings, but am bothered by the usurping by prominent male literary figures of an exclusive right to the rhetoric of exile. Literature in exile is written by men *and* women and should be recognized as such, instead of being presented as a stereotypical male construct, one that can never represent the complexities of this literary phenomenon.

20. I am aware of a few recent publications of Polish women poets in translation (see Chapter 1) and occasional remarks about women writers from that country here and there. However, the larger picture of Polish and other East European émigré and dissident literature is decisively male and celebrates strongly politicized figures, such as the Polish Lithuanian Czesław Miłosz, the Russian Joseph Brodsky, who is now considered an "American" poet, or the Czech Milan Kundera. This narrow approach is not so much a fault of the émigrés themselves, although it is true that they could do more to foster a more inclusive view of literature in exile, as it is a result of the American way of creating or even, in Werner Sollors's term, "inventing" East Europe. Such a view often oversimplifies and distorts the complex stories behind the prominent dissident figures' past and emigration. (For example, see "Who Speaks for Whom," 132, for a

glimpse at Milan Kundera as an ambivalent political figure who had been "an indulged and rewarded child of the Communist regime until 1968.")

21. Benstock, "Expatriate Modernism," 20, 25. Although Benstock's argument is about the writers of modernism, I find it very relevant to postwar literature in general and to Kuncewicz, who emerged from Polish modernism, in particular.

22. Radner, "Exiled from Within," 252.

23. For a discussion of the "posttotalitarian mind," see Goldfarb, *Beyond Glasnost*, 161–96, who argues that in the countries such as Poland, Hungary, or Czechoslovakia the resistance to the regime and to its Newspeak created an alternative posttotalitarian frame of mind under communist domination. He singles out Poland as creating the most advanced posttotalitarian political and cultural situation. The simplistic division of writers into the "good" ones—who went abroad—and "collaborators"—who stayed on under the regime—was unfortunately the perspective through which many Polish authors were judged. The ones who chose to remain in their country for various reasons were often considered "traitors," especially by those who left and became celebrated dissidents in the West. I will discuss the specific case of Maria Kuncewicz as one such writer later in this chapter.

24. Kuncewicz, *Fantomy*, 186. Subsequent quotations from this work are cited in the text, abbreviated *Fant*.

25. Julia Kristeva's theory about an "exile who asks, 'where,'" presented in *The Powers of Horror*, could also be applied here. As Kristeva claims, "The more he strays, the more he is saved. . . . For it is out of such straying on excluded ground that he draws his jouissance" (8). Kristeva's idea could inspire a completely different study—one about her theory of "jouissance" in exile and the exile as a "deject" who is a "deviser of territories, languages, works"—but I acknowledge it in these pages as another "signal" from an East European exiled woman.

26. Quoted in Zaworska, ed., *Rozmowy z Marią Kuncewiczową*, 42.

27. The exact translation of this novel's title from Polish should be *The Foreigner*, but in this case, as in a few others, I have decided to use the titles of available English editions.

28. Gurr, *Writers in Exile*, 14, 15. See also Friedman, "Exile in the American Grain," for a discussion of H.D.'s expatriatism, which, as with Kuncewicz, meant that "she needed to be an outsider to write."

29. Kuncewicz, *Klucze*, 19. Subsequent quotations from the Polish edition are cited in the text, abbreviated *K*, Polish. *The Keys* was first published in Polish (1943) and then in English (1946). Because the two editions are slightly different, I will refer to both.

30. Kuncewicz, *The Keys*, 74. Subsequent quotations from this edition are cited in the text, abbreviated *K*, English.

31. I chose to rely on my own translation of this passage from the Polish because the English translation published by Hutchinson is curiously edited. It omits the fragments about the "British country" and London underground stations, possibly considered too ironic or crude for the English reader.

32. It is interesting to note that the passage describing the matinee at the Comédie Française and referring to French military men praising metaphors at the theaters during the "drôle de guerre" (which appeared in both the Polish and English versions)

was removed from the French translation, *Les Clés*, perhaps because it was seen as a negative generalization about that country's attitude to war. Kuncewicz mentions this omission in *Fantomy*.

33. Kristeva's discussion of the "abject" in *The Powers of Horror* could be expanded here.

34. An interesting reading of such displacement of the "I" as a subject into the position outside of itself can be found in Silverman's reading of Emile Benveniste in *The Subject of Semiotics*, 43–53.

35. In Polish this term is *czas narodowy*, meaning "national time" or "the nation's time."

36. See also Zaworska, ed., *Rozmowy z Marią Kuncewiczową*, 221, 224.

37. *Robienie gęby*—"making face"—is a term that Kuncewicz borrows from Witold Gombrowicz, who uses it to refer to the state of being duped by others and being forced to assume a grotesquely distorted (and alienating) identity.

38. Kuncewicz, *Zmowa nieobecnych*, title page. (This motto is omitted in the English translation.)

39. Kuncewicz, *The Forester*, 5. Subsequent quotations from this work are cited in the text, abbreviated *F*.

40. Miłosz, *The History of Polish Literature*, 430–31. Miłosz introduces the subject of women writers before he discusses Kuncewicz: "Literary critics were puzzled by the invasion of women novelists who secured for themselves positions as the most widely read authors of fiction. Whether the often advanced economic explanation is valid or not (women supposedly had more time to write, while their husbands were busy being the breadwinners), the list of female writers is considerable" (430).

41. Kuncewicz, *The Olive Grove*, ix–x. Subsequent quotations from this work are cited in the text, abbreviated *OG*.

42. See, for example, Nyren, review of *The Olive Grove*, *Library Journal*, 2275, and Hale, "The Momentum of Murder," 39–40, who complains that "the network of past bitterness and betrayal, like Pat's family situation, sometimes seems too complex. It is only when these plot chores have been disposed of that the novel becomes as fascinating as its material" (40). It is interesting to note how Hale is in favor of a direct and "realistic" depiction of the factual material in fiction.

43. A reading of this novel through the rhetoric of original sin would make an interesting study.

44. These events took place in 1946, as reflected in the title of the Polish version: *Tristan 1946* (1970). (The date is omitted in the English translation.) Kuncewicz wrote the novel in Polish while living in the woods near Victoria, British Columbia, then rewrote it for her English-speaking readers.

45. *Tristan* is told by the "voices" of Kathleen, Michael, and some of their friends, but the larger narrative, embracing these voices, is spun by Wanda. Like the careless servant in the romance, Wanda-Brangien brings the lovers together; in *Tristan* she also survives their tragic "death" to tell the story, and can thus be seen as its metaphorical author.

46. Kuncewicz, *Tristan*, 273.

47. Radner, "Exiled from Within," 254, 256. See also Marcus, "Alibis and Legends."

48. Kuncewicz, *Przeźrocza* (Slides), 85. Subsequent quotations from this work are cited in the text. The phrase "waves of ether" can be translated more idiomatically as

"on the air," but I decided to keep the old-fashioned flavor of the reference to early-day radio broadcasts.

49. Zaworska, ed., *Rozmowy z Marią Kuncewiczową*, 52, 138, 187, emphasis mine.

50. Kuncewicz, *Listy do Jerzego*, 112. Subsequent quotations from this work are cited in the text.

51. See Baym, "Melodramas of Beset Manhood."

52. Marcus, "Alibis and Legends," 276, 270.

53. Gardiner, "On Female Identity and Writing by Women," 185. I am also indebted here to the works of Susan Gubar, Teresa De Lauretis, Dorothy Dinnerstein, Carolyn Heilbrun, Julia Kristeva, Simone de Beauvoir, and other feminist critics.

54. Quoted in Zaworska, ed., *Rozmowy z Marią Kuncewiczową*, 50.

55. See ibid., 186, 249. It is interesting to note Kuncewicz's opinion about interviews as "traps" set for the writer by clever interviewers who work out a preconceived narrative that the writer is obliged to fill in with her answers to carefully designed questions. In this way, still another external narrative of otherness becomes written through the interviewer's "fiction," which is then passed on to the readers—who, of course, often await a reconfirmation of their own "fictions" about the writer (ibid., 100).

56. Kuncewicz, "Exile without Tears," 14.

57. Storm Jameson, introduction to *The Stranger*, 7.

58. Storm Jameson, "The Cost of Freedom," 9.

59. Kuncewicz, "Refugees as World Citizens," 6a.

60. Storm Jameson, introduction to *The Stranger*, 13.

61. For a similar stance, see Barańczak, *Breathing under Water*, 9–15.

62. Kuncewicz, "Exile without Tears," 14.

63. Barańczak, *Breathing under Water*, 14–15.

64. Steinfels, "The Fall of the Ironic Curtain," 102.

65. Kuncewicz's other publications in English are *Polish Millstones* (1942), a short pamphlet-story on the Polish women's heroism during the war; a play, *Thank You for the Rose* (1945); and two anthologies, *Modern Polish Prose* (1942) and *The Modern Polish Mind* (1962). All her works in translation are out of print.

66. An anonymous review of *The Stranger* seems especially ironic: "Ably executed—but not pleasant reading, though the market for *Strange Woman* [possibly a reference to Ben Ames Williams's adventure and romance novel of 1941] and its ilk may find this Polish character challenging." See *Kirkus*, 1 July 1945, 275.

67. Burger, review of *The Olive Grove*, by Maria Kuncewicz, *New York Times Book Review*, 11 Aug. 1963, 22.

68. Miller, "Gruesome Episode in Southern France," 4, emphasis mine.

69. Review of *The Forester*, *Times Literary Supplement*, 29 Jan. 1954, 25; Yezierska, review of *The Forester*, 31.

70. Page, "Other Titles on the Fiction List," 26.

71. Review of *The Conspiracy of the Absent*, *Times Literary Supplement*, 29 Sept. 1950, 609.

72. See also Pick, "Unhappy Woman," 29. This is an interesting, albeit a little hostile, review of *The Stranger*. The critic classifies the theme as "the happy unhappy, 'frustrated' woman . . . belong[ing] to French novel writing of the 1890's; . . . [the] technique stems from Proust, although Mme. Kuncewicz's is a thinned-out and sentimental Prousteism." I believe he also alludes ironically to Virginia Woolf in his last

sentence: "Yet all its [the novel's] nuances and facets do not make for a whole—which (this goes for novels, too) is supposed to be more than the sum-total of the parts." Instead of attempting to see the writer for herself and her work as the individual piece of literature it was meant to be, Pick relates his difficulties in determining what Kuncewicz's writing reminded him of.

73. "Flight through Europe," *Times Literary Supplement* 23 Feb. 1946, 86.

74. Unfortunately, some of the methods of fighting communism abroad were reminiscent of the ones used by the regimes to suppress dissent. For example, in the years 1968–70 the Paris *Kultura* printed the so-called Czarna Lista (Black List) of writers who were publishing texts that supposedly proved their authors' collaboration with the regime. It is always stimulating to have ideological adversaries or enemies, but nobody seemed to have thought about freedom of speech and like issues while implementing the publication of this list, which oddly resembled the ones on which the émigrés themselves figured in every censor's "black book" back home.

75. The abbreviations refer to the law issued on 31 Aug. 1981 by the Central Office for the Control of the Press, Publications, and Entertainment (the censorship bureau) and modified in 1983. (For the exact censorship restrictions and a list of authors who were forbidden to appear in print between 1975 and 1977, see Niczow, *Black Book of Polish Censorship*, and Curry, trans. and ed., *The Black Book of Polish Censorship*.) Omissions due to censorship were fairly common in the books published by PAX and, in the early 1980s, were marked regularly in the Catholic weekly *Tygodnik Powszechny*. I remember waiting for this journal every week with my friends and collectively poring over the mysterious remains of articles that had been censored; only the titles were printed, accompanied by the abbreviation of the censorship law. For a demystifying view of Kuncewicz's "collaboration," see also Zaworska, "Żeby wiedzieć co u was."

76. Kuncewicz to Hugh McLean, 4 April 1969. Professor McLean kindly shared this letter with me.

77. Ibid.

78. Ibid.

79. Interestingly, the history of writing *The Olive Grove* involves two English versions, as the first one was (somewhat significantly) lost during Kuncewicz's journey to the United States in 1955. She recalls that event in *Natura*: "A terrible moment, even though not a person died but only a year. What died were the twelve months of reworking the Polish nature into an English story." Her son, Witold, replies: "You know, Mom . . . now you are laughing about it, because you wrote that story of yours again, later on, supposedly even a better one. But I, at that time, . . . I know these things . . . I knew what it was like. The boys came onto the deck, turned the faucet on and hosed the pages down, and what was left floated in the air. Like you . . . father . . . I . . . . Us, too, either something would hose us down from the deck, or we were floating in the air" (92–93, ellipses in original).

80. Review of *The Conspiracy of the Absent*, *Times Literary Supplement*, 29 Sept. 1950, 609.

81. Sapieha, "Polish Author Presents Stormy Petrel in Flight," sec. 6, p. 5.

82. Review of *The Conspiracy of the Absent*, *Kirkus* 15 Sept. 1950, 567.

83. One of Maria Kuncewicz's students at the University of Chicago was James Rice. Now a professor of Russian at the University of Oregon, he is a living witness to this

writer's ingenious blending of fact and fiction. She mentions "Jimmy" in *Fantomy*, *Natura*, and *Fantasia alla polacca* (1979).

84. Storm Jameson, introduction to *The Stranger*, 10.

85. Kristeva, *The Powers of Horror*, 8–9. Kristeva offers an intricate theory of subjectivity that can be developed into a study of internal exile.

86. Kristeva, *About Chinese Women*, 203, 209.

## Chapter 6

1. Hoffman, *Exit into History*, 138. Subsequent quotations from this work are cited in the text, abbreviated *EH*.

2. Hoffman, *Lost in Translation*, 179. Subsequent quotations from this work are cited in the text, abbreviated *LT*.

3. Kristeva, *Strangers to Ourselves*, 195. Subsequent quotations from this work are cited in the text, abbreviated *SO*.

4. Kristeva describes her arrival from Bulgaria and her initiation into the pantheon of French intellectuals in her autobiographical novel, *The Samurai*. Although this text gives interesting insights into her life as an academic and a woman immersed in the fascinating Parisian scene of the sixties and seventies, it disappoints as a novel about otherness and exile. Bulgaria is mentioned only on the first few pages, and the heroine seems to miraculously metamorphose into a French woman without much intercultural struggle.

5. The "strange within us" is Kristeva's term in the English translation by Leon Roudiez.

6. For examples, see Hoffman's discussion of Vladimir Nabokov, Milan Kundera, and Czesław Miłosz in *Lost in Translation*, 115–16, 197–98.

7. As I argued in Chapter 2, Antin presents the Old World both as oppressive and hostile and, less obviously, as a place full of intense sensual memories of childhood.

8. Although free from the constraints we saw in the case of Antin or Yezierska, Hoffman's book still fits "our time," as she admits herself. Obviously, she is bound by a subtle dominant narrative that makes her write a certain story, a tale about "today." Like any writer who is living at a particular moment and at a particular place, she is expected to attest to her reality and meet at least some of her readers' expectations.

9. Gladsky calls this theme "look[ing] at Polishness from the inside, recording the evolution of New World ethnic consciousness and the emergence of the ethnic self in transition," but he does not differentiate between its rendering in Hoffman and Yezierska (*Princes, Peasants*, 36).

10. I discuss Hoffman's approach to Nabokov more fully in the next chapter.

11. It is interesting to note how Nabokov often used images of pregnancy to describe his writing in Russian. However, in his case, it is the "Russian Muse" who lies with him and who bears his literary offspring. The author is the father, but his body is not involved in the process of birthing the text; his task does not extend beyond conception. Thus he needs and uses the female body of the muse as a necessary medium to produce writing. See Nabokov's letters to Edmund Wilson, quoted in Beaujour, *Alien Tongues*, 97.

12. Hoffman also mentions that Antin conceals an alternative story behind her super-

ficial narrative of successful Americanization and that we can glimpse that story in Antin's introduction. Having already argued a similar point in Chapter 2, I was happy to discover that Hoffman was also inspired by Antin's alternative reading of *The Promised Land*. However, I do not think that Hoffman reads Antin as carefully as she should be read. There are more points in Antin's text besides the introduction where we can clearly see how Antin's desire to write an antistory is defeated by the necessity to compromise with the dominant mode of an immigrant tale that she was expected to follow.

13. Elaine Scarry's argument about the relation between pain and imagination could be applied here: "Pain and imagining are the 'framing events' within whose boundaries all other perceptual, somatic, and emotional events occur; thus, between the two extremes can be mapped the whole terrain of the human psyche" (*The Body in Pain*, 165).

14. Spivak and Gunew, "Questions of Multiculturalism," 413.

15. See also Havel, "Words on Words."

16. See also Hoffman's "My Poland, Then and Now," an astute article on the post-revolutionary political and socioeconomic changes in Poland.

17. Mukherjee, *Jasmine*, 90–91.

18. Kristeva, *Nations without Nationalism*, 9–10. Subsequent quotations from this work are cited in the text, abbreviated *NN*.

19. For perspectives on studies describing Polish-Jewish relations, see Braumberg, "Jewish Revelations," and Cesarani, "What Went Wrong in Warsaw," and Michnik, "Poland and the Jews," an especially brilliant piece. See also Cahn, "New Poland, Old Problems," and O'Connor, "Two People, Two Stories." Deák's "Strategies of Hell" is a comprehensive review of Holocaust literature concerned with general European anti-Semitism.

## Chapter 7

1. Nabokov, *Pnin*, 25–26. The novel was first published serially in the *New Yorker* in 1953–55, then issued by Doubleday in 1957. Subsequent quotations from this work are cited in the text.

2. See Boyd, *Vladimir Nabokov*, 298–99, for a description of Nabokov's love for detail in planning Pnin's appearance for the cover of the novel's first edition. In his review of Boyd's biography, Adams refers to similar criticism of Nabokov: "Like many deft writers, Nabokov has often been accused of mere cleverness, of 'having nothing to say'" ("The Wizard of Lake Cayuga," 4). See also Gass, *Habitations of the Word*, for a reading of Nabokov's story "The Vane Sisters." Gass sees the story as doubling the "dialectical interference of text with intention, intention with text" due to the author's control over his composition; this control is "not that of a fatherly Czar but that of the secret police." As Gass emphasizes, "Nabokov's passage is a performance . . . and a good one" (276, 284).

3. Tanner, *City of Words*, describes Nabokov's writing as games on the "lexical playfields," which "erect a verbal world . . . to triumph over vertigo, diffusion, and victimization" (33, 38–39). He sees this quality as the most important Nabokovian influence on a generation of American writers. (Tanner examines Nabokov in a chapter that also explores Jorge Luis Borges's work.)

4. Quoted in Boyd, "The Year of *Lolita*," 32.

5. Boyd, *Vladimir Nabokov*, 7. I talk about the happy ending to Nabokov's career in general, but am aware that *Pnin* was written before he achieved financial independence.

6. See Boyd, "The Year of *Lolita*," 31–33. Boyd emphasizes how rapidly *Lolita* turned into a best-seller, which meant that Nabokov would not have to teach any more and would be able to devote himself solely to writing and his lepidoptera. This is an interesting change of pace in the career of a writer who had struggled for many years to make ends meet.

7. Obviously, mine is just one more reading of Nabokov among many that emphasize his immigrant status and stress that, just like any other newcomer, he had to go through an acculturation process. Although this reading cannot pretend to describe the full curve of his life, it elicits the often neglected dimension of the author whose class often prevented the critics from considering him an "immigrant" (a term that has a definite lower-class connotation and would not fit Nabokov's aristocratic origin).

In my next study I plan to compare the biographical and fictitious narratives about and by Nabokov to the model immigrant tale in Cahan's *The Rise of David Levinsky*, in which the main character becomes a millionaire, an economic feat that marks his Americanization. However, David has to pay a price for his financial coup—he has to renounce his scholarly ambitions, and he never realizes his dream of going to college. In Nabokov's later versions of the male immigrant story, *Pnin* and *Lolita*, the characters actually capitalize on their knowledge and learning, just as their creator did. Other examples of typical male narratives are the ones already mentioned in previous chapters: Carnegie's *Autobiography* and Bok's *The Americanization of Edward Bok*. On the other hand, Roth's *Call It Sleep* provides an interesting contrast with these predictable tales, since Roth uses a child's mind as a narrative device and emphasizes the mother's experience, which gives his text a significant "feminine" quality. See also Holte's classifications of gendered acculturations in *The Ethnic I*.

8. It is interesting to note how gender differences were often analogous to the political ones in expatriate writers. For example, Kuncewicz was not active politically and did not fight communism or pronounce her anticommunist views widely while in the United States (behavior that some of the Polish émigrés, such as Czesław Miłosz, hold against her). On the other hand, Nabokov's political declarations are more compatible with the stereotype of a staunch anticommunist. Unlike other intellectuals in America of that time, he was an ardent advocate of the Vietnam War. In a telegram to Lyndon Johnson Nabokov wished the president a "speedy return to the admirable work you are accomplishing" (quoted in Boyd, *Vladimir Nabokov*, 503). See also ibid., 311, where we learn that Nabokov's anticommunism was so strong that he detested Roman Jakobson for the latter's visit to the Soviet Union; if necessary, he would also have had his son, Dimitri, enlist in the FBI to fight that ideology.

9. One could argue that a form of gender oppression is also present in Cahan's *The Rise of David Levinsky*, as David never marries, having been unable to find a mate. Nevertheless, his masculinity is never doubted (he is virile and passionate), and his problems stem more from the problem of the class he represents, new Russian-Jewish money, than from the nature of his sexual identity.

10. See also Craveri, "Women in Retreat," 67, for an interesting perspective on writing about women. In her review of *A History of Women in the West* she praises the editors' efforts to challenge the reductionist view of a masculine-feminine dichotomy,

which claims that only women can and should write about women. A perspective that Farge and Davis propose involves "[a] study [of] the social roles of both men and women in connection with each other" and the view that to give as accurate a picture of the times as possible we should "investigate the relationships between the sexes and their differences." Although social sciences and literature differ as far as their conceptions of "social roles" and "subjectivity" are concerned, it is interesting to turn back and read the male texts from within the feminist perspective. Such an approach cannot ever provide an accurate picture of a particular historical or cultural moment, but it can give us a chance to appreciate otherness in each gender and in their relation to each other.

11. I would like to draw here on Spivak's argument about reading the world as a book, what she terms a "risky reading" in her essay "Reading the World" (*In Other Worlds*, 95–102). Spivak says: "The world actually writes itself with the many-leveled, unfixable intricacy and openness of a work of literature. If, through our study of literature, we can ourselves learn and teach others to read the world in the 'proper' risky way, and to act upon that lesson, perhaps we literary people would not forever be such helpless victims. . . . One must fill the vision of literary form with its connections to what is being read: history, political economy—the world" (95). Although I do not think that "literary people" have always been, or still are, "helpless victims," I am aware that the "risky reading" I am offering in this chapter is just another attempt to read the world and to make my readers see how we can do it differently. In this sense, this part of my study proposes a context for the female story discussed earlier, that provided by the traditionally privileged male narrative, which in itself is just a part of the larger text written by the interacting cultures and literatures.

12. Karlinsky, ed., *The Nabokov-Wilson Letters*, 241.

13. It is also worth noticing how, in Nabokov's first text written in English, *The Real Life of Sebastian Knight* (1941), the problem of linguistic identity is made central in a writer's life. The narrator, who is a half-brother of the deceased author, the Anglo-Russian Sebastian Knight, while struggling himself with writing his brother's biography in English, encounters the traces of Sebastian's painful attempts to acquire this language, to erase the stigma of a foreigner. For an interesting reading of this aspect of Nabokov's novel, see Kristeva, *Strangers to Ourselves*, 33–38.

14. The Nansen Passport was devised for displaced artists after the Second World War. Nabokov calls it "that miserable thing, the Nansen Passport (a kind of parolee's card issued to Russian émigrés)" (*Pnin* 46).

15. We can also read Pnin's otherness quite differently, as temporary and meant to inspire feelings of empathy and acceptance in the reader. With his emphasis on Timofey's inner life, by means of providing the insights into his daily habits ("Pninizing" his American rooms, his squirrel-like library research method, his sunlamp, and the ritual of brushing his clothes), his émigré society, and even his "shadow behind the heart," the author gives the American reader a chance to erase Pnin's otherness. There are good reasons to accept such an interpretation, since the reader even has a chance to peer a few times into Nabokov's character's cranial "space helmet" and follow his most intimate moments. However, I would still argue with this interpretation because the very fact that the reader feels empathy for Pnin is based on and results from his otherness. He is endearing precisely in his quaint way of speaking and due to his vulnerability as a "delicate imported article worth paying for in domestic cash" (11). Although we

see reasons for who he is, as Nabokov takes great pains to show us, Pnin remains the other in his constant movement from place to place and even in escaping from writer-narrator Sirin at the end of the novel; thus his otherness is his strength and his escape an affirmation of his fascinating Pninian defiance of being pigeonholed by critics or "captured" by the readers.

16. The Cinderella motif in this passage is related to the "squirrel design" that Nabokov weaves through his novel. For a discussion of the connection between squirrels and "Cendrillon's shoes," see Nicol, "Pnin's History," 95–96. Pnin has also been compared to Cinderella in Boyd, *Vladimir Nabokov*, 283; and see also Barabtarlo, *Phantom of Fact*, 243.

17. See also Field, *Nabokov*, where Victor is seen as an orphan: "Liza's trip to see Pnin . . . was not an idle whim, for shortly after she speaks with him about assuming some financial responsibility for Victor, she leaves Wind and is 'about to be married in Buffalo to a man named Church.' From what we know of Liza Bogolepov there is every reason to assume that, for all practical purposes, Victor has been orphaned" (138).

18. Victor's dreams are echoed in Kinbote's fantasies about the king of Zembla in *Pale Fire*.

19. I emphasize the contrast between the two characters because it perpetuates the movement of Nabokov's complex narrative and shows us how, precisely because we get a lot of Pnin and very little of Sirin, they represent female and male roles within it. An alternative reading might contend that Pnin does not need Sirin to be appreciated, that the novel is only his story. Such an interpretation is valid, but I would argue that it could do more justice to Timofey if it acknowledged how Nabokov uses Sirin to complicate and expand the construction of his central character.

20. Other examples of conformist Russians in America are the Komarovs, Pnin's colleagues at Waindell. They represent the type of immigrants who "would throw Russki parties . . . with Russki hors d'oeuvres and guitar music and more or less phony folk songs—occasions at which shy graduate students would be taught vodka-drinking rites and other stale Russianisms; and after such feasts, upon meeting gruff Pnin, Serafima and Oleg (she raising her eyes to heaven, he covering his with one hand) would murmur in awed self-gratitude: 'Gospodi, skol'ko mï im dayom!' (My, what a lot we give them!)—'them' being the benighted American people. Only another Russian could understand the reactionary and Sovietophile blend presented by the pseudo-colorful Komarovs, for whom an ideal Russia consisted of the Red Army, an anointed monarch, collective farms, anthroposophy, the Russian Church and the Hydro-Electric Dam" (71). Nabokov's biting irony is very apparent in this passage, as he mocks the "colorfulness" of the Komarovs. However, it is also interesting to note his exclusionary "only another Russian could understand" and his subtle aristocratic disdain for Oleg, "a Cossack's son, . . . a very short man with a crew cut and a death's-head's nostrils," and his wife, "large, cheerful, Moscow-born . . . who wore a Tibetan charm on a long silver chain that hung down to her ample, soft belly" (71).

21. This description of Pnin was based on numerous Russian prototypes whom Nabokov knew in person. Timofey looks very much like Roman Jakobson, for example.

22. This particular passage invites a Kristevan reading of the symbolic and semiotic—the female body as lacking boundaries, open and undefinable in opposition to

the bounded male one. See Kristeva, *Desire in Language*, 124–47. Kristeva also argues for "an analytical theory of signifying systems and practices that would search within the signifying phenomenon for the *crisis* or the *unsettling process* of meaning and subject rather than for the coherence or identity of either *one* or a *multiplicity* of structures" (125). My proposed reading of *Pnin* traces the meaning of Timofey's story in the Kristevan process of acquiring a new meaning in a dialogue with the female narratives.

23. See also Boyd, *Vladimir Nabokov*, 271–72, for an argument about *Don Quixote* as an inspiration for Pnin. Nabokov was supposedly outraged by the cruelty of the pursuers and ridiculers of the knight of La Mancha and accused Cervantes of insensitivity. However, look what he does with Pnin. Even if he is sympathetic, one cannot help laughing and hoping that one's English is so much better.

24. The title of the first edition of Rowson's novel was *Charlotte: A Tale of Truth*. I have no idea whether Nabokov knew this text, but he was obviously, as his sneers prove, very familiar with the convention of a didactic romance, and I give him credit for that. It is also fascinating to see how the whole story of the romance between Pnin and Liza, including their journey to America, seems to be directly "lifted" from and a clear parody of Charlotte's story and the entire genre. (Is it an accident that Lolita's mother is named Charlotte Haze and loves romances?)

25. See White, "Nabokov," 5–27, for an interesting discussion of Nabokov's use of parody. As White notes, "Wit, scorn, and the parody of romance can be a way of rescuing romance" (12). It is easy to see how we could replace the word "romance" with "sentiment." By thwarting the sentimental plot and by making fun of it, the author of *Pnin* actually leaves a way for himself to use it and to perpetuate it. See also Hyde, *Vladimir Nabokov*, 149–70, for an analysis of Nabokov's texts as formalist "skazy," which call attention to their own fictionality "by means of persistently foregrounding the inventiveness of the teller" (149). In such a context, Hyde sees Pnin "as a puppet turned parable" very much in the way he sees Gogol's characters work (158).

26. Nabokov's derogatory remarks about Liza's poetry supposedly attacked Anna Akhmatova's verse, and the stylized Akhmatovian "poems" he included in *Pnin* as examples of Timofey's poetess-wife's craft upset the poet. See also Karlinksy, ed., *The Nabokov-Wilson Letters*, 212–13, for Nabokov's fierce attack on nonliterature: Faulkner, Hugo, Malraux, "impotent Henry James," and "the Rev. Eliot." Interestingly, Nabokov mentions the sentimental novel *Uncle Tom's Cabin*, which "may be necessary in a social sense, but . . . [which] is not literature."

27. Oates, "A Personal View of Nabokov," 104.

28. But, as is always the case with Nabokov, he never remains the same, so his opinions about "Jane," and possibly some other writers and topics, evolved into admiration. See Karlinsky, ed., *The Nabokov-Wilson Letters*, 17–18.

29. Quoted in Boyd, *Vladimir Nabokov*, 289.

30. Like Pnin, the writer himself was very anxious about hiding his St. Petersburg Russian-French accent. He was also tortured by the memory of his brother, Sergey, a homosexual who died in a concentration camp, and by his inability to extricate his nephew from communist Czechoslovakia. See ibid., 88–89, 91, 126.

31. See also Beaujour, *Alien Tongues*, 91–101, for an interesting reading of Nabokov's novelistic career as a process of denial and acceptance of his bilingual writing identity.

# Conclusion

1. I agree here with Hazel B. Carby's statement that studying separate traditions is essentialist and ahistorical. But I also think that it is possible to study one's critical position in relation to the tradition one identifies with, or is a member of, without falling into the traps that Carby cautions against. See Carby, *Reconstructing Womanhood*, 15–19.

2. I have borrowed the term "contact zones" from Pratt, "Arts of the Contact Zone," 34.

3. Kristeva, *Nations without Nationalism*, 50–51.

4. I want to emphasize here my gratitude to the readers of my manuscript who have, like some readers of this book will, disagreed with the theoretical assumptions and arguments I use in presenting my case about East European immigrant women writers. I still defend what I do, but acknowledge that I have learned a lot from the opinions that have been provided by my critical "others." They helped me realize that I would like my work to open rather than prevent critical arguments and constructive disagreements.

5. Handlin, *The Uprooted*, 3.

6. Morrison, *Playing in the Dark*, 33–39.

7. Morrison's argument suggests also that the study of African American literature necessitates an inquiry into the whiteness against which writers and readers of the black tradition had to define themselves, and be read, as well. This way of looking at racial dynamics as involving both constructs inextricably is akin to West's argument in *Race Matters*, where he comments on the black and Jewish conflict: "The best of black culture, as manifested, for example, in jazz or the prophetic black church, refuses to put whites or Jews on a pedestal or in the gutter. Rather, black humanity is affirmed alongside that of others, even when those others have at times dehumanized blacks. To put it bluntly, when black humanity is taken for granted and not made to prove itself in white culture, whites, Jews, and others are not that important; they are simply human beings, just like black people" (78).

8. Morrison, *Playing in the Dark*, 90, 43.

9. Ibid., xii.

10. Gladsky, *Princes, Peasants*, 288.

11. For a theoretical framework on African American–Jewish relations, see West, *Race Matters*, 71–79.

12. Smith, introduction to *Incidents in the Life of a Slave Girl*, xxvii–xl.

13. Showalter, "Review Essay," *Signs* 1 (1975): 435, quoted in ibid., xxxiv.

14. See, for example, Carby, *Reinventing Womanhood*, 8–10, which criticizes Barbara Smith's "Toward a Black Feminist Criticism" (1977) for its essentialist confinement of, as Carby puts it, "black feminist criticism to black women critics of black women artists depicting black women" (8).

15. Lorde, *Sister Outsider*, 34.

16. Ibid., 27.

17. Enloe, *The Morning After*, 18–19.

18. Ibid., 21–22.

19. I want to emphasize here that my discussion of this instance is meant as an illus-

tration of a general, possibly oversimplified, tendency of cultural representation and not as an attack on Enloe's argument.

20. It seems that we are finally moving beyond simplistic perceptions of cultural otherness: "The understanding of freedom in the West has become the definition of 'unfreedom' in socialist societies." See Goldfarb, *On Cultural Freedom*, 7. See also Goldfarb, *Beyond Glasnost*.

21. Barańczak, *Breathing under Water*, 14–15.

22. See note 20.

23. Fox-Genovese, *Feminism without Illusions*, 256.

# BIBLIOGRAPHY

## Primary Sources

Antin, Mary. "The Amulet." *Atlantic Monthly*, Jan. 1913, 31–41.

———. *From Polotzk to Boston*. Boston: W. B. Clarke & Co., 1899.

———. "The Lie." *Atlantic Monthly*, Aug. 1913, 177–90.

———. "Malinke's Atonement." *Atlantic Monthly*, Sept. 1911, 300–319.

———. *The Promised Land*. Boston: Houghton Mifflin, 1969.

———. "The Soundless Trumpet." *Atlantic Monthly*, May 1937, 560–69.

———. *They Who Knock at Our Gates*. Boston: Houghton Mifflin, 1914.

———. "A Woman to Her Fellow Citizens." *Outlook*, 2 Nov. 1912, 482–86.

Hoffman, Eva. *Exit into History: A Journey through the New Eastern Europe*. New York: Viking, 1993.

———. *Lost in Translation: A Life in a New Language*. New York: E. P. Dutton, 1989.

———. "My Poland, Then and Now." *Lear's*, July 1991, 104, 102–3 (mispaginated).

Kuncewicz[owa], Maria. *The Conspiracy of the Absent*. Trans. Maurice Michael and Harry Stevens. New York: Roy Publishers, n.d.

———. *Cudzoziemka* (The Stranger). Warsaw: Książka i Wiedza, 1984.

———. *Don Kichote i niańki* (Don Quixote and the Nannies). Lublin: Wydawnictwo Lubelskie, 1989.

———. *Dwa Księżyce* (Two Moons). Lublin: Wydawnictwo Lubelskie, 1989.

———. "Exile without Tears." In *The Pen in Exile: An Anthology*, ed. Paul Tabori, 14–16. [London]: International P.E.N. Club Centre for Writers in Exile, 1954.

———. *Fantasia alla polacca* (A Polish Fantasy). Warsaw: Czytelnik, 1979.

———. *Fantomy* (Phantoms). Lublin: Wydawnictwo Lubelskie, 1989.

———. "50-Lecie niepodległości" (The Fiftieth Anniversary of Independence). *Twórczość*, Dec. 1968, 113–15.

———. *The Forester*. Trans. H. C. Stevens. London: Hutchinson, 1954.

———. *The Keys: A Journey through Europe at War*. Trans. H. C. Stevens. New York and London: Hutchinson International Authors, 1946.

———. *Klucze* (The Keys). Lublin: Wydawnictwo Lubelskie, 1990.

———. *Leśnik* (The Forester). Warsaw: PAX, 1983.

———. *Listy do Jerzego* (Letters to George). Warsaw: PAX, 1988.

———. *Natura* (Nature). Lublin: Wydawnictwo Lubelskie, 1989.

———. *Nowele i bruliony prozatorskie* (Short Stories and Prose Notebooks). Ed. Helena Zaworska. Warsaw: Czytelnik, 1985.

———. *The Olive Grove*. New York: Walker, 1963.

———. *Polish Millstones*. Trans. Stephen Garry. London: P. S. King & Staples, 1942.

———. *Przeźrocza* (Slides). Warsaw: PAX, 1985.

———. "Refugees as World Citizens." *London Times*, 10 Mar. 1949, 6a.

———. *Rozmowy z Marią Kuncewiczową* (Conversations with Maria Kuncewicz). Ed. Helena Zaworska. Warsaw: Czytelnik, 1983.

———. *The Stranger*. New York: L. B. Fischer, 1945.

———. *Tristan*. New York: George Braziller, 1974.

———. *Tristan 1946.* Warsaw: Czytelnik, 1970.

———. *W domu i w Polsce* (At Home and in Poland). Warsaw: Czytelnik, 1958.

———. *Zmowa nieobecnych* (The Conspiracy of the Absent). Warsaw: PAX, 1957.

———, ed. *The Modern Polish Mind: An Anthology.* Boston and Toronto: Little, Brown, 1962.

———, ed. *The Modern Polish Prose.* Birkenhead: English-Polish Publications Committee, 1945.

Morton, Leah [Elizabeth Stern]. *I Am a Woman—and a Jew.* New York: Marcus Wiener, 1986.

Nabokov, Vladimir. *Lolita.* Greenwich, Conn.: Fawcett, 1959.

———. *Pale Fire.* New York: G. P. Putnam's Sons, 1974.

———. *Pnin.* New York: Doubleday, 1957.

———. *The Real Life of Sebastian Knight.* Norfolk: New Directions, 1956.

———. *Speak Memory: An Autobiography Revisited.* New York: G. P. Putnam's, 1966. Originally published as *Conclusive Evidence.* New York: Harper & Bros., 1951.

Stern, Elizabeth [Gertrude Levin]. *This Ecstasy.* New York: J. H. Sears, 1927.

———. *A Marriage Was Made.* New York: J. H. Sears, 1928.

———. *My Mother and I.* New York: Macmillan, 1925.

———. *When Love Comes to Woman.* New York: J. H. Sears, 1929.

Yezierska, Anzia. *All I Could Never Be.* New York: Brewer, Warren, & Putnam, 1932.

———. *Arrogant Beggar.* New York: Doubleday, Page, 1927.

———. *Bread Givers.* New York: Doubleday, Page, 1925.

———. *Children of Loneliness.* New York and London: Funk and Wagnalls, 1923.

———. *Hungry Hearts.* Boston and New York: Houghton Mifflin, 1920.

———. *Hungry Hearts and Other Stories.* New York: Persea Books, 1985.

———. *How I Found America: Collected Stories of Anzia Yezierska.* New York: Persea Books, 1991.

———. *The Open Cage: An Anzia Yezierska Collection.* Ed. Alice Kessler Harris. New York: Persea Books, 1979.

———. *Red Ribbon on a White Horse.* New York: Scribners, 1950.

———. Review of *The Forester*, by Maria Kuncewicz. *New York Times Review of Books*, 12 Sept. 1954, 31.

———. *Salome of the Tenements.* New York: Boni & Liveright, 1923. Reprint, Chicago: University of Chicago Press, 1982.

## Secondary Sources

Abel, Elizabeth, ed. *Writing and Sexual Difference.* Chicago: University of Chicago Press, 1982.

Adamic, Louis. *From Many Lands.* New York: Harper and Bros., 1940.

———. *A Nation of Nations.* New York: Harper and Bros., 1945.

———. *Two-Way Passage.* New York: Harper and Bros., 1941.

Adams, Robert M. "The Wizard of Lake Cayuga." Review of *Vladimir Nabokov: The American Years*, by Brian Boyd. *New York Review*, 30 Jan 1992, 4.

Adams, Timothy Dow. *Telling Lies in Modern Autobiography.* Chapel Hill: University of North Carolina Press, 1990.

Alarcón, Norma. "The Theoretical Subject(s) of This Bridge Called My Back and

Anglo-American Feminism." In *Making Face, Making Soul. Haciendo Caras: Creative and Critical Perspectives by Feminists of Color*, ed. Gloria Anzaldúa, 356–369. San Francisco: Aunt Lute Foundation Books, 1990.

Alexandrov, Vladimir E. *Nabokov's Otherworld*. Princeton: Princeton University Press, 1991.

"America's Possibilities for the Immigrant." *Nation*, 30 Aug. 1917, 105.

Appel, Alfred, Jr., and Charles Newman, eds. *Nabokov: Criticism, Reminiscences, Translations, and Tributes*. London: Lowe & Brydone, 1970.

Bakhtin, M. M. *The Dialogic Imagination*. Ed. Michael Holquist. Austin: University of Texas Press, 1981.

Bannan, Helen M. "Elizabeth Gertrude Levin Stern." In *American Women Writers*, ed. Lina Mainiero, 4:165–67. New York: Frederick Ungar, 1982.

Barabtarlo, Gennadi. *Phantom of Fact: A Guide to Nabokov's* Pnin. Ann Arbor: Ardis Publishers, 1989.

Barańczak, Stanisław. *Breathing under Water and Other East European Essays*. Cambridge: Harvard University Press, 1990.

Barańczak, Stanisław, and Clare Cavanagh, trans. and eds. *Spoiling Cannibals' Fun: Polish Poetry of the Last Two Decades of Communist Rule*. Evanston: Northwestern University Press, 1991.

Bassnett, Susan, and Piotr Kuhiwczak, trans. and eds. *Ariadne's Thread: Polish Women Poets*. London and Boston: Forest Books/UNESCO, 1988.

Bayley, John. *Selected Essays*. Cambridge: Cambridge University Press, 1984.

Baym, Nina. "Melodramas of Beset Manhood: How Theories of American Fiction Exclude Women Authors." In *The New Feminist Criticism: Essays on Women, Literature, and Theory*, ed. Elaine Showalter, 63–80. New York: Pantheon Books, 1985.

Beajour, Elizabeth Klosty. *Alien Tongues: Bilingual Russian Writers of the "First" Immigration*. Ithaca: Cornell University Press, 1989.

Beeson, Trevor. *Discretion and Valour: Religious Conditions in Russia and Eastern Europe*. Philadelphia: Fortress Press, 1982.

Bellamy, Joe David. *The New Fiction: Interviews with Innovative American Writers*. Urbana: University of Illinois Press, 1974.

Bellow, Saul. *The Bellarosa Connection*. New York: Penguin Books, 1989.

Benstock, Shari. "Expatriate Modernism: Writing on the Cultural Rim." In *Women's Writing in Exile*, ed. Mary Lynn Broe and Angela Ingram, 19–40. Chapel Hill: University of North Carolina Press, 1989.

Bercovitch, Sacvan. Afterword to *Ideology and Classic American Literature*, ed. Sacvan Bercovitch and Myra Yehlen. Cambridge: Cambridge University Press, 1986.

———. "The Rites of Assent: Rhetoric, Ritual, and the Ideology of American Consensus." In *The American Self: Myth, Ideology, and Popular Culture*, ed. Sam B. Girgus, 5–42. Albuquerque: University of New Mexico Press, 1981.

Berezowski, Maksymilian. *Ameryka pięknych snów* (America of Beautiful Dreams). Warsaw: Książka i Wiedza, 1989.

Bergland, Betty. "Ideology, Ethnicity, and the Gendered Subject: Reading Immigrant Women's Autobiographies." In *Seeking Common Ground: Multidisciplinary Studies of Immigrant Women in the United States*, ed. Donna Gabaccia, 101–21. Westport, Conn.: Praeger, 1992.

Berman, Myron. *The Attitude of American Jewry towards East European Immigration, 1881–1914*. New York: Arno Press, 1990.

Bevan, David, ed. *Literature and Exile*. Amsterdam and Atlanta: Editions Radopi B. V., 1990.

Blicksilver, Edith, ed. *The Ethnic American Woman: Problems, Protests, Lifestyles*. Dubuque: Kendall/Hunt, 1978.

Boelhower, William. *Immigrant Autobiography in the United States*. Venice: Tipo-Litografia Armena, 1982.

———. *Through a Glass Darkly: Ethnic Semiosis in American Literature*. New York: Oxford University Press, 1987.

Bok, Edward. *The Americanization of Edward Bok: An Autobiography*. New York: Scribner, 1920.

Bonner, Elena. *Mothers and Daughters*. Trans. Antonia W. Bouis. New York: Knopf, 1992.

Borkowska, Grażyna. "Dlaczego skrywamy pragnienie wolności? Kobiecym Piórem" (Why Do We Hide Our Desire for Freedom? With Woman's Pen). *Polityka*, 21 July 1993, Kultura I–II.

Boyd, Brian. *Vladimir Nabokov: The American Years*. Princeton: Princeton University Press, 1991.

———. "The Year of *Lolita*." *New York Times Book Review*, 8 Sept. 1991, 1, 31–33.

Boydston, Jo Ann, ed. *The Poems of John Dewey*. Carbondale: Southern Illinois Press, 1977.

Braumberg, Abraham. "Jewish Revelations." *Times Literary Supplement*, 22 Nov. 1991, 26.

Brettell, Caroline B., and Patricia A. deBerjeois. "Anthropology and the Study of Immigrant Women." In *Seeking Common Ground: Multidisciplinary Studies of Immigrant Women in the United States*, ed. Donna Gabaccia, 41–63. Westport, Conn.: Praeger, 1992.

Bridenthal, Renate, and Claudia Koonz, eds. *Becoming Visible: Women in European History*. Boston: Houghton Mifflin, 1977.

Brodsky, Joseph. *Less Than One*. New York: Farrar Straus Giroux, 1986.

———. "'The Post-Communist Nightmare': An Exchange." *New York Review of Books*, 17 Feb. 1994, 28–30.

Broe, Mary Lynn, and Angela Ingram, eds. *Women's Writing in Exile*. Chapel Hill: University of North Carolina Press, 1989.

Brown, Francis J., and Joseph Slabery Roucek, eds. *Our Racial and National Minorities*. New York: Prentice-Hall, 1937.

Brooks, Peter. *Reading for the Plot: Design and Intention in Narrative*. Cambridge: Harvard University Press, 1992.

Brownlow, Kevin. *Behind the Mask of Innocence*. New York: Alfred A. Knopf, 1990.

Bruss, Elizabeth W. *Autobiographical Acts: The Changing Situation of a Literary Genre*. Baltimore: Johns Hopkins University Press, 1976.

Bruss, Paul. *Victims: Textual Strategies in Recent American Fiction*. Lewisburg: Bucknell University Press, 1981.

Burger, Otis K. Review of *The Olive Grove*, by Maria Kuncewicz. *New York Times Book Review*, 11 Aug. 1963, 22.

Cagidemetrio, Alide. "A Plea for Fictional Histories and Old-Time 'Jewesses.'" In

*The Invention of Ethnicity*, ed. Werner Sollors, 14–43. New York: Oxford University Press, 1989.

Cahn, Susan. "New Poland, Old Problems." *On the Issues*, Spring 1991, 13–15.

Carby, Hazel V. *Reconstructing Womanhood: The Emergence of the Afro-American Woman Novelist*. New York: Oxford University Press, 1987.

Carnegie, Andrew. *Autobiography of Andrew Carnegie*. New York: Houghton and Mifflin, 1920.

Carpenter, Bogdana. *Monumenta Polonica. The First Four Centuries of Polish Poetry: A Bilingual Anthology*. Ann Arbor: Michigan Slavic Publications, 1989.

Cesarani, David. "What Went Wrong in Warsaw." *Times Literary Supplement*, 22 Nov. 1991, 26.

Chambers, Ross. *Story and Situation: Narrative Seduction and the Power of Fiction*. Minneapolis: University of Minnesota Press, 1984.

Clayton, Jay. *The Pleasures of Babel: Contemporary American Literature and Theory*. New York: Oxford University Press, 1993.

Cliff, Michelle. "A Journey into Speech," In *The Greywoolf Annual Five: Multicultural Literacy*, ed. Rick Simmons and Scott Walker, 57–62. St. Paul: Greywoolf Press, 1988.

Clifford, James. *The Predicament of Culture: Twentieth-Century Ethnography, Literature, and Art*. Cambridge: Harvard University Press, 1988.

Craveri, Benedetta. "Women in Retreat." Trans. Joan Sax. *New York Review of Books*, 19 Dec. 1991, 67–71.

Curry, Jane Leftwich, trans. and ed. *The Black Book of Polish Censorship*. New York: Vintage Books, 1984.

*Czarna księga cenzury PRL* (The Black Book of Censorship of People's Poland). 2 vols. London: ANEKS Political Quarterly, 1977.

Davie, Donald. *Slavic Excursions: Essays on Russian and Polish Literature*. Chicago: University of Chicago Press, 1990.

Deák, István. "Strategies of Hell." *New York Review of Books*, 8 Oct. 1992, 8–20.

Dearborn, Mary V. "Anzia Yezierska and the Making of an Ethnic American Self." In *The Invention of Ethnicity*, ed. Werner Sollors, 105–23. New York: Oxford University Press, 1989.

———. *Love in the Promised Land: The Story of Anzia Yezierska and John Dewey*. New York: Free Press, 1988.

———. *Pocahontas's Daughters: Gender and Ethnicity in American Culture*. New York: Oxford University Press, 1986.

De Lauretis, Teresa. *Alice Doesn't: Feminism, Semiotics, Cinema*. Bloomington: Indiana University Press, 1984.

D'Emilio, John, and Estelle B. Freedman. *Intimate Matters: A History of Sexuality in America*. New York: Harper and Row, 1988.

Deutsch, Babette. "An Unimpressive Autobiography." Review of *I Am a Woman—and a Jew*, by Leah Morton. *New York Herald Tribune Books*, 19 Dec. 1926, 17.

Di Pietro, Robert J., and Edward Ifkovic, eds. *Ethnic Perspectives in American Literature: Selected Essays on the European Contribution*. New York: MLA, 1983.

Donald, Miles. *The American Novel in the Twentieth Century*. Vancouver: Douglas David & Charles Limited, 1978.

Duffy, Richard. "You Can't Be an Immigrant Twice: An Interview with Anzia Yezierska." In *Children of Loneliness*, by Anzia Yezierska, 261–70. New York and London: Funk and Wagnalls, 1923.

DuPlessis, Rachel Blau. *Writing beyond the Ending: Narrative Strategies of Twentieth-Century Women Writers*. Bloomington: Indiana University Press, 1985.

Eakin, Paul John. *Fictions in Autobiography: Studies in the Art of Self-Invention*. Princeton: Princeton University Press, 1985.

Enloe, Cynthia. *The Morning After: Sexual Politics at the End of the Cold War*. Berkeley: University of California Press, 1993.

Ferraro, Thomas J. *Ethnic Passages: Literary Immigrants in Twentieth-Century America*. Chicago: University of Chicago Press, 1993.

Field, Andrew. *Nabokov: His Life in Art*. Boston: Little, Brown, 1967.

Filipiak, Izabela. *Śmierć i Spirala* (Death and the Spiral). Biblioteka Feministyczna. Wrocław: Wydawnictwo A, 1992.

Filipowicz, Halina. "Fission and Fusion: Polish Émigré Literature." *Slavic and East European Journal* 33 (Summer 1989): 157–72.

———. "Przeciw 'literaturze kobiecej'" (Against l'écriture féminine). *Przegląd Polski*, 18 Feb 1993, 10–11.

Fine, David F. *The City, the Immigrant, and American Fiction, 1880–1920*. Metuchen, N.J., and London: Scarecrow Press, 1971.

"Flight through Europe." *Times Literary Supplement*, 23 Feb. 1946, 86.

Foley, Barbara. *Telling the Truth: The Theory and Practice of Documentary Fiction*. Ithaca: Cornell University Press, 1986.

Fowler, Lois J., and David H. Fowler, eds. *Revelations of Self: American Women in Autobiography*. New York: State University of New York Press, 1990.

Fox-Genovese, Elizabeth. *Feminism without Illusions: A Critique of Individualism*. Chapel Hill: University of North Carolina Press, 1991.

Freibert, Lucy N., and Barbara A. White, eds. *Hidden Hands: An Anthology of American Women Writers, 1780–1870*. Brunswick, N.J.: Rutgers University Press, 1985.

Friedman, Susan Stanford. "Exile in the American Grain: H.D.'s Diaspora." In *Women's Writing in Exile*, ed. Mary Lynn Broe and Angela Ingram, 87–112. Chapel Hill: University of North Carolina Press, 1989.

Funk, Nanette. "The Fate of Feminism in Eastern Europe." *Chronicle of Higher Education*, 2 Feb. 1994, B1–2.

Gabaccia, Donna, ed. *Seeking Common Ground: Multidisciplinary Studies of Immigrant Women in the United States*. Westport, Conn.: Praeger, 1992.

Gardiner, Judith K. "On Female Identity and Writing by Women." In *Writing and Sexual Difference*, ed. Elizabeth Abel, 177–91. Chicago: University of Chicago Press, 1982.

Gass, William H. *Habitations of the Word: Essays*. New York: Touchstone Books, 1985.

Gates, Henry Louis, Jr., ed. *"Race," Writing, and Difference*. Chicago: University of Chicago Press, 1986.

———, ed. *Reading Black, Reading Feminist: A Critical Anthology*. New York: Meridian, 1990.

Gibian, George, and Stephen Jan Parker, eds. *The Achievements of Vladimir Nabokov: Essays, Studies, Reminiscences, and Stories from the Cornell Nabokov Festival*. Ithaca: Center For International Studies, 1984.

Gilman, Charlotte Perkins. *The Living of Charlotte Perkins Gilman: An Autobiography*. New York: D. Appleton-Century Company, 1935.

———. *Women and Economics*. Ed. Carl N. Degler. New York: Harper and Row, 1966.

Gilman, Sander L. *Difference and Pathology: Stereotypes of Sexuality, Race, and Madness*. Ithaca: Cornell University Press, 1985.

———. *Jewish Self-Hatred: Anti-Semitism and the Hidden Language of the Jews*. Baltimore: Johns Hopkins University Press, 1985.

———. *The Jew's Body*. New York: Routledge, 1991.

Girgus, Sam B., ed. *The American Self: Myth, Ideology, and Popular Culture*. Albuquerque: University of New Mexico Press, 1981.

———. *Desire and the Political Unconscious in American Literature: Eros and Ideology*. New York: St. Martin's Press, 1990.

———. *The New Covenant: Jewish Writers and the American Idea*. Chapel Hill: University of North Carolina Press, 1984.

Glad, John, ed. *Literature in Exile*. Durham and London: Duke University Press, 1990.

Gladsky, Thomas S. *Princes, Peasants, and Other Polish Selves: Ethnicity in American Literature*. Amherst: University of Massachusetts Press, 1992.

Goldfarb, Jeffrey C. *Beyond Glasnost: The Post-Totalitarian Mind*. Chicago: University of Chicago Press, 1989.

———. *On Cultural Freedom: An Exploration of Public Life in Poland and America*. Chicago: University of Chicago Press, 1982.

———. *The Persistence of Freedom: The Sociological Implications of Polish Student Theater*. Boulder: Westview Press, 1980.

Gomolka, Stanislaw, and Antony Polonsky, eds. *Polish Paradoxes*. New York: Routledge, 1990.

Gomori, George, and Charles Newman, eds. *New Writing of Eastern Europe*. Chicago: Quadrangle Books, 1968.

Goodman, Charlotte. "Anzia Yezierska." *Dictionary of Literary Biography*, ed. Daniel Walden. Vol. 28. Detroit: Book Tower, 1984.

Gornick, Vivian. *Fierce Attachments: A Memoir*. New York: Simon and Schuster, 1987.

———. Introduction to *How I Found America: Collected Stories of Anzia Yezierska*. New York: Persea Books, 1991.

Grabes, H. *Fictitious Biographies: Vladimir Nabokov's English Novels*. The Hague and Paris: Mouton, 1977.

Graff, Gerald. "Narrative and the Unofficial Interpretive Culture." In *Reading Narrative: Form, Ethics, Ideology*, ed. James Phelan, 3–11. Columbus: Ohio State University Press, 1989.

Gronowicz, Antoni. *Modjeska: Her Life and Loves*. New York: Thomas Yoseloff, 1956.

Grzeloński, Bogdan, ed. *Ameryka w pamiętnikach Polaków. Antologia* (America in the Diaries of Poles: An Anthology). Warsaw: Wydawnictwo Interpress, 1988.

Gubar, Susan. "'The Blank Page' and the Issues of Female Creativity." In *Writing and Sexual Difference*, ed. Elizabeth Abel, 73–91. Chicago: University of Chicago Press, 1982.

Gurr, Andrew. *Writers in Exile: The Identity of Home in Modern Literature*. Atlantic Highlands, N.J.: Humanities Press, 1981.

Guttmann, Allen. *The Jewish Writer in America: Assimilation and the Crisis of Identity*. New York: Oxford University Press, 1971.

Hale, Hope. "The Momentum of Murder." *Saturday Review of Literature*, 22 June 1963, 39–40.

Handlin, Oscar. Foreword to *The Promised Land*, by Mary Antin. Princeton: Princeton University Press, 1969.

———. *Immigration as a Factor in American History*. Englewood Cliffs: Prentice-Hall, 1959.

———. *Race and Nationality in American Life*. Boston: Little, Brown, 1957.

———. *The Uprooted: The Epic Story of the Great Migrations That Made the American People*. Boston: Little, Brown, 1951.

———, ed. *Children of the Uprooted*. New York: George Braziller, 1966.

Havel, Vaclav, et al. *The Power of the Powerless: Citizens against the State in Central-Eastern Europe*. Ed. John Keane. New York: Armonk, 1985.

———. "Words on Words." In *Writings on the East. Selected Essays on Eastern Europe from* The New York Review of Books, 7–19. New York: Rea S. Hederman, 1990.

Heilbrun, Carolyn G. *Writing a Woman's Life*. New York: W. W. Norton, 1988.

Henriksen, Louise Levitas. *Anzia Yezierska: A Writer's Life*. New Brunswick and London: Rutgers University Press, 1988.

———. Afterword to *The Open Cage*, by Anzia Yezierska. Ed. Alice Kessler-Harris. New York: Persea Books, 1979.

Higham, John. *Strangers in the Land: Patterns of American Nativism, 1860–1925*. New York: Atheneum, 1975.

Hite, Molly. *The Other Side of the Story: Structures and Strategies of Contemporary Feminist Narrative*. Ithaca: Cornell University Press, 1989.

Holte, James Craig. *The Ethnic I: A Sourcebook for Ethnic-American Autobiography*. New York: Greenwood Press, 1988.

Holton, Milne, and Paul Vangelisti, eds. *The New Polish Poetry: A Bilingual Collection*. Pittsburgh: University of Pittsburgh Press, 1978.

Holquist, Michael, and Katerina Clark. *Mikhail Bakhtin*. Cambridge: Harvard University Press, 1984.

Homberger, Eric. "Charles Reznikoff's *Family Chronicle*: Saying Thank You and I'm Sorry." In *Charles Reznikoff: Man and Poet*, ed. Milton Hindus, 327–42. Orono, Maine: National Poetry Foundation, University of Maine, 1984.

Hyde, G. M. *Vladimir Nabokov: America's Russian Novelist*. London: Marion Boyars, 1977.

"The Immigrant." *New York Times*, 14 Apr. 1912, 228.

Iser, Wolfgang. *Prospecting: From Reader Response to Literary Anthropology*. Baltimore: Johns Hopkins University Press, 1989.

Jarry, Alfred. *The Ubu Plays*. Trans. Cyril Connolly and Simon Watson Taylor. New York: Grove Press, 1968.

James, Henry. *The American Scene*. Bloomington: Indiana University Press, 1968.

———. *The Speech and Manners of American Women*. Ed. E. S. Riggs. Lancaster: Lancaster House Press, 1973.

Jameson, Fredric. *The Political Unconscious: Narrative as a Socially Symbolic Act*. Ithaca: Cornell University Press, 1981.

Janaszek-Ivaničková, Halina. "La Contemporanéité et les archétypes ou le mythe de

Tristan et Iseut dans l'Œuvre de Maria Kuncewiczowa" (Contemporaneity and Archetypes or the Myth of Tristan and Yseult in the Work of Maria Kuncewicz). *Neohelicon* 3–4 (1975): 189–201.

Jehlen, Myra. Introduction. *Ideology and Classic American Literature*, ed. Sacvan Bercovitch and Myra Jehlen, 1–18. Cambridge: Cambridge University Press, 1986.

Kamel, Rose. "'Anzia Yezierska, Get Out of Your Own Way': Selfhood and Otherness in the Autobiographical Fiction of Anzia Yezierska." In *Studies in American Jewish Literature*, ed. Daniel Walden, 3:40–50. Albany: State University of New York Press, 1983.

Karamcheti, Indira. "Caliban in the Classroom." *Radical Teacher* 44 (1993): 13–17.

Karlinsky, Simon, ed. *The Nabokov-Wilson Letters: Correspondence between Vladimir Nabokov and Edmund Wilson 1940–1971*. New York: Harper and Row, 1979.

Kazimierczyk, Barbara. *Dyliżans Księżycowy* (A Moon-Coach). Warsaw: Instytut Wydawniczy PAX, 1977.

Kent, Donald Peterson. *The Refugee Intellectual: The Americanization of the Immigrants of 1933–1941*. New York: Columbia University Press, 1953.

Kessler-Harris, Alice. Introduction to *Bread Givers*, by Anzia Yezierska. New York: Persea Books, 1975.

———. *Out to Work: A History of Wage-Earning Women in the United States*. New York: Oxford University Press, 1982.

———, ed. *The Open Cage: An Anzia Yezierska Collection*. New York: Persea Books, 1979.

Knapp, Bettina L. *Exile and the Writer: Exoteric and Esoteric Experiences. A Jungian Approach*. University Park: Pennsylvania State University Press, 1991.

Kolodny, Annette. *The Land Before Her: Fantasy and Experience of the American Frontiers, 1630–1860*. Chapel Hill: University of North Carolina Press, 1984.

———. *The Lay of the Land: Metaphor as Experience and History in American Life and Letters*. Chapel Hill: University of North Carolina Press, 1975.

Kosiński, Jerzy. *Being There*. New York: Bantam, 1988.

———. *The Painted Bird*. London: W. H. Allen, 1966.

———. *Steps*. New York: Modern Library, 1983.

Kostrzewa, Robert, ed. *Between East and West: Writings from Kultura*. New York: Hill and Wang, 1990.

Kott, Jan, ed. *Four Decades of the Polish Essay*. Evanston: Northwestern University Press, 1990.

Kraditor, Aileen S. *The Ideas of the Woman Suffrage Movement, 1890–1920*. New York and London: Columbia University Press, 1965.

Kristeva, Julia. *About Chinese Women*. Trans. Anita Barrows. New York: Urizen Books, 1977.

———. *Desire in Language: A Semiotic Approach to Literature*. New York: Columbia University Press, 1980.

———. *Nations without Nationalism*. New York: Columbia University Press, 1993.

———. "A New Type of Intellectual: The Dissident." In *The Kristeva Reader*, ed. Toril Moi, 292–300. New York: Columbia University Press, 1986.

———. *The Powers of Horror: An Essay on Abjection*. Trans. Leon S. Roudiez. New York: Columbia University Press, 1982.

———. *The Samurai*. Trans. Barbara Bray. New York: Columbia University Press, 1992.

———. *Strangers to Ourselves*. Trans. Leon S. Roudiez. New York: Columbia University Press, 1991.

———. "Why the United States." In *The Kristeva Reader*, ed. Toril Moi, 272–91. New York: Columbia University Press, 1986.

Krzyżanowski, Julian. *Dzieje literatury polskiej* (History of Polish Literature). Warsaw: Państwowe Wydawnictwo Naukowe, 1979.

Kundera, Milan. *The Art of the Novel*. New York: Grove Press, 1988.

Latawiec, Bogusława. "Żywy dom" (The Living House). *Arkusz*, 28 Dec. 1993, 3.

Lazarus, Emma. "The New Colossus." In *The Ethnic American Woman: Problems, Protests, Lifestyles*, ed. Edith Blicksilver, 307. Dubuque: Kendall/Hunt, 1978.

Lazarus, Josephine. "From Plotzk to Boston." *Critic*, Apr. 1899, 317–18.

Le Sueur, Meridel. "A Remembrance." Preface to *Living My Life: An Autobiography of Emma Goldman*, by Emma Goldman. Salt Lake City: Peregrine Smith, 1982.

Levenberg, Diane. "Three Jewish Writers and the Spirit of the Thirties: Michael Gold, Anzia Yezierska, and Henry Roth." *Book Forum* 6 (1982): 233–44.

Levine, Madeline G. *Contemporary Polish Poetry 1925–1975*. Ed. Irene Nagurski. Twayne's World Author Series: A Survey of the World's Literature. Boston: Twayne, 1981.

Lewis, W. B. *The American Adam*. Chicago: University of Chicago Press, 1955.

Lionnet, Françoise. *Autobiographical Voices: Race, Gender, Self-Portraiture*. Ithaca: Cornell University Press, 1989.

Lilly, Paul R., Jr. *Words in Search of Victims: The Achievement of Jerzy Kosinski*. Kent and London: Kent State University Press, 1988.

Limanowska, Barbara. "Dlaczego w Polsce nie ma feminizmu" (Why Doesn't Feminism Exist in Poland?). *Pelnym Glosem*, Summer 1993, 3–24.

Lorde, Audre. *Sister Outsider: Essays and Speeches by Audre Lorde*. New York: The Crossing Press, 1984.

Lupack, Barbara Tepa. *Plays of Passion, Games of Chance: Jerzy Kosinski and His Fiction*. Bristol: Wyndham Hall Press, 1988.

Lyra, Franciszek. "Following the Cycle: The Ethnic Pattern of Polish-American Literature." *MELUS*, Winter 1985, 63–71.

Marcus, Jane. "Alibis and Legends: The Ethics of Elsewhereness, Gender, and Estrangement." In *Women's Writing in Exile*, ed. Mary Lynn Broe and Angela Ingram, 269–94. Chapel Hill: University of North Carolina Press, 1989.

Marx, Leo. *The Machine in the Garden*. New York: Oxford University Press, 1964.

Masterson, Martha Gay. *One Woman's West: Recollections of the Oregon Trail and Settling the Northwest Country*. Ed. Lois Barton. Eugene: Spencer Butte Press, 1986.

Mayewski, Pawel, ed. *The Broken Mirror: A Collection of Writings from Contemporary Poland*. New York: Random House, 1958.

M. G. S. Review of *My Mother and I*, by Elizabeth Stern. *New York Call*, 9 Sept. 1917, 15.

Michnik, Adam. "Poland and the Jews." *New York Review of Books*, 30 May 1991, 11–12.

Milbauer, Asher Z. *Transcending Exile: Conrad, Nabokov, I. B. Singer*. Miami: University Press of Florida, 1985.

Miller, Warren. "Gruesome Episode in Southern France." *New York Herald Tribune Books*, 23 June 1963, 4.

Miłosz, Czesław. *The History of Polish Literature*. London: Macmillan, 1969.

———, ed. *Postwar Polish Poetry: An Anthology*. Berkeley: University of California Press, 1983.

Minh-ha, Trinh T. *Woman, Native, Other: Writing Postcoloniality and Feminism*. Bloomington: Indiana University Press, 1989.

"Miss Mary Antin Wrote Noted Book." *New York Times*, 18 May 1949, L27.

Modjeska, Helena. *Memories and Impressions of Helena Modjeska: An Autobiography*. New York: Macmillan, 1910.

Monticone, Ronald C. *The Catholic Church in Communist Poland 1945–1985: Forty Years of Church-State Relations*. New York: Columbia University Press, 1986.

Moody, John, and Roger Boyes. *The Priest and the Policeman: The Courageous Life and Cruel Murder of Father Jerzy Popieluszko*. New York: Summit Books, 1987.

Morrison, Toni. *Playing in the Dark: Whiteness and the Literary Imagination*. New York: Vintage Books, 1992.

Morson, Gary Saul. Introduction to "Russian Cluster." *PMLA* 107 (March 1992): 226–31.

Morton, Donald E. *Vladimir Nabokov*. New York: Frederick Ungar, 1974.

Mukherjee, Bharati. *Jasmine*. New York: Fawcett Crest, 1989.

Natanson, Wojciech. "Niezliczone style pisarki: o Marii Kuncewiczowej" (Innumerable Styles of Woman Writer: About Maria Kuncewicz). *Życie Literackie*, 17 Sept. 1989, 10.

Neidle, Cecyle S. *America's Immigrant Women*. Boston: Twayne, 1975.

Nicol, Charles. "Pnin's History." In *Critical Essays on Vladimir Nabokov*, ed. Phyllis A. Roth, 93–104. Boston: G. K. Hall, 1984.

Niczov, Aleksandar. *Black Book of Polish Censorship*. South Bend: And Books, 1982.

Novak, Michael. *The Rise of the Unmeltable Ethnics: Politics and Culture in the Seventies*. New York: Macmillan, 1975.

Nyren, Dorothy. Review of *The Olive Grove*, by Maria Kuncewicz. *Library Journal*, 1 June 1963, 2275.

Oates, Joyce Carol. "A Personal View of Nabokov." In *Critical Essays on Vladimir Nabokov*, ed. Phyllis A. Roth, 105–8. Boston: G. K. Hall, 1984.

O'Connor, Mark. "Two People, Two Stories." *Commonweal*, 12 July 1991, 440–42.

Ohmann, Richard. "English after the USSR." *Radical Teacher* 44 (1993): 41–46.

Packman, David. *Vladimir Nabokov: The Structure of Literary Desire*. Columbia and London: University of Missouri Press, 1982.

Page, Ruth. "Other Titles on the Fiction List." Review of *The Stranger*, by Maria Kuncewicz. *New York Times Book Review*, 5 Aug. 1945, 26.

Pfanner, Herbert Grundmann, ed. *Kulturelle Wechselbeziehungen im Exil—Exile across Cultures*. Bonn: Bonvier Verlag, Herbert Grundmann, 1986.

Phelan, James, ed. *Reading Narrative: Form, Ethics, Ideology*. Columbus: Ohio State University Press, 1989.

Piasecki, Waldemar. "Obywatelka świata, cudzoziemka ziemi wybranej" (Citizen of the World, Foreigner of the Chosen Land). *Panorama Polska*, Nov. 1989, 34–35.

Pick, Robert. "Unhappy Woman." *Saturday Review of Literature*, 4 Aug. 1945, 29.

Polacheck, Hilda Satt. *I Came a Stranger: The Story of a Hull-House Girl*. Ed. Dena J. Polacheck Epstein. Chicago: University of Illinois Press, 1989.

Pratt, Mary Louise. "Arts of the Contact Zone." *Profession* 91 (1991): 34.

"The Promised Land." *Independent*, 22 Aug. 1912, 445.

Radner, Hilary. "Exiled from Within: The Woman's Novel." In *Women's Writing in Exile*, ed. Mary Lynn Broe and Angela Ingram, 252–67. Chapel Hill: The University of North Carolina Press, 1989.

Reed, Ishmael. "America: The Multinational Society." In *The Greywoolf Annual Five: Multicultural Literacy*, ed. Rick Simmons and Scott Walker, 155–60. St. Paul: Greywoolf Press, 1988.

Review of *The Conspiracy of the Absent*, by Maria Kuncewicz. *Times Literary Supplement*, 29 Sept. 1950: 609.

Review of *The Conspiracy of the Absent*, by Maria Kuncewicz. *Kirkus*, 15 Sept. 1950, 567.

Review of *The Forester*, by Maria Kuncewicz. *Times Literary Supplement*, 29 Jan. 1954: 25.

Review of *My Mother and I*, by Elizabeth Stern. *Cleveland*, July 1917, 100.

Review of *The Stranger*, by Maria Kuncewicz. *Kirkus*, 1 July 1945, 275.

Roosens, Eugeen E. *Creating Ethnicity: The Process of Ethnogenesis*. Frontiers of Anthropology 5. Newbury Park: Sage Publications, 1989.

Roosevelt, Theodore. Foreword to *My Mother and I*, by Elizabeth Stern. New York: Macmillan, 1925.

Rosen, Philip. *The Neglected Dimension: Ethnicity in American Life*. Notre-Dame: University of Notre Dame Press, 1980.

Roth, Henry. *Call It Sleep*. New York: Avon Books, 1962.

Roth, Philip. *The Facts: A Novelist's Autobiography*. New York: Farrar, Straus and Giroux, 1988.

——— . *Reading Myself and Others*. New York: Farrar, Straus and Giroux, 1975.

——— , ed. *The Polish Complex*, by Tadeusz Konwicki. Writers from the Other Europe. New York: Penguin, 1984.

Roth, Phyllis A., ed. *Critical Essays on Vladimir Nabokov*. Boston: G. K. Hall, 1984.

Rowson, Susanna. *Charlotte Temple: A Tale of Truth*. Ed. David Stineback. Albany: NCUP, Inc., 1964.

Royce, Anna Peterson. *Ethnic Identity: Strategies of Diversity*. Bloomington: Indiana University Press, 1982.

Rubenstein, Roberta. *Boundaries of the Self: Gender, Culture, Fiction*. Urbana: University of Illinois Press, 1987.

Said, Abdul, and Luiz R. Simmons, eds. *Ethnicity in an International Context*. New Brunswick: Transaction Books, 1976.

Salvatori, Maridina. "Women's Work in the Novels of Immigrant Life." *MELUS*, Winter 1982, 39–58.

Sapieha, Virgilia. "Polish Author Presents Stormy Petrel in Flight." *New York Herald Tribune Weekly Book Review*, 5 Aug. 1945, sec. 6, p. 5.

Sawicka, Elżbieta. "Tak się życiem nasycić i zmęczyć" (To Live to the Fullest, to Get Tired of Life). *Tygodnik Polski*, 31 July 1989, 38.

Scarry, Elaine. *The Body in Pain: The Making and Unmaking of the World*. New York: Oxford University Press, 1985.

Schofield, Mary Ann. "Underground Lives: Women's Personal Narratives, 1939–45."

In *Literature and Exile*, ed. David Bevan. Amsterdam and Atlanta: Editions Radopi B. V., 1990.

Schwartz, Helen J. "Mary Antin." In *American Women Writers*, ed. Lina Mainiero, 1: 61–62. New York: Frederick Ungar, 1982.

Schoen, Carol B. *Anzia Yezierska*. Boston: Twayne, 1982.

Scholes, Robert. *The Fabulators: The Illiberal Imagination*. New York: Oxford University Press, 1967.

Seabrook, William. *These Foreigners*. New York: Harcourt, Brace, 1938.

Seller, Maxine Schwartz, ed. *Immigrant Women*. Philadelphia: Temple University Press, 1981.

———. *To Seek America: A History of Ethnic Life in the United States*. N.p.: Jerome S. Ozer, 1977.

Showalter, Elaine. "Feminist Criticism in the Wilderness." In *The New Feminist Criticism: Essays on Women, Literature, and Theory*, ed. Elaine Showalter, 243–70. New York: Pantheon Books, 1985.

Silverman, Kaja. *The Subject of Semiotics*. New York: Oxford University Press, 1983.

Slotkin, Richard. *The Fatal Environment: The Myth of the Frontier in the Age of Industrialization*. New York: Atheneum, 1985.

———. *Regeneration through Violence: The Mythology of the American Frontier, 1600–1860*. Middletown: Wesleyan University Press, 1973.

Smith, Henry Nash. *Virgin Land: The American West as Symbol and Myth*. Cambridge: Harvard University Press, 1950.

Smith, Sidonie. *A Poetics of Women's Autobiography: Marginality and the Fictions of Self-Representation*. Bloomington and Indianapolis: Indiana University Press, 1987.

Smith, Valerie. Introduction to *Incidents in the Life of a Slave Girl*, by Harriet Jacobs. New York: Oxford Univrsity Press, 1988.

Sochen, June. "Identities within Identity: Thoughts on Jewish American Women Writers." In *Studies in American Jewish Literature*, ed. Daniel Walden, 3:6–10. Albany: State University of New York Press, 1983.

Sollors, Werner. *Beyond Ethnicity: Consent and Descent in American Culture*. New York: Oxford University Press, 1986.

———. Foreword to *Through a Glass Darkly: Ethnic Semiosis in American Literature*, by William Boelhower, 1–4. New York: Oxford University Press, 1987.

———, ed. *The Invention of Ethnicity*. New York: Oxford University Press, 1989.

Spivak, Gayatri Chakravorty. *In Other Worlds: Essays in Cultural Politics*. New York: Methuen, 1987.

Spivak, Gayatri Chakravorty, and Sneja Gunew. "Questions of Multiculturalism." In *Women's Writing in Exile*, ed. Mary Lynn Broe and Angela Ingram, 412–20. Chapel Hill: University of North Carolina Press, 1989.

Środa, Magdalena. "Feministki, kobiety, wiedźmy" (Feminists, Women, Witches). *Polityka*, 21 July 1993, Kultura I–II.

Steinfels, Margaret O'Brien. "The Fall of the Ironic Curtain." *Commonweal*, 8 Feb. 1991, 102–7.

Storm Jameson, Margaret. "The Cost of Freedom." In *The Pen in Exile: An Anthology*, ed. Paul Tabori, 9–13. [London]: International P.E.N. Club Centre for Writers in Exile, 1954.

———. Introduction to *The Stranger*, by Maria Kuncewicz. Translated by B. M. A. Massey. New York: L. B. Fischer, 1945.

Suleiman, Susan Rubin. "Can You Go Home Again? A Budapest Diary 1993." *Postmodern Culture* 3, no. 3 (May 1993). Available from pmc@unity.ncsu.edu.

———. "Excerpts from the Motherbook." *Hungarian Quarterly* 34 (Winter 1993): 123–33.

Surdykowski, Jerzy. *Duch Rzeczypospolitej* (The Spirit of Respublica). New York: Bicentennial Publishing, 1989.

Szałagan, Alicja. "Cudzoziemka Marii Kuncewiczowej. Powstanie, dzieje, recepcja" (Maria Kuncewicz's *The Stranger*: Genesis, History, Receptions). *Pamiętnik Literacki* 77, bk. 3 (1986): 241–76.

Tabori, Paul, ed. *The Pen in Exile: An Anthology.* [London]: International P.E.N. Club Centre for Writers in Exile, 1954.

Tannner, Tony. *City of Words: American Fiction 1950–1970.* New York: Harper and Row, 1971.

Terlecki, Tymon. *Literatura polska na obczyźnie 1940–1960.* London: B. Świderski, 1964.

Theweleit, Klaus. *Male Fantasies: Women, Floods, Bodies, History.* 2 vols. Trans. Stephen Conway. Minneapolis: University of Minnesota Press, 1987.

Thomas, William Isaac. *The Unadjusted Girl: With Cases and Standpoint for Behavior Analysis.* Boston: Little, Brown, 1923.

Thompson, Eva M. "The Writer in Exile: The Good Years." *Slavic and East European Journal* 33, no. 4 (Winter 1989): 499–515.

Tökés, Rudolf L., ed. *Opposition in Eastern Europe.* Baltimore: Johns Hopkins Univeristy Press, 1979.

Tompkins, Jane P. *Sensational Designs: The Cultural Work of American Fiction, 1790–1860.* New York: Oxford University Press, 1985.

Tyrmand, Leopold, ed. *Explorations in Freedom: Prose, Narrative, and Poetry from Kultura.* New York: Free Press, 1970.

Umansky, Ellen. Introduction to *I Am a Woman—and a Jew*, by Leah Morton. New York: Marcus Wiener, 1986.

Vaculik, Ludvìk. *A Cup of Coffee with My Interrogator: The Prague Chronicles of Ludvík Vaculik.* Trans. Goerge Theiner. London: Readers International, 1987.

Walden, Daniel. "Jewish Women Writers and Women in Jewish Literature: An Introduction." In *Studies in American Jewish Literature*, ed. Daniel Walden, 3:1–5. Albany: State University of New York Press, 1983.

———, ed. "Twentieth-Century American-Jewish Fiction Writers." *Dictionary of Literary Biography.* Vol. 28. Detroit: Book Tower, 1984.

Warren, Rosanna, ed. *The Art of Translation: Voices from the Field.* Boston: Northeastern University Press, 1989.

Weatherford, Doris. *Foreign and Female: Immigrant Women in America, 1840–1930.* New York: Schocken Books, 1986.

Webber, Jeannette L., and Joan Grumman. *Woman as Writer.* Boston: Houghton Mifflin, 1978.

Wedel, Janine R., ed. *The Unplanned Society: Poland during and after Communism.* New York: Columbia University Press, 1992.

Weinberg, Sydney Stahl. "The Treatment of Women in Immigration History: A Call for Change." In *Seeking Common Ground: Multidisciplinary Studies of Immigrant*

*Women in the United States*, ed. Donna Gabaccia, 3–22. Westport, Conn.: Praeger, 1992.

Weissbort, Daniel, ed. *The Poetry of Survival: Post-War Poets of Central and Eastern Europe*. New York: St. Martin's Press, 1991.

West, Cornel. *Race Matters*. Boston: Beacon Press, 1993.

White, Edmund. "Nabokov: Beyond Parody." In *The Achievements of Vladimir Nabokov: Essays, Studies, Reminiscences, and Stories*, ed. George Gibian and Stephen Jan Parker. Ithaca: Center for International Studies, 1984.

"Who Speaks for Whom." *Wilson Quarterly*, Summer 1990, 132.

Wisniewska, Celina, ed. *Polish Writing Today*. Baltimore: Penguin Books, 1967.

Wittke, Carl. *We Who Built America: The Saga of the Immigrant*. New York: Prentice-Hall, 1946.

Wójcik, Włodzimierz, ed. *W stronę Kuncewiczowej: Studia i szkice* (Toward Kuncewicz: Studies and Sketches). Katowice: Uniwersytet Śląski, 1988.

Woodbridge, Elizabeth. "The Promised Land." *Yale Review* 2, no. 2 (Oct. 1912): 175–76.

Woolf, Virginia. *Three Guineas*. New York: Harcourt Brace Jovanovich, 1966.

*Writings on the East: Selected Essays on Eastern Europe from* The New York Review of Books. New York: Rea S. Henderman, 1990.

Yelin, Louise. "Exiled in and Exiled from: The Politics and Poetics of *Burger's Daughter*." In *Women's Writing in Exile*, ed. Mary Lynn Broe and Angela Ingram, 395–411. Chapel Hill: University of North Carolina Press, 1989.

Zangwill, Israel. Introduction to *From Polotzk to Boston*, by Mary Antin. Boston: W. B. Clarke, 1899.

———. *The Melting-Pot*. New York: Macmillan, 1926.

Zaworska, Helena, ed. *Rozmowy z Marią Kuncewiczową* (Conversations with Maria Kuncewicz). Warsaw: Czytelnik, 1983.

———. "Śmierć 'Kuncewiczówki'" (Death of "Kuncewiczówka"). *Gazeta Wyborcza*, 12 Mar. 1992, 9.

———. "Żeby wiedzieć co u was" (To Know What Was Happening with You). *Arkusz*, 8 March 1994, 4.

# INDEX

Mary as a Jewish prodigy, 61–64, 67, 69; two-part structure of, 55, 66–67, 68–72, 73, 308 (n. 58)
—*At School in the Promised Land*, 53
—"Snow," 53
—"Soundless Trumpet, The," 306 (n. 40)
—*They Who Knock at Our Gates*, 3, 34, 53, 310 (n. 23)
—"Woman to Her Fellow Citizens, A," 307 (n. 52)
Anti-Semitism, 23, 50, 84–85, 86, 122, 134, 135, 141, 168, 233, 254–55, 317 (n. 5), 324 (n. 19)
Armstrong, Nancy, 297 (n. 2)
Austin, Jane, 328 (n. 28); *Pride and Prejudice*, 267
Autobiography, 6, 15, 228–29, 231, 233, 294, 304 (n. 6), 316 (n. 63). *See also* Antin, Mary; Hoffman, Eva; Kuncewicz, Maria; Yezierska, Anzia

Bakhtin, Mikhail, 6, 25, 298 (n. 6); Bakhtinian theory of the novel, 13, 15–16
Baldwin, James, 288
Balkans, 3, 23, 62
Bannan, Helen M., 87, 88
Barańczak, Stanisław, 16, 26, 178, 205, 293
Baym, Nina, 297 (n. 2)
Benstock, Shari, 179, 319 (n. 21)
Benveniste, Emile, 320 (n. 34)
Bercovitch, Sacvan, 27, 284, 301–2 (n. 33)
Bergland, Betty, 56, 59, 307 (n. 42), 308 (n. 64)
Bildungsroman, 80, 82, 151, 231
Boelhower, William: *Through a Glass Darkly*, 42, 303 (n. 1)
Bok, Edward, 63, 119, 303 (n. 49), 311 (n. 11), 325 (n. 7)
Borowski, Tadeusz, 178
Boyd, Brian, 256, 276, 324 (n. 2), 325 (n. 6), 328 (n. 23)
Brodsky, Joseph, 6, 266, 300 (n. 22), 318 (n. 20)
Bromwich, David, 117
Brooks, Peter: *Reading for the Plot*, 311 (n. 10)
Budapest, 256

Buddenbrook, Antonina, 174
Bulgaria (Bulgarian), 14, 227, 250, 258, 323 (n. 4)
Burger, Otis K., 207

Cahan, Abraham, 21, 34, 119, 269, 310 (n. 1), 325 (n. 7); *The Rise of David Levinsky*, 34, 269, 303 (n. 49), 305 (n. 15), 325 (nn. 7, 9)
Canon: literary critical debate, 21, 33, 178, 285, 287, 289; as a male construct, 25, 178, 318 (nn. 19, 20). *See also* American literature; American novel; East Europe: intellectuals from; East Europe: writings from
Carby, Hazel V., 288, 329 (nn. 1, 14)
Carnegie, Andrew, 19, 63, 119, 303 (n. 49), 311 (n. 11), 325 (n. 7)
Castle Garden, 117
Cather, Willa, 122
Catholicism, 25, 28, 167, 193–96, 212, 213, 229, 233, 252, 272; and censorship in Poland, 211–12, 322 (n. 75)
Censorship (censor), 211–15, 322 (nn. 74, 75)
Central Europe, 62, 167, 168, 172, 218, 255
Chaplin, Charlie: *Immigrant, The*, 303 (n. 47)
Childbirth, 45, 273; as metaphor for writing, 163, 201, 247, 323 (n. 11)
Childcare, 45. *See also* Mother
Chopin, Kate, 311–12 (n. 13); *The Awakening*, 308 (n. 60)
Christian, Barbara, 282
Christians, 49, 60, 61
Civil War, 304 (n. 8)
Clark, Katerina, 15
Class. *See* Lower class; Antin, Mary: *The Promised Land*; Stern, Elizabeth Gertrude Levin: *My Mother and I*; Yezierska, Anzia
Clayton, Jay, 17, 25, 298 (n. 14)
Cliff, Michelle, 80, 81
Clifford, James, 17
Clothing manufacture, 45. *See also* Sweatshop
Cold War, 7, 19, 20, 23, 24, 35, 167, 168,

Miscegenation, 7, 19, 31, 47, 69, 93, 94, 119, 122, 128–31, 140–47, 148–50, 152, 155, 159, 177, 232, 244, 312 (n. 23), 313 (n. 27). *See also* Marriage; Mediation

Modernism, 319 (n. 21)

Moro, Aldo, 214–15

Morrison, Toni, 286–87, 288, 291, 329 (n. 1)

Morson, Gary Saul, 16

Morton, Leah (Eleanor Morton), 309 (nn. 3, 4). *See also* Stern, Elizabeth Gertrude Levin

Moscow, 290

Moses, 157

Motherhood, 48, 50. *See also* Mother

Mothers (mothering), 45, 60, 66, 72, 80, 89–91, 93, 94–107, 181, 196–98, 251, 274

Mukherjee, Bharati, 248, 249

Multiculturalism (multicultural), 19, 41, 227, 239, 249; immigrant literature in, 8, 282–83, 288–91

Nabokov, Vladimir, 8, 33, 34, 35, 237, 238, 285, 303 (n. 51), 305 (n. 15), 318 (n. 18), 323 (nn. 6, 11); characterization, 263–64, 267–73, 326–27 (nn. 15, 19, 21), 328 (n. 23); critical approaches, 263–64, 266–67, 275–76, 324 (nn. 2, 3), 325 (n. 6), 327 (n. 16), 328 (nn. 25, 31); dialogism, 265, 266–67, 270–71, 276–77; endings, 263, 264, 265, 266, 267, 268, 270, 274, 276, 325 (n. 5); exile, 265, 267–71, 276; "feminized" male, 36, 272, 274; gender reversals in narrative, 269–71, 270, 273–75, 276; life, 264–67, 275–76, 325 (n. 8), 326 (n. 14), 328 (nn. 26, 28, 29); male narrative of acculturation, 263, 265–66, 268–71, 326 (13); revision of male immigrant narrative, 264, 269, 273–77; search for home, 268–70

—*Lolita*, 36, 264, 265, 266, 267, 270, 275, 325 (nn. 6, 7)

—*Pale Fire*, 265, 270, 325 (n. 7), 327 (n. 18)

—*Pnin*, 8, 33, 34, 35, 263, 264, 265, 266, 267–77, 325 (n. 7)

—*Real Life of Sebastian Knight, The*, 270, 326 (n. 13)

Nansen Passport, 267, 326 (n. 14)

Narrative: as dialogue of genders, 33–37, 266–67, 294–95; of female liberation, 30, 32–33, 81; patterns of, for males and females, 19–20, 30–31, 33–37, 44, 66–67, 79, 80–81, 88, 119–20, 169–72, 233–40, 249, 264–65, 266–67, 268–71, 303 (n. 49); rags-to-riches, 34, 63, 119, 236–37, 265. *See also* Acculturation; Antin, Mary; Hoffman, Eva; Nabokov, Vladimir; Otherness; Stern, Elizabeth Gertrude Levin; Yezierska, Anzia

National Academy of Arts and Sciences, 54

National Americanization Committee, 53

National Geographic programs, 292

National Security League, 53

Nationhood, ix–xi, 17, 55–58, 60–64, 90–92, 123–36, 284–85, 289–95. *See also* Hoffman, Eva; Kuncewicz, Maria

Native Americans, 41

Nativism, 3–4, 23, 41, 29, 53, 62–63, 84, 85, 131, 168, 176, 254, 304 (n. 7); against immigrant women, 46–47, 48–49, 178–79, 305 (n. 19). *See also* Anti-Semitism; "New racism"; Racism; Xenophobia

Natural History Club: in Antin's *The Promised Land*, 53, 71, 72, 73, 206

Nazis, 167, 168, 183, 185, 188, 189, 190, 203

Neidle, Cecyle S., 21, 56–57, 314 (n. 35)

"New Colossus, The," 132, 169

"New racism," 49, 62–63, 85, 305 (n. 20)

Newspeak, 319 (n. 23)

New Woman, 23, 48, 60, 148, 149

New World: as a literary critical concept, 284; as other, 88, 121, 132, 234; patriarchal oppression in, 14, 20, 34, 82, 108; as place of rebirth, 5, 14, 20, 132. *See also* America; Patriarchy; Promised Land

New York School of Philanthropy, 82

Norris, Frank: *McTeague*, 308 (n. 60)

## DATE DUE

| | | | |
|---|---|---|---|
| | | | |
| | | | |
| | | | |
| | | | |
| | | | |
| | | | |
| | | | |
| | | | |
| | | | |
| | | | |
| | | | |
| | | | |
| | | | |
| | | | |
| | | | |
| | | | |
| GAYLORD | | | PRINTED IN U.S.A. |